RADICAL BREWING

RECIPES, TALES, AND WORLD-ALTERING MEDITATIONS IN A GLASS

Randy Mosher

brewers publications

A Division of the Association of Brewers Boulder, Colorado

Brewers Publications

Division of the Association of Brewers

PO Box 1679, Boulder, CO 80306-1679

(303) 447-0816; Fax (303) 447-2825

www.beertown.org

Printed in the United States of America

10 9 8 7 6 5 4 3 2 1

Library of Congress Cataloging-in-Publication Data

Mosher, Randy.
  Radical brewing : recipes, tales, and world-altering
meditations in a glass / by Randy Mosher.
      p. cm.
  Includes bibliographical references and index.
  ISBN 0-937381-83-7 (alk. paper)
  1. Brewing--Amateurs' manuals. I. Title.

  TP570.M65 2004
  641.8'73--dc22

      2004003466

Technical Editor: Gordon Strong

Book Project Editor: Ray Daniels

Copy Editor: Jill Redding

Cover and Interior Designer: Randy Mosher/Randy Mosher Design

Production: Julie Korowotny

Direct all inquiries or orders to the above address.

To all the brewers,
past and present,
who have pushed
the boundaries in
search of something
great to drink.

RADICAL BREWING

RECIPES, TALES, AND WORLD-ALTERING MEDITATIONS IN A GLASS

Randy Mosher

TABLE OF CONTENTS

Table of Contents

Entlüftungs
Rohr

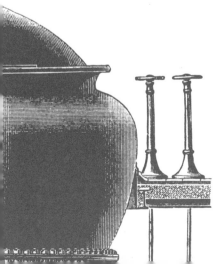

ACKNOWLEDGEMENTS

A work like this cannot exist in a vacuum. *Radical Brewing* draws inspiration both from the past and from the happy vitality of the American homebrewing movement, a unique and wonderful chapter in the long history of beer. Hopefully this work offers an accurate glimpse of this energetic movement.

My sincere thanks to the technical editor on this project, Gordon Strong. His diligent scrutiny saved me from more than one embarrassing misstep. A big thanks also goes to Ray Daniels for believing in and supporting this project—and for everything else over the years.

Thanks to Bat Bateman, Chuck Boyce, Ray Spangler, Tim Steininger, Gordon Strong, Thomas Vista and Paul Williams for some very outrageous recipes. And to Ed Bronson and Ray Daniels for the loan of some rare old brewing books. A special debt is owed to the late Bill Friday, the devoted and generous beer-bibliophile, who awakened some very old texts from their microfilm slumber and brought them back to life by allowing myself and others access to their fascinating contents.

Thanks also to Pete Crowley, Fred Eckhardt, Michael Jackson, Lyn Kruger, Bill Pengelly, Fred Scheer and Chuck Skypeck for assistance or inspiration of one kind or another.

And finally, thanks to the homebrewing members of the Chicago Beer Society and the brewers from the many other clubs across the country with whom I have had the good fortune to have shared many beers and illuminating discussions over the years.

FOREWORD

The Marvel of Mosher

By Michael Jackson

The world desperately needs more Moshers. If only we had more Moshers, the Tasmanian tiger might return from extinction. Mike Tyson at his peak would be able to step into the ring with Muhammad Ali. We would be able to see and hear the great performers who pre-dated the recording of sound. I might even now be sipping a pre-Prohibition beer and checking whether Buddy Bolden could be heard across Lake Ponchartrain. Or I might be sampling Harwood's Porter in a London pub, or an India Pale Ale aboard a clipper heading for Calcutta.

To be truthful, I know only one Mosher. He is Randy, which in the United Kingdom, where I live, means feeling sexy. I know nothing of his private life, but there is passion in the heart of this seemingly quiet, kindly man. His activities are probably a threat to our morals. Passion, imagination, and tenacity are a challenge to the established order. So are people whose definition of progress is not acquiescence.

As a teenager, I learned this when I saw an item on television about a London pub in which the walls were lined with friezes showing merry monks. The pub was scheduled to be demolished to make way for road widening. In the TV programme, a slightly crazy-looking English poet was arguing that the pub was a temple to the pleasures of drinking and should be saved. It was. The poet's name was Betjeman. I thought at the time that we needed more Betjemen.

We don't call them that; we know them as conservationists. A pity. I prefer Betjemen. Until now, there has been no name for people who go a stage beyond conservation, and somehow bring back pleasures that have been lost.

A revivalist? Randy does more than that. He and I once presented a tasting of rare Northern European beer styles, using examples that he had brewed. One of the styles was Grodzisk, from Poland. I had tasted the last commercially-brewed Grodzisk; Randy had only read about the style. Despite this, he made a beer that tasted like the Grodzisk I had enjoyed.

A beer archaeologist? People like Randy can find old "recipes" for some of the beers that have been lost, but they are very hard to interpret. The brewer of a century ago knew what "Mr. Smith's malt" tasted like, but we do not. Nor do we know that characteristics of hops that long preceded today's varieties.

A scholar? Randy's researches represent diligent scholarship, and make possible a Jurassic Park of beer styles.

So what is he? He is a Mosher.

INTRODUCTION

We're taught from childhood that what is good can't be fun. It's a lie. Homebrewing combines good *and* fun into one sparkling amber liquid. We can all drink to that.

Okay, so it isn't saving-babies-in-Africa good, but American homebrewers have profoundly changed the beer scene for the better. What we've accomplished, along with making it pretty easy to get a palatable beer just about anywhere in this country, is nothing less than keeping beer, a twelve thousand year-old cultural treasure of humanity, from slipping into a coma of mechanized industrial anonymity.

Beer is a deep, wide river that flows through human culture. It appears along with the earliest signs of civilization, and is enjoyed and venerated in nearly every society with access to its makings. To think that might have been subsumed into the drab one-size-fits-all world of modern commerce is an outrage, but we came very close. Fortunately, things are on a happier track now.

If you're a homebrewer, give yourself a hearty whack on the back. You've earned it. You have experimented, evangelized, and prophesied. Some of you have even given up jobs your moms were perfectly proud of to put on the big rubber boots and brew beer in tiny breweries, a truly generous act. You've celebrated the joy of great beer, paid your hard earned cash for it when you needed to, and demanded it from the places you frequent. Craft beer could never have happened without you.

It is a huge accomplishment to have prodded some of the most massive corporations on earth—the industrial brewers—into doing things they'd really rather not have done. For a hundred years, Big Beer set the direction—paler, lighter, less bitter—with the swagger of inevitability. And then, horrors! Geeks in their basements were suddenly in charge. At the first frenzied peak of craft brewing, all the big guys wigged out and made stouts, bought micros, and generally acted as if the world was coming to an end.

It is probably for the best that the 45 percent annual growth of craft beer didn't continue, as craft brewing might have gotten big enough to make it worth crushing, but (whew!) the pressure's off and now the big brewers' marketing geniuses can get back to cannibalizing their core brands with the latest licensed alcopop fad of the day and doing business in the safe confines of their cubicles. Dangers remain, but we have carved out a niche for craft beer with some staying power. In Europe, as hallowed styles fade away, American craft brewing is serving as an inspiration and a model for the future of specialty beer over there as well.

My Definition of Craft Beer in America

If a homebrewer (current or former) gets to decide what the beer tastes like, it's craft beer.

And behind it all are homebrewers, with restless curiosity and infectious enthusiasm. We are determined to make something meaningful, something real. And we're doing it pretty well.

But make no mistake, corporate blandness is on the march. If left unanswered, it will wrap its cubicle walls around real culture and squeeze the life completely out of it. This is not speculation; it's a business plan. People who are aware are fighting back. For boring beer, radical brewing is the necessary antidote.

Once you turn your hand to it, you can expect great things. The exact same ingredients and techniques available to commercial brewers are available to amateur brewers as well, and this, combined with knowledge and enthusiasm, is the reason good homebrew is the rival of any commercial beer on the planet. American homebrewers have been relentless in their pursuit of quality beers, both iconic and iconoclastic, resulting in a subculture just exploding with enthusiasm and creativity.

So what does it mean to be a radical brewer? Well, I can tell you stories of people who have custom built "garages" suited only for brewing, of a brewer who makes sublime beers from nothing more than seeds and organic fertilizer, of a half-million BTU burners, and of 1,500 homebrewers celebrating their favorite drink in the Southern California scrubland, But to me, the only requirement for being a radical brewer is to pursue the art with passion. The great joy of it is discovering what your own unique path will be.

Brew Big, Buy Small: Support Your Local Micro

Throwing a brick through the window of a Starbucks may be satisfying for a few mindless sociopaths, but it won't accomplish diddly-squat. Why? Because it's not action; it's just *reaction*.

You still have to buy beer sometimes; so as a customer you need to make your choices carefully. You can surrender your dough to some vast industrial conglomerate that owns who-knows-what-else, or you can help support a dedicated entrepreneur who's a part of your community, who is crazy for the good stuff (just like you), and who isn't trying to water it down to utter blandness. Buying genuine microbrew is not just a matter of being nice—it's self interest. If you don't support them, they'll be gone, and then what will your choices be like?

Be cantankerous. Demand craft beer wherever you go, and don't be afraid to be a pest about it. Learn where good beer comes from. Consider who you're giving your money to. Turn your friends on to the pleasures of craft beer. *It matters.*

A PROMISE

This book has two goals. The first is to help you brew great beer. Wacked-out, elegant, seductive, mind-blowingly delicious beer. The second is to help you understand that beer is an art form, a gastronomic treasure, a political act, a mystical ritual, a food, and a fundamental human craft. This, in turn, will help you brew even better beer.

If you're just beginning your brewing journey, this book will take you through the steps needed to get comfortable making beer. For those of you who have been brewing for a while, this book should be a treasure trove of ideas, techniques, and recipes, both historically-based and pure American homebrew anarchy. For those interested, there should be plenty of tools here to develop your own voice as a brewer. As an artist in beer.

This is not a book for drooling imbeciles. I promise not to oversimplify things or gloss over the thorny bits so you can feel superior. Making beer is about doing things for yourself. As my welding teacher says, "*They* just want you to sit on your ass and watch TV, and buy their stuff. If you can work with your hands, you can control your own life." So you are going to have to learn to work out a recipe. Get yourself a point of view. Become your own brewmaster. I'm not going to spoon feed everything to you.

This is art. It's not paint-by-numbers!

On the other hand, do not expect this book to exhaustively cover every style; that has been done very well elsewhere. I've included styles that are either object lessons, technical showcases, new to the homebrewing community, or just essential beers every brewer should know how to make.

I have omitted a fair amount of detail on technical matters, opting to include only what I have found essential to brewing good beer in a homebrew setting. As with styles, the technical side of brewing has been covered many times, far better than I ever could. Frankly, I have seen some home-brewers get obsessed with rather minor process issues and kind of miss some of the more important questions, like what to brew.

So get your kettle shined up and prepare to dive into the world of beer. Ready yourself for the delightful act of discovery that is Radical Brewing.

HOW TO BREW

Brew as if beer is a gift from a benevolent universe. Because it is.

Brew as if it's a magic spell. Incant the names: barley, hops, water, yeast, fire. These primal elements converge in a miraculous way to create beer. Just because you understand how enzyme molecules catalyze complex chains of reactions in every stage of the brew, it doesn't make their million-to-one reaction energy lowering ability any less astounding. Every time you brew, you invoke an uncountable number of miracles.

Brew like a good shepherd, with billions of tiny creatures at your mercy. The yeast you sprinkle on your brew is not inert muddy goo. It's alive, and each cell claims a proud royal lineage, nurtured for millennia by our brewing forebears. Give it a comfortable home, with plenty to eat, and it will do its part without hesitation.

Brew as an act of benevolence. For all of recorded history, beer has had the power to soothe, to please, to bring people together. It was, and remains, a nurturing staple crafted by brewers of faith, the cloistered few whose calling it was to contemplate the universe. Over the ages, beer has brought civilization to nomads, succor to travelers, and a revolution to our own young country, with dark plans and brilliant declarations hatched in public houses, then sealed with a pint. Or two.

Brew like an artist, with your senses and your whims. Brewing is not engineering; there are no equations for flavor. You have to grope your way through every new brew with an intuitive sense of what's good, with rhythm, harmony, and contrast, and then get the parts to transcend their individuality and add up to something sublime.

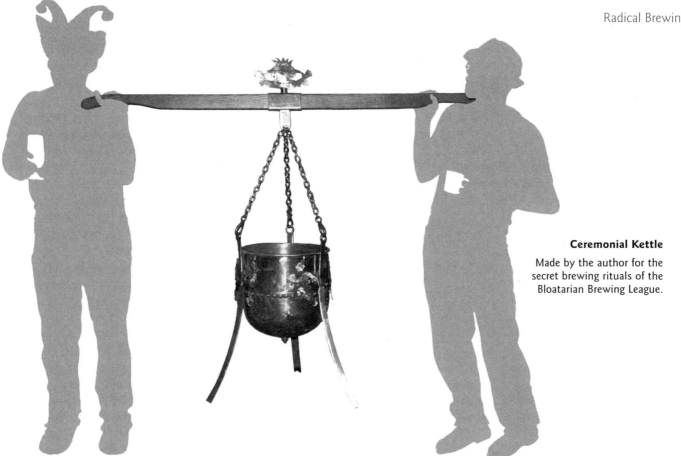

Ceremonial Kettle
Made by the author for the secret brewing rituals of the Bloatarian Brewing League.

Brew with balance. Play the sweet malt against the bitter hop, but also consider the rough bitterness of roasted malt, the spiciness of ale fermentation, the fatness of well-lagered Munich malt. As the universe is balanced, so should be your beer.

Brew with simplicity. Those four *Reinheitsgebot* substances: malt, water, hops, and yeast, have the power to create a spectacular range of flavors, textures, and sensations. Paring it down to the minimum needed to achieve a great result is the sign of a true master. Even with these limited ingredients the brewing toolkit is huge; malting, kilning, mashing, boiling, and fermentation give you unlimited options for shaping your brews.

Brew with reckless abandon. Over the millennia, nearly every foodstuff and herbal substance known has been put into beer. Magic beers with mystical—and often psychoactive— ingredients were part of the ancient classical mysteries. Beer has a central role in ceremonial occasions around the world. Berries, roots, bark, seeds, mushrooms, even chickens, eggs, and oysters have all been thrown into the brewpot in the quest for some unusual taste, sensation, cure, tonic, or magical effect. And while our need to chemically connect with the spiritual dimension has diminished in our modern society, there remains much to explore for the sake of flavor.

Brew with meaning. Beer is deeply intertwined with our humanity across the globe. Yes, brewing can be a job or a hobby, but it is also an act certifying your participation in the family of mankind. Beer brings people together, as you will find once you have a steady supply of homebrew at hand.

Brew beer with all of this in mind, and the world will remain an amazing place.

Chapter 1

An Embellished History of Beer

Homebrewing dates back as far as beer itself, probably about twelve thousand years ago.

Some academics suggest it was the ingestion of mind-altering substances that led to the creation of the human consciousness. Their view may be on the fringe, but psychoactive chemicals played prominent roles in many early religions. In Christianity, the central ritual of communion revolves around the ingestion of two transformative materials, one of them—wine—with proven psychoactive properties.

My own crackpot view on the birth of civilization is supported by some actual academics. I imagine the nomadic tribesmen as fiercely freedom-loving, with the wind-in-the-hair lifestyle of modern day bikers, tough enough to deal with the brutal realities of nature. Is freshly baked bread, nice as that is, enough enticement to trade Harley for hoe and join the backbreaking ranks of the farmer? In my view it is not. Toss in a refreshing and relaxing beer to ease your troubles and woes and, well, that's a proposition worth talking about.

I further contend that the lubricating nature of alcohol allows people to coexist in the otherwise crushing density of cities. This is as true now as it was in Ur of the Chaldees.

Beer has always been shaped by geography and climate. Each species of grain is adapted to a particular climatic zone, with wheat favoring milder climes while oats and rye thrive in harsh Northern regions. Barley is pretty hardy, but does need a richer soil than rye or oats. Hops, too, are sensitive to latitude, as they require a particular summer day-length to trigger cone production. Each herb, fruit, and other ingredient has a preferred habitat, and in the days before the easy transport of commodities, every drink tasted of its own unique flora.

Despite this, much of the pattern of beer's popularity defies explanation. Why was Egypt and so much of the rest of the early Middle East so crazy for beer, while the Greeks and Romans started early with wine and have pretty much stood by it for the last three thousand years? Was it a technological improvement that originally allowed them to store and enjoy the wine throughout the year? Was it just the masses mimicking the luxurious drinking practices of the elite, and later the desire to cling to the culture of the faded empire long past its glory? Or was it just the fact that once you get the grapes, wine is about the easiest thing there is to make?

And what of the Barbarian nations? The French have always found plenty of uses for beer, if not respect. Even today, France supplies much of the barley used to turn out the radiantly artistic beers of Belgium. So why no beer culture in Gaul?

The Germans can make a pretty good cask of wine. Was their

headlong lust for beer a means of spurning the decadent ways of the South, reminding themselves of their raggedy triumph over the largest empire the world had ever known? Could this have happened without a real national identity until the late Middle Ages? And could there be a shred of resonance in this idea today, or is the beer tradition running on the fumes of sheer dogged traditionalism?

A couple hundred years ago, the differences were chalked up to the fundamentally diverse constitutions of the various "races": beer being suited to the Dutch, while unhopped ale was the healthier drink for the Englishman, blah, blah, blah. This is hogwash, of course, but beer functioned as liquid bread, an important part of a whole nutritional system consisting of many interdependent parts, and any kind of change would tend to upset a carefully balanced equilibrium. Plus, people tend to be rather set in their ways, as well as contemptuous of foreigners. As an example, it took about a hundred years for hops to become accepted in England.

There is a certain churning fashionability affecting beer styles in most places, and this also has a generational component to it. Of course we don't have any detail when we look at truly ancient tastes, but when we get to about five hundred years ago, we see beer fashions changing two or three times a century. There's always an old-fashioned beer, staunchly defended by the old guys, who take the style with them when they pass from history. Unless, as often happens, the once-senescent beer is recast by an enthusiastic new generation eager to reconnect with their past, or who just

The Birth of Beer: Location: a really fertile part of the Fertile Crescent, 10,000 B.C.E.. It must have gone something like this:

"Senacherib, you lazy son of a scarab!

"I've had it up to my shooskas with this lousy nomadic life. We never have anything nice. No coffee table, no comfy chair, not even a teevee! Camel hair tents, camel hair rugs, camel hair shorts! My life is an itchy hell, husband of mine, and you're to blame. Can't we just settle down, maybe quit the Ur's Angels, get one of those new mud brick split levels, like the Joh'Nzanh's?"

"Awwww, Angie, you know I just got new chrome mud flaps for Harl'eh and Dav'd-Zon. Look how shiny! This desert dude was born to ride!"

"Come, sit, eat. I got some of that new barley grain down at Honest Ur's Bargain Hut. Very trendy. A deal, too. I think it got wet in last year's rainstorm. Looks like it sprouted. Made you some nice gruel from a recipe in Good Tentkeeping. Mmmm, steaming hot."

"Splakh! I hate nouvelle cuisine. You know I'm a lamb and lentils man. I'm outta here! Hey guys, c'mon, let's ride out to the oasis. I think they're grillin' goatburgers tonight."

RRRRRRvvvvrrrrmmmm! (To be perfectly accurate, camels peeling out sound more like flup, flup, flup.)

As Senacherib and the rest of the gang flups off into the desert, Angie, frustrated by another failed effort to tame her free-spirit husband, dumps the remaining barley into his uneaten bowl of gruel and sets it outside the tent. She cries herself to an itchy sleep under the cool desert moon.

The next day the goop has taken on a life of its own, sputtering and throbbing under the hot Mesopotamian sun. "Interesting," she thinks. "But this needs more work." She takes the pulsating mash and filters it into a clay jug through her camel-hair headcloth, then digs the pointy end of the jug into the cool sand. As a final attempt to save the situation, she tosses in some chopped dates, coriander seeds, and the bitter herb rue into the mix.

A couple of days pass before Senacherib and the rest of his rowdy pals trundle back to the encampment, a bloated gazelle strapped across the back of one of the camels (actually she smelled them before she heard them).

"Heyyy Angie! Yo, I'm home! What is there to drink around here?"

"Just a little something I brewed up. Here." He takes the jug and after a cautious sniff takes a long, cooling draught of the tangy, tickling beverage. She has a twang of conscience, thinking maybe she didn't really want to poison him completely to death.

"Uargh, not bad. Kinda fizzy. Whoa, I gotta sit down. Hey, guys, try this..."

You know the rest of the story. Senacherib gets a little sick, but in a good way. He and Angie settle down into their mud-brick double-wide next to a very large pile of barley and the rest of the Ur's Angels, forming a happy little village of bubbling barley-juice drinkers. They go on to invent the wheel, civilization, and after a very long hot spell, the fridge.

A MOSTLY TRUE BEER HISTORY TIMELINE

c. 10,000 B.C.E.   Glaciers melt, barley pops up everywhere. Neolithic people take flat rocks and pound it into hearty nourishing gruel.

9999 B.C.E.   Neolithic people sick of gruel. Wonder what else they can do with barley.

9998-9000 B.C.E.   Tried everything: gruel loaf, gruel au jus, gruel fritters, gruel pâté, gruel in aspic. Charred meat is still by far the most popular food.

8999 B.C.E.   Final contestant in barley cook-off comes up with a winner: crock-aged festering sprouted barley-cake bisque with bitter herbs, actually much more enjoyable than it sounds. Dubbed *beer*, it's *much* better than gruel. The formerly neglected Goddess of Gruel becomes fashionable new Goddess of Beer, now in big demand at parties everywhere across Fertile Crescent.

5000 B.C.E.   Formerly nomadic people of ancient Middle East settle down to avoid having to lug around heavy jugs of beer. Civilization officially begins.

3000 B.C.E.   Egyptians start to build mighty civilization based on the motivating power of beer. The whole place gets drunk and stacks rocks into giant pointy pyramid things, frightening desert nomads. As a joke, they appoint a hippopotamus named Seth as the god of beer. Nation wakes up a thousand years later with a helluva hangover.

1740 B.C.E.   Sneaky Babylonian brewery accountants encourage use of straw and papyrus chaff as cost-saving measure in breweries. Hammurabi gets mad and writes code of laws describing which body parts to chop off as punishment for such infractions.

45 B.C.E.   Degenerate Egyptian ruler-god mistakenly trades Queen Cleopatra to Roman wine-drinking weasel for a six-pack of something "much better than beer."

50 C.E.   Roman Emperor Julian says beer "smells of goat," starting long tradition of effete wine snobs bad-mouthing beer. Rome becomes filthy with wealthy, effete wine snobs, and begins its long and inevitable decline.

410-455   Beer drinkers from the barbaric North ride their Harleys into Rome and smash up the place but good.

700-900   Vikings learn to make beer from grains and tree parts. Heaven envisioned as giant beer joint, with glorious death in battle as the cover charge. Thousands rush to join the army.

Dark Beer Ages. Monks support religion by brewing beer using creepy-sounding medieval ingredients like Bog Myrtle. Strong beers reserved for Abbots and other bigshots.

600-1400

Monastic brewery accountants come up with the idea of "small beer" to give out to penitents as a cheaper substitute for expensive hair shirts.

Monopoly maintained on the sale of high-priced beer "gruit" herbs, guaranteeing the church a piece of the action on every beer sold in whole Dark Ages area.

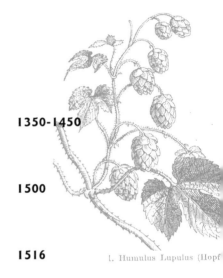

Hops replace other herbs, weakening the church's grip on beer revenue, eventually allowing free-willed scalawags like Martin Luther to vandalize church doors, inexplicably opening the floodgates of the Renaissance.

1350-1450

Lager beer emerges from damp and chilly caves in Germany. Soccer not yet the national sport, so England fails to see the point. A little later, Scotland—way into damp and chilly—takes it up enthusiastically.

1500

Bavarians enact the fabled Reinheitsgebot beer purity act, creating the foundation for serious-sounding advertising puffery 475 years in the future.

1516

L. Humulus Lupulus (Hopf

Flemish immigrants bring hopped beer to England. Ale lovers in Britannia show their appreciation by making up derisive ditties and rioting.

1524

New World Indians show Walter Raleigh how to make cheap watery beer from maize, and American beer is born. Raleigh later beheaded, but the warning was ignored by later brewers.

1587

Pilgrims stuck on small, stinky ship bobbing slowly across the Atlantic, sort of lost and really, really thirsty. They look for landmark, but can only find small ugly rock and decide to land anyway. They show their devotion to their religious principles by postponing church-building in order to make the brewery their first permanent structure.

1620

In London, the story of Ralph Harwood inventing porter is invented. Due to poisonous additives in beer, people start hallucinating, and worse. Consumers rail against the use of such adulterants in beer, which are eventually outlawed.

1722

American colonists pretty sick of stale, highly taxed English beer. They hold a meeting in the local tavern and plot to dump all the ale in the harbor as a protest. After a few more rounds, someone comes up with the much better idea of dumping tea into the harbor, and history is made.

1773

Beer Timeline, Continued:

1750–1800   The thermometer, hydrometer, and steam power all come to English porter breweries as the industrial revolution takes hold. Brewery accountants get nice corner offices. German brewers come and take notes. Belgium yawns, decides not to clean the spiderwebs off their fermenters.

1814   Giant beer vat collapses in London. Dozens drown, but in a pretty cool way. Impoverished hordes signal their approval by violently struggling for gutter space to drink the spilled beer.

1847   England's Glass Tax is repealed, encouraging bottled beer and starting a trend toward paler, clearer beers (which reached its zenith with Miller's 1994 introduction—and withdrawal—of Clear Beer.)

1840-1860   Germans immigrate to America, and lagers displace English-style ales. English finally start to feel better about losing Revolutionary War.

1873   "Golden Era of American brewing" peaks with 4,131 breweries.

1890s   Refrigerated railcars and national marketing signal the beginning of national breweries. Local breweries send out press releases stating they will survive thanks to "the undying loyalty of their local customers."

1915-1917   World War I rationing cuts strength of beer, and brewers rush to convince us we like it this way. Local brewers start to report some of their local customers are dying off. "Golden era of American brewery accountants" begins.

1919-1933   Prohibition ushers in era of gangsters, speakeasies, and homebrewing. The cocktail flourishes as the only way to hide the strong, bathtubby taste of bathtub gin.

1934   Beer can invented. Joe Six-Pack born in Steubenville, Ohio.

1976   American bicentennial year is low ebb of beer quality and diversity, as 90 percent of the beer brewed in the United States comes from just five companies.

1976   First American microbrewery opens, then soon closes. Lured by the sweet, malty smell of success, many others are inspired to open their own breweries.

1995   Industrial breweries jump on increased consumer demand for quality beer by redoubling efforts to find clever animal mascots for their red beers.

crave what they believe to be a new sensation, which is a perfect picture of our present situation.

Gender and beer is another interesting area of study. There were beer deities of both sexes in the ancient Middle East: Sumerian Ninkasi was female, as were the brewers and alehouse proprietors; the Egyptian beer hippo-god Seth was male. The gender of the brewer seems to have depended on the scale and degree of commercial activity. When brewing was a household chore, it was invariably a female responsibility. On a larger scale, especially after industrialization, it became exclusively male. In between was a kind of fuzzy area where gender roles could go either way, depending on the society. In the Middle Ages, small-scale commercial brewing was practiced by women, and it seems to have been a real lifeline for widows and other unattached—and financially marginal—women. At the same time, larger breweries flourished in monasteries, always the domain of men. Today's homebrewers tend to be men, mainly, I believe, because hobbies of all kinds seem to be more captivating for men. Honestly, I wish the situation were different; most of the women I know who brew are really good at it. One of them uses "Beer Diva" as an e-mail address, and I have to say this is not an idle boast.

So beer's relationship to society poses the kind of questions that give anthropologists, sociologists, and historians purpose—and that also drive them crazy. The history of beer's role in society is a difficult pursuit. Once you start looking into history, you realize how much is gone forever, and how much effort it takes to connect the well-separated dots of the past.

Some of the oldest laws of any kind pertain to brewing and serving beer. The famous Code of Hammurabi contains prohibitions against overcharging in alehouses. Poor quality beers—especially those watered down or adulterated—seem to have been major problems throughout history. Nowadays, watered beer is a point of pride with some people; it commands more than 40 percent of the American beer market.

Beer has always been a free-flowing gusher of government funding; at this writing there are proposals in many legislatures to raise the taxes on beer once again. People's desire for beer and other alcohol is so strong that they will willingly shoulder a huge burden of taxation. This started early. By the early Middle Ages, governmental or religious monopolies were established for the production and sale of gruit, the spice mixture used to flavor ale. It was a mandatory ingredient, and the high prices charged by the gruit monopoly constituted a tax of sorts. These monopolies were later extended to hops in many places.

A multitude of different schemes for extracting money from brewers and their customers have been used over the years, and these usually had an impact on the strength and character of the beers. Taxes on malt, wort gravity, hops, glassware, alcohol content, and even on the volume of the mash tun have all played a role in the development of present day beer styles.

In the Dark Ages, we discover a huge range of beers seasoned with plants other than today's ubiquitous hop. Exotic seasonings like meadowsweet, bog myrtle, and wild rosemary complemented the more familiar ginger, nutmeg, and clove in these medieval brews. Beers were thought of as much more than simple drink. Indeed, every

Bronze Age Beakers and Jugs

Ritual vessels for beverages suggest a liquid of great importance. Recent evidence from Neolithic ceremonial vessels has revealed traces of meadowsweet, an herb known to have been used in mead and beer.

Medieval Ale Glasses
(above and opposite)

An elegant glass has always
made the beer taste better!

culinary, medicinal, or magical herb has at one time or another found its way into a beer of some sort. The legendary fearlessness of Northern beer-drinking tribes like the Picts and Vikings were often ascribed to the strength of their ale and mead, frequently bolstered by psychoactive plant substances. It is believed that the legendary Viking warriors, the *Berserkers*, were hopped up on ale laced with *Ledum palustre*, or wild rosemary.

It's impossible to say exactly how these medieval beers would have tasted, although there are plenty of dogged recreationists out there brewing old recipes as well as they can decipher them. I ascribe to the view that people liked a good beer back then as much as they do now, and despite severe limitations in raw materials and technology, clever and dedicated individuals were able to turn out beers worthy of poetry. Documents from the past reveal that governments had a keen interest promoting quality products, as the town's reputation was on the line.

Guilds were entrenched by the start of the fourteenth century; on the Continent, these guilds—and sometimes whole towns—specialized in either red (barley) or white (usually wheat) beers. Although there were many exceptions, white beers tended to be more of a northern product than a southern one.

All across the North Sea coast, cities banded together to form a trading organization called the Hansa (or Hanseatic League), whose focus was trading by ship. Many of the towns—Hamburg, Bremen, Rostock, Lübeck, and others—were known as brewing centers, and this trade spread Germanic brewing traditions far afield, especially to the north and east. Beer was also exported to England. Many of the Hansa towns—especially the ones like Hamburg, which were early hop trading centers as well—helped spread the gospel of hopped beer.

As trade and manufacturing became more structured, so did the business of beer, changing from a household craft to a purely commercial enterprise, although breweries in large estates survived until about 1900. Brewsters, women who formed the backbone of the brewing craft in the Middle Ages, did not make the transition.

Meanwhile, in the caves of southern Germany, perpetually chilly conditions led to the evolution of a particular type of yeast adapted to cooler temperatures. This bottom-fermenting yeast was first mentioned in the fifteenth century, but it took another century or two before it became dominant in the area. Appreciated for its clean, smooth flavors, this new "lager" (from the German word meaning "to store") beer would come to dominate the entire brewing world, pushing top-fermenting ales into the realm of specialty beers, save for a few holdout regions, but this came much later.

In 1722, porter was born, so the story goes. This might have been just another curious regional specialty, except that it happened in London, one of the largest cities on earth, where a little thing called the Industrial Revolution was just starting. England was coming down from a massive hangover spawned by a curious experiment featuring homebrewed gin and unregulated retailers. The effect on the health of the population was disastrous, and the Crown was motivated to promote the more temperate beverage of beer. Hogarth's famous pair of engravings, *Gin Lane* and *Beer Street*, sum up the mood of the day pretty well.

Spurred by advances in technology and a burgeoning urban population, porter rode the tidal wave of a whole new kind of factory brewing. For the working classes, industrial employment and crowded urban conditions meant they lacked the time, space, and resources to brew beer at home. This fueled the thirst for professionally brewed beer.

As London boomed, so did the brewers, becoming among the most heavily capitalized businesses in the world. As they rushed in to take advantage of this swelling industry, competition became more intense, and brewers scrambled for any financial advantage. Business interests prevailed. As in all times and places, there were righteous brewers as well as scoundrels. The bad ones flaunted the laws against additives, and loaded the beers with everything from chile peppers to opium. As early as the fifteenth century there were prohibitions against "unwholesome" beer, and this was further codified by a 1710 law which forbade anything other than hops to be used for bittering, although the use of broom and wormwood was allowed by publicans. It wasn't until the early 1800s that the government cracked down on druggists selling all manners of toxic additives to brewers, effectively ending the problem. Lifting the tax on hops didn't hurt, either.

Black malt, patented in 1817, meant that porter could be brewed largely from the high-yielding pale malt, lowering the cost of production significantly. This changed porter's flavor but the public didn't seem to mind. Sugar, a valuable product of England's colonial empire, was also added to the mix as a cheap fermentable adjunct, further bringing down the quality.

The word "stout" as cant for a strong beer was in use fifty years before the birth of porter. Later, of course, it came to specifically stand for a particularly strong dark substyle of porter, and eventually far surpassed porter in popularity, thanks to the Irish.

Pale ale, which had largely remained the domain of the country gentleman throughout porter's rise, became the next great fad, pushed along by the availability of affordable glass drinking vessels. Now the more countrified pale ale brewers became fair game for acquisition and development.

The immense wealth of the large mechanized brewers allowed them to focus on things besides beer, and they began to play at high finance, first swallowing each other up, then turning to smaller game in a cannibalistic orgy of consolidation and brewery extinction that continues in Britain, as elsewhere, to this very day.

In Continental Europe similar forces were at work, although less dramatically. The Germans came gawking to London in the mid-1700s and took back many bits of industrial technology, but the consolidation there didn't reach the same kind of feeding frenzy until very recently.

Pillar Ale Glass, c. 1860

Modern industrial technology was used to create glassware that showcased the new pale ales and Pilseners.

In 1842, a pale lager brew was cooked up in the town of Plze (Pilsen), Bohemia. By World War I, this newly fashionable Pilsener dominated the world beer market. The close of the nineteenth century saw the demise of a large number of regional specialties everywhere. People were less interested in the quaint and sometimes quirky products of their hometowns, and now wanted the new, pale, clear, mass-produced modern beers.

Two world wars on top of many earlier conflicts led to rationing and tax policies that encouraged weaker beers. Germany's unification and incorporation of Bavaria in 1871 led to the adoption of the Reinheitsgebot nationwide, killing off a number of spiced and specialty brews in the North.

In America, the number of breweries peaked at 4,131 in 1873. Aided by innovations like refrigerated railcars and large advertising budgets, established regional breweries muscled their way onto the national scene. By the time Prohibition began in 1919, there were only 1,568 left. After it was repealed in 1933, less than half reopened, but many were in a severely weakened condition and didn't last long.

American Saloon Staff, c. 1900

Besides profit considerations, other factors led to American beer's decline in intensity and variety. World War I led to a suppression of German culture here, and the popularity of Germanic styles such as Münchner seems to have vanished with it. Since before 1550, corn, a near-flavorless adjunct, had been a great favorite with the boys in the accounting department and with brewers trying to tame the high protein barley that thrives here. Two world wars had the same effect here as in Europe: weaker beers. And with the horrifying excesses of prohibition sandwiched in between, people largely forgot what real beer was like.

Consumers of the mid-twentieth century were enraptured with the new consumer culture, and were only too eager to cast off the past. Like my father, who planed the claw feet off the family's Victorian dining-room chairs, postwar Americans wanted modern products for their sparkling modern lives. Dave Brubeck on the hi-fi, Formica on the dinette, and name-brand, crystal-clear canned beer chilling in the fridge. By the 1970s, there were just a handful of breweries in this country, virtually all of them producing pretty much the same beer.

Just when things were at their darkest, a young Fritz Maytag bought the very run-down Anchor Brewery in San Francisco, which had been inconsistently producing a remnant of the Gold Rush era called "steam beer." With an immense amount of effort—and no small amount of cash—Maytag managed to turn Anchor into the cornerstone of the craft brewing movement.

In the late 1970s, homebrewing began to inspire dreams of craft brewing. Not knowing it was impossible, Jack McAuliffe started New Albion Brewing in Sonoma, California. This company didn't last long, but by then the fuse was lit. By the mid 1980s, craft breweries were springing up like mushrooms on the West Coast and elsewhere.

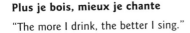

Plus je bois, mieux je chante

"The more I drink, the better I sing."

The late 80s and early 90s were a period of booming growth for craft and home brewing alike. Such success attracted a lot of people who had no business in the business, and there followed a wave of brewery closings. To this day, there is still a lot of used equipment lying around. So the industry has retrenched and settled into a more sober period of modest growth. The people who are making imaginative, well-crafted beers and marketing them with a bit of verve are doing just fine. I think it can honestly be said that there has never been a better time to drink beer in America than the present. And the future looks even brighter.

In a strange way it may be a good thing that America's brewing tradition had the artistic life just about squeezed out of it by the industrial brewers. This was liberating, as American home and craft brewers felt completely free to invent a new style of brewing unhindered by the need to preserve a vanishing folk tradition. In Britain, real ale was (and is) imperiled, so the logical step was to form an organization dedicated to preserving the tradition. CAMRA (the Campaign for Real Ales) succeeded in rescuing real ale from the scrap heap, but at the same time, this movement was anything but encouraging to innovation, although by now this has started to change.

The old familiar mergers and consolidation are rampant on the Continent. There have been a lot of woeful tales from Belgium of late, as treasured and eccentric products have been eradicated or mainstreamed. The bock is just starting to hit the fan in Germany, which is extremely vulnerable due to the sameness of so many of its beers. With a lot of effort and a little luck, the same kind of creative energy that has made the American craft beer so vibrant will find a way to bring some vitality to these proud brewing nations.

Chapter 2

WHAT IS THIS THING CALLED BEER?

Brewmaster c. 1870

Beer is the vast family of fermented beverages made from plant starch, usually derived from grain. It is a worldwide phenomenon; nearly every society with access to grain, from the Himalayas to the Andes, makes beer. In Africa, millet is the preferred grain. In South America, corn and manioc beers are most common. In Asia, from Japan to Tibet, rice is the grain of choice. Elsewhere, palm, agave, cassava/manioc, sorghum, and rye are all used to make beer. The variety is mind-bending. Eskimos, as far as I know, have no traditional beer, having apparently tried and discovered that it is impossible to get alcohol from walrus blubber.

In addition to the flavor and modest amount of alcohol it offers, beer is also valued as a food—liquid bread—and as a safe, potable beverage, as the brewing process renders water reliably safe to drink.

All types of grain and many edible roots contain starch, which are sugars linked into chains. The molecules are too long for yeast to eat, so a process is needed to break starch into fermentable sugar. In barley malt beer, we hijack the mechanism the plant itself uses to make its own energy reserves available to the sprouting plant. In the rice-based Japanese *saké* and Himalayan *chang*, special fungi supply the enzyme. *Chicha*, the indigenous corn beer of Latin America, uses human saliva as the enzyme source.

For beers broadly in the European tradition, barley reigns supreme with wheat a significant second and others like rye and oats making occasional appearances. In most cases, the grains are malted before brewing. In malting, the grains steep in cool water until they sprout and just begin converting from a seed into a small plant before being quickly dried and lightly toasted. The malting process activates starch-dissolving enzymes in the grain and makes the kernels more crumbly and receptive to water. The drying, or *kilning*, creates that lovely range of malty flavors we treasure in beer.

WHAT MAKES A BEER?

Great beer is a delight to the senses. As we are highly visual creatures, the most obvious characteristic of a beer is its color. The whole range, from pale golden yellow to the inkiest black, comes from malt kilned in a variety of ways; mixing various shades gives the brewer a huge palette to work with. And of course, these colored malts display a huge range of different flavors and aromas as well.

"Strength" can describe either alcoholic content or the density of the unfermented wort, called original gravity. They are closely related, as the more material that's available to ferment, the more alcohol that can be created. It's not a rock-solid relationship, because various factors influence how much of the potential sugars are eventually transformed into alcohol. A rough rule of thumb is that an original gravity of 1.050 (12 °P) will result in an alcohol content of 5 percent; at 1.070 (17 °P), alcohol is around 7 percent. So it goes up and down the scale. With increasing gravity come not only increasing alcohol but more intense flavors as well.

It is important to remember that color is not strength. Although draft Guinness may taste strong to some, it actually has less alcohol than most (so-called) industrial Pilsener-style beers. Color reflects simply the amount of roasted or toasted malt used, which in most beers amounts to less than 25 percent of the recipe.

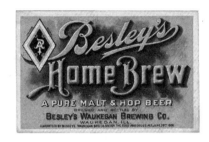

BODY AND TEXTURE

As beer hits your tongue, there is a perception of weight and texture that is different from a flavor sensation. There may be a certain viscosity or oiliness on the palate. In some beers there are mouth-puckering (or *astringent*) qualities that may add to perceptions of weight or just be distracting. And of course sweetness also adds a feeling of weightiness in the mouth.

Beer is a *colloid*, a suspension of small particles (in this case, proteins) in a liquid. The proteins form a loose net that knits the liquid into a semi-solid. Gelatin is a familiar example. The colloidal state is an important contributor to beer body as well as head formation and longevity. Unfortunately, it is a house of cards, degrading over time—this is the "snow" you sometimes see in a really old bottle of Eurobrew. The colloidal state is also temperature dependent, often throwing a haze when the beer is chilled. This sort of misbehavior is frowned upon in commercial beer, so manipulation of the colloid composition by commercial brewers is one of the finer points of the science. Most homebrewers are generally unconcerned about the details, except those who want to master the subtleties of lager brewing. But then this is a breed of brewer looking for trouble the same way mountain climbers do.

Grains—especially in their unmalted state—contain *beta glucans* and *pentosans*, gummy polymers of sugar that can cause problems for the brewer. In the mash, their high viscosity may make it hard to separate the sugar-rich wort from the spent grains. In the finished beer, these gums can add a creamy or even an oily texture. This can be a problem in cheap, canned corn beer, but in styles such as Belgian witbiers and rye beers, the oily texture can be a welcome addition.

Carbonation adds texture and a certain measure of flavor to beer. Carbon dioxide gas actually dissolves in the beer as carbonic acid, adding fizz and an acidic bite. The quantity can be easily controlled by the brewer and is usually driven by style. British ales are usually lightly carbonated, which allows their subtle complexity to shine. In larger quantities, dissolved CO_2 can mask other flavors, especially hops—another reason why mainstream beers taste so bland. Wheat beers are highly carbonated, but are usually poured from the bottle in such a way as to remove some of the excess gas by the time the beer is in the glass.

Units of Measurement in Beer

Quality	Unit	Comment
Alcohol	% by Volume	The international standard
	% by Weight	America, from 1933 to about 1995
Gravity of Wort	OG (Original Gravity)	Specific Gravity, often expressed minus the decimal point
	°Plato	Sugars, in percentage—new standard
	°Balling	Sugars, in percentage—old standard
	Belgian Degrees	Original Gravity, decimal shifted: 1050 = 5° Belgian
	Brewers Pounds	Sugars, expressed as pounds/British barrel. One Brewers Pound per Bbl = 10028 OG.
Wort Color	SRM	Modern spectrophotometric method, corresponds roughly to the old Lovibond series.
	°Lovibond	Old arbitrary system of colored glasses to be compared visually to beer samples. Still used to refer to malt color in the United States.
	EBC	European Brewing Convention color measurement standard. Approximately double at any given color, but not precisely correlated to °SRM
	Malt Color Units	°SRM x Lb ÷ gallons. Very rough measure of total malt color added to beer. The higher up the color scale, the less accurate it gets. See p 62.
Hop Bitterness	IBU	Parts-per-million of iso-alpha acid present in the finished beer. Spectrophotometrically determined.
	HBU	Homebrew Bittering Units. Estimation of hop bittering substances added. Not accurate by itself as a predictor of beer bitterness. Alpha Acid % x ounces ÷ gallons. Also called Alpha Acid Units (AAU).
Carbonation	Volumes CO_2	Amount of CO_2 dissolved in beer, the volume of the gas compared to the volume of the liquid. Since the density of the gas (and the liquid too for that matter) varies by temperature, the same volume of gas will be at a higher pressure when the temperature is higher. Typical beer carbonation levels are at 2.2 to 3.0 volumes. See p 68.

BEER FLAVOR

As you taste, it is important to distinguish between flavor and aroma, although it may be hard to pull them apart at times. Flavor is defined by certain chemical interactions in the mouth, primarily on the tongue. There used to be four recognized flavors: sweet, sour, salty, and bitter. It turns out there's another, *umami*, that is found in soy sauce, fish, seaweed, and MSG, and that is very important in Japanese and other Asian cuisines. The chemical responsible for this is glutamate, an amino acid.

I would show you one of those textbook tongue diagrams where the organ is broken into areas according to which flavor it detects best, but it turns out that's all wrong. So much for health class. The little bumps on your tongue are called papillae, and they contain the sensing apparatus for the different flavors. They are not concentrated by type, but are spread all over the tongue.

Sweetness and bitterness are the primary players in beer flavor. The sweetness of malt and the bitter hop resins form a yin and yang of balance every brewer has to deal with in every single brew. Additionally, most dark malts have roasty/toasty qualities that fall on the bitter side of the balance equation.

Sweetness in beer comes mainly from unfermented sugars. During mashing, the brewer can make the brew more or less fermentable. Yeast love maltose, the primary sugar that comes from malt, but will not ferment some of the other sugars liberated during brewing.

Bitterness comes primarily from the addition of hops (or rarely, other bitter herbs) to beer. These green fluffy cones contain bitter resins and aromatic compounds that change chemically and dissolve in the wort when boiled. More important than bitterness is balance. The balance between malt sweetness and hop bitterness is the backbone of any beer recipe, but other components like tannin, roasty/toasty flavors, acidity, smoke, alcohol, and others may also have roles to play in some beers. As the gravity of the beer goes up, so does the amount of bitterness needed to balance it.

Salt (sodium chloride) can play a role in beer flavor, as it is often present in brewing water to one degree or another. It doesn't affect the chemistry of the mash, but in small amounts, salt can give the impression of a full-bodied richness, and has been employed as a seasoning ingredient in some very light beers to achieve just this effect.

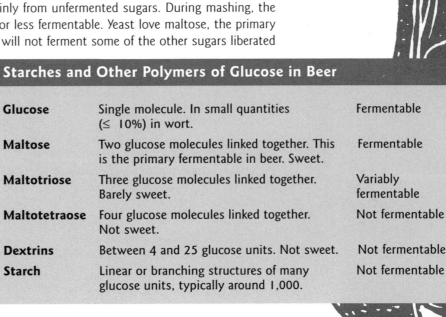

Bellarmine Jug

From 1400 to 1600, these pot-bellied stoneware jugs were used to transport and serve beer and wine across Northern Europe.

Starches and Other Polymers of Glucose in Beer

Glucose	Single molecule. In small quantities (≤ 10%) in wort.	Fermentable
Maltose	Two glucose molecules linked together. This is the primary fermentable in beer. Sweet.	Fermentable
Maltotriose	Three glucose molecules linked together. Barely sweet.	Variably fermentable
Maltotetraose	Four glucose molecules linked together. Not sweet.	Not fermentable
Dextrins	Between 4 and 25 glucose units. Not sweet.	Not fermentable
Starch	Linear or branching structures of many glucose units, typically around 1,000.	Not fermentable

ELEMENTS OF AROMA

In contrast to the limited universe of five flavors, the spectrum of aromas humans can detect is essentially unlimited. Beer plays into this by offering several hundred known aroma chemicals, which can be grouped into several classes.

The Laws of Aroma in Beer

1. You want some.

2. Use more than you think. It will go away.

3. Complexity is good.

4. Complicated is bad.

Alcohols Various forms, from ethanol to longer chains, called fusel alcohols, with more intense aromas (think isopropyl alcohol).

Aldehydes Family of fruity and perfumey aromas. Most common in beer is acetaldehyde, which has a fresh, green-apple aroma.

Diacetyl The chemical that gives movie popcorn its buttery zing. May add a certain richness in very small amounts, but if noticeably buttery it's usually an indicator of a contamination or yeast stress problem. Also a natural product of normal fermentation; in lagers, there is a need for a short period of elevated temperatures (twenty-four hours at 68 to 70° F or 20 to 21° C) to allow it to be reduced to less objectionable chemicals.

Esters Fruity or sometimes spicy aromas mostly due to yeast activity. At high levels in Belgian yeasts, especially when fermented at higher temperatures.

Ethyl acetate	Fruity, nail polish remover
Isoamyl acetate	Banana
Ethyl hexanoate	Ripe apple

Organic acids A result of yeast and bacterial activity, which may be pleasant or unpleasant depending on context and concentration.

Acetic	Vinegar
Butyric	Rancid butter or cheese
Capric, caproic, caprylic, capranoic	Goaty (like goat cheese); sweaty
Isovaleric, isobutyric, 2-methyl-butyric	Horse (from *Brettanomyces*)
Lactic	Yogurt, sour cream
Valeric	Stinky cheese

Phenol A wide range of chemicals, many of which are noxious—smoky or medicinal, for example. Desirable ones may be produced by specialized yeasts such as strains used in Bavarian weizens or Belgian ales.

4-vinyl guiaicol	"Clove" aroma found in weizens
4-ethyl phenol	Barnyard; a marker for *Brettanomyces* activity

Pyrazines, etc. Malt aroma chemicals from bready to malty to nutty, to toasty to roasty. These are formed exclusively from malt kilning, even in the palest malts. Malt extract has been largely stripped of aroma, which is why a pound of crystal malt or a mini-mash makes such a dramatic improvement.

Terpenoids Hop aromatics, mainly, which differ greatly according to variety. Hop aromas come from the plant and dissolve into the beer unscathed. However, boiling does drive them out again, which is why aromatic hops are added at the end of the boil, and sometimes even (as in dry hopping) during fermentation. Excess CO_2 gas given off during fermentation will also scrub hop aroma out of beer. And time, of course, does its damage too.

This list does not include spiced, fruit, or infected beers (see p 74), although in both cases many of the chemical classes are the same.

THE FINE ART OF DRINKING BEER

It takes effort to brew your own beer, so you might as well make sure you serve it in the best possible manner. A well-crafted beer, when served at the proper temperature, in the proper glass, with a proper head, can be a thing of wonder.

Start with a clean glass—very clean. If there are bubbles clinging to the side, it's not clean. The dirt provides nucleation sites for bubbles, which will drain a beer of its fizz prematurely. Modern dishwashing detergent is pretty good, so this shouldn't be too tough. If you're washing by hand, make sure the detergent is thoroughly rinsed; if not it can collapse the head. And be sure to dry the glass by hand as well, because minerals from dried-up water spots can count for dirt.

The choice of glassware has of late been made into a pseudoscience as tricky and opaque as quantum chromodynamics, with a numbing variety of strangely shaped vessels accompanied by dire warnings lest you commit the unforgivable faux pas of serving, say, a lambic in a gueuze glass. As much a fan of drinking glasses as I am, I have to tell you this is a rather modern conceit, concocted in the last half of the twentieth century. Before about 1750, little distinction was made between even wine and beer, with glasses holding whatever was being passed around the table. People felt lucky to have a glass at all.

However, in some countries brewers are very particular about the serving methods used for their beers, even specifying the glass shape. In Belgium, every beer has its own glass, and in some bars if the proper glass is already in use, you'll have to pick another beer. Of course glass selection is not all frippery. Certain styles do show well in their "traditional" glassware, but you should treat these suggestions for what they are, and not inviolable laws.

Most important is matching glass size to beer strength. You wouldn't (well, shouldn't) drink barley wine by the pint, so small glasses are best. The strong October beers of England were drunk from glasses holding barely 2 ounces. Some beers have a lot of carbonation, which demands a glass with some additional headspace. Topers in Berlin quaffed their low-alcohol weissbier from huge tumblers holding a gallon or so, capacious enough for an immense bouffant of foam. It is best to pour out all of a bottle of homebrew at one time, as the yeast is almost always unattractive and some-

Ale Glass, c. 1840, possibly Pittsburgh

times adds a muddy taste, so having a large enough glass is very important. Having some extra headspace also allows for aromas to collect, giving the sniffer a sniffable experience.

Various tapers can either compact or support the head. A Pilsener glass with its ice cream cone shape supports a large, fluffy head. Inward tapering glasses will force the head together as it rises in the glass, as well as helping to keep the aroma inside the glass. A tulip-shaped glass both concentrates and supports the head.

If you're doing a judging or critical tasting, a 6-ounce wineglass is the internationally approved standard for beverage sensory analysis, but given the nature of most homebrew judgings, simple hard plastic cups are a necessary evil.

Serving temperature is also very important. To some degree this is dictated by tradition—cellar temperature for British real ales, for example—but generally weaker beers are served cooler than stronger ones. A fine, fruity British ale will taste weird and lifeless if served ice cold. So will a German lager for that matter, which is why they're served at about 45° F (7° C). Dark, malty, or strong beers may be served warmer than pale ones. High carbonation levels require colder serving temperatures to prevent overfoaming.

"We have besides cups made of horns of beastes, of cockernuts, of goords, of eggs of estriches; others made of the shells of divers fishes brought from the Indies and other places, and shining like mother of pearle. Come to plate, every tavern can afford you flat bowles, french bowles, prounet cups, beare bowles, beakers; and private householders in the citie when they make a feast to entertain their friends, can furnish their cupboards with flagons, tankards, beere cups, wine bowles, some whits, some percell gilt, some gilt all over, some with covers, others without, of sundry shapes and qualities."

— Heywood, Philocothonista or Drunkard Opened, Dissected and Anatomized (1635)

Pouring Pour right down the middle of the glass. You want to release some carbonation and get a good head going. Let it settle, and keep pouring. Patience will be rewarded with a dense, long-lived head and a less gassy beer.

Storage Cool and dark is the rule here. But the truth is that most homebrew is at its prime some time before you get your hands on it. If you've ever tasted beer at the brewery, you know this. Nonetheless, proper storage can keep deterioration at a minimum.

Keep lagers cold The cold conditioning of these styles is an essential part of the brewing process. To do this correctly requires a temperature-controlled environment such as a dedicated refrigerator.

Keep ales cool A basement is the ideal location. Storing ales at near-freezing temperatures will cause a harmless but unsightly protein haze to develop, interfering with the perfect drinking experience. All the processes of aging in beer are accelerated by heat, so keep your beer away from radiators and other hot spots.

Avoid temperature changes Repeated heating and cooling will cause the protein complexes in beer to destabilize and come out as haze. One trip in and out of the fridge won't kill a beer, but try to avoid temperature swings if you can. In the East and Midwest, cellars serve well for cellaring. Elsewhere, a closet or room toward the center of the home will have to do until you add that second refrigerator. In warmer climates, space in wine storage lockers is available for rent at reasonable prices.

Avoid light   Sunlight and fluorescent tubes shine with a lot of blue-green light that can quickly turn a beer "skunky." Brown bottles are good protection, but green ones generally stink. And where there's light, there's often heat, which is bad for beer.

Give it time   Most beer is not really meant for long-term storage, but most homebrew benefits from a few months of aging. Obviously, since the word "lager" means "to store," such beers benefit from between two months to a year of cold storage. Very strong beers such as barley wines and imperial stouts really need a year at least, and sometimes are splendiferous at ten.

Beer Serving Temperatures	
Pale Lager	40–45° F (4.5–7° C)
Dark Lager	45–50° F (4.5–10° C)
Strong Lager	50–55° F (10–13° C)
Wheat Beers	40–50° F (4.5–10° C)
Real Ale	50–55° F (10–13° C)
Cream, Blonde Ales	40–45° F (4.5–7° C)
Belgian Abbey Dubbel	50–55° F (10–13° C)
Belgian Pale Ales	40–45° F (4.5–7° C)
Belgian Abbey Tripels	40–45° F (4.5–7° C)
Lambic (all)	40–50° F (4.5–10° C)

These temperatures are a little on the cool side to allow for warming up slightly when they are poured.

An Overview of Brewing

WHY HOMEBREW?

You probably have an idea—maybe even a mission—behind your desire to brew. Lofty or humble, it's a testament to the depths of beer's cultural roots that people get so many different kinds of satisfaction from brewing. Here are a few reasons to brew—yeah, like you need another one.

Brew what you want The marketing geniuses at the world's industrial breweries haven't a clue as to what kind of beer you like. Even if they did, the best they could do would be to dump it into a pot with a hundred thousand other preferences and brew an accountant-approved approximation of the resulting mélange—which is exactly what they do. By brewing it yourself, you can have what you want, when you want it. You are the niche market supreme. You can brew for yourself, your lover, your parents, your new brewing friends, or the guests at your company picnic. Every real or imagined style is within your reach: dunkel, Pilsener, smoked habañero ale, strong pale ale, wheat porter. If you seek out rare and exotic beers, your own nanobrewery can be the source for the most rarefied beers in the world.

Brew for knowledge Brewing adds a huge new dimension to your understanding of beer. Wine is largely about agriculture and weather; brewing is all about process: the way malt is made and kilned, the way beer is mashed, at what time hops are added to the boil, the temperature of fermentation. These and dozens of other factors have profound effects on every beer. The best way to learn, as we know, is by doing. By brewing.

Sharpen your palate Whether nervously watching for flaws in one's own brew, or trying to untangle the secrets of a favorite commercial beer, brewing makes one highly attuned to the many tastes that come together in beer. Chocolate malt, Cascade hops, and a hundred other ingredients cease to be meaningless names, but snap into focus as living entities imparting their unique personality traits to beer.

Relive the past The past is lost to us forever, but brewing gives us a unique power to raise the dead. Beers of fifty, a hundred, or a thousand years ago may be brought to life, not with total accuracy perhaps, but near enough to transport you to another age quite effectively. You don't have to imagine how it felt to quaff a strong, dark, smoky, herb-infused gruit ale from medieval Germany. If you brew, you can track down some bog myrtle, cook one up, and taste it for yourself.

Express your true nature Brewing is a direct creative act, a far cry from the tangential purposes to which our cubicle-bound labors are usually applied. You can get an inspiration for a new beer, go home and brew it, and in a few weeks delight yourself and your friends with your masterpiece. But more than merely a simple pleasure, homebrewing is beer as art, a high calling of our nature.

Be the life of the party Your friends will brag about you shamelessly, even as they unapologetically "forget" to bring beer to your place. But for membership in the glorious community of brewers, it's a small price to pay. A passion for brewing, combined with the social bond created by the simple act of sharing a beer, creates a true kinship among brewers.

Brew as a meditation Except for those mad moments when the kettle boils over for the sixth time, brewing is a very relaxing and rewarding activity. Monastic traditions have long recognized the power of manual labor to fortify the soul. Take the harvest of the earth, mix it with pure water, bind and purify it with fire, and transform it with the mystery of yeast, once known as "Godisgood." There's plenty to contemplate here. And I can tell you, a shelf full of freshly bottled ale is a deeply calming sight.

Brew better than the next guy For those of a competitive bent, homebrewing offers plenty of opportunities to test your mettle. And nothing will whip your brewing skills into shape like the pressure of a looming competition. Even if you're not a Type-A personality, competitions can give you informed and impartial feedback on your beers and how well they match the styles you're shooting for.

King Gambrinus

This myth-shrouded figure is the patron symbol of the brewer's art.

Embark on a new career Most microbreweries began as a gleam in some homebrewer's eye. You too can give up your fast-track software or biotech career to wear the rubber boots of the brewer. If you are thinking of starting a small brewery, it is essential—even if you don't plan to be the brewer yourself—that you learn to brew. Craft brewing is a very product-focused business, and you can't afford not to know as much as possible about how the product is made.

Simply the best beer Without a doubt, well-made homebrew is the best beer in the world. With some practice, you can brew with greater control, and with more and better ingredients than the typical microbrewery. Your beer can be superbly conditioned, adjunct-free, unfiltered, and unpasteurized. Blowing the dust off a five-year-old homebrewed barley wine and wallowing in its mature, malty essence is a treat seldom equaled in the world of mere commercial products.

THE BREWING PROCESS IN A NUTSHELL

To strip it to its essence, brewing is a two-stage process. First, hot water is mixed with crushed barley and allowed to stand in a process called mashing. The temperature of this operation is critical, and usually takes place in the neighborhood of 150° F (65.5° C). In under an hour the enzymes convert most of the malt starch into sugar, and the mash becomes sweet as a result. In the second stage, the liquid—now called wort—is collected and boiled with the hops.

That's the simple version. Other changes in the mash occur at three other temperature points, although they aren't necessarily involved in every brew. At low temperatures, 95 to 100° F (35 to 38° C), gummy substances like glucans and pentosans are degraded, lowering the viscosity of the mash, which may make sparging easier and more efficient. At 113 to 131° F (45 to 55° C), proteolytic enzymes chop up some of the long protein molecules into smaller chunks. The length of a protein (or fragment) determines whether it will contribute to the body of a beer, aid in head formation and retention, or simply be a nuisance as a haze former when the beer is chilled. In the old days when protein levels were higher and malting tended to be less consistent, more complicated mashing schedules were needed to produce acceptable beers. With modern malts, a protein rest may actually do damage, breaking up proteins needed for a good head and body. For this reason, a protein rest is not used in most of the recipes in this book. For today's mega-brewers and others who wish to produce a shelf-stable, chill haze-free product with extreme efficiency, protein management is crucial. You have to decide whether you share those concerns. For most homebrew, a simple infusion mash works perfectly.

The other key temperature is the mash out. This is usually accomplished by the addition of near-boiling water at the end of the mash. This raises the temperature of the goods to 165 to 170° F (74 to 76.5° C), which has two effects. First it stops enzymatic activity, fixing the ratio of fermentable to unfermentable sugars. It also helps gelatinize some of the remaining starch and gums, allowing for a free-flowing sparge, an important asset.

Factors Affecting Starch Conversion and Wort Fermentability

		MORE FERMENTABLE ◄ ► LESS FERMENTABLE	
Temperature	145° F (63° C)		159° F (70.5° C)
Time	2 Hours		30 Min
Dilution	3 Qts/Lb		1 Qt/Lb
pH*	5.3–5.5		above 5.5, below 5.2

* pH is actually not this simple, and the optimum varies by temperature. Fortunately it doesn't require a lot of managing. Use proper techniques in other respects, and pH will usually take care of itself.

Great Brewing Words

Barm	Yeast
Bung	Wooden plug for a cask
Coolship	A shallow pan for cooling wort
Gyle	A brew, batch, or fermenting vessel
Lobb	To add yeast
Shive	Bung with a hole into which is inserted a spile
Spile	A peg inserted into a shive used to regulate carbonation
Tun	A mashing vessel; in older terms could also refer to a fermenter
Wort	Unfermented beer

During the starch-conversion rest, there are plenty of subtle details brewers can use to fine-tune their beer. Fermentability is the main character that can be affected by the way the mash is conducted. Time, temperature, dilution, and pH can all have a modest effect; they are usually combined if a particularly sweet or dry beer is desired.

At the end of the mash, the grain bed is drained of its sugary juice, now called wort, and hot water is added to rinse any remaining sugars out of the grain, a process called sparging. More practical details are in the how-to section on mashing, p. 37.

If you're an extract brewer, somebody has done all this work for you, and this is where you take over.

The wort is transferred to a kettle and brought to a boil. In modern brewing (that is, after 1500), hops are the bittering herb of choice, but many other herbs and spices have been used throughout history. Bitterness is required to balance the sweetness of malt, and some herbs, like hops, have antiseptic properties that allow the beer to keep longer without spoiling. The bitter materials in the hops, the alpha acids, have to isomerize (change shape chemically), rendering them bitter and soluble in the wort. Although some bitterness develops quickly, it takes two to three hours to reach maximum bitterness.

Hops are usually added in several doses. Hop aromatics are volatile and waft away during the boil. The bitter alpha acids take a while to work their way into the beer. In order to have both, one needs to make multiple additions—typically at sixty-to-ninety minutes, fifteen-to-thirty minutes, and at two-to-five minutes or just as the heat is turned off.

During the boil, proteins from the malt combine with hop tannins and precipitate out of solution, appearing as clumps of stuff called hot break that looks—and is—like egg drop soup. This may be accelerated by adding a coagulant such as Irish moss to the kettle for the last ten minutes or so of the boil.

The wort is then cooled as rapidly as possible, usually with a wort-chiller circulating cold water, although in the old days it was simply placed in shallow pans called coolships. Sticking your kettle into a snowbank works pretty well, too. If the cooling is rapid enough, additional protein will precipitate. This is called the cold break.

After the wort is cooled and transferred to a fermenter, yeast is added. At first, it just reproduces right there in your beer. Once it has used up all available oxygen, it attacks the sugars with a vengeance. At full tilt, it can generate a large, foamy head that can rise a foot or more. As it feeds, yeast produces carbon dioxide and alcohol along with small amounts of many other chemicals that give beer much of its subtle flavor and aroma. The insanity goes on for a few days, then, having scarfed up the most digestible sugars, the yeast calms down and nibbles on the leftovers. Eventually, there's nothing left to eat; it gets up from the table and settles to the bottom of the tank. Total time: about a week for a normal strength beer to get through this primary fermentation. It takes another three weeks or so for the same beer to be ready to drink.

The temperature of fermentation and subsequent aging affects the beers flavor and

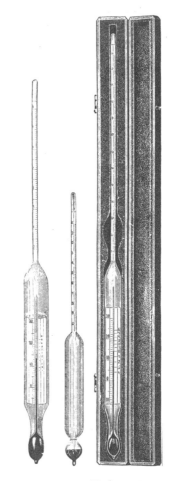

Hydrometers

These glass instruments are used to determine the gravity of a wort.

Ale and Beer Fermentation Temperatures

Type	Fermentation	Conditioning
Ale	55–80°F (13–26.5° C)	55–68° F (13–20° C)
Lager	48–52°F (9–11° C)	33–38° F (0.5–3.5° C)

What is an Enzyme?

Enzymes are proteins that act as catalysts, facilitating chemical reactions. They are prime movers for just about all of the chemical reactions in life, a number of which are key to brewing. There are a few you need to get to know personally.

Enzymes are not general-purpose catalysts; each one is tailored to a particular chemical reaction, or even a single step of one. Each chemical reaction has to overcome a certain energy level to get from one stable form to another. Between is an unstable state—think of climbing and then balancing on top of a high wall. Enzymes work by stabilizing this transitional state, lowering the energy needed (the height of the wall) for a reaction to occur by as much a million-fold or even more.

Enzymes are active in malting. Proteolytic (protein-degrading) enzymes attack the walls of starch granules, making the starch available during brewing. Other enzymes are activated during malting, getting them ready to produce a plant—or a beer. Unless you're malting your own, this is really all you need to know.

The mash is a different story. There, all the enzymes are involved in chopping up longer molecules.

Enzyme	Target Molecule	Useful Temperature Range
Beta Glucanase	Glucans (gums)	95–113° F (35–45° C)
Protease, Peptidase	Proteins	115–131° F (46–55° C)
Beta Amylase	Starch (more fermentable wort)	140–149° F (60–65° C)
Alpha Amylase	Starch (less fermentable wort)	149–160° F (65–71° C)

These enzymes all operate at different temperatures, and have specific requirements for mash dilution, pH, and other parameters. If all this sounds hopelessly complex, it is. If you're a producer of industrial yellow beer, you've got to know it cold. But as a small-scale brewer you can rely on millennia of traditional practice to guide you through the basics, and then you only have to make a few decisions.

Most important are the amylolytic, or starch-dissolving enzymes. There are two of them, and since they operate at slightly different temperatures, you can shift the burden from one to the other by mashing at a higher or lower temperature. Alpha amylase works by chopping up starch molecules willy-nilly, resulting in fragments of randomly varying size. Beta amylase is a fastidious nibbler, working from the end of the starch molecules and biting off one maltose sugar with every nip. Maltose is the sugar that yeast most likes to eat, meaning that favoring beta amylase will produce a very fermentable wort. Favoring alpha amylase, on the other hand, will leave more of the longer sugars and dextrins (halfway between starch and sugar), which means that some of the wort sugars will be unfermentable, thus resulting in residual sweetness in the finished beer.

aroma. At higher temperatures, yeast produces much more of the secondary chemicals that impart fruity or spicy notes to the beer. This is the primary difference between ales and lagers.

You could drink the beer at this point, but it would be disgustingly flat. To carbonate the beer, carbon dioxide must be added. In homebrewed bottled beer, a measured amount of sugar is added to the batch before it's placed into bottles. Fermentation restarts, and there's no place for the gas to go, so it dissolves in the beer, making it lively. This usually takes another two weeks. Draft beer can be carbonated in a similar process, or by simply hooking up a tank of CO_2 to the keg and allowing a week or so for the gas to permeate the beer.

STUFF

No gear, no hobby.

Homebrewing sometimes seems like a hobby for equipment-crazed, mechanomaniacal, re-animating Frankensteins. I must admit I am guilty of crimes along these lines, but I am happy to tell you that this is not normal. You do need a certain kit of tools, but I promise you don't need to learn to weld unless you want to.

For every junkyard junkie with a TIG torch in hand, there are dozens of happy kitchen brewers who make great beer the way Fred Astaire danced—smooth and graceful, never breaking a sweat. The homebrew shop in your area will offer basic and deluxe equipment kits, and are often a great source of information and contacts with other brewers in your area. You might even call them and ask about a homebrew club in your area, then go to a meeting and see what's up. Ask lots of questions. If you really feel like you need hands-on help, offer to split your first batch with someone in exchange for their assistance.

Every homebrew shop on the planet sells a basic starter package. This should include:

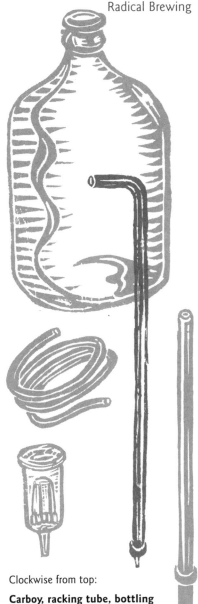

7- to 10-gallon capacity fermenter, typically plastic (or better, a 6.5-gallon glass carboy)
Rubber stopper with hole
Fermentation lock
Racking cane, hose, shutoff clip
Bottling wand
Bottle capper plus caps
Carboy brush (if a carboy is included in the kit)
Hydrometer and jar

Kits don't typically contain these items, but you'll need them:

3- to 6-gallon stainless steel pot (enameled steel will work as long as it's unchipped)
Stainless steel spoon sized to fit your pot
Two cases plus a six-pack of non-screw-off beer bottles. You can buy them empty or full.
A powdered brewery cleaner such as Five Star PBW or B-Brite
Unscented household bleach or homebrew sanitizer
Stainless steel pot scrubber (copper's okay as well), and a small all-stainless hose clamp
A reasonably accurate thermometer such as one suited for cooking.

Clockwise from top:

Carboy, racking tube, bottling wand, fermentation lock, hose

The quality of these items is usually decent enough, and there aren't an awful lot of different models from which to choose. I do recommend two additions or upgrades. First, if the kit doesn't include one, get a large glass 6- to 7-gallon carboy. The ones usually sold are recycled chemical jugs that hold 25 liters and have a screw-on cap

"Wing" Capper

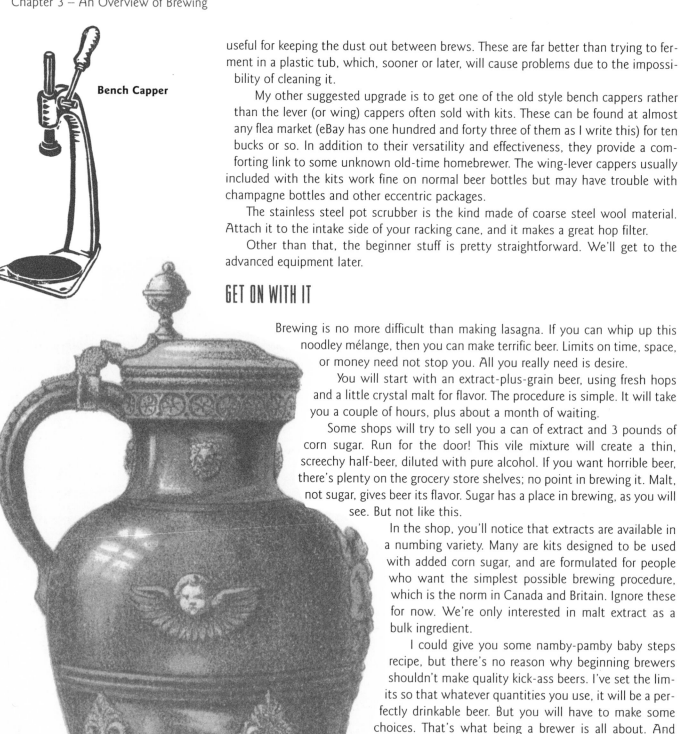

Bench Capper

useful for keeping the dust out between brews. These are far better than trying to ferment in a plastic tub, which, sooner or later, will cause problems due to the impossibility of cleaning it.

My other suggested upgrade is to get one of the old style bench cappers rather than the lever (or wing) cappers often sold with kits. These can be found at almost any flea market (eBay has one hundred and forty three of them as I write this) for ten bucks or so. In addition to their versatility and effectiveness, they provide a comforting link to some unknown old-time homebrewer. The wing-lever cappers usually included with the kits work fine on normal beer bottles but may have trouble with champagne bottles and other eccentric packages.

The stainless steel pot scrubber is the kind made of coarse steel wool material. Attach it to the intake side of your racking cane, and it makes a great hop filter.

Other than that, the beginner stuff is pretty straightforward. We'll get to the advanced equipment later.

GET ON WITH IT

Brewing is no more difficult than making lasagna. If you can whip up this noodley mélange, then you can make terrific beer. Limits on time, space, or money need not stop you. All you really need is desire.

You will start with an extract-plus-grain beer, using fresh hops and a little crystal malt for flavor. The procedure is simple. It will take you a couple of hours, plus about a month of waiting.

Some shops will try to sell you a can of extract and 3 pounds of corn sugar. Run for the door! This vile mixture will create a thin, screechy half-beer, diluted with pure alcohol. If you want horrible beer, there's plenty on the grocery store shelves; no point in brewing it. Malt, not sugar, gives beer its flavor. Sugar has a place in brewing, as you will see. But not like this.

In the shop, you'll notice that extracts are available in a numbing variety. Many are kits designed to be used with added corn sugar, and are formulated for people who want the simplest possible brewing procedure, which is the norm in Canada and Britain. Ignore these for now. We're only interested in malt extract as a bulk ingredient.

I could give you some namby-pamby baby steps recipe, but there's no reason why beginning brewers shouldn't make quality kick-ass beers. I've set the limits so that whatever quantities you use, it will be a perfectly drinkable beer. But you will have to make some choices. That's what being a brewer is all about. And there's no sense messing around with dry yeast unless you can't get anything else. For good clean flavor and known pedigreed strains, liquid is absolutely the way to go.

30

| RECIPE | **[Your Name Here]—*Your First Radical Brew*** |

Yield: 5 gallons (19 liters)
Gravity: 1.050
Alcohol/vol: 5.5 to 5.8%
Color: Gold to brown
Bitterness: It's up to you
Maturation: 6 to 8 weeks

Ingredients:

5.0 lb (2.3 kg) pale dry unhopped malt extract (or 6-7 lb of liquid malt extract)

0.5–1.5 lb (227–680 g) (depending on how malty you want it) crystal malt, any color you choose. Darker malt will make darker beer, of course. Smell, taste, and buy what appeals to you. This will be the signature flavor of the beer. Buy pre-ground if they have it; otherwise you can crack it lightly with a coffee grinder or more percussive means. It just needs to be crushed a little, not ground to a powder.

1 knit bag or cheesecloth to hold grain

4–8 oz (113–227 g) high quality aroma hops such as Kent Goldings (English), Saaz (Czech), Hallertau (German), or Cascade (American). More hops will make a more bitter, aromatic beer. I recommend whole hops, but pellets are fine. Just use 25 percent less. Do not use high-alpha hops here. If you don't want plenty of hop aroma, cut the final addition down to 1 oz (28 g) or less.

To figure your hop quantities, see the chart below:

This hop bitterness chart follows the procedure outlined below, with the hops added in stages:

1/4 for 60 minutes

1/4 for 20 minutes

1/2 at the end of the boil

Use this chart to find quantities for your preferred bitterness level.

Hop Bitterness Chart (follows 1/4 + 1/4 + 1/2 use below)

		Estimated IBUs Contributed by:		
Variety	AA%	4 oz (113g)	6 oz (170 g)	8 oz (227 g)
Kent Goldings	5	28	42	56
Saaz	3	17	26	34
Hallertau	4.5	25	38	50
Cascade	5.5	31	46	62

For reference, here are some IBU levels in common commercial beers: Budweiser 11; Heineken 17; Beck's 24; Bass Ale 27; Guinness draft 35; Sierra Nevada Pale Ale 38; Pilsner Urquell 40; Anchor Steam 40; Anchor Liberty 54; Arrogant Bastard 75.

Use one package of liquid ale yeast. There are tons to choose from, so it can be kind of intimidating. Generally, English yeasts are slightly fruity and complex; German ale yeasts are super clean; Belgian ones vary, but are often full of earthy spiciness. Some accentuate malt, others hops, and some have their own assertive character. There's a lot of information on the Wyeast and White Labs Web sites, and your shop owners will have some experience too. Anyway, pick one; it's just a batch of beer. You don't have to overthink it right now; there's plenty of time for that later.

6 gal (28 L) filtered (dechlorinated) tap water

Procedure:

This recipe assumes you can boil at least 2.5 gallons (9.5 liters) of liquid (this will require a 12-quart pot or larger).

First, be sure everything is clean. New equipment should just require a rinse to knock off any dust, but if you're recycling somebody else's carboy, use PBW or other oxygenated cleaner (like Oxy-Clean or unscented automatic dishwasher detergent) to get the scum off. Once clean, sanitize your carboy (or plastic fermenter). Mix 2 teaspoons unscented household bleach with a quart of water, and swish this around in the carboy to sanitize. If you purchased a brewery sanitizer, follow directions for mixing and use. Chlorine is powerful stuff, and it won't take more than a minute or two. Drain and rinse three times with tap water—it's generally sterile enough for this purpose. Then run 2.5 gallons of the tap water from the filter into your kettle, which needs to be clean but not sanitized, and 3 gallons into the freshly sanitized carboy/fermenter.

Place the ground malt into the knit or cheesecloth bag and tie shut, using cotton string if you need to. Add this to the water in the kettle.

Place the kettle on the stove, and turn on the heat. Slowly raise to about 200° F (93° C). Pull out the grain bag and place it in a saucepan so it can drain. Squeeze it gently, and add any liquid you can get out of it back into the kettle. Add the dry (or liquid) malt extract, stirring to keep it from scorching. Keep the heat on and raise to a boil. The moment the wort reaches boiling is the most dangerous part of brewing. Boilovers can happen in a flash, which is why brewers use the term "jump" to describe the effect. Once you hit a boil, turn the heat down a little and add a sprinkling of hops. Usually this will make the beer want to jump out of the pot, as the hops provide plentiful nucleation sites for the steam bubbles. Watch the wort until it settles down to a comfortable boil, then add one-fourth of your total hop amount. Note the time.

After 40 minutes, add another one-fourth of the hops. This will provide both bitterness and aroma. As the boil nears completion, you will notice globs of fluffy stuff that looks (and is) very much like the drops in egg drop soup. This is proteinaceous material that has combined with tannins in the hops, coagulating into the flakes you see swimming around in there. There is a type of marine algae called Irish moss that brewers have long used to aid this process. A small amount is added in the last 10 minutes of the boil. Personally, I have not noticed a speck of difference in the finished beer, but it is kind of cool, and it does make bigger flakes of the stuff.

After another 20 minutes, add the rest of the hops and turn off the heat. This will contribute aroma but add very little bitterness.

There are a million schemes for chilling wort. The simplest is to just allow it to cool as it sits, but rapid cooling is important for lots of reasons. As it cools it reaches a point where it's vulnerable to various infectious beasties, and there are chemical reasons too. A rather unpleasant vegetal-smelling compound called DMS (dimethyl sulfide) is formed at elevated wort temperatures. Normally driven off by boiling, it can stink up a beer if the wort is allowed to cool too slowly. Slow cooling may lead to hot wort aeration and problems of oxidation that could show up as stale, cardboardy flavors later on. Rapid cooling also facilitates the precipitation and eventual removal of excess protein gunk, called the cold break.

One simple method is to put the kettle into a sink or laundry tub full of cold water, and keep adding ice to the water while gently stirring the wort. In northern winters, snow can be used.

Wort chillers can be purchased or built. The simplest sort consists of 20 to 30 feet of 3/8" diameter copper tubing coiled so it will fit into the brew pot, with half of a garden hose clamped onto each end. This is lowered into the wort before the end of the boil to sanitize the device. Cold tap water is then run through it, which will usually chill the wort in under half an hour. More complex counterflow chillers work faster, but are more difficult to sanitize and use.

At this point a hydrometer is used to check the wort gravity, which should be cooled to the temperature specified on the instrument. Since density is dependent on temperature, hydrometers are calibrated to a particular temperature, usually 68° F (20° C). Professional models often have a thermometer and a correction scale built into them.

Once cooled to 80° F (26.5° C) or below, stir the wort briskly in a circular motion with the racking cane (sanitize it first), which will cause much of the hops and trub (coagulated protein) to pile up in the middle. Allow things to settle

RECIPE [Your Name Here]—Your First Radical Brew

and then attach the sanitized racking cane to the hose, with its little clip clamped just down from where the hose joins the cane, but in the "open" position. The potscrubber should be fit over the end of the cane, and if needed, clamped with a small, all-stainless hose clamp. Fill the hose and cane with water, clip the clamp, then insert the cane into the wort toward the outside edge of the kettle, avoiding the pile of trub, and the other end into the fermenter, which has been placed at a lower level than the kettle. Unclip the clamp, and wort will flow. You can now pitch the yeast into the fermenter.

Once full, put the lid on (if you're using a plastic tub), then add the sanitized lock and stopper. I like to fill the locks with cheap vodka, as it will kill most anything that should get in there, but will not harm the yeast as bleach water will. Wort that is warmer than the surrounding air will shrink as it cools, sucking some of the lock liquid into the fermenter, so look the next day to see if it needs topping up.

Now comes either the easy part or the hard part, depending on your personality—waiting for the yeast to do its business. With fresh yeast, you should expect some activity within 24 hours, which will be indicated by a thin film of yeast on top, and some activity in the fermentation lock indicating that there is escaping CO_2 gas. Within a couple of days the activity should be quite dramatic, with foam as much as 6 inches thick on top, and a rapid bubbling of the lock. The quantity of yeast you pitch and the fermentation temperature will determine the vigor of this activity.

After about two weeks, the yeast will slow down and the surface will begin to clear. When the fermentation lock stops bubbling, it's time to bottle or keg. See the instructions on p 67 for this. Congratulations, you're a brewer!

Scene from John Taylor's Brewery, Albany, NY, 1868

Acres of wood!

THE RACKING CELLAR.

HOW NOT TO SCREW IT UP

Better beer is something most homebrewers seek. With the right approach and a little help, your first beers should taste pretty good, with some room for improvement. Like anything worth doing well, there are a million little details that all add up to a better outcome. Here are a few of the issues—no, let's call them opportunities—you might want to tackle.

Freshness does make a difference with malt extract syrups Stale extract will make beer that smells of ballpoint pen ink. Domestic extracts are usually fresher than imports, but not always. The shop staff will know—or should. Dry extract stays fresh indefinitely as long as it's kept dry and, unlike syrups, you can use as much or as little from a package as you like. Many shops carry drums of liquid extract, which usually don't sit around long enough to get stale.

Canned kits are not always a great solution If you want to try one, the proper way to use it is this: hold the can firmly in one hand, and with the other, pull off the plastic lid and grab the packet of yeast inside between thumb and forefinger. Toss it in the trash. Second, peel the paper label from the can and chuck it in the trash bin, having first noted whether the extract is hopped or unhopped, pale or dark. You are now holding a usable can of raw material.

Chill As previously noted, getting your wort cooled quickly is critical to a clean tasting beer. A long waiting time at elevated temperatures makes the wort vulnerable to infection by microbes that are waiting to pounce. DMS can reach problematic levels if the wort is allowed to linger while warm. How quick is quick enough? There's no precise answer, but half an hour is probably a good target. There are several methods described on p. 32.

Put the effort into sanitation Clean, well-sanitized equipment is essential for making flawless beer. Equally important (but often neglected) is getting the sanitizer thoroughly rinsed off.

You will never have too much yeast Starting your fermentation with plenty of yeast minimizes the chance that bad bugs will take over and produce off-flavors. Liquid yeasts have brewery pedigrees and come in many more varieties, and are now suitable for pitching right from the package, although the "smack-pack" type does require a few days to get itself ready for your brew. If you are using dry yeast, use two or even three packets per 5-gallon batch, and be sure to ask the shop owner which brand is giving the best results. Dry yeast should be rehydrated in hot (110° F or 43.5° C) water before adding to your beer.

Repitch There is no easier way to assure a quality fermentation than to repitch a clean layer of yeast from a just-finished brew. I usually repitch the yeast from a secondary of a beer being transferred to a keg on brew day. You can repitch from a primary, but I recommend pouring the slurry into a tall beaker and allowing it to settle for a few hours. The floaters and sinkers should be discarded; use the creamy, smooth layer in the middle, as this contains the most viable yeast and least amount of bad-tasting crud.

Aerate that wort Loading your chilled wort up with oxygen allows the yeast to get going much more quickly, reducing the chances of infection while allowing you to drink your beer much sooner. For various ways to accomplish this, see p. 67.

Go draft A draft system removes one of the most onerous chores from the brewing process, bottling. See p. 68.

Forget high-alpha hops If you're an international mega-brewer playing the price game on millions of barrels of beer a year, you can ignore this advice. But your beer will taste better with low-alpha hops. You will definitely get more hop flavor and aroma by using 4 ounces of Saaz instead of 1 ounce of Chinook, as the aromatic oils do not necessarily scale up along with the alpha acids in the high-alpha hops. And they don't call them "noble" hops for nothing; they do taste great.

Taste critically Scrutinize your own beers, other homebrews, and commercial beers. Don't forget to taste the malts and smell the hops—both as raw ingredients and in finished beers. Try and pin down what you like. You don't have to write it down, but for some people it helps.

Get competitive Enter a homebrew competition. There's a chance for glory, but more importantly, you'll get feedback from experienced judges including an objective description, a listing of flaws, and how the beer fits into the category in which it's entered. See p. 284 for more on competitions.

Keep records There are a lot of variables, and it's just about impossible to recall all of them by the time the beer's ready. If you brew a killer batch, you want to be able to repeat it, or even improve it. You can use the sheet on [p. 71], make your own, or do it in a spreadsheet or PDA.

Don't rush it While your beer may be drinkable in a month or so, the general rule is "The homebrew is ready when you've drunk the last bottle." Another month or two may make a significant improvement. Stay ahead of demand and start a second batch before your first is finished. You'll thank yourself later.

Beer loves company Brew with a friend, a sweetheart, or a spouse. It lightens the load and improves the enjoyment of the finished product. There's much more on group activities in Chapter 19.

Just keep brewing There's no substitute for a hands-on approach. Strive to make every beer better than the last, and it probably will be.

Hierarchy of Homebrew Complication

Approach	Supplies You Will Buy	Technique/Equipment
Extract Kit	The kit: a can of hopped extract that comes with a package of yeast.	Simple: mix and ferment. Little or no boil. Basic equipment kit does the job. A six-year-old could do this.
Extract Components	A can of extract, some hops and yeast—each of your own choosing.	Easy, but may include a full-length boil (60-90 minutes). Chiller recommended. Limited aroma and flavor possibilities.
Extract + grain	Extract, hops, grains, and yeast.	Elementary: steep grains in hot water, remove and boil with hops. Grain bag and maybe a bigger pot needed.
Partial Mash	Same as above, but with more grain.	Transitional: volume and temperature control, sparging technique, etc. A grain bag will do, but purpose-built mash equipment starts to look good.
All-Grain Brewing	No extract, just grain (about 10 pounds for a 5 gallon batch), plus all the hops you'll need and some yeast.	Craftsmanship: a full mashing rig and careful technique required for ideal results, but most master it in just a few batches.

THE BEST OF BOTH WORLDS: EXTRACT PLUS MINI-MASH

This is the next big step beyond the bag of crystal malt added to the boil. The idea is to do a small-scale mash, which in every other respect is just like a full mash. The benefit is that because you're actually doing starch conversion, a mini-mash allows you to use a wider range of malt types instead of being restricted to crystal and roasted malts. Using this method, you can brew credible versions of most of the beers in this book.

The ideal setup is a 1- or 2-gallon picnic cooler jug. A 1-gallon cooler will hold a little over 4 pounds of grain, enough for most recipes. It also has the advantage of being small enough to accept one of those stainless steel expanding vegetable steamer inserts, which makes a perfect filter screen. For larger-sized coolers, you can build or buy a screen or manifold.

The procedure is the same as a normal infusion mash. Mix 1 quart of hot (165° F or 74° C) water per pound of grain, stir well, then take its temperature. If it's lower than the target specified in the recipe, add hot water until you hit the right temperature. Let this sit for forty-five minutes to an hour, then start to drain. The first wort will likely have some suspended solids in it, so put this back on top of the mash. When the wort runs clear, start adding it to your brew kettle. Gradually add another gallon of water to the grains, this time at 180° F (82° C), which will sparge out the remaining sugars. All this wort goes into your kettle, and the extract gets mixed in.

If, like most extract brewers, you're boiling only 3 gallons for a 5-gallon batch, you will need to slightly boost the hop quantities. In a smaller volume, the wort will be at a higher gravity in the boil, which means lower hop utilization rates. Add 20 percent more hops than the recipe specifies.

MASHING MADE EASY

If you've even halfway followed these instructions, your beer's pretty good—at least your deadbeat pals are sucking them down like there's no tomorrow. You've got a few batches under your belt, literally. Life is good.

But there are nagging thoughts. That the beers could be even better, fresher-tasting, more complex. That you'd like to really get in control of your recipes, to know exactly what you're putting in your beer. That you'd really like to brew the way the big boys do. But something is holding you back…

It's that M-word: Mashing. The beast in the homebrew closet. A snarling tangle of chemistry, hoses, uncertainty, and chances for things to go terribly wrong.

Well, a monster can be a pussycat if you just scratch its ears the right way.

I won't kid you and say that mashing doesn't take longer and require a bit more equipment, but it isn't all that complicated. By using adjunct grains in your extract beers, you're sort of doing it already. Think of it as just scaling up.

Converting All-Grain Recipes to Extract + Mini-Mash

Radical Brewing lists extract alternatives to all-grain recipes when practical, but you will at some time or place run into an all-grain recipe you'd like to brew with extracts. Although mashing gives you the most control over the flavor of your brews, the use of a high-quality malt extract combined with a mini-mash of the specialty grains specified in the recipe will result in a beer that will be very hard to tell apart from its full-mash cousin.

To convert a recipe, simply use pale malt extract instead of the pale or Pils malt specified in the recipe, using the following percentages:

Product replacing pale malt	Reduce quantity to:
Liquid malt extract	85 percent of recipe
Dry extract replacing pale malt	65 percent of recipe

If the recipe calls for a large proportion of Munich or mild malt, substitute amber dry malt instead of pale. Then do a mini-mash with the specialty grains in the recipe. If you wish to use dry malt extract instead of liquid, use 20 percent less than the amount of malt in the grain recipe. Munich, Vienna, mild, biscuit, and aromatic malts all contain enough enzymes to convert themselves, while darker malts do not, although really dark malts like black patent may be used without converting. If the specialty grains in the recipe are mostly of the medium dark variety—amber or brown, for example—it may be desirable to add a pound of Pils malt to help with converting the starch. Crystal malt is preconverted, so it needs no mashing.

If the recipe you're converting calls for a large amount of Munich malt, you may want to substitute 1 pound of pale crystal plus 2.25 pounds (1 kilogram) of dry malt extract for every 5 pounds of Munich malt, which will come close to the flavor and color.

Mashing is the heart and soul of the brewing process. Just to review, here are the basics: malted grain is crushed and mixed with hot water to arrive at a mash at about 150° F (65.5° C). At this temperature, enzymes that have been activated during the malting process spring into action and snip the long starch molecules into smaller ones composed of variably fermentable sugars. At higher temperatures (150 to 160° F or 65.5 to 71° C), the wort produced is less fermentable; at lower temperatures (140 to 150° F or 60 to 65.5° C) it's more fermentable. There are lots of complicated subtleties, but the fact is that if you get within 10 degrees of 150° F (65.5° C) and hold it for a hour, you'll get a liquid that will ferment into a perfectly lovely beer, without any of the tangy, stale, thin flavors the average canned malt extract delivers.

Lazy brewers should take note that the longest portion of mashing is felicitously called a "rest," during which you can do likewise, or get lunch, or clean bottles, or anything but fuss with the mash, as it really doesn't need your help for this, thank you very much.

You will need two things you may not have: a reasonably accurate thermometer and a modified cooler to mash in. The newer type of cooking thermometer/timer with the probe on a cable is perfect, and you can justify its purchase as a cooking device as well. Even radio-linked remote versions are available.

If you have a large plastic cooler, you simply need to add a sort of drainage manifold to it, which most brewers do by dry-fitting copper plumbing pipe into a trident-shaped thingy that roughly fits the bottom of the cooler, the long tubing pieces being cut halfway through their diameter with a series of hacksaw cuts spaced about an inch apart to provide drainage. The narrow end of the trident is force-fit into the cooler's drain spigot, with the aid of a short piece of plastic tubing if needed. You could drive yourself nuts trying to figure out the best way to do this, but there's almost no way to totally screw it up.

If you have a couple of clean 5-gallon buckets lying around, they'll make a fine mash tun as well. Add a spigot or a piece of hose with a pinch clip at the bottom of the one that will become the bottom vessel. Then carve out the bottom of the top bucket to resemble a three-armed peace sign, and attach a piece of bronze window-screen to the inside by stitching it on with a piece of the wire you pulled off the edge of the screen, using small drilled holes in the plastic to stitch into. If you're really nuts, get a 1/8" drill and make a zillion holes, but be warned that by the third hour this gets really boring—unless you have much better drugs than I have access to. If you're planning on making stronger beers with this method, be aware that the 5-gallon size of this unit may be a bit small for your purposes, so you may want to go down to the local restaurant supply store and get something in the 7- to 10-gallon (26- to 38-liter) range. There are also inexpensive, commercially available false bottoms designed to work in buckets or round coolers.

If you need more specific directions on building your mash tun, get on the Web and poke around; there are a million different ways to solve this problem. There are also companies that sell parts and kits to do this. But do remember: simple works just fine.

The conventional wisdom is that in order to do a mashed beer, you must sparge (rinse the sugars out of the spent grain) and collect more than the full volume of your finished beer, then boil it down to the final amount. This is the most efficient, but not necessarily the laziest, way to do it, which is to waste some malt by collecting and boiling a concentrated wort—say 3 gallons—then diluting it with cold water at the end of the boil.

This does three things:

1. Speeds up the brew by eliminating the time-consuming sparging process, which can be like water torture for some impatient brewers.

2. Lets you use a smaller pot on a normal stove.

3. Speeds the chilling process, so a wort chiller is not absolutely necessary.

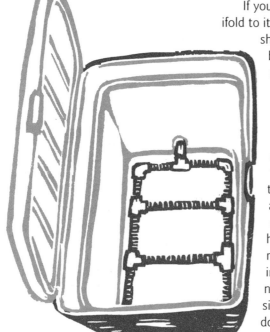

Picnic Cooler Mash Tun

Perhaps the most common mash tun used by all-grain brewers, this is made by adding a manifold of dry-fit copper plumbing pipe to drain the wort. The straight sections of pipe have been cut halfway through with a hacksaw (space cuts about 1/4" apart) to provide drainage.

A 5- or 10-gallon circular beverage cooler may also be used as a mash-tunn, substituting a false bottom for the copper manifold.

Like I said, this wastes a bit of malt, so recipes have to be calculated differently. If you collect and boil just 3 gallons instead of 6 and then dilute, you will need to use about 1.4 times as much malt as a particular recipe calls for. Multiply the hop amounts by 1.1 to make up for the lower utilization you'll get with the smaller brew kettle; if you're boiling the full 5 gallons use the hop quantities as specified. Your mileage may vary, so after you do one or two of these you may find you need to adjust the conversion formula a bit. Because this is not the mainstream technique, the recipes in this book are not formulated for this "no-sparge" technique.

The procedure described here has been much discussed on the homebrew forums of late, and many advocates also feel it makes beer with a cleaner, purer taste, as it leaves behind potentially husky, tannic flavors that can harm a delicate beer if over-sparged.

THE BASIC INFUSION MASH

In contrast to the "no-sparge" method, normal mashing procedures call for a hot water rinse—called a sparge—of the grain to ensure that most of the fermentable sugars end up in the beer and not on the compost pile. This usually adds about an hour to the process, which most brewers feel is a worthwhile tradeoff for the 35- to 45-percent increase in efficiency over the no-sparge method.

Up to the point where you start running off the wort, the two procedures are exactly the same. But instead of simply draining the grain bed dry, hot water at approximately 175° F (79.5° C) is gently ladled or sprinkled onto the surface until the full volume of the beer batch, plus a gallon or so which will be lost in the boil, is collected. During this time it is important to keep the goods from falling below 145° F (63° C), at which point starches will start to gel, making runoff difficult. It is also important not to let the water level fall below the top of the grain bed. You get better runoff when the grain is allowed to float, and removing the water allows the grain to compact under its own weight, slowing runoff. You can ignore this at the very end, as runoff goes quicker when most of the soluble materials have been rinsed out.

MASHING MADE DIFFICULT

An infusion mash will get you through most of the kinds of beer you would want to brew, but there are times when a more complex mashing procedure might be called for:

- When using large amounts (25 percent or more) of unmalted grain in a recipe.

- When attempting to brew certain styles, such as German dark lagers, in the most completely authentic manner, which would be a single, double, or triple decoction mash.

- When dealing with less modified malts that require more intensive mashing methods.

Eleven Ways to Avoid a Stuck Sparge

I just about quit homebrewing in disgust more than once, usually about four hours into a miserable sparging experience, accompanied by considerable verbal fireworks. There's nothing worse than being ready to move on and being subjected to the water torture of a sluggish drip, drip, drip. It drove me nuts. As a brewer of exotic beers, I was asking for it by using unmalted and huskless grains, but I knew there had to be a better way.

So I began a quest involving both technique and equipment. It took a while, but I finally got it licked, and now sparging is one of the most enjoyably satisfying parts of the process. Here's some of what I learned along the way. You don't necessarily need to do all of these to have a pleasant sparge, but if you're having problems, start looking at these items, implementing what you can until things become bearable. Now if only I could make cleanup this easy!

1. Be sure your grain is correctly ground. The idea is to crush the malty center of the kernels evenly into pinhead-sized particles, while keeping the husks as intact as possible for good filtering action. This always involves a tradeoff, but a reasonable balance can be achieved. I find roller mills are best. There are magicians who can coax well-milled malt from a Corona-style mill, but they are rare. Anything with a slicing or shearing action should be avoided.

The roller settings are critical, and should be fine-tuned with every change of grain. Generally roller mills don't do such a great job with huskless grains as wheat, which should be ground very finely. For adjunct grains, I use an old grocery-store coffee mill that works brilliantly for this.

2. Don't make the bed too deep. Four inches will give you all the filtering action you need. More than 8 or so and you're asking for trouble. When I redid my lauter tun, I made it half again as wide as my brew kettle so as to have the proper surface area; this size difference occurs in commercial breweries as well. I know you have to load it up to make that juicy barley wine or Abbey-style quadrupel, but why don't you do as the Belgians do and use a tasty sugar for the last 10 to 20 percent of the gravity? A good unrefined sugar can add a caramelly twist while enhancing drinkability.

3. Use a mash-out rest after conversion. Most commercial techniques raise the goods to 170° F (77° C) or thereabouts to stop enzyme activity, and importantly, to keep any remaining starch or glucans liquified. See Number 4.

4. Keep the temperature up. If you let the goods drop below 145° F (63° C) or so, they'll begin to gel, with unpleasant consequences. Insulation is of obvious benefit. Keeping your sparge water at 170 to 180° F (77 to 82° C) is critical.

5. Start your runoff slowly. At the beginning, get just a trickle going, then slowly increase. Having the wort flowing at a high rate before the filter bed is set creates a considerable vacuum that can compact the bed into a bricklike substance.

6. Don't let the bed drain dry. A free-flowing filter bed is dependent on the grains being suspended (floating) in the

In the first case, a procedure called an adjunct or cereal mash is used. This is the technique used by brewers of American style lagers, and was created to deal with the large amounts of unmalted rice or corn used in these beers. The technique also works very well for Belgian styles such as witbier that use lots of unmalted wheat.

The procedure involves making two separate mashes. One mash with unmalted grain and a small amount of malt is raised through a series of temperature rests and then boiled for a few minutes. Meanwhile a malt mash is underway and sitting at protein rest temperature, 122° F (50° C). Then the boiled adjunct grains are added to the malt mash, which brings the whole thing up to starch conversion temperature, about 150° F (65.5° C) (or whatever the recipe calls for). Details are given in connection with Belgian Witbier on p. 205.

Decoction mashes were traditional for centuries in Germany. In a decoction, a por-

sparge water. Remove this liquid support and the bed collapses from its own weight. If this happens mid-sparge, flood the goods to get them floating, stir to unclump, then reset the sparge as if you were just starting.

7. Add a vent to the bottom of your lauter screen. This involves running a tube just barely through to the underside of the lauter screen to a level well above the top of the goods, and fitting the top end with a clip, plug, or valve. Then, if you experience the kind of excessive vacuum described in Number 5, you can open the tube and release the vacuum.

8. Make a vacuum break into the grant. Don't have the runoff tube submerged in the receiving vessel, as the water pressure above the bottom of the tube will prevent liquid from draining freely. My solution is to use a "T" fitting on my drain hose, positioned above the highest possible liquid level in the receiving vessel, with the top leg going up to the lauter tun, the bottom leg with a stub of tubing to determine the height of it—to make it sure it clears the liquid—and with the side leg of the T left open to act as the vacuum break.

9. Add a vacuum gauge (manometer) to the underside of the lauter screen. This is a geeky one, I admit, but it helped the lesson of Number 5 really sink in for me. They're used in commercial-scale breweries for the same purpose. You can watch the thing as you start the runoff, and if you start to pull a vacuum, the needle starts to swing. At this point you can slow the flow and release the pressure to bring things back to normal. I used a pressure gauge from a CPR training dummy. It was set to register low positive pressure, but I took it apart and bent some things so it reads very slight vacuums now. I'm not sure what sort of pressure scale you're looking for, probably "inches of water." Having a calibrated scale is unimportant; you just want to make sure the needle moves visibly with the kind of suction required to drink soda—not a milkshake—through a straw.

To install, run a small tube to just below the bottom of the lauter screen. Run it up to the top of the lauter tun and connect it to a T fitting. Connect the gauge to one leg, and a valve connected to the atmosphere on the other leg, which can then be used to vent the space below the screen. See Number 7.

10. When all else fails, try rice hulls. Actually, they are a cheap and easy fix for whatever ails your sparge, although they're a particular godsend to the brewing of beers with wheat, rye, oats, or other gooey adjuncts. Use 0.5 to 2 pounds per 5-gallon batch, depending on quantity and stickiness of the adjuncts. This emulates traditional practice with wheat beers, for example, in which husks were reserved after threshing to be added to the mash for the purpose described here.

11. Underlet. Sometimes adding sparge water from underneath the false bottom can refloat the mash, making further sparging a little easier.

tion—25 to 35 percent—of the mash is removed and stepped up through a series of rests, and then briefly boiled before being mixed back into the rest of the mash, which raises its temperature. They allow mashing to be conducted in wooden vessels and still have several different temperature steps. The boiling of the grains softens the hard ends of undermodified malt, increasing efficiency, and adds a certain caramelly quality to the finished beer.

Decoctions are always fussy affairs, and can take up to six hours. With modern well-modified malt, they are not needed for efficiency's sake, and there are other ways to do a step mash. But the extra caramelly qualities a decoction can add may be worth the effort in subtle malt showcases such as a Munich dunkel or a Czech Pilsener. More detail on decoction mashing can be found in Chapter 8.

Chapter 4

Basic Ingredients

Malt, water, hops, yeast. Although many other ingredients can be used in beer, these four do the heavy lifting. Quality, of course, is important, but it's not a simple matter. Each of these ingredients has many properties important in brewing. Some of these qualities are apparent, and can be smelled or tasted. Others are more chemical in nature, and require an understanding of the underlying science in order to select and use them to best advantage.

MALT, GLORIOUS MALT

Malt is barley that has been sprouted and dried. Other grains such as wheat, oats, and rye may be malted, but barley is the workhorse of the brewhouse. The malting process tricks the seed into sprouting, during which it readies its starchy reserves to fuel the expected new growth. Enzymes attack the wall of the little sacs holding the starch, while other enzymes are unfolded and pumped up, ready to disassemble the starches into sugars the new shoot can assimilate. The maltster takes it right to the brink, to where the little sprout is about to pop from beneath its protective husk, and then, wham! *Germinatus interruptus*. It all comes to a stop as the malt hits the kiln, driving off the water and ending the plant's chance at a life. The heat and desiccation preserve all this wonderful chemistry in a suspended state so that when the brewer adds water, it's all there ready and waiting to make beer.

The Flavor of Malt Color The kilning may be done with just enough heat to dry out the malt, and can even be accomplished with the sun or in the rafters of a dry barn for that matter. But most modern malt is kilned with sufficient heat to develop at least a little color. Today most maltsters offer a kaleidoscopic range of malt colors and flavors, making possible an infinite variety of beers. This embarrassment of riches brings certain problems—how best to mix and match to achieve one's goals?

Understanding the chemistry of malt flavor and color certainly helps to get a handle on this. Barley is nearly flavorless in its raw state—think beef barley soup without the beef, onions, vegetables, and seasonings. Malting develops a few flavor chemicals, but on the whole, air-dried malt is a pretty bland product. Just about all of the flavors we

associate with malt—bready, malty, nutty, toasty, roasty, and all the rest—are the result of chemical reactions that occur during kilning.

Understanding this requires entering a deep thicket of chemistry known as the Maillard reaction, also called non-enzymatic browning. This is the reaction responsible for caramel, bread crusts, roux, meat browning, and many other very familiar and heartwarming edibles. It's also what makes frozen orange juice taste different than fresh, and what gives that stale can of malt extract its thin, ballpoint-pen aroma. A rough outline is shown here to give you some idea of the complexity of the actual chemistry. Don't be afraid.

Although, as you can see, the specifics are hideously complex and still incompletely understood by science, the essence of it—the part that sheds light on brewing—is remarkably easy to grasp.

If you take any sort of sugar, combine it with nitrogen-bearing protein debris and add heat, things will start to happen. After a long slalom of fancy chemistry, two classes of end products emerge. First are melanoidins—large, highly colored polymeric molecules with no perceptible flavor or aroma. The structure of these, as much as it is known, is varied and complex, and honestly not all that important. Some display more reddish tints in a beer; others are more yellowish.

The aromatic chemicals are much more knowable. They consist of a large group of small, ring-shaped molecules typically containing nitrogen, sulfur, or oxygen, giving us the familiar range of aromas from the lightest maltiness to the deepest roast. These are extremely potent aroma chemicals, some with thresholds as low as .002 parts per billion. Without them, beer would be vastly different.

The key fact to know is that every combination of time, temperature, pH, concentration, sugar, and nitrogenous compound will create a different set of flavor chemicals. This creates the huge range of different flavors we can taste in malt and beer.

All of this Maillard chemistry points out the importance of considering much more than simply color when working out a grain bill. Identical-looking worts may have very different flavor and aroma profiles, and in most beer styles the particular nature of this key malt flavor is crucial to fitting into the style. You can make a beer that looks like a Märzen from Pils malt and a pinch of black, but it will in no way taste the part.

To put a further point on it, even similarly colored malts may have very different flavor and aroma qualities. Biscuit or amber malt (25° SRM) is kilned dry for a sharp toasty or nutty aroma that is perfect for brown ales or ESBs. The malt sometimes

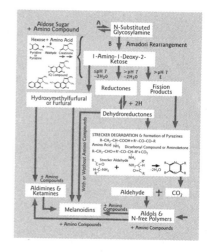

Maillard Chemistry for Beginners

A *simplified* chart on Maillard chemistry gives you some idea of the complexity of the science. Some of this is still being argued over. And you thought it was just a beer!

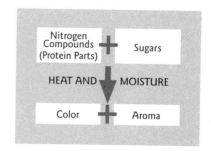

Maillard Chemistry for Experts

This chart shows what you really need to know.

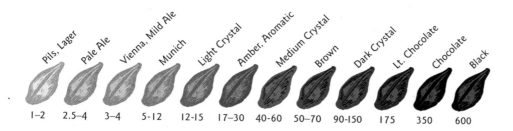

Pils, Lager	Pale Ale	Vienna, Mild Ale	Munich	Light Crystal	Amber, Aromatic	Medium Crystal	Brown	Dark Crystal	Lt. Chocolate	Chocolate	Black
1–2	2.5–4	3–4	5–12	12–15	17–30	40–60	50–70	90–150	175	350	600

Malt Color by the Numbers

This shows the appearance and numerical values for many common malt types. Some of the numbers have been simplified. In reality, each malt type exists as a range of color rather than a single number.

Malt Types for Brewing

GRAIN TYPE & COUNTRY	Extract lb/5 gal	Extract kg/20 liter	Color EBC	Color °L	COMMENTS & DESCRIPTION
PILSENER MALT (Two-row) Europe, Britain	1.0071	1.73 °P	2–3.5	1.0–2.0	Pale straw color. The base for most pale lagers. High diastatic power allows mashing with up to 40 percent grain adjuncts. Traditionally decoction mashed; modern versions well-modified—OK for infusion mashing.
LAGER MALT (Two-row) United States	1.0070	1.71 °P	2.5–3.5	1.4–2.0	Best mashed with decoction or step mash, and a 116–131°F/47–55°C protein rest may help avoid chill-haze in paler beers. High diastatic power allows mashing with up to 35 percent grain adjuncts.
LAGER MALT (Six-row) North America	1.0068	1.66 °P	2.5–3.8	1.4–2,2	Very high diastatic power. Well suited to the co-mashing of rice or corn adjuncts, up to 60 percent. Inferior in flavor to two-row; may impart husky flavors. Decoction or step-mash with protein rest used to avoid chill-haze.
PALE ALE MALT England, Belgium	1.0073	1.78 °P	4.5–8	2.5–3.8	Slight nutty flavor; brews a pale amber beer. Low % N makes protein rest unnecessary. Not well-suited to the co-mashing of adjuncts. Infusion mash is traditional.
VIENNA MALT Europe, North America	1.0071	1.73 °P	5–8	3–4	Adds malty caramelly richness and sweet maltiness, along with pale amber color. Enzyme content is low, but sufficient for self-conversion.
MILD ALE MALT England	1.0070	1.71 °P	10–20	4.3–8	Darker color, sweeter, nuttier taste than pale ale malt. Low diastatic power; poorly suited to the co-mashing of grain adjuncts. Protein rest unnecessary.
MUNICH MALT Europe, North America	1.0070	1.71 °P	12–15 17–25	5–7 8–12	Imparts malt aroma and gentle toasty taste, and amber color. Roasted moist for rich aroma. Gives beer a reddish color, in quantity. Not enough enzymes for adjuncts, but will convert itself. Some supplier offer two colors.
AROMATIC MALT Belgium, Germany	1.0070	1.71 °P	55–80	17–26	A darker Munich type. Moist-roasted. Extremely full, rich flavor and aroma. Some (Belgian) versions called "Aromatic" are really Munich type. Weyermann's version called "Melanoidin." Should convert itself.
AMBER/BISCUIT MALT England, Belgium, U.S.	1.0066	1.61 °P	40–80	20–30	Toasty/nutty flavor, without the strong aroma of Munich malts. Roast pale ale malt at 200° F for 15–20 minutes, then raise to 250°–300° F for a few more minutes. Briess' version called "Victory." Should convert itself.
BROWN MALT England	1.0066	1.61 °P	110–170	50–70	Traditionally made by rapidly heating pale ale malt to 350° F over an oak fire, and held for 2 hours or until a rich brown color is reached. An old-fashioned malt, it was the dominant malt in porter until 1750 or so. Very toasty. Great for brown ales. May not convert itself.

Malt Types for Brewing (Continued)

GRAIN TYPE & COUNTRY	Extract lb/5 gal	Extract kg/20 liter	Color EBC	Color °L	COMMENTS & DESCRIPTION
PALE CHOCOLATE MALT England	1.0066	1.61 °P	400–500	150–188	Paler version of chocolate. Less harsh, but still loads of coffee-like roasted character. Best used in small quantities (≤ 1 lb/5 gal). Will not convert itself. Pale shades of German röstmalz are very similar in character.
CHOCOLATE MALT England, Europe, North America	1.0061	1.49 °P	750–1100	300–500	Made by roasting pale ale malt until a deep chocolate color is reached. Sometimes harsh; black patent malt is darker, but often smoother tasting.
RÖSTMALZ (Carafa®, etc) Germany	1.0061	1.49 °P	1000–1200	375–450	German interpretation of chocolate malt. Available in several colors (medium shade described here), as well as de-husked for smoother flavor. Used to adjust color and add a deep roastiness to lagers and other brews.
BLACK (PATENT) MALT England, Europe, North America	1.0061	1.49 °P	1200–1500	500–600	The darkest, most pungent and bitter of all malts. Made by roasting pale malt at a high temperature until nearly black, but not burned. Some versions are debittered for smoothness, and are preferable for most brews.
BLACK ROASTED BARLEY England, U.S.	1.0061	1.49 °P	1300–1600	550–650	Similar to black malt, but barley is unmalted. Has drier, less rich character. Very dark color. Classic in Irish stouts.
DEXTRINE MALT (CARA-PILS®)	1.0067	1.63 °P	3–5 8–20	1.7–3.4 4–8	Nearly colorless crystal malt type used as a body builder in pale lagers such as Pilseners. Improves the head, too. Not a great deal of flavor. Two color ranges exist.
CRYSTAL MALT					All varieties are made by heating undried malt to mash temperatures and allowing to convert before raising to roasting temperatures. When cooled, sugars harden and give it a crystalline texture. May be made from two- or six-row barley. Contains high proportion of unfermentable dextrins. There are a wide variety of crystal malts, each with a unique flavor profile—malts of similar color may have very different flavors. Very useful in adding personality to beer. High-intensity aromas make them especially useful additions to extract beers.
Pale	1.0066	1.61 °P	40–80	20–30	
Medium	1.0066	1.61 °P	90–150	40–60	
Dark	1.0066	1.61 °P	160–250	65–90	
Extra Dark	1.0057	1.39 °P	300–400	110–160	

known as aromatic or melanoidin is just a little paler, at roughly 20° SRM, but is much maltier, rounder, and richer—really more of a dark Munich malt, a result of being roasted with a high level of moisture.

The differences are dramatically demonstrated in crystal malts. Each maltster does things a little differently, which is reflected in the final products. As a fun and easy club event, hold a crystal malt tasting. Get as many different makes of crystal as you can round up, group them by color, and start tasting. You will be amazed by the variety, even among identically colored ones. Every good brewer I know constantly tastes the ingredients. Make this a part of your brewing habits.

MORE HOPS!

Ah, hops. Their resiny bitterness and spicy, floral, or herbal aromas are a large part of what draws many of us into the hobby. American industrial beers use hops at or below the threshold, leaving many of us with a hunger for the flavor of those small, green cones. Fortunately, it is easily satisfied in our own brews.

Hops are the green, fluffy, cone-shaped catkins (technically *strobiles*) of the climbing vine *Humulus lupulus*, the only sibling of marijuana in the *Cannabaceae* family. Hops are more distantly related to nettles, elms, mulberries, and others. The vines regrow every year from fleshy underground runners called *rhizomes*, shooting up to twenty feet or more in height. Hops need a certain summer day-length to produce cones and their cultivation is restricted to bands between 35° and 55° latitudes, in both Northern and Southern Hemispheres. This is roughly from North Carolina to Hudson Bay, or southern Spain to northern Germany. If you have soil, sun, and something for them to climb on, they make a lovely ornamental plant as well as a useful one (see Chapter 16).

Hops contain two groups of substances of primary interest to brewers. First are thick tarry resins known as alpha and beta acids, which provide bitterness. Alpha acid is the more important of the two bitter substances, and it plays the primary role in the bittering of beer. Beta acids are present in smaller quantities, are less soluble in beer than alpha acids, and generally come to the fore only when old hops are used in a beer. Second is the wide range of aromatic oils that impart their magic to the nose of a well-brewed beer. This mix of oils differs by variety, region, soil, and other variables. Both components are subject to degradation by heat, oxygen, and time. Generally, hops are kept chilled or even frozen to preserve their bittering power and aroma.

Hop resins have a preservative effect due to their antibacterial action, which especially affects lactic acid bacteria. This preservative ability led to the hop being the dominant herb of beer. Prior to their widespread use, the only other method of preserving beer was to make it massively strong, above 10 percent alcohol or so, and even at that strength the preservation was not particularly effective. This reduction of strength may have been one of the things that caused such resistance to the introduction of hops. In England, even King Henry VIII got personally involved and banned the pernicious weed from the royal ale brewhouse. But his grandfather recognized the military value of a beer that would keep for months rather than days and issued a ban on the bad-mouthing of the new hopped beer

A traditional Kentish Oast, or hop drying kiln.

Sign on a Fin-du-Siecle building in London. Hop traders are called "Hop Factors" in England.

introduced by Flemish immigrants. Hops have reigned supreme for more than five hundred years.

Hops also contain polyphenols (tannins) that combine with some of the excess malt proteins and precipitate out of the wort during the boil (hot break) and at chilling (cold break), removing large amounts of unwanted haze-forming materials and also producing better foam characteristics.

Hops are dioecious, meaning there are distinct male and female plants, but the cones are borne only by the females. Male plants are of no use for brewing, and if allowed to pollinate the females, cones with seeds will be produced—adding nothing to their brewing value. Males are sometimes used in proximity to females, since they have the ability to increase cone production to some degree.

Hops are a somewhat tender plant, and are subject to a number of diseases and pests, many of which are aggravated by damp climates. As a result, they tend to be heavily sprayed.

At the end of the growing season, the plants are cut off at the base and brought to a stationary picker, which strips off the cones and discards the rest. The cones are then kiln-dried and stuffed tightly into large cloth bags called pockets in order to save space and protect them from air, which degrades both bitterness and aroma. Hydraulic presses are the norm now, but a century ago a person called a "hop treader" literally stomped the hops into the pockets.

Some hops are processed into pellets. The cones are finely ground up and forced through dies at high pressure, squirting out the other end as small green pellets that look like rabbit food. These hop pellets stay fresh longer, but there is some concern that the process may sap some aroma and introduce certain rough, green flavors released by the rupturing of cell walls.

Further processing yields more concentrated material that is destined for larger and larger breweries and that is of less and less interest to us. Supercritical CO_2 is used as a solvent to separate all the oils and resins from the fibrous material. This may be used as-is, or separated into bittering and aromatic components. The bitter fraction may be purified and isomerized, making it soluble in beer without boiling. The ultimate in hop processing results in fractionally distilled hop aroma components, which are useful for taking to the ballpark and dumping in your yellow beer, but precious little else.

There are really two main crops from an agribusiness viewpoint. High-alpha hops are grown for their resin content—typically 9 to 15 percent alpha acid— and these tend to be turned into non-varietal extract and are treated very much as a commodity crop. Varietal aroma hops are a premium product valued for their delicate, refined aromas. Many come from regions that have been famous for centuries—East Kent in England; Hallertau, Spalt and Tettnang in Germany; and the town of Saaz in the Bohemia region of the

The shoes of the Hopfentreader, from the Hallertauer district

Before the advent of mechanical presses, hops used to be literally stomped into the large cloth bags called "pockets."

Hop Tokens from Saaz

Czech Republic. Aroma hops generally have an alpha acid content of 5 percent or less.

There are also certain varieties with intermediate alpha acid levels (6 to 9 percent) and decent aromas, and these are known as dual use hops. Northern Brewer, Cascade, and newer varieties such as Centennial and Mount Hood all have nice aromas and find a useful place in the homebrew arsenal.

Work is ongoing in all regions to develop new varieties. A lot of this effort is centered around high-alpha hops, disease resistance, harvesting ease, or other agricultural qualities. Some new aromatic varieties have come into cultivation, especially in the American Northwest. One of the elusive goals in the United States has been to develop a hop that will produce a true European noble hop character, which is not the case when varieties such as Saaz and Hallertau are grown here. Crystal, Liberty, Vanguard, and Mount Hood come pretty close to the Hallertau goal; Ultra and Sterling have very nice, spicy Saaz qualities. Craft brewers in America have been eager to try out new varieties such as Santiam, Ahtanum, and Amarillo in their quest for unique personalities for their beers.

This varietal aroma is one of the most important tools you have to shape the aroma profile of your beer. Hops all smell like hops, but each variety has its own character. This is something you have to learn from your own personal experience. Old hands in the hop industry know to grab a small handful, rub briskly between the palms, open their hands slightly, thrust their noses into the gap, and sniff deeply, getting a real snootful.

Hops are used by adding them to the wort as it boils. More than simply dissolving, the heat causes a chemical change called isomerization, which allows the formerly non-bitter, insoluble resins to become highly bitter and dissolve into the wort. It takes up to ninety minutes for hops to release their full bitterness into the boiling wort, but the process begins in just a few minutes. A vigorous boil enhances the process. A simmer won't cut it.

Hop Varietal Aroma Character

Country	Archetype	Character
American	Cascade	Resiny, floral, citrus/grapefruit
Czech	Saaz	Clean, spicy, mellow
English	East Kent Goldings	Bright, green, softly spicy
German	Hallertau	Mellow, herbal, almost minty

This chart represents the four most typical hop varieties but is by no means complete. Many intermediate and atypical varieties exist. New varieties are constantly being developed, so it's a good idea to consult a resource like Hopunion for current detailed information on hop varieties and their uses.

Hop Token, 1794

Hop pickers were often paid in tokens or scrip— good only at the company store.

The heat of the boil also liberates and dissolves aromatic oils, but these will also be driven off by the heat. For this reason hops are added several times during the boil: in the beginning for bitterness, and toward the end of the boil for flavor and aroma. For additional aroma, hops may be added after boiling is finished, either by just dumping them into the kettle or by putting them in a device called a hop

Hop Variety Characteristics

VARIETY	ORIGIN	BREWING USE	ALPHA ACID %	STORAGE STABILITY	COMMENTS & DESCRIPTION
ADMIRAL (RH 40)	England	Bittering	11.5–14.5	••	Newer high-alpha type, a more potent replacement for Target.
AHTANUM	U.S.	Dual	5.7–6.3	••	Privately developed dual use hop; very similar to Cascade.
AMARILLO	U.S.	Bittering	8–11	•	High-alpha hop with similar floral/citrus aromas to Cascade.
AURORA	Slovenia	Dual	7–9	•	"Super Styrian," Northern Brewer parentage. Mild European flavor.
BRAMLING CROSS	England	Aroma	5–7	••	Wild Manitoba/Golding cross. Blackcurrant, lemony aroma.
BREWER'S GOLD	Germany, China	Dual	5.5–8	—	English/wild Canadian cross. Pungent English character.
CASCADE (CFJ 90)	U.S.	Dual	4–6	—	Unique American floral character, defines U.S. Pale Ale style.
CENTENNIAL	U.S.	Dual	8–10	•••	Similar to Cascade, but higher alpha. Formerly called CFJ 90.
CHINOOK	U.S.	Dual	11–14	••	High alpha with resiny grapefruit aroma. Golding ancestry.
CLUSTER	U.S.	Dual	6–8	••••	Original American hop. A certain sharpness often called "cattiness."
COLUMBUS	U.S.	Bittering	14–16	••	Newer super high-alpha variety. Finding favor with microbreweries.
CRYSTAL	U.S.	Aroma	3–3.5	—	Newer variety with fine Hallertauer character. Ultra clean!
FIRST GOLD	England	Dual	6.5–8.5	••••	Dwarf hop with fine English Golding character. WGV heritage.
FUGGLE	England, U.S.	Dual	3.5–5.5	•	Traditional hop for darker beers. Less refined aroma than Goldings.
GALENA	U.S.	Bittering	10–14	••	Brewer's Gold ancestry. Pungent English flavor.
GOLDING	U.S., Canada	Aroma	4–6	•••	U.S.-grown version of the English classic. Mild, pleasant flavor.
HALLERTAUER MITTELFRÜH	Germany	Aroma	4–5	•	Original noble aroma hop. Being replaced with newer varieties.
HALLERTAUER TRADITION	Germany	Aroma	4–5.8	••••	Disease-resistant, more aromatic replacement for Hallertauer.

Hop Variety Characteristics (Continued)

VARIETY	ORIGIN	BREWING USE	ALPHA ACID %	STORAGE STABILITY	COMMENTS & DESCRIPTION
HALLERTAUER MAGNUM	Germany	Bittering	10–12.6	••••	High-alpha variety with some German taste characteristics.
HERALD	England	Bittering	11–13	••••	New high-alpha dwarf with acceptable flavor. Sister of Pioneer.
HERSBRUCKER	Germany, U.S.	Aroma	2.5–5	•••	Traditional German variety. Drier, spicier than Hallertauer.
KENT GOLDING	Kent, England	Aroma	4.5–6.5	—	The traditional English aroma hop, reserved for pale ales.
LIBERTY	U.S.	Aroma	3.5–5.5	•	American Hallertauer clone. Somewhat floral and fruity.
LUBLIN/LUBELSKI	Poland	Aroma	3–5	—	Polish hop with Saaz origins. Refined spicy flavor.
MOUNT HOOD	U.S.	Aroma	3–4.5	—	An American Hallertauer clone with similarities to Hersbrucker.
NORTHERN BREWER	U.S., Germany	Dual	7.5–8.5	•••	Neutral-tasting multipurpose hop. Used in California common.
NUGGET	U.S., Germany	Bittering	9–10.5	•••	High-alpha hop with delicate but pleasant aroma.
PERLE	U.S., Germany	Dual	5–7.5	•••	Hallertauer replacement with higher alpha and spicier flavor.
PHOENIX	England	Dual	8.5–11.5	••••	New dual use with very attractive English aroma character.
PIONEER	England	Dual	8–10	•••	New dwarf variety with clean bitterness and mild English aroma.
PRIDE OF RINGWOOD	New Zealand	Dual	7.5–10	—	Tasmanian wild/English cross. Rough and spicy English character hop.
PROGRESS	England	Dual	5–7.5	•••	WGV/American cross. Similar to Fuggle, but a little sweeter.
SAAZ	Czech Republic	Aroma	3.5–5	—	The classic spicy/herbal hop of Pilsener beers.
SANTIAM	U.S.	Dual	5–7	•	Newer dual-use hop with strong similarity to German Tettnang.
SHINSU WASE	Japan	Aroma	4.5–6	•	Saaz/American ancestry. Spicy, refined character.
SLADEK	Czech Republic	Dual	9–9.5	•••	Newer Czech dual purpose hop with some Saaz character.

Hop Variety Characteristics (Continued)

VARIETY	ORIGIN	BREWING USE	ALPHA ACID %	STORAGE STABILITY	COMMENTS & DESCRIPTION
SPALTER	Germany	Aroma	3.5–5.5	•••	Highly valued traditional German noble hop, important in altbiers.
SPALTER SELECT	Germany	Aroma	3.5–5.5	•••	Disease-resistant cultivar of Spalt, closer to Hallertauer in aroma.
STERLING	U.S.	Dual	6–9	••	Newer dual use hop with Czech Saaz character.
STRISSELSPALT	France	Aroma	3–4	••	The main French variety, probably related to Hallertauer.
STYRIAN GOLDING	Slovenia	Aroma	4.5–6	••	A Fuggle with a rich Golding character. Common in Belgian ales.
TAURUS	Germany	Bittering	12-15	•	Ultra-high-alpha hop with some German character.
TETTNANGER	Germany, U.S.	Aroma	3.5–5	••	Traditional aroma hop with a soft spiciness. Great in weissbier!
ULTRA	U.S.	Aroma	2.2–3.1	••	Newer aroma variety with a very nice Saaz character.
VANGUARD	U.S.	Dual	5–6	NA	Newer dual use hop with German Hallertau Mittelfrüh character.
WGV (Whitbread Golding Variety)	England	Dual	5–7.5	••	Traditional English hop with sweet, fruity aroma. A little coarse.
WILLAMETTE	U.S.	Dual	4–6	••	American-grown version of Fuggle. Very similar, but softer.
WYE CHALLENGER	England	Dual	6.5–8.5	•••	Dual-use English hop with fruity aroma.
WYE NORTHDOWN	England	Dual	7–10	••	Generally regarded as the best of the English dual-use hops.
WYE TARGET	England	Bittering	10–12	—	Mellow. Early high-alpha variety, mostly goes into extract products.

STORAGE STABILITY:

—	Terrible
•	Poor
••	Fair
•••	Good
••••	Excellent

English Hop Ale Bottles, Early Twentieth Century

These were more akin to soda than beer. Wouldn't you like to see these in the vending machines?

Hop Pickers, c. 1850

For generations, whole families of working-class Londoners were lured to the hop fields for a working vacation.

back, which hooks up to the outlet of the kettle and allows the hot wort to filter over the hops on its way to the chiller. Hops may even be added to the finished beer, a procedure called dry hopping.

Hops in the Recipe

Many new brewers just go nuts and load up on the bitter resiny flavors, and of course there's nothing wrong with this. But after you've had your fill at the trough, you may seek a more balanced and sophisticated approach. Or not.

You don't always want a lot of hop aroma, but it's striking how often beers entered in homebrew competitions have no discernable hop aroma even if the style requires it. Something's amiss; brewers are either using the wrong hop varieties or are using insufficient quantities in the late stages of the boil for the aroma needed.

Many recipes will add the largest quantity of hops at the beginning of the boil, then smaller amounts in the middle and at the end. This results in most of the bitterness coming from the first hop addition, and with a relatively small amount of hop aroma in the finished beer. At some point I started calculating hop bitterness and decided on how much bitterness I wanted out of each hop addition, all of which is explained in the *Cypherin'* section, p. 64. If you want, say, a third of your bitterness to come from each of the early, middle, and late hop additions, the quantities used change dramatically—relatively small amounts in the early addition, fairly large quantities in the second (half-hour) addition, and very large amounts in the final aromatic dose.

My personal opinion is that there are few legitimate homebrew uses for high-alpha hops. Developed at the request of brewery accountants, they're just one more example of the "Department of Improvements" wrecking a good thing by trying to jam their kind of progress down our throats. Most high-alpha hops have somewhat coarse personalities and feel a little out of place for many traditionally inspired beers. And why shouldn't they? They're just raw feedstock for the extraction process.

That said, they have a place as bittering hops for very bitter beers such as India pale ales, imperial stouts, and the like. I usually stay away from them, although I perversely enjoy them as aroma hops in American-style IPAs. The grapefruit-like (the Europeans call it "cat-piss") aroma of varieties like Chinook add a citrusy touch. And to be fair to the hop researchers, varieties with better aromatic profiles continue to be developed. But generally I stick to my guns; if you want a nice hop flavor and aroma, use high-quality low-alpha hops, and lots of 'em.

If I didn't make the point a few paragraphs ago, I think whole hops will make better beer than pellets. It's not that pellets are awful, but due to the violent processing, they seem to have a rougher flavor than whole. On the other hand, they stay fresh longer and some varieties may only be available in pellet form since they're easier to ship from faraway places like Slovenia or New Zealand—so you may need to use them from time to time. Some brewers also like pellets because they're less messy in the kettle; however, since they're chopped fine, they may actually be harder to filter out. A stainless steel or copper scouring thingy attached to the end of your racking tube makes a simple and effective filter, so this really shouldn't be a problem.

Many beginner recipes suggest the use of a hop bag. These don't work all that well. Unless the bags are of extremely fine mesh, pellets leak right out, and whole hops don't get the opportunity to roil around the kettle as they need to in order to get incorporated into the wort. So, skip the bag. If you're chilling in the pot, either in a sinkful of water or with an immersion wort chiller (p. 32), stirring in a circular motion will whirlpool the hop detritus and other solids into a cone-shaped pile in the center of the kettle, and you can then siphon carefully from the edge of the kettle.

An interesting old technique that has recently been rediscovered is called *first wort hopping*. This involves adding a portion of the bittering hops to the kettle when the very first runnings of the mash start to trickle in. For some mysterious reason, this

Hop Usage Methods

Technique	Description	Result
First Wort Hopping	Added as wort hits kettle	Flavor; plus some aroma and bitterness
Full Boil	Added at start of boil	Bitterness
Mid-Boil	Added 15–30 min. from end	Bitterness + aroma
End-of-Boil/Post Boil	Added last 5 min. or end	Aroma
Hop Tea	Hops boiled in water	Mostly aroma. Limited effectiveness
Dry-Hopping	Hops added to secondary	Very fresh hop aroma

seems to fix the flavor of the hops into the final beer. I have experimented with this, and tasted a lot of beers brewed this way, and it does seem to add a profound hop flavor. If you wanted to simulate this in an extract brewing method, the best thing would be to simmer a third of your first hop addition with a half-gallon (2 liters) of water with a dollop of extract added for about half an hour, then add the rest of the ingredients and brew as usual.

There are lots of radical old techniques for hop use. Some antique recipes will recommend steeping the hops overnight in the cold water used as brewing liquor. Authentic Berliner weisse recipes from the old days recommend adding hops right into the mash, which will help in lautering this naked grain. These beers were often unboiled before fermentation, and of course the hops would have had a preservative effect as well, especially in knocking down the massive load of lactic acid bacteria that comes with the grain. But even with the hops, such a beer would have needed to be consumed quickly.

Dry-hopping has long been used to preserve and add flavor to beer. Hops are simply added to the storage vessel, or more typically, to the serving cask, where they impart lots of fresh hop aroma. This technique is most typical of English real ales, such as bitters, pale ales, and IPAs. It may be used wherever a little boost of hop aroma is desired. Quantities are in the range of 0.25 to 1 ounce (7 to 28 grams) per 5 gallons (19 liters) (although some hopheads will double that), with the very finest aroma hops reserved for this purpose.

Many homebrewers worry that dry hopping will sully their fresh, clean beers, and it is logical to fear that throwing in handfuls of a raw farm product would invite micro-biological havoc. In practice, such contamination is rare, and there seems to be little risk in the practice. Use only the freshest, best quality hops. You can place them in hop bags to keep them from clogging up the "out" hole.

IS IT OR IS IT NOT THE WATER?

Well, yes. And no.

Water can add to, or more likely detract from, the flavor of a beer, and brewers of every scale are well-advised to take it into consideration before they brew. In the old days just coming up with potable water was a big deal, and cities famous for brewing were inevitably situated near sources of clean water. The beer in those cities evolved to take advantage of the chemistry of the local water, as the science wasn't under-stood well enough to manipulate it. Although the chemistry of water—called liquor when destined for brewing— is complex if you really want to dig into it, for most of us there are just a few simple things to keep in mind.

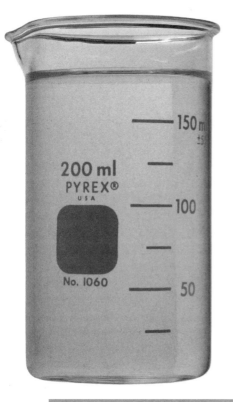

Water falls from the sky in a relatively pure form, soft and free from minerals. During its journey through streams, rivers, lakes, caves, and other deep geological strata, it absorbs minerals from the surrounding rock. Volcanic rocks tend to give up very little; sedimentary rocks, formed by the precipitation and biological deposition of minerals from water eons ago, are more ready to redissolve back into whatever's flow-ing by. Most commonly this rock is limestone (calcium carbonate) or dolomite (mag-nesium carbonate). More rarely deposits of gypsum (calcium sulfate) may be found, and these also add their rocky tang. Such minerals impart a quality to water called hardness. This has for a long time been measured by how readily soap will form lath-er, as this is of some importance for domestic water users.

Hard water may be divided into carbonate, or tem-porary, hardness; and sulfate, or permanent, hardness. As one would expect, temporary hardness can be coaxed into loosening its grip and leaving the water, while permanent is as it sounds. Many of the great brewing centers of the world, including Munich, Dublin, London, Saint Louis, and Milwaukee have water with temporary hardness. Most of the midwestern United States, situated on a giant slab of Paleozoic limestone, falls into this camp. Surface water, from rivers or reservoirs, tends to be more dilute in its min-eral content than well water, and is usually unencum-bered by noxious bit players like sulfur or iron, either of which can be ruinous to beer flavor. Carbonate will make water more alkaline, indi-cated by a higher pH.

"Possibly the best water in England is that at Castleton, in Derbyshire, commonly called, the Devil's Arss, &c...I have seen the Ale made of Castleton Water as clear in three days after it was bareled as the Spring Water was itself, and impossible to be known by the Eye in a Glass from the finest Canary Wine."

—Edward Whitaker, 1700

Carbonates may or may not be a problem depending on what sort of beer you're brewing. The most noticeable effect is to alter the character of hops, emphasizing harsh, astringent qualities that are pretty unpleasant in beer. In the case of London, Munich, and Dublin, the beers that developed around the local water were dark beers. This is because dark malts have sufficient acidity to bring the whole system into balance, and whether hoppy, like Irish stout, or malty, like Münchner, these dark beers are smooth on the finish without any raspy bitterness.

It's a very different story for sulfate (permanent) hardness. The brewing location famous for such water is Burton-on-Trent, long famous for pale, bitter beers. With sulfate water, the hops can express themselves free of any astringency. If you've ever tasted a well-kept cask of Bass ale, you can detect a hint of plaster—calcium sulfate—in the lovely nose, and then, wham, the hops, smooth and clean. Burton water is highly variable and massively mineral-like, with dissolved solids often over 2000 ppm, and sulfate content higher than 600 ppm. Should you be blessed (or cursed) with such liquor, you can either brew Burton style ales, or dilute it way down with distilled water.

The water of Plzen, another brewing center famous for pale, bitter beer, is almost completely mineral free. Although this would seem to be ideal, it is actually so pure that the enzymes may have a little trouble getting going. To cope, brewers there developed a hideously complex triple decoction mash, which, coupled with a steely, undermodified Moravian malt, turns out the most exquisite golden nectar. This traditional technique can be done at home, but it is not for the faint of heart.

Carbonate in brewing water may easily be reduced by the homebrewer. To stay soluble, the mineral depends on dissolved carbon dioxide, a mild acid. If you remove the CO_2 by boiling, the carbonate falls right out, familiar to most of us as the chalk that appears on the bottom of the teakettle. This process is aided by the addition of a small amount of calcium—in the form of calcium hydroxide or calcium chloride—which gives the carbonate ions something to combine with. Gypsum will work as well. How much to add depends on how much carbonate is present. This can be calculated down to the milligram, which is rarely necessary for homebrewing. The moderately carbonate water, found in all the Great Lakes and upper midwestern river systems (note that well water from the same region is usually two to three times as hard), will require roughly 1 teaspoon (3.5 grams) of calcium chloride or 2 teaspoons (8 grams) of gypsum per 5 gallons (19 liters) of water to help precipitate the carbonate. It should be noted that boiling will not remove all the carbonate, but it will usually knock it down to the point that a pale bitter beer is feasible.

Other minerals may also have an effect on beer flavor. Salt is often present in small amounts and can contribute a savory roundness to beer. It was previously used in certain light-gravity European beers to add an impression of body, and in the case of the East German white ale called gose, the drinker could even select the level of saltiness. In the old days, salt was added, usually in combination with flour, to "cleanse" casks, or to get the yeast to stop working and settle out. The water of Dortmund has a fairly high salt content, which may in part account for the full, rich taste of its beers. Salt cannot be easily removed from water, but fortunately is rarely found in quantities that

pH

pH is the scale used to describe the acidity or alkalinity of a substance, a measure of the concentration of hydrogen ions. The 14-point pH scale is logarithmic, which means that each number represents a ten-fold increase in concentration. A pH of 7 is neutral, with lower numbers increasingly acidic, and higher ones alkaline.

would affect the brewing process.

Metals such as copper and zinc are important in trace amounts as yeast nutrients, which is another reason to avoid distilled water. But too much of them can cause fermentation or flavor problems. Iron is fairly common in well water, and is not a welcome addition to brewing water; manganese is less common but is similarly harmful to flavor, clarity, and yeast. Other metals may be present in areas associated with mining, and are often at levels that can be tasted. If in doubt, get an analysis.

Aluminum has gotten a bad rap because of its supposed association with Alzheimer's disease. Work by some homebrewers has shown that even if this link was proven (which it is not), very little aluminum leaches into beer, even when brewing in unlined aluminum kettles. Aluminum may appear delicate and frail, but it actually surrounds itself with a nearly impregnable layer of aluminum oxide—the same mineral as rubies—that is extremely nonreactive.

Tin, which is not considered a particularly harmful metal for humans, may cause the beer to become hazy. It is the primary constituent of lead-free or soft silver solder.

Heavy metals such as lead, cadmium, mercury, and others do show up in low levels in municipal water supplies, and their levels are mandated by law. Certain mountainous areas may have high levels of toxic metals due to the underlying geology. Heavy metals are not removed by a charcoal filter alone, but higher grades of drinking water filters often contain ion-exchange components that do the job. There's no specific problem with these metals and the brewing process. You just don't want to consume more than a vanishingly small amount of them.

Fluoride is added to tap water in most cities (where they don't consider it a communist plot) to prevent tooth decay. This seems not to affect the brewing process, yeast, finished beer, or party loyalty in any way.

The most disruptive chemical in tap water is free chlorine, which is added as a disinfectant. Brewing with chlorinated water (or not rinsing your chlorine sanitizer well enough) will result in a beer that smells like adhesive bandages, not something you want in your homebrew. Fortunately a charcoal filter removes chlorine and chloramine, as well as traces of nasty organics such as PCBs and pesticides, which, although regulated, are sometimes present in tap water. Any hardware store or home center will carry activated charcoal drinking water filters ranging from small, inexpensive icemaker filters to larger and more expensive under-counter units. If you do nothing else in terms of water treatment, use a filter.

An Ancient Beer Saga

The Finnish-Hungarian national epic poem, the *Kalevala*, contains a charming tale of the discovery of fermentation. The brewer, Osmotar, has whipped up a batch of his finest, but it's a dud:

"*What will bring the effervescence,*

Who will add the needed factor,

That the beer may foam and sparkle,

May ferment and be delightful?"

But the "sparkling maiden" Kalevatar, aided by various magic virgins and small furry animals, comes to the rescue. She tries various remedies, starting with fir cones and pine branches.

"*But it brought no effervescence,*

And the beer was cold and lifeless."

Actually, she's close. Evergreen parts are still used to flavor beer, and twigs have also been used as a resting-place for yeast, tossed into the beer as a sort of magic stick. An eighteenth-century recipe book states: "*…it is a common practice to twist hazel twigs so as to be full of chinks and then to steep them in ale-yeast during fermentation. The twigs are hung up to dry, and then they are put into the wort instead of yeast.*"

Thereupon, our heroine is struck with another bright idea:

"*Gather yeast upon thy fingers,*

Gather foam from lips of anger,

From the lips of bears in battle…"

GODISGOOD: THE MYSTERY OF YEAST

Yeast is not so much an ingredient as a process. Its job in brewing is to turn sugar into alcohol. Along the way, wort is transformed from a sickly sweet syrup into something balanced and beautiful. It is alive, as we now know, reacting to its surroundings, stamping a deep and lasting imprint in the finished product, then getting out of the way when its work is done. Yeast is so magical it was called Godisgood before Louis Pasteur (and Schwann and Latour before him) discovered the true nature of yeast. Science took it out of the metaphysical realm, but it's still pretty amazing.

Research has revealed yeast to be an astonishingly complex and active entity. It's a fungus, a type of life that shares some characteristics with both the plant and animal kingdoms. It's a fantastic chemical factory, using an amazing number of chemical processes to feed itself and reproduce.

Ancient people were clearly aware of yeast; the Sumerians had fifty words related to it. For millennia, bread and beer were intertwined, and it is unlikely that there was a distinction made in the type of yeast used, especially when fermentation provided bakers with big jugs of active yeast. You almost had to brew in order to bake.

After the trashing of Rome by beer-drinking barbarians from the North, the classical world collapsed and yeast settled in for a long, slow evolution. In the damp limestone beer "caves" of southern Germany, this evolution took an interesting turn. The constant chilly temperatures favored a cold-tolerant yeast, one that did its work on the bottom of the beer rather than on top. By the fifteenth century, this had become the predominant yeast in that region, giving rise to one of the world's great families of beer—lagers.

In England, another tool for the selection of yeast worked in the opposite direction. Brewers there used various contraptions to "cleanse" the fermenting beer of yeast in preparation for aging. Most of these used some method or another for removing yeast from the top of the beer. The simplest method is manual skimming, but increasingly complex schemes were employed, culminating in the Burton Union, an improbable arrangement of barrels and swan necks that encouraged the yeast to rise out of the bungholes on top of the barrels.

Every set of local conditions bred its own blend of brewer's yeast, sometimes with wild yeast and bacteria mixed in. Remnants of this ancient way of brewing exist today in the Lambic beers of Belgium. In these unique brews, the region's wild yeast is

Saga, continued:

Except for the obvious element of danger, this isn't a half-bad idea. Saliva has been used for millennia as a source of starch-splitting enzymes as well as microbes. But this too fails. Then she hits on a real hummer:

"Osmotar, the beer-preparer,

Placed the honey in the liquor;

Kapo mixed the beer and honey,

And the wedding-beer fermented;

Rose the live beer upward, upward,

From the bottom of the vessels,

Upward in the tubs of birchwood,

Foaming higher, higher, higher,

Till it touched the oaken handles,

Overflowing all the cauldrons;

To the ground it foamed and sparkled,

Sank away in sand and gravel."

The wedding took place and everyone drank a lot beer and lived happily ever after. Wild honey, with its abundance of bee-gathered yeasts, got the beer going.

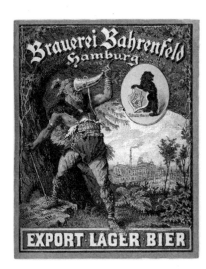

A nineteenth-century lager label evokes a much earlier time.

encouraged to come through slats in the eaves and inoculate the wort cooling in shallow pans in the attic. Wild yeast and bacteria have also taken up residence in the walls, barrels, and (so they say) cobwebs of these rustic breweries. The beer undergoes a complex chain of fermentation whereby one microorganism breaks down materials in the beer to create ideal conditions for the next. In a year or two the beer arrives at a stable, drinkable condition. Lambic tastes dramatically different than conventional beer, with lots of acidity, unfamiliar aromas, and a vinous, bone-dry palate. For more on this, and how to brew it, see Chapter 15.

Around 1885, Emil Christian Hansen isolated a single-cell strain of lager yeast, and it has been propagated this way ever since. Industrial brewing has favored clean, straightforward yeasts, but some eccentric strains of brewing yeast are still thriving. Many of the artisanal beers of Belgium showcase the amazing variety of flavors yeast is capable of producing. Bavarian weizen, with its unique, clove-like aroma, is another delightful example. Many of these strains are currently available as commercial products through homebrew suppliers.

In the dark ages of homebrewing, we were stuck using dried yeast. This is yeast that has been dehydrated in such a way as to keep it alive but dormant, so that it will reactivate on contact with warm water, ready for brewing. Dried yeast is not always bad, but it does have limitations. First, few choices are available, and only rarely are they specific brewing strains. Second, homebrewers are the smallest customers for dried yeast, with distillers and bakers accounting for most of the volume, so the strains may not always be the ones we'd choose. Third, the dehydration process asks a lot of the poor little critters, which means strains may be selected more for their ability to survive this brutal treatment rather than solely for their brewing value. Fourth, this yeast will deteriorate in time, so it's important to find the freshest pack you can.

Dried yeast should be rehydrated in warm water at 100 to 110° F (38 to 43° C). There is no need to add sugar or malt extract, and there is some evidence to suggest that it may even be harmful. I usually just put a measuring cup or beaker half full of tap water in the microwave and bring it to a boil. After it boils, I put a small piece of aluminum foil over the top and let it cool. Sprinkle the yeast over the surface. In a few minutes, it will start to bubble. Let it cool to fermentation temperature before pitching.

That said, it is possible to brew perfectly fine beer with dried yeast. But if you take this hobby seriously, you'll want the purity, provenance, and subtlety of liquid yeast.

There are hundreds of different beer yeast strains in use at breweries around the world. These strains are maintained at universities such as Weihenstephan in Germany, as well as commer-

Liquid Yeast

Both Wyeast and White Labs offer a variety of high quality, pedigreed brewing yeast.

cial yeast labs like Wyeast and White Labs, who package them for sale to brewers. For long-term storage, freezing in liquid nitrogen is the preferred method. At normal, even refrigerated temperatures, yeast loses its viability quickly, and needs frequent reculturing to maintain a healthy state.

Among the many flavor differences between strains are emphasis of hop or malt flavors; fruitiness, spiciness, and other aromatic qualities; levels of the buttery chemical diacetyl; and attenuation, which affects the dryness and alcoholic strength of the beer. Flocculation is yeast's ability to clump together and fall out of suspension when finished fermenting, and is an important characteristic, especially for commercial breweries. Additionally, the yeast may vary in its reaction to fermentation time, temperature, vessel shape, size or depth, strength of beer, CO_2 pressure, and many other factors. The manufacturers have good detailed information on their Web sites about flavors, beer types, and other characteristics. Choosing the perfect yeast for a brew is complicated, and if you're trying to really fine-tune a brew you may have to brew several batches so you can try different yeasts.

Louis Pasteur
Much of his groundbreaking work centered on beer.

"Pontoon" Room, John Taylor Brewery, Albany, N.Y., 1868

These primary fermenters spewed yeast which was collected and repitched, assuring the propagation of strongly top-fermenting yeast.

Chapter 5

HOW TO BUILD A BEER

IT'S ART, I TELL YOU—PUTTING A RECIPE TOGETHER

A great beer is more than the sum of its parts. Hitting the parameters for a style—color, gravity, and bitterness—may put you in the running for a ribbon, but it won't take best of show. A great beer has some extra magic that makes an impression on the drinker. Brewing is too much work to settle for mediocrity; dull beers are easy enough to buy ready-made. With the proper approach and quality ingredients, every batch can tap dance on the tongues of your amazed friends in an unforgettable performance.

Brewing is an art form. Color, texture, form, contrast, harmony, and surprise are all available for the artistic brewer to employ. Your audience has a specific set of senses with which to appreciate your art, as well as expectations that can be affected with names, packages, glassware, and the like. Your job as a brewer is to put them together into a coherent aesthetic experience.

So where to start? You can't underestimate the value of the *big idea*. You should be able to describe your beer idea in a short phrase: "a milkshake-smooth strong porter," for example. Once you have that, every decision should support the *big idea*. In this example, you might want to use raw wheat and oats, then lager for three months to take out every last kink. When you think about it this way, you end up making decisions that really add to the personality of the beer.

Balance is crucial for all gustatory experiences. Of course, there's malt and hops, neatly countering each other. You're not always trying to even things out; sometimes you want a seriously malty or hoppy beer. But there does come a point where things get lopsided, and of course, there's some subjectivity in where the line is drawn. You also have to remember that the balance will change as the beer ages. Hops lose about half of their bitterness every year a beer ages, which can be significant in a very strong beer meant for long aging. Other flavors fade as well, causing the maltiness to increase.

Balance can have more than two sides. You can get a three-way going with malt sweetness, hop bitterness, plus roasted or toasted malt flavors, which is one of the things that keeps dark, malty beers from being cloying. And when you throw in things like fruit, acid, smoke, hot chiles, or other deviant ingredients, the beer's balance can hang on very different hinges.

Consider drinkability. This obviously has different meaning for an ordinary bitter than for a barley wine, but the concept applies to both. While sugar has been the *bête noire* of the homebrew revival, Belgian brewers feel no such false pride and use it to good effect in many strong ales.

Using the best grade of ingredients can have a profound effect. Maris Otter barley is low yielding and difficult to grow, which is why it has largely been supplanted by other varieties. But in the right sort of beer where it is properly showcased, it can present a depth and complexity that can't be achieved any other way. One use for luxury ingredients is in relatively light session beers, where you're trying to find ways of having enough depth of flavor, but at the same time end up with a beer than can be drunk by the pint without fatiguing the palate of the drinker. On the opposite end of the spectrum, barley wines benefit from top-grade malt, a point insistently made in the old brewing manuals.

There's a continuum of quality in malt. In general, American malt, having been selected and malted to suit American brewers, just doesn't have the same depth of flavor as its European counterparts. In a beer all loaded up with crystal malt and Cascade hops this hardly matters, but for a delicate blonde ale with nothing to hide behind, you'll be much happier with the more flavorful malt.

Take a cue from cooking—layer flavors for greater depth. Don't use just one malt when two would do. But be sensible about it. Paler malts are more delicately flavored than dark ones. And consider the context as well. Two ounces of Munich malt will enrich a Pilsener, but will be undetectable in a stout.

Special ingredients often require special techniques in order to get what you want out of them. Raw wheat, for example, is resistant to infusion mashing, and requires something more intensive to extract fermentable material and the protein that adds that great creamy texture.

I always like to add a twist so subtle that no one is going to figure it out. Consider Guinness stout, with its subtle 3 percent infusion of soured beer, which adds a snappy crispness to this seductive black beer. You're always looking for depth.

CYPHERIN': CALCULATION IN THE BREWERY

In order to get to the point where all this magic artistry can take effect, you have to engineer the foundation. The basics of beer styles are built on the parameters of gravity, color, and bitterness. These three qualities are predictable with varying degrees of accuracy. No formulation system is dead-on accurate; the important thing is that they are repeatable in any given brewhouse.

All of this calculator punching may seem like needless work, but the arithmetic actually frees up your creative brain for more important tasks. You can learn to think in percentages, and formulate recipes based on the big picture of where you want to end up.

Since you are working with numbers in your recipe, it is helpful to try to calibrate your senses. Learn what a 45 IBU beer tastes like, and what a 20° SRM beer looks like. Find a book that has specific information about various brands and take notes as you drink.

Gravity can be predicted with some precision. Liquid malt extract will vary only by the amount of water in it, which runs between 77 and 82 percent. Each type of grain can contribute a specific amount of

Beer by the Numbers

This chart is a rough guide to beer color as expressed by the numbers. As with the malt chart, the numbers have been simplified, and all these styles exist as a range rather than a single number.

US Pils	Czech Pils	Pale Ale, Bitter	Märzen	Brown Ale	Munich Dunkel	Schwarzbier	Porter	Stout	Imperial Stout	
3	4	9	12	18	20	24	32	40	70	°SRM

extract, between 68 and 82 percent of its weight, and this is tested by the maltsters. These extract figures are listed in the malt chart on p. 44 & 45. You will never reach this theoretical maximum, but the amount by which you miss is relatively constant for similar techniques.

If you've already brewed an all-grain batch, it's easy to go back and calculate your efficiency. Just add up the amount of extract that theoretically would have been yielded, and then look at what you actually got. Divide actual by theoretical, and that's your efficiency. Be sure to pay special attention to the exact quantity of wort produced. Being just a quart off in a 5-gallon recipe represents a potential 5-percent error.

An efficiency of 75 to 80 percent of laboratory extract is about where most home-brewers end up, and 75 percent is the figure used to calculate the recipes in this book. The efficiency is about 5 percent higher if a decoction mash is used.

Another key characteristic you can play with is attenuation, or the extent to which malt sugars in the wort are fermented by the yeast. Malt extracts vary greatly in their fermentability, from 57 to 81 percent. Highly attenuated beers tend to be dry on the palate, and have the maximum amount of alcohol for their gravity. Less attenuated beers drink heavier and sweeter, with less alcohol. It should be obvious which beer styles can take advantage of those qualities. With extract beers it's a matter of choosing a single product or a blend that matches the profile you're aiming for. In all-grain beers the fermentability may be manipulated by the time and temperature of the saccharification rest, plus other factors. See p. 37.

Calculating color is a bit problematic, but there are ways you can achieve meaningful results as long as you don't expect real science. Malt Color Units (MCUs) are a simple way to express the total pounds times color of malt in a recipe. Simply multiply malt color in SRM times pounds for each grain, add them all up, and divide by the number of gallons in the recipe. Simple, right?

ASBC* Color Measurement Standard in a Nutshell

Sample is decarbonated and centrifuged or filtered (if needed) to remove haze, which will affect readings. The sample is inserted into a 1 cm sample cuvette. This is loaded into a spectrophotometer and absorbance is read at a blue wavelength of 430 nanometers.

The Absorbance value is multiplied by two factors: x 1.27 to compensate for the 1 cm cuvette size (original standard was written for 1/2"); and then x 10, which was applied to help the photoelectric method correlate better to the old Lovibond glass comparison standards. The resulting number is the beer color, ° SRM.

Few spectrophotometers can give a reading beyond 20, and most are far more accurate in the lower end of the scale. For this reason, samples of darker beers must be diluted with distilled water before reading. Everyone seems to agree that there is sort of nonlinearity, but the prevailing attitude is just to wink and move on.

*American Society of Brewing Chemists

Well...two problems: malt color numbers are about as predictive of the colors in a finished beer as the names on crayon colors, a fact that makes most people in the malting and brewing business just sigh in resignation. The second is that malt color just doesn't add up in a linear fashion. The more you add, the less color really shows up, so you end up with a calculated color as much as three or more times higher than the beer will actually measure. People in the know postulate that there is some sort of interaction of color molecules at high concentrations, and probably some precipitation of color compounds (melanoidins) during boiling or later, but nobody really seems to know.

At the very low end of the scale (2 to 4° SRM), the calculations work out fine. For us homebrewers, this isn't all that relevant, because at these levels, things like batch variations and kettle caramelization are large enough factors to throw this into chaos. It's the amber and darker beers where the calculations are needed most.

Based on work that I, and later Ray Daniels, have done, and verified by personal experience, here's a conversion chart that offers a rough translation between MCU and SRM beer colors. As you can see, the darker you get, the more discrepancy between predicted and actual color.

So all you do is translate your desired beer color from SRM to MCU, then start adding up the malts, starting with the medium colored ones, adding enough of the palest ones to get to your desired gravity, then adjusting the color with the darker malts. It's a little tricky at first, but it will give you more reliable results than just guessing.

And as a general rule, I personally like to get most of my color from the malt that is not the darkest one in the recipe. To my taste, they're just more profound this way, but it's clearly a personal preference.

You should be aware that there are loads of other factors that affect beer color:

- **Mash Efficiency** — More efficient = darker
- **Batch-to batch variation of malt** — Lighter or darker
- **Yeast** — Lighter or darker
- **Kettle caramelization** — Longer, more vigorous boil = darker
- **Mash & boil pH** — Higher pH = darker
- **Aging time** — Aging reduces color
- **Finings or filtration** — Either may reduce color

Am I saying you can ignore these? Yes I am. Anheuser-Busch can't, but you can. This color prediction business will get you only so far. If you're really trying to nail that Ninkasi award, you'll be well advised to do some trial batches and make adjustments based on your own experience, as brewers have always done.

°SRM (Standard Reference Method—ASBC)

0 10 20 30 40 50 60 70 80 90 100

0   50   100   150   200   250   300

HCU (°Lovibond x lbs ÷ Gallons)

Calculated vs. Actual Color

This chart gives an approximate translation between color calculated in a recipe and the actual color of the finished beer. It's not scientific, but it does give useful results.

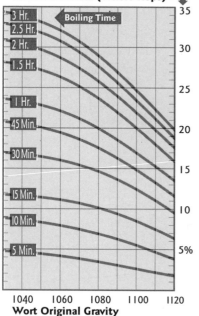

Utilization Rate (Whole Hops)

Boiling Time

3 Hr.	35
2.5 Hr.	
2 Hr.	30
1.5 Hr.	
	25
1 Hr.	
45 Min.	20
30 Min.	
	15
15 Min.	
10 Min.	10
5 Min.	5%

1040   1060   1080   1100   1120
Wort Original Gravity

Hop Utilization Chart

Find the utilization % at the intersection of the boil time and wort gravity lines. NOTE: chart is for whole hops; utilization for pellets will be 24% greater.

ON TO A RECIPE

What I'm getting at is that it's a good idea to try to define the signature malt character you would like to taste in your beer, and build your recipe around it.

It doesn't have to be just one thing. You can aim for a symphony of malty flavors, balancing rich warming maltiness with a whiff of sharp roastiness to create a balanced old ale or Scotch ale, for example. Or chunk up the austere purity of Pilsener malt with an overlay of Munich or Vienna. Maybe you want to do as one brewer did after hearing me rant on the subject, and put some of every kind of malt you can find into the beer and just be done with it. That's complex! The possibilities are endless, so it helps to have a plan.

Consider especially the middle malts. In porter and stout, expecting pale and black malt to do all the work can leave one a bit disappointed. Putting a thick, creamy layer of something or other in there can give this a lot more personality. There are lots of choices here: amber/biscuit, aromatic, and the crystals can all fill this role. You might even consider replacing half or more of your pale malt with something with a dab more color; mild ale malt was a common choice in Britain in the nineteenth and twentieth centuries. Its color (5 to 7° SRM) gives it rich, malty qualities very much like Munich, and this will fatten and add fascination to these sometimes drab working-class beers.

I usually calculate color and gravity at the same time. I start with the medium-colored grains, and I usually have a pretty good idea of how much I want to use for flavor and color. Add up the gravity from them, and subtract from the gravity target to get the amount of base malt required. Then add up the color from those two and calculate the amount of the darkest malt required to get you where you want to go, colorwise. You can just ignore the gravity contributed from less than a pound of really dark malt.

I love to use specialty grains for special purposes: wheat for head, oats for creaminess, rye for spiciness. And don't forget that roasted specialty grains such as wheat or oats (see Chapter 11) have flavors that are quite distinct from roasted malt.

Hop bitterness can be predicted accurately enough to be useful. Each hop has an assayed alpha acid content, and the main factors that determine how much of this bitterness gets into the beer can be taken into account in your calculations. They are:

- **Boil time**   Longer (up to 1.5 hours) means better utilization
- **Wort gravity**   Higher (above 1.030) means lower utilization
- **Quantity**   More is more, up to about 100 IBU
- **Pellets vs. Whole** Pellets will yield about 25 percent more IBU than whole

Bitterness in beer is measured by the parts-per-million of iso-alpha acids, a fairly complicated process involving a very expensive ultraviolet spectrophotometer. The measurement is called International Bitterness Units, or IBU. Some IBU levels in common beers are shown on p. 31.

To calculate hop bitterness, you need to have the alpha acid content, which will come from your supplier, or you can get typical values from the hop chart on

p. 49. You also need the utilization rate, which is based on the boil time and wort gravity. See the chart on p. 64. Then, get out the calculator. Each addition and variety must be calculated individually. A correction factor is applied to make the numbers work out to standard IBU units. Different corrections are used depending on whether you're using ounces or grams as your measurement.

Hop Quantity and IBU Calculation—Examples

Hop quantity, in ounces x Alpha acid % x Utilization % x Correction factor: 15.8 = IBU (predicted)

Example: 1 oz x 5 AAU [=5] x 25% [=1.25] x Correction factor: 15.8 = 19.75 IBU

Hop quantity, in grams x Alpha acid % x Utilization % x 0.55 = IBU (predicted)

Example: 28 g x 5 AAU [=140] x 25% [=35] x Correction factor: 0.55 = 19.25 IBU

Then you add the hop additions up, and that's your total estimated IBU number.

Other factors can affect utilization, including pH, boil vigor, wort protein, cold break, yeast type, and more. Overall the effect from these are small and more or less consistent for any given brewery, so they'll just have to be ignored, as this hop calculation is complicated enough already. However, boiling the hops in a hop bag noticeably reduces bitterness, so bump up your hop quantities by perhaps 25 percent in this case. Also, time takes a toll on hop bitterness before and after they are added to the beer. Depending on variety and storage conditions, hops can lose up to half of their bittering power in a year. And the same thing happens in the beer. There's no precise way to calculate this, but if you know you are working with old hops, or are brewing a beer that will be aged for a long time, heavy up on the hops.

For hops, I like to calculate each hop addition (full boil, thirty minutes, five minutes, for example) as a percentage of total alpha acid. As you move the focus from the beginning toward the end of the boil, the hop quantities increase, giving you much better flavor and aroma (remember this isn't always what you want). This uses more hops, but who's on a budget?

Hop character is far more elusive. In the case of our milkshake-like wheat porter, I might choose Northern Brewer, as I find it has a sort of bittersweet chocolate character that will complement the milkshake idea. Varietal choices should generally follow national style traditions: German hops for German beers, and so on.

IT'S ALL ABOUT PROCESS

Water can contribute its magic by completely screwing up an otherwise fine brew if attention is not paid to the minerals present (see p. 54). Other process issues also play important roles. Don't forget to include things like mash temperature, boil time,

Calculator Wheels

You can work out the particulars of gravity and bitterness with a pencil and paper. A handheld calculator makes this reasonably easy, but these circular slide rules I cooked up make the job really simple, especially when calculating backward from IBU to hop quantities.

Brewing calculator programs are available to run as freestanding applications on the PC, or as a template for Excel. These work well, but they do tie you to your computer or handheld PDA, neither of which are exactly wortproof.

Hot Side Aeration—What, Me Worry?

This is, as it sounds, the exposure of hot wort to oxygen during various phases of the brewing process, such as mash stirring and wort transfer. This has been a bit of a bogeyman of late, with some people going to *extreme* lengths to prevent it. The question is, will it cause problems in homebrewed beer, especially oxidized flavors as the beer ages? Breweries certainly take it seriously, but then they have a lot more to worry about in terms of product stability. The jury is still out as to whether HSA is injurious to your average batch of homebrew, but I think it's safe to say it isn't a huge problem, a view supported by the fact that the phenomenon was not even discovered by brewing science until fairly recently. But it also makes sense to try to avoid techniques that are likely to expose hot wort to an undue amount of air if alternative methods can be found.

A vast storage cask in Heidelberg, Germany, c. 1900.

and fermentation temperature as part of the recipe process; they should work in service of the *big idea* just as much as any ingredient.

Don't expect to get it perfect the first time. Breweries that make really great beer are obsessed with tinkering with their recipes. Think like the great jazz clarinetist Benny Goodman. Keep it the same until you can improve on it, then wail, man, wail.

FERMENTING

Yeast love wort. It contains sugars that form the main nutrient source, along with protein fragments called amino acids, fatty chemicals called lipids, and traces of inorganic minerals such as zinc and copper. All of these components are important, and a deficiency of any one of them can cause the yeast to perform poorly. Fortunately this is not a problem with most beers, so yeast nutrients are rarely needed for brewing.

Another important element is oxygen, without which yeast cannot reproduce. For this reason, it is important to adequately aerate your wort, which should always be done after the wort is cooled, because aeration of hot wort has the potential to cause problems. There are various ways to aerate chilled wort. Vigorous splashing, dribbling, or spraying the wort into the fermenter will add some oxygen. An aquarium pump with an air stone does a better job; a tank of oxygen is the geek solution and the way it's done at commercial breweries.

Temperature is the great regulator of yeast activity. At the simplest level, yeast take up sugar and split it into carbon dioxide and ethanol. But along the way, yeast make lots of other chemicals that have a profound effect on the flavor of beer. And most of these aromatic chemicals, from fruity esters to solvent-like fusels, are created in greater amounts at higher temperatures. This is the key difference between ales and lagers.

Ales, fermented relatively warm, have a far more complex aroma than lagers. At cool temperatures, the accent in lager remains on malt and hops, without the fruity, spicy aromatics that characterize ales. While specific yeasts for each are normally used, it is the temperature that makes the real difference. Certain ales—altbiers, for example—are fermented cool and have more of a lager-like quality. Others, like Anchor Steam, employ a lager yeast at warm temperatures and consequently have much more of an ale-like flavor profile.

Some yeast strains accentuate malt, while others favor hops. Certain varieties bring woody, spicy, fruity, or other characteristics to the brew. It takes a long time to become familiar with them, but don't be afraid to interrogate your homebrew pals about their experiences.

There has always been a great debate among homebrewers about whether a one-stage (primary only) or two-stage (primary plus secondary) fermentation method should be used. Conventional wisdom says that racking the beer off to a carboy after the yeast drops will produce a cleaner-tasting beer, and, since the secondary carboy is full to the brim, will keep away oxygen-born problems like acetobacteria. This is all theoretically true, but in my own experience, it really isn't necessary to do this with beers that will be ready to bottle or keg within a month, which is the majority of normal-strength beers. The problem of off-flavors from trub and autolysed yeast is more of an issue with pale, delicate beers, but many of these get lagered in a secondary anyway so the problem kind of solves itself. The oxygen argument may be more pertinent in a plastic bucket, which may do a poorer job of keeping a blanket of CO_2 over the beer, especially if you keep lifting the lid to check the progress.

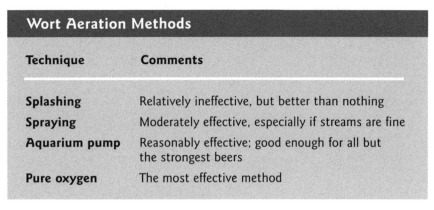

Wort Aeration Methods	
Technique	**Comments**
Splashing	Relatively ineffective, but better than nothing
Spraying	Moderately effective, especially if streams are fine
Aquarium pump	Reasonably effective; good enough for all but the strongest beers
Pure oxygen	The most effective method

Normally, the primary fermenter is filled about three-quarters full, and a lid or stopper with a fermentation lock is fitted on it, allowing CO_2 gas to escape. Occasionally you will get a beer that ferments vigorously, or you may desire to make a 5-gallon batch in a 5-gallon carboy. Either way, you will have foam gushing out of the top of the lock, a grossly unsanitary mess. The usual remedy for this is to use a large-diameter hose jammed into the neck of the carboy, the other end dunked into a plastic bucket partially filled with bleach water, forming a large fermentation lock. Ever since a professional brewer described to me the thick raft of bacteria he found growing in a bucket of strong bleach solution, I have been wary of its omnipotence in the sanitation department.

The solution is a closed blow-off. This requires a vessel such as a gallon jug fitted with a two-hole stopper. A metal or plastic tube goes through one hole, descending nearly to the bottom, and is connected at the top to a hose coming from the carboy. I just use a lock in a stopper, but without the internal parts, leaving a tube sticking up to slide the hose over. On the blowoff jar, a fermentation lock fits into the second hole and keeps the whole system clean and isolated from the surrounding environment. The long tube goes to the bottom because if the two openings are close together in the jug, the foaming goo sometimes can gush right up through the lock.

Closed Blow-off

The key to this is the two-holed stopper on the smaller container. A fermentation lock is fitted to one; a dip tube goes in the other, and serves to prevent yeast foam from being pushed out of the lock.

BOTTLE-CONDITIONED BEER

This is pretty straightforward. A carefully measured amount of sugar or malt extract is added to the finished beer, and this is put into bottles and sealed. The added sugar will ferment, creating carbon dioxide gas that will dissolve in the beer, creating fizziness. The usual method is to bring a small saucepan with a couple of cups of water along with the priming sugar in it to a boil, then allow to cool to blood heat, covered. It is then added to the beer, stirring gently to avoid introducing too much air into it, and filled into bottles. Unless the beer being bottled is very old (like a year), or very strong (over 10 percent), there is no need to add fresh yeast. It usually takes about two weeks for the full effect of the carbonation to take hold.

Priming (Corn Sugar) Quantities per 5-Gallon Batch for Various Carbonation Levels					
Units	**Very Low**	**Medium Low**	**Medium**	**Medium High**	**Very High**
Oz/5 gallons	3.0	3.75	4.5	5.25	6.0
Cups/5 gallons	0.45	0.55	0.67	0.78	0.90
Grams/20 liters	80	100	120	140	160

DRAFTING AN ALE

A Homebrew Draft System

This consists of a soda keg attached to a tank of CO_2 gas through a regulator, which lowers the pressure to appropriate serving levels of 5 to 15 psi. A hose with a plastic "cobra" tap delivers the beer.

With another kit of gear, you can bypass the tedium of bottling and serve your beer on draft. The standard homebrew setup is based on castoff soda serving tanks, most commonly known by one of the manufacturer's names, Cornelius—corny kegs, for short. They're most commonly found in 5-gallon size, although 3- and (rarely) 10-gallon ones turn up. They all have a removable lid and two quick disconnect fittings. Carbon dioxide gas hooks up to one, and the liquid comes out the other. The soda business has largely abandoned this system, so there are lots of them available cheap. Rubber O-rings may need to be replaced, especially if the tank held something pernicious like root beer or grape soda, which forever taints the rubber parts.

The gas setup consists of a steel or aluminum gas bottle, designated by the amount of liquid CO_2 the tank will hold. Five-pound tanks offer a nice compromise between portability and capacity. A pressure regulator screws onto the gas tank and drops the pressure from several hundred psi down to useful pressures. The gas tanks must be pressure-tested every five years, so check the date of the last test stamped into the shoulder if you're buying a used one. You want the most recent test date possible.

You can carbonate the beer naturally by priming just like bottles, but this adds a layer of yeast that tends to get sucked into the serving tube until the very end of the keg. The more common method is to rack the finished beer into the corny, then hook up the gas. With nice cold beer and the gas set at 12 psi it will take between one and two weeks to fully saturate with gas. If you're in a hurry, you can crank it up as high as 50 psi (the tanks are rated for 75 psi), and the gas will dissolve more quickly. If you're *really* in a hurry, a few minutes of vigorous rocking of the keg from end-to-end will jumpstart the process. For the deeply impatient, a carbonating stone can be attached to a lengthened "gas in" tube, and this can get the beer drinkable in just a few hours. Before going into serving mode be sure to turn down the pressure to 10 to 12 psi and vent the keg. And if you're speed-carbonating, try not to overcarbonate the beer, because it's hard to get the gas out of the beer once it's in there.

REAL ALE

This is easy to duplicate in the homebrewery. In fact, you have to work pretty hard to make unreal ale. For homebrewed cask ale, allow the fermentation to finish in a carboy, then rack into a Cornelius tank with a low dose of priming sugar (see bottling). Keep the keg sealed, and if possible, monitor the pressure with a gauge on the gas inlet. A pressure of 7 to 9 psi is ideal. To serve by gravity, position the keg horizontally, with the liquid fitting at the bottom, and attach a hoseless gas fitting to vent it. If you have a beer engine, you can leave the keg vertical. Your beer will be brighter if you saw off the bottom one inch of the dip tube inside to keep from continuously drawing up the settling yeast. You can also hook up a beer engine, which looks really cool, but it isn't really necessary and adds nothing to the taste or texture of the beer.

With this vented serving, air will enter the beer, encouraging contamination, so you must drink it within a week. If you want to savor the brew for a longer time, you must make other arrangements. Instead of venting, hook it up to the gas at a low pressure—2 to 5 psi—while serving, then disconnect it when you're done for the day so the beer won't soak up additional gas.

Traditional firkins (10.8 U.S. gallons) or pins (5.4 U.S. gallons) are manageable for homebrewers, but are not generally set up for connecting to CO_2, so if you wish to use CO_2 blanket pressure, you'll have to rig up a fitting for the bunghole.

ABOUT THE RECIPES IN THIS BOOK

In order to save space, I have omitted a fair amount of repetitive detail in the individual recipes. Also, I have necessarily made some assumptions which may turn out to differ from your own brewhouse experience, and therefore may require some adjustments of ingredient quantities.

In addition to all-grain versions of all the recipes, I have attempted to offer simpler extract + grain recipes where I thought a reasonable approximation could be made. However, there are some recipes I though might not be worth the effort, so for those, no extract equivalent is given. If you wish to attempt extract versions of these, I refer you to the all-grain to extract conversion suggestions offered on p. 37. This method may be used for converting all-grain recipes from other sources as well.

Malt, grains, and efficiencies The recipes are calculated based on a 75 percent efficiency; that is, a yield of extract equal to 75 percent of laboratory Hot Water Extract (HWE), which is the most common measure that maltsters supply with their malt. If you have been brewing for a while, you may have some idea of what your brewhouse efficiency is. Simply calculate a previous recipe using the method outlined on p. 61 to find your efficiency, then make adjustments accordingly. Chances are your system will differ from my assumptions by less than 10 percent, so you may be able to live with the discrepancy.

Hop alpha acid (% AA) content and quantities The alpha content used to calculate the bitterness is stated for each hop variety in the recipes. Note that these are idealized numbers, and that hops will vary by origin and year. These figures are for fresh hops, and hops that are a year old may be 20 to 50% less bitter (this also depends on storage conditions). You may wish to make adjustments.

All hops are calculated for whole hops rather than pellets, so if you wish to use pellets for any hop addition, reduce the stated quantity by 25 percent. All the hop calculations have been performed with the hop wheel shown a couple of pages back. This has been demonstrated to give bitterness calculations as accurate as any home-brew system out there, but I must stress that there are a lot of variables. If you find you are getting too much or too little bitterness, then make adjustments to hop quantities accordingly.

Mashing and brewing procedures There are three basic procedures given in the recipes: an all-grain, and either an extract + steeped grain, *or* an extract + mini-mash. The all-grain procedure, unless specified otherwise, follows the basic infusion mash detailed on p. 39. Unless different temperatures are given, assume a single mash at 150° F (65.5° C) of sixty minutes duration. A water-to-grain ratio of 1.5 quarts per pound (0.65 liters per kilogram) is a good general quantity, although for beers mashed at higher temperatures, the ratio can go as low as 1 quart per pound (0.45 liters per kilogram); for lower temperatures, the mash can become more dilute: 2 quarts per pound (0.85 liters per kilogram). For all mashed recipes, keep in mind the importance of a mash out of 170° F (77° C) at the end of mashing. This will stop the enzyme activity and keep the starch liquified, which will make sparging easier.

The extract + steeped grain procedure is outlined on p. 32. The extract + mini-mash procedure is covered on p. 36. Follow the detailed procedures just mentioned unless the recipe specifies something different.

Yeast, fermentation, and aging For the most part, I have not made specific yeast strain recommendations for the individual recipes. Within the general type listed in the recipe, you should consult the detailed specifications posted on the White Labs and Wyeast sites; they are more detailed and up-to-date than this book could ever be. Yeast selection is a fine art. Recipe, batch size, temperature, pitching conditions, and above all, personal preference all play a role in how a yeast will perform—and how the finished beer will taste. I have mentioned it before, but I cannot overstress the importance of freshness.

Worksheet I highly recommend that you fill out a worksheet with every brew, recording the details of ingredients and procedures. Although the fine points may seem at the time to be etched permanently into your brain, I can assure you that by the next day or the next month your memory will be a hopeless jumble. Use the sheets. As a convenience, a downloadable PDF of the worksheet at right (but sized for 8.5" x 11" reproduction) is available for your use at www.radicalbrewing.com.

RADICAL BREWING

Mash Time & Temperature

°F									°C
210									100
200									
190									90
180									80
170									
160									70
150									
140									60
130									
120									50
110									
100									40
90									
Hrs	0	.5	1	1.5	2	2.5	3	3.5	4

Brew/Mash Type

Total Lbs/Bbl

Strike Water   Qt/.Lb

= Rest Temp   = Diff

Mash Ph   Wort Ph

Boil Length

Irish Moss?

Water

Yeast

OG chart

Gravity — °Plato / OG / Alcohol Potential — %

Gravity — °Plato	OG	Alcohol Potential — %
24	1100	13.0
22	1090	12.0
20	1080	11.0
18	1070	10.0
		9.0
16	1060	8.0
14		
	1050	7.0
12		6.0
10	1040	
		5.0
8	1030	4.0
6	1020	3.0
4		2.0
2	1010	1.0
0	1000	0.0

Beer Name   Brew Date

Beer Style   Brewer

Batch size   Target OG/°P

Lb/kg	OG/°P	Ingredient		Color

Qty	Oz/g	Hop /Seasoning	α Acid	P/W	Min.	Util.	IBU

Stage	Date	OG/°P	% Alcohol Potential	Temp °F/°C
Primary				
Racked				
Racked				
Bottled				
Kegged				

Notes

Is it Any Good?

Drinking is different than tasting. Sure, you do taste when you drink (hopefully), but what we're talking about here is a real focused attitude behind a trained set of senses, usually with a specific purpose in mind. It may be to judge the winners and losers of a competition, to fine-tune your own brews, or to try and grasp the nuances of a commercial style. No matter what you're doing with it, a little education can be very helpful.

What is there to work with? To use a computer analogy, you can break it down into hardware and software. The hardware is chemistry and physiology, in which specific molecules interact with receptors in the nose and mouth in sensitive lock-and-key arrangements, firing off neurons that travel up the nerve chain. The software is psychology, the weird baggage of perception and conception we deal with all the time. In reality, the hardware/software boundary is a little fuzzy, as neurons link upwards into higher and higher processing centers in the nerves and brain.

THE BASICS OF CRITICAL TASTING

We all know the familiar four flavors of sweet, sour, bitter, and salty. There is one additional flavor called *umami* (often described as savory) that is especially prominent in Asian cuisine, as it is naturally present in seaweed, oily fish, and MSG. All of these tastes are sensed on the tongue, offering a limited range of sensations.

Aroma is vastly more complex, with upwards of ten thousand perceptible odors detectable by our olfactory sense. In fact, much of what we think of as taste is really aroma, and people who have lost their sense of smell have difficulty tasting anything, as you may have noticed when suffering a bad cold.

The molecules that trigger aroma sensations travel in through your nostrils and into your nasal cavities from the back of your mouth. When tasting, you can concentrate the aromas by a technique called aspirating, in which you hold some of the liquid in the bottom of your mouth while gurgling air through it as you slowly inhale. It takes a while to get the hang of this, but it really does heighten the experience.

Your sense of smell is wired differently from your other senses. Olfactory signals go to three places in the brain, all of them very primitive: the hypothalamus, seat of appetite, anger, fear, and pleasure; the hippocampus, regulator of memories; and the brainstem, controller of basic bodily functions such as breathing. Because they interface with such low levels of the brain, aromas have the ability to stimulate powerful psychological responses, memories, and emotions, far more than other senses. This provides us with a powerful tool to draw people into our art, and probably accounts for much of beer's appeal.

This neural wiring explains why a single whiff can trigger vivid childhood memories, and our overwhelming revulsion to aromas like decomposing corpses or brackish water—incidentally the most potent aroma molecule known. These are not learned.

We come pre-wired with them. Similarly, aromas associated with high nutrient foods—fats, for example—trigger positive feelings without so much as a bite. There's a reason they tell you to bake bread before you have an open house for the home you're trying to sell.

The clever taster can use these telegraphic memories to help decode aromas in beer. Perhaps a smell makes you think of your grandma's house. Is it summer or winter? Inside or out? Is it a flower, something for dinner, potpourri, air freshener? Let your mind drift and you just might be able to put your finger on it. Learning to judge beer is an interesting act of self-discovery.

In addition to aroma and taste, other physical sensations play a role in the perception of beer. Mouthfeel sensations such as carbonation, body, astringency, and temperature all affect the experience that is beer. Certain chemicals have unpleasant effects: the harshness of polyphenols, the oiliness contributed by high levels of diacetyl, and the eye-watering effect of ethyl acetate (nail polish remover), a common component of ale.

Our eyes are at work here too, and play a larger role than we would like to admit. By seeing a beer, certain taste expectations are created: the light maltiness of a pale beer, the roastiness of a stout, the creaminess of a slow-poured head.

If you're Fred Eckhardt, even sound offers an appreciable dimension of beer.

English Ale Glasses, Nineteenth Century

Matching the beer to the glass is one of the fine arts of tasting.

YOUR STRANGE BRAIN

Even though taste and aroma sensations are laden with the baggage that comes along with any psychological process, they are chemically driven at their base level, and a right-thinking beer judge ought to be able make an even-handed account of what's in the glass, right?

Well, yes and no. Even with your head screwed on right, there are many factors that introduce a considerable amount of non-linearity in the way we perceive aromas and tastes. Some of these are:

Variable thresholds Perceptions vary from person to person. As an example, 20 percent of the population is unable to smell phenol, a common and not always welcome aroma in beer. You may be insensitive or super-sensitive to some of the chemicals found in beer. And of course, having the receptors does not guarantee that one will recognize a scent when present. Those of you who have gone through the effort to become a beer judge know just how important training a palate can be.

Concentration effects The amount of a chemical can determine not just the intensity, but the *quality* of its aroma. One chemical, o-aminoacetophenone, tastes grainy in parts-per-trillions, like tacos in parts-per-millions, and like Concord grape juice in parts-per-thousands. In my own tasting experience, diacetyl and DMS seem to exhibit this behavior, too.

Matrix effects These are interactions in which the individual aroma chemicals change each other into something different than any of them alone. Although there

The Dirty Dozen of Beer Off-Flavors & Aromas

The cellar door startled the cat with its hoarse creaking, and I felt the rush of cool earthy air from within. Reaching carefully through the cobwebs, I plucked a seemingly innocent bottle from its long repose, and pondered the sleeping golden liquid in the dim subterranean twilight. With a quick snap of my wrist and a snakelike hiss, the ale obediently slid into my waiting glass. No innocent nymph, this beery banshee fairly shrieked with a chemical so vile, so repulsive as to be pure evil. It was my old nemesis, Phenol. My anguished cry reverberated throughout the ancient stone grotto, "Whyyyyyyyyyyyyy..."

If something like this—although perhaps a bit less Poe-like—has ever happened to you, read on. Like all the other major metaphysical dimensions of the universe, beer sometimes shows a darker side. Errors in brewing, biological contamination, or poor storage conditions all may contribute off flavors and aromas to beer. There are a number of fairly common ones whose presence is often indicative of specific problems. Learning to recognize them can be crucial to preventing them in the future, Here's a list of common beer defects—by no means complete—and a suggestion of how to easily prepare a sample for this nosing.

These spiked samples are strictly sniffers—DO NOT DRINK!

NAME	COMMENTS & DESCRIPTION
ACETALDEHYDE	This is a green apple-scented chemical that can be created by normal yeast, or more intensely (and rarely) by bacterial infection. Interestingly, Budweiser uses this aroma to impart a crisp, "snappy" quality. Use: one small green apple Jolly Rancher candy smashed and dissolved overnight in a little water; add to sample beer.
ACETIC	A vinegar aroma caused by infection—intentional, in the case of Belgian lambics and sour brown ales—by acetobacteria. Use: a couple of teaspoons of distilled vinegar in a sample beer.
CHEESY	An aroma of limburger or rancid butter caused by oxidized hops, usually as a result of poor storage conditions. Use: actual limburger, but unwrap it outside, please.
CHLOROPHENOL	An aroma of medical adhesive tape usually caused from inadequate rinsing of chorine (bleach) sanitizer. Use: a roll of old-fashioned adhesive tape displays the odor quite well.
DIACETYL	This buttery aroma can be desirable in low concentrations in some ales, but if it sticks out too far, it's usually regarded as a defect. Produced by yeast, but especially by certain bacteria. Use: butter flavor extract (the kind used for baking), one to four drops or dry equivalent of one-eighth teaspoon. Note that diacetyl's quality changes with quantity, and for that reason it might be useful to do a series at different dilutions.
DMS (di-methyl sulfide)	A vegetal aroma that can result from brewhouse procedure (a weak boil, wort held at high temps without boiling) or, in extreme cases, from a slow yeast start or contamination. Actually regarded as a positive in some pale European lagers, where, in small quantities, it adds a certain richness. Use: juice from canned corn added to light beer.
OXIDIZED	A papery, wet cardboard flavor/aroma, the result of over-aged beer, enhanced by overexposure to air during the brewing process. Oxidized flavors vary from beer to beer and can manifest themselves as harshness, thinness, astringency, a flat taste, or other hard-to-pin-down qualities. Use: the oldest, dustiest European beer in the

The Dirty Dozen of Beer Off-Flavors & Aromas

NAME	COMMENTS & DESCRIPTION
OXIDIZED (continued)	liquor store, ideally with haze or flakes on the bottom (don't use weizen, because the haze is intentional). Go for beer in brown bottles only, as the ancient green-clad ones are often skunked as well as oxidized.
GOATY/SWEATY	This is not as rare a condition as we would like, both for homebrew and micro brew, although, thankfully, it's getting rarer. It's caused by Lactobacillus and Pediococcus bacterial infections, which produce capryllic and other organic acids with strong sweaty or animal (goat-like) aromas. Use: there are no artificial substitutes, so you'll have to come up with a bad beer.
PHENOLIC	A broad category of flavor gremlins. The worst of them—3, 5 dimethoxyphenol—is an indicator of wild yeast infection, and smells like an electrical fire. Other, more subtle, even pleasant ones, can come from certain yeast strains (weizen) or honey. Use: a nice fresh Weizen for the clove-like yeast character; honey diluted 1:4 in water; for the really nasty one, perhaps a piece of phenolic circuit board, the amber colored kind, freshly rasped or broken for intense aroma. Use: don't bother to dunk them in beer, just sniff the objects.
SKUNKY (methyl mercaptan)	The result of light hitting dissolved hop compounds, resulting in a rubbery, skunky aroma. Use: European beer in green bottle, placed in sunlight for an hour, then chilled and served normally.
SOLVENT	Esters are produced by yeast at higher temperatures, and contribute floral or fruity notes to ales. In extreme cases, this becomes a solvent-like character, due to concentrations of ethyl acetate. Use: a few drops of old-fashioned nail polish remover (non-perfumed) in a beer. This is as much a sensation as an aroma; I always feel my eyes tearing up long before I actually smell it. Solventy aromas can also come from fusel alcohols.

are nine hundred identified chemicals in coffee, there is no known flavor chemical "coffee"—nothing that, by itself, tastes coffee-like. On p. 169 is a recipe for gingerbread ale, in which a mixture of cinnamon, ginger, nutmeg, and other spices is added to a beer. It tastes exactly like gingerbread. The first time I tasted the beer, the aroma sent me back to my childhood—it was quite striking. It was the exact proportions of these ingredients that created the effect. DMS is also subject to a matrix effect in beer. In pale beers, it has a familiar aroma of cooked corn; in dark beers, the aroma is more like tomato juice. Matrix effects are also involved in "meaty" aromas, which involve many of the same kinds of (Maillard) chemicals as the flavors of malt.

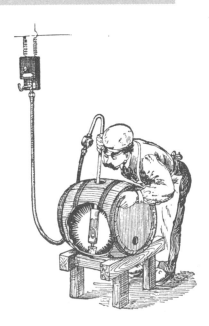

Masking This is a phenomenon in which one chemical covers up, or diminishes the effect of, another. Vanilla is a remarkably effective one and can cover a multitude of minor sins in a beer, if you don't mind turning your slightly defective brew into a spiced beer. High hop rates can mask oxidation; high carbonation can mask hops.

Adaptation/potentiation After smelling a substance for a while, the receptors become desensitized. As you know, when hops first hit the kettle, the smell is strong

and wonderful. After a while, you can't smell them, but if you leave, then walk back into the brewery, wham! They hit you again. This is why first impressions are so important in judging. If you're having trouble picking up a scent after trying for a while, give your nose a rest by smelling something else, then coming back to it. Amazing, but it works.

Moving on to the realm of the psychological, we get to the truly irrational stuff:

Cross-sensory effects How would you grade a black Pilsener? The official judging form would give it 2 points off. Yet since the visual sense uses more of our brain than all other senses combined, we sometimes tend to believe our eyes at the expense of other senses.

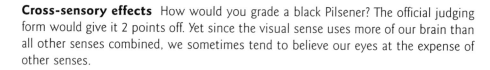

The "halo" of name and identity Remember the mystique Coors once had for those of us east of the Mississippi? My college friends and I once drove a thousand miles for it in 1973. What did you drink when you drank junk beer (c'mon, admit it, everybody did)? Have you tasted one recently? Do you have the foggiest idea what it was you once liked about it? The fire brewing? The beechwood aging? Was it the champagne of beer? The sky blue waters?

Packaging Labels and interesting, meaningful names can improve your beer—yes, *even homebrew.* Such trimmings give a context and set up expectations that are very real—a way to direct the perceptions of your audience. This is art, not trickery! If you have grungy bottles with shards of labels stuck on them, what does that say? Do you respect your beer? Why should I?

An Outline of Beer Evaluation

Judging may be formal or casual, but in either setting it is helpful to break the experience into several steps, which are outlined below.

Beer evaluation should be done in a room without too many distractions, and most importantly, free from pervasive odors such as cigarette smoke or food. Small wine glasses are ideal, but clear, odor-free plastic cups are the norm. Be sure to have water and bland crackers or bread available for palate cleansing if a number of beers will be judged.

In formal settings, beers are evaluated in flights of 10–15, invariably presented blind (identities hidden from judges). An experienced judge can deal with two or three such flights in a setting, depending on the thoroughness of the judging system.

NAME	COMMENTS & DESCRIPTION
AROMA	Do this before anything else, because some aromas dissipate very quickly. Are the aromas pleasant or not? Do they match the style? Do they add up to a pleasant overall sensation? Try to pick apart the aromas; note the familiar and the unfamiliar. If you can't put your finger on something, try to picture in your mind some time and place where you can remember the scent. Sometimes this helps put a name to an aroma.
APPEARANCE	Is the beer cloudy or clear? How's the head? Does the color match the style guidelines?
FLAVOR	Pay attention to the way the flavor changes: initial impression, mid-taste, and aftertaste. Are these pleasant? Do the flavors form a harmonious whole?
MOUTHFEEL	This is body, carbonation, head, and similar textural sensations. Do they work with other qualities of the beer? Are they appropriate for the style?
OVERALL	Do all the parts work together? Is there a depth to the beer? Is this something you will remember later? Is this a beer you would actually drink? Does it do justice to the style?

JUST THE BEGINNING

This is just the beginning of a study of beer flavor defects and their origins. Getting your nose sharpened up is the best place to start, but you'll probably want to get a little more detail, especially if you're having a problem with something you identify here. George and Laurie Fix's books (*Principles of Brewing Science* and *An Analysis of Brewing Techniques*) offer great, gooey gobs of detail. The organizations listed below can help connect you with organized judging programs and competitions, the very best way to go further in this area.

BJCP Beer Judge Certification Program:
www.bjcp.org

AHA American Homebrewers Association:
www.beertown.org

Basic Drinkers

In most times and places there is a need for a quenching beer than can be consumed in quantity without putting the drinker into a compromised state too quickly. Sometimes these everyday brews are truly watery, with little to recommend to a serious beer lover. Some, by contemporary reports or recipes, must have been awful. But the limitations of low-gravity brewing can spur the brewer to produce beers of great artistry and seductiveness.

EXTRAORDINARY ORDINARIES: BRITISH BITTER

Throughout England's history, for reasons of privation, taxation, profit, or temperance, beers have often weakened over time, typically settling into a gravity range between 1.030 to 1.040 (7 to 9.5 °P), far below the swaggering new brews of America's new brewers.

Using less material forces the brewer to make the most of what he or she uses. The best ingredients—carefully assembled, processed, and fermented in a way that maximizes their best qualities—is the basic plan. Serving the beer in superb condition is the crowning touch. Here's an expansion of that scheme, along with a trick or two.

Use the best malt British bitter, when well made, is a shining standard for modest-gravity beer with great depth and personality, much of it due to the character of the malt. Some of the best ones use an old, difficult-to-farm variety called Maris Otter. Beers made from it have a nutty depth that's hard to describe. Yes, it's more expensive, but for a home-brewer, it's just a matter of pennies. In general, British and other European malts will bring more flavor to a beer. American malts have their place in brewing, but remember, most are specifically cultivated to brew cold, fizzy, flavorless beers. *Caveat maltor.*

Use the best hops Not only are the flavors of low-alpha aroma hops usually better, but if you use them, you will have a larger quantity than if you use high-alpha hops—which means a greater amount of hop flavor in the finished beer. And you can use fairly large quantities of finishing hops (1 to 2 ounces per 5 gallons) in the last half-hour of the boil without adding a lot of extra bitterness.

Use lightly colored malts for much of the color The color added by a tablespoon of black malt or a pound of crystal might seem similar, but there's a vast difference in flavor. This applies all along the color scale. One of the reasons a Munich *dunkel* tastes so rich is that it contains a very high proportion of Munich malt, a relatively lightly kilned product. Another malt that's not widely used enough is mild ale malt. It's similar in color to Munich, and was traditionally used as a base malt for milds and stouts (in the twentieth century), where it laid down a full, malty base to build upon.

Layer flavors Choose your ingredients so that each one contributes to the overall effect. For a smooth, chocolatey mild ale, start with the mild ale malt I just mentioned, where it gives a round richness similar to the sweet component of the chocolate flavor. Add to that some amber/biscuit malt, also a traditional component of such beers, for a toasty mocha flavor, sort of the mid-range of the chocolate taste. Top it off with a small amount of smooth, roasty black, or Carafa malt to evoke the sharp roastiness of bittersweet chocolate. One might automatically think of using chocolate malt here,

---

RECIPE — Tire-Biter Bitter

There are endless subtle variations to this style, and there is no such thing as a definitive recipe. Feel free to tweak any of the ingredients to make your own variation.

Yield: 5 gallons (19 liters)

Gravity: 1.045 (10.75 °P)

Alcohol: 3.7 to 4.3%

Color: Tawny amber

Bitterness: 37 IBU

Yeast: English ale

Maturation: 3 to 4 weeks

All-Grain Recipe:

8.0 lb (3.6 kg)	83%	Maris Otter pale ale malt
1.0 lb (0.45 kg)	11%	pale crystal malt
0.25 lb (113 g)	6%	biscuit/amber malt

Malt Extract + Steeped Grain Recipe:

4.75 lb (2.2 kg)	73%	pale dry extract
1.5 lb (0.68 kg)	11%	pale crystal malt
0.25 lb (113 g)	16%	biscuit/amber malt

Hops:

1.0 oz (28g)	90 min	Northdown (6.5% AA)
0.5 oz (14 g)	30 min	East Kent Golding (5% AA)
0.5 oz (14g)	30 min	East Kent Golding (5% AA)

---

but I find this to be somewhat sharp and not particularly chocolatey in character. The character of hops plays into this as well. I would use Northern brewer, which has a certain chocolatey bitterness. Further, I would choose a yeast that accentuates the sweetness of malt, such as the Fuller's strain. Layered. Luscious.

Boost the body A little more body and sweetness can make a beer drink bigger than it really is. During World War I, the British were very interested in Belgian witbier techniques, which at the time were turning out palatable beers with gravities around 1.025. They did this by mashing in, then draining off, all the enzyme-rich liquid and

boiling it, which denatured the enzymes; but preferentially leaving alpha amylase, which would produce a poorly fermentable wort, resulting in the beer being somewhat sweet and full-flavored.

There are a number of other, saner techniques for this. Mashing at higher temperatures—155 to 158° F instead of 150° F—is one. Crystal malt and Carapils (dextrin malt) are proven body-boosters. The judicious use of a little lactose can enrich a beer. Adjuncts such as oat, wheat, or rye contain proteins and gummy carbohydrates that can enhance body and head retention. Salt in small quantities (one-eighth to one-half teaspoon per 5 gallons) will boost mouthfeel, a trick used by brewers of *gose* beer, a light brew from eastern Germany. Many old brewing books make the same claim for coriander, and indeed it does find its way into several very light styles, although it has not been a regular feature of commercial British ales for almost three hundred years.

Pay attention to condition Fortunately, fining and filtration are seldom necessary in homebrewing, so the concern about stripping the life from our beers this way isn't an issue. Nonetheless, it's especially important with this lighter sort of beer that they be carbonated appropriately for the style, then served with a perfect layer of foam in the correct glassware at an ideal temperature. Your pint beckons!

(NOT SO DUMB) BLONDE ALES

A blonde ale is the love child of India pale ale conjugated with a pale lager. Lighter versions of burly pale ales called dinner ales or sparkling ales were brewed from about 1860 to 1900. They were designed to be served fresh, without long aging, and were light enough to be quenching and refreshing. As the American brewing industry shifted into the hands of German immigrants familiar with the altbiers (ales) of Cologne/Köln, brewers cast pale ales in a Continental mold rather than an English one. To my mind, there is little theoretical difference between Kölsch, cream ale, and blonde ale.

We are talking about a golden ale of moderate gravity with a smooth, sweet malt character—not too much carameliness—modestly hopped, with a pleasant floral, non-English hop bouquet. Top-fermenting yeast working at coolish temperatures (55 to 60° F) provides a kiss of fruitiness.

If beers could talk, many of the blondest would sound like this: "Hi, I'm like, oooh..you're so...heehee...giggle."

Poor darlings. Cast off like orphans by thoughtless brewpubers who fling them in the tanks at the last minute "to make the partners happy," or to placate those pitiful customers who "don't know what good beer is," blonde ales all too frequently are perceived to lack deep inner beauty. This is a shame, because blonde beers can be as deeply soulful as their brunette cousins, just as worthy of a lustful, longing *well-informed* gaze.

So, fellow homebrewers, it is up to us, as usual, to take things into our own hands, and brew beer the way it is supposed to be.

Much more than darker beers, the character of a blonde ale hangs on the quality of the malt that forms the bulk of the grist. With nothing to mel-

There is a historical precedent for the term blonde ale. Wouldn't you know it's French?

low or obscure it, the pale malt character jumps right out at you, and if the malt is not up to the challenge, it may fall a little flat.

Such delicate beers offer scant cover for off-flavors. Cleanliness, sanitation, and especially pitching adequate amounts of healthy yeast are crucial to a taste unencumbered by annoyingly un-blonde flavors. You've been warned. Now that I've told you how impossible it is, let me reassure you that it really isn't all that difficult; with just a few tricks and techniques you can brew a truly memorable blonde ale.

For those of you brewing all-grain beers, your best bet is either Belgian or German Pilsener malt for a base. I wish I could say otherwise, but American malt just doesn't measure up. I have found it impossible to get the kind of intense-but-innocent malt flavor from American malt. It takes European malts, grown and malted for beers like this, to really deliver. I like to add Munich, Vienna, or pale crystal malts to richen things up a bit, but it's easy to overdo it and make the beer overly caramelly or too dark. If you are using a really fine Pilsener malt, you need very little of those. A little wheat (malted or unmalted) gives the head a foamy lift.

Water is key. Pale beers lack the acidity provided by dark malts, so the effects of alkaline hard water become unpleasantly prominent, especially as the hop rate rises. Either use soft water, or treat your carbonate water (see p. 55).

I like to emphasize hop aroma over bitterness in these beers. I usually aim for 20 to 30 IBU in blonde ales, which gives you plenty of toothsome bitterness without

---

R E C I P E	**Bambi's Best Blonde Ale**		

Yield: 5 gallons (19 liters)

Gravity: 1.048 (13 °P)

Alcohol/vol: 4.3 to 4.9%

Color: Gold

Bitterness: 30 IBU

Yeast: Altbier or Kölsch

Maturation: 3 to 4 weeks

Procedure: Mash grains at 152° F (67° C) for an hour. If you want beer to be clear when chilled, add a protein rest of 15 to 20 minutes at 122°F (50°C) first, but be aware that there may be a tradeoff in the form of slightly less body and head retention. Sparge as usual. Boil for one hour. A longer boil will add richness, but also color.

All-Grain Recipe:

8.0 lb (3.6 kg)	80%	German/Belgian Pilsener malt	
1.0 lb (0.45 kg)	10%	German/Belgian Munich malt	
0.5 lb (227 g)	5%	pale crystal malt	
0.5 lb (227 g)	5%	wheat, flaked or malted	

Malt Extract + Mini-Mash Recipe:

1.6 lb (0.72 kg)	54%	extra pale dry extract	
1.5 lb (0.68 kg)	19%	German/Belgian Pilsener malt	
1.5 lb (0.68 kg)	17%	German/Belgian Pilsener malt	
1.0 lb (0.45 kg)	10%	pale crystal malt	

Hops:

1.0 oz (28 g)	60 min	Crystal (or Hallertau type) (3.5% AA)	
1.25 oz (35 g)	20 min	Crystal (or Hallertau type) (3.5% AA)	
1.5 oz (42 g)	20 min	Saaz (3% AA)	
0.5 oz (14 g)	end of boil	Crystal (or Hallertau type) (3.5% AA)	
0.5 oz (14 g)	end of boil	Saaz (3% AA)	

Good old ALE Makes beauty fresh: It causes love. It fools dissension. It cheers the heart. It feeds the flesh: It lengthens life. It's death's prevention. It makes a beggar seem a king. Boys it hardens. Fools it sharpens. ALE so rare a thing.

—Inscription on an ale jug, circa 1900

blowing out the delicate malt taste. Heaping up hops at the end of the boil will impart a lovely hop aroma. Dry-hopping may be used, but these beers don't need *that* much aroma.

The choice of hops is pretty wide open, but the noble aromatic varieties make the most elegant beers. Saaz, Tettnang, and the Hallertau clones such as crystal or Vanguard all make delightful beers. Cascades will do a nice job as well, if you want that American touch. I usually stay away from the high-alpha hops; their citrus/resiny tastes overwhelm a delicate beer.

Develop extra flavor from processes. Brewer and owner Chuck Skypeck of Bosco's in Memphis has an unusual touch for his house blonde beer—it's stone-brewed. Hot glowing rocks are added to the brew kettle, where they throw a hissy fit. The resulting caramelization adds a lovely layer of caramel to an already well-brewed beer. Small wonder this is Bosco's most popular beer.

In such a subtle beer as blonde ale, the choice of yeast plays an important role. Pedigreed liquid brewing yeasts can accentuate malt or hops, sweeten or dry out a beer, or add their own spicy, woody, or fruity flavors. My own tastes lean toward the malt-accentuating character of a strain like Wyeast 1968 or White Labs WLP002, which are the Fuller's strain. Another good choice is, as you may have guessed, a Kölsch yeast. But the choice is wide open and quite up to you.

Lower fermentation temperatures seem to bring out the best in the light, malty character of a blonde, although some strains—like Fuller's—may settle out and stop working below about 65° F (18°C). I especially like to cold condition them, much as they would in Germany, and this works wonderfully with the Kölsch yeast strains.

R E C I P E — Mister Squinty Contemporary Summer Ale

Yield: 5 gallons (19 liters)

Gravity: 1.048 (13 °P)

Alcohol/vol: 3.9 to 4.6%

Color: Pale gold

Bitterness: 43 IBU

Yeast: English ale

Maturation: 3 to 4 weeks

Mash grains at 146 to 148° F (63 to 64.5° C) for 90 minutes (the temperature is a little on the low side to maximize fermentability). Mash out at 175° F (79.5° C), then sparge. Boil is one hour, with three hop additions.

All-Grain Recipe:

4.0 lb (1.8 kg)	62%	Maris Otter pale ale malt
2.0 lb (0.90 kg)	25%	Pilsener malt
10.0 oz (283 g)	8%	malted wheat
0.5 lb (227 g)	5%	piloncillo, demerara or similar unrefined sugar, added to kettle

Malt Extract Recipe:

4.0 lb (1.8 kg)	76%	extra pale dry extract
1.25 lb (0.55 kg)	24%	liquid wheat extract

Hops:

1.25 oz (35 g)	60 min	Challenger (7.5 % AA)
0.5 oz (14 g)	30 min	Challenger (7.5 % AA)
0.5 oz (14 g)	5 min	Challenger (7.5 % AA)
0.5 oz (14 g)	5 min	Saaz (3% AA)

With English ale yeast, temperatures around 65° F (18° C) are recommended. German Kölsch or alt yeast can handle relatively cool temperatures of 55 to 60° F. If fermentation seems sluggish in this range, raise the temperature slightly. Rack to secondary, allow to clear, and bottle or keg as usual. After carbonation has been completed, lager for a few weeks at 33 to 40° F.

After that, there's nothing but the waiting and the drinking.

A FLASH OF BRILLIANCE: BRITISH SUMMER ALE

A shaft of golden light rips through a thin patch of the blotchy white sky. On the beach below, towels unfurl to reveal bumpy legs cased in vampire-white flesh that broils to prawn pink in the hazy brilliance. Released from the dark closet of winter, seekers young and old sit and squint, dazed, mole-like in the mossy sea air. It's a perfect summer day in England.

The moment begs for a perfect summer ale—crisp, dry, refreshing, but sturdy enough to satisfy, a citric hop aroma leaping from a dazzling white meringue.

It's not English, but it does kind of sum up the mood.

R E C I P E	Summer Ale, What-if Version, c. 1830		

Yield: 5 gallons (19 liters)

Gravity: 1.065 (15.5 °P)

Alcohol/vol: 5.4 to 6.2%

Color: Gold

Bitterness: 53 IBU

Yeast: English ale

Maturation: 8 to10 weeks

Mash grains at 150 to 152° F (65.5 to 66.5° C) for 60 minutes. Mash out at 175° F (79.5° C), then sparge. Boil is one hour, with two hop additions.

Either recipe can be fermented with your favorite ale yeast, although a hop-accentuating strain, such as the one originating from Bass, might be just the thing here.

All-Grain Recipe:

6.0 lb (2.7 kg)	50%	Maris Otter pale ale malt
2.0 lb (0.90 kg)	35%	Pilsener malt
1.0 lb (0.45 kg)	8%	malted wheat
1.0 lb (0.45 kg)	8%	piloncillo, demerara or similar unrefined sugar, added to kettle

Malt Extract Recipe:

3.75 lb (1.7 kg)	56%	extra pale dry extract
2.0 lb (0.90 kg)	29%	liquid wheat extract
1.0 lb (0.45 kg)	15%	piloncillo, demerara or similar unrefined sugar, added to kettle

Hops & Spices:

2.5 oz (71 g)	60 min	Fuggles or Styrian Goldings hops (5.5% AA)
2.0 oz (56 g)	5 min	East Kent Goldings (5% AA)
0.25 oz (7 g)	5 min	crushed coriander
0.25 oz (7 g)	5 min	candied ginger

A style like this seems so right, so suited to the timeless cycle of the seasons, it's hard to believe summer ale is actually a modern creation, not yet twenty years old. John Gilbert of Hop Back Brewery created his famous Summer Lightning in the late 1980s, and it remains the standard for this style.

Paler than most English bitters, summer ales are likely to be a little more intensely hopped as well. Most versions hover between 4.5- and 5-percent alcohol. Hops have center stage, with moderate to high bitterness backing up loads of fresh, citric aroma. Late kettle additions, and perhaps even dry hopping, contribute to this forward expression of hop personality. East Kent Goldings, with their spicy, resinous aromas, have always been the hop of choice for top-grade British beers. Challenger is a much more recently developed variety (1972), and with a flavor that's described as "fruity, almost scented, with spicy overtones," it's going to fit nicely into our recipe for a contemporary summer ale.

It's an easy beer to brew, although true excellence depends on top-flight ingredients. A base of British pale ale malt is the place to start. Maris Otter is generally regarded as the most nuanced in flavor, with light caramelly and nutlike qualities. A dash of Pilsener malt will lighten the color and contribute a fresh, bright maltiness. Use a little bit of unrefined sugar to add crispness without sacrificing character, and top it off with a few percent of wheat malt that will help your beer settle into a compact, creamy head.

The possibility also exists for "secret" ingredients. British law long forbade the use of seasonings other than hops in commercial beers, a Reinheitsgebot of sorts. This law was put into effect in 1710 as a reaction to the adulteration of beers with substances (many of them toxic) intended to give beer an additional kick. Spiced beers have a long history in Britain, and the use of seasonings such as coriander, ginger, and grains of paradise continued in private breweries up to the mid-nineteenth century. These particular spices blend extremely well with the kind of light, breezy beer we're talking about here, and feature in the second mock-historical brew I've concocted for your amusement.

For both beers, soft water is preferred, as hard water will result in harsh hop bitterness.

To make an extract version of either of these beers, substitute 85 percent as much pale malt syrup as the total malt, then toss a half-pound of crushed pale crystal into your kettle (in a grain bag) and remove just before it gets to a boil. Sugar and hop/spice additions remain as they are.

Scottish sparkling ale bottle, c. 1900. This bottle was never opened!

A SPARKLE IN YOUR ALE

Sparkling ale is a trade term for a bottled beer that seems to have originated in Scotland as a somewhat lighter, more drinkable product than many of the brutally strong ales of the day. The trend had begun in mid-eighteenth century London with India pale ales, which then spread to, and were displaced by, beers from Burton-on-Trent. Modest in gravity by the standards of the day, and hopped at double or even triple the rate for more old-fashioned brews, these new-style beers fed a craving for something happening and hip.

The Scots, never to be outpaced in the business arena, followed suit with their own IPAs, plus a range of other styles including dinner ales, table beers, and various lagers. Sparkling ale was being bottled and sold by Younger and McEwans and others by at least 1885, and was exported in large quantities to America and the Empire. Homegrown versions turned up around that time in the United States and in Australia, where the beer still survives at Coopers and a couple of breweries in Adelaide. But, alas, no longer in Scotland.

I must confess my recipe details are a bit sketchy. This is one of the great frustrations of historical beer research. Old books often give great detail on mashing heats and water quantities, but almost never give a cogent description of the beer being brewed. Ingredients are described in trade terms that no longer exist. It's just a reflection of the fact that the books weren't written for us. So, there's going to be some interpolation here.

The "sparkling" designation is applied only to bottled beers and seems to have indicated a highly carbonated product. The Scots were pioneers in the bottle manufacturing business, and by 1850 were turning out well-made stoneware bottles capable of fairly high pressure.

Let's start with Scottish versions. My bottle of Wm. Younger Monk Brand, which I'm estimating at 1885 to 1890, lists an alcohol percent of 8.25. The Wahl-Henius Handy Book lists a 1901 version at 18.03 °B (1.075), with an alcohol by weight as 6.84 (8.6 percent by volume), so in those few years the gravity had dropped. A version by McEwans comes in at a beefy 21.6° B (1.090) and 7.8-percent alcohol by weight (9.6 percent by volume). Both show moderate amounts of lactic acid, 0.15 percent and 0.38 percent, respectively (contemporary lambics and Irish

"Fill with mingled cream and amber,
I will drain that glass again.
Such hilarious visions clamber
Through the chamber of my brain
Quaintest thoughts—queerest fancies
Come to life and fade away;
What care I how time advances?
I am drinking ale today."

—Edgar Allan Poe

RECIPE — Wee Twinkling Winkie Scottish Sparkling Ale

Yield: 5 gallons (19 liters)
Gravity: 1.082 (19.5 °P)
Alcohol/vol: 5.6 to 6.4%
Color: Deep golden amber
Bitterness: 50 IBU
Yeast: Scottish ale
Maturation: 2 to 3 months

Mash slightly high at 154 to 155° F (68°C) for an hour. Raise to mash-out, 170 to 175° F (76.5 to 79.5° C), then sparge. Add sugar to kettle. Boil 1.5 hours. Ferment with cold-tolerant yeast at 58 to 65° F (14.5 to 18.5° C) for primary, slightly lower for secondary, if possible. Try to age this beer for three months before consuming.

All-Grain

12.0 lb (5.5 kg)	86%	pale ale malt (English or Belgian preferred)
1.0 lb (0.45 kg)	7%	German sour malt
1.0 lb (0.45 kg)	7%	partially refined sugar: demerara, turbinado, piloncillo, jaggery, added to kettle

Malt Extract + Styeeped Grain Recipe:

6.5 lb (2.9 kg)	68.5%	pale malt extract
1.0 lb (0.45 kg)	10.5%	German sour malt
1.0 lb (0.45 kg)	10.5%	pale crystal malt
1.0 lb (0.45 kg)	10.5%	partially refined sugar: demerara, turbinado, piloncillo, jaggery, added to kettle

Hops:

1.5 oz (42.5 g)	90 min	Kent Goldings (4% AA)
2.0 oz (56.5g)	30 min	Kent Goldings (4% AA)

stouts both were about 1.0 percent, by comparison), which suggests wood aging with some *Brettanomyces* activity. This acid would have given these beers a refreshing tang that can be easily achieved by the use of German sour malt or food-grade lactic acid. Hop rates are elusive, but an "X" Scottish ale of similar gravity from mid-century came in at 2.8 to 4.0 ounces per 5 gallons, which would have put it in the neighborhood of 40 to 60 IBU.

Scottish beers were invariably referred to as full-flavored. This could have had a number of causes, one of which was almost certainly a lower fermentation temperature, 5 to 10° F below English beers on average. The Scots had a lager tradition that

---

RECIPE — Telltale Ale—American Sparkling Ale

Yield: 5 gallons (19 liters)

Gravity: 1.057 (13.5 °P)

Alcohol/vol: 4.2 to 4.8%

Color: Pale gold

Bitterness: 54 IBU

Yeast: American ale

Maturation: 6 to 8 weeks

Mash in at 122° F, hold for 30 minutes. Raise to 154° F (66° C), hold for 30 minutes. Raise to 162° F (72° C), hold for 30 minutes, then sparge. Boil one hour. Ferment with lager yeast, primary at 44° F, then lager for two to three months at 39° F (4° C). Bottle with slightly higher than normal amount of corn sugar (three-fourths cup per 5 gallons).

All-Grain Recipe:

7.75 lb (3.5 kg)	74%	U.S. six-row Pils malt
2.25 lb (1.0 kg)	21%	flaked corn (in mash) or 1.5 lb corn sugar (added to kettle)
0.5 lb (227 g)	5%	pale crystal malt

Malt Extract + Steeped Grain Recipe:

6.25 lb (2.8 kg)	72%	pale dry extract
1.0 lb (0.45 kg)	11%	pale crystal malt
1.5 lb (0.68 kg)	17%	corn sugar, added to kettle

Cluster hops would have been used in the old days (use the same quantities as below). If you dislike them as much as I do, use this mix instead:

1.0 oz (28 g)	60 min	Northern Brewer (7% AA)
0.5 oz (14 g)	60 min	Willamette (7% AA)
0.5 oz (14 g)	20 min	Northern Brewer (7% AA)
0.5 oz (14 g)	20 min	Willamette (7% AA)

---

began much earlier than in England, as well as a much stronger bottled beer market.

Scotland had been trading enthusiastically with the north countries for hundreds of years, and one of the prime goods was beer. I think even the use of Monk's Brand as a trade name is a reference to Continental brewing tradition, as such monastic references are rare in Britain. Machine-made bottles that could stand up to higher pressure, cheaper sugar from the Empire, and newly developed filtering equipment also contributed to the craze for paler, crisper beers—India pale ale and others—that began the century before in England.

In America, sparkling ale held a position between lager and stock ale, and was a product designed to compete with the increasingly popular lager. Gravities were lower than imported versions, around 14 °B (1.057), about the same as cream ale. The difference was an extended lagering at 39° F. Three months is given as a typical aging

time. It is logical to think that German brewmasters would have added their own touches to the ales they brewed. And for the sake of efficiency as well, production was in accordance with mainstream U.S. lager brewing practice. As with most American beers, a percentage (25 to 30) of corn grits or sugar was an integral part of the style. Hop rates were 1 to 1.5 pounds per barrel, or 2.5 to 3.8 ounces per 5 gallons, plenty hoppy at around 30 to 50 IBU. Three months' lagering would knock the edges off.

For both beers, soft water is preferred, as hard (especially carbonate) water will result in harsh hop bitterness.

RECIPE — Rye Pale Ale

The bright pepperiness of rye is accentuated by the spice of traditional English hops here.

Yield: 5 gallons (19 liters)

Gravity: 1.065 (15.5 °P)

Alcohol/vol: 5.3 to 6.0%

Color: Deep gold

Bitterness: 43 IBU

Yeast: American ale

Maturation: 8 to 12 weeks

If you're using unmalted rye, you'll get more out of it if you grind it fine and cook it up like porridge before adding it to your mash. A crockpot works well for this. Rye will make the mash sticky and sluggish, so it's especially important to keep the mash bed temperature above 160° F (71° C) during the sparge.

All-Grain Recipe:

10.0 lb (4.5 kg)	80%	pale ale malt
1.0 lb (0.45 kg)	8%	pale crystal malt
1.5 lb (0.68 kg)	12%	malted (preferred) or flaked rye
0.5 lb (227 g)	—	rice hulls

Extract + Mini-Mash Recipe:

5.0 lb (2.25 kg)	60%	pale dry extract
1.5 lb (0.68 kg)	18%	malted (preferred) or flaked rye
1.0 lb (0.45 kg)	11%	US 6-row malt
1.0 lb (0.45 kg)	11%	pale crystal malt
0.5 lb (227 g)	—	rice hulls

Hops:

0.75 oz (21 g)	60 min	Fuggle (5% AA)
1 oz (28 g)	30 min	Challenger (7.5% AA)
1 oz (28 g)	5 min	Challenger (7.5% AA)

A standard infusion mash can be used, but a three-step approach will better deal with the rye. Mash in at 90°F/32°C, hold for 30 minutes; step up to 122°F/50°C, hold for 30 minutes; then step up to main mash, a little low, at 147°F/64°C for 90 minutes.

Fifty-Fifty American Pale Ale By now, you should be able to brew this in your sleep. The formula is simple. A good quality pale ale malt as a base, with something caramelly like a pale crystal for color, offset perhaps by a bit of biscuit or very dark crystal, plus a heaping of nice fresh Cascade hops—although you might be a devil and perversely throw in some Chinook or other grapefruity high-alpha hops for aroma at the end of the boil. Ferment it with the so-called Chico yeast (from Sierra Nevada, Wyeast 1056, or White Labs WLP001) and you've got beer. Easy as pie and pure heaven in a glass.

KICK-ASS IPAs

Don't ya just love American beers these days? Having lost none of their aggressive, in-your-face pugnaciousness, many now wrap that big personality in a velvet glove, an elegance not much valued in the early "just gimme some hops" days of the craft beer scene. And it's the big, hoppy flagship beers, the beer the brewer brews just because she (or he) likes it, that most often receive this extra finesse. First among them are many lovely variations on the IPA theme.

R E C I P E	IRA–India Red Ale

The potent carameliness contributed by a big dollop of Munich malt and dark crystal allows us to add even more hops and still maintain some sort of balance in this beer. Grist should be 60 percent pale ale malt, 30 percent Munich malt, 10 percent dark crystal or mix of crystals. I'd go with Cascade or Liberty hops all the way here, as this one's as American as they come.

Yield: 5 gallons (19 liters)

Gravity: 1.065 (15.5 °P)

Alcohol/vol: 5.3 to 6.0%

Color: Deep reddish-amber

Bitterness: 75 IBU

Yeast: American ale

Maturation: 8 to 12 weeks

All-Grain Recipe:

6.5 lb (2.9 kg)	50%	pale ale malt
5.0 lb (2.3 kg)	39%	Munich malt
0.75 lb (0.34 kg)	10.5%	medium crystal malt
0.5 lb (227 g)	5.5%	dark crystal malt
2.0 oz (57 g)	1%	black patent malt

Extract + Mini-Mash Recipe:

6.5 lb (2.9 kg)	50%	pale dry extract

Plus: everything from the all-grain recipe except the pale malt

Hops:

2.0 oz (57 g)	60 min	Cascade (6% AA)
2.0 oz (57 g)	30 min	Cascade (6% AA)
2.0 oz (57 g)	5 min	Goldings (4% AA)

Of course, there's nothing wrong with your basic India Pale Ale. This bright, hoppy style created a smash in both its homelands—England and India—and forced a lasting change in the brewing industry everywhere. It's unquestionably a delightful and historic drink. But one could make a case that IPA was a crucial step in the long slide to lightness in the same way that, an NPR commentator said, *"Chet Atkins ruined country music,"* by applying sophisticated arrangements and production techniques into twangy hillbilly tearjerkers, leading to today's bland pickup-truck pop. By making dingy dark beers into something unfashionably déclassé, IPA stoked the thirst for lighter and weaker products, and well, you know the rest of the story.

But that's another debate, for another time—worthy of a few pints of gentlemanly discussion at least.

Of course we homebrewers are never content with the status quo—from whatever era—and are always eager to break a few rules. So here is a handful of ways to mangle and abuse the idea of India pale ale, yet still come up with something pretty great to drink.

Belgian-American IPA This takes advantage of the grapefruity character of some of the West Coast high-alpha hops, and expands on the theme. Start with a European Pilsener malt, and add 10 percent of the kind of dark Munich malt called "aromatic." For hops, I would go with a mix of Saaz and one of the grapefruity U.S. hops such as

RECIPE	**Belgian-American IPA**		
Yield: 5 gallons (19 liters)	*All-Grain Recipe:*		
Gravity: 1.060 (14.5 °P)	9.75 lb (4.4 kg)	87%	Pilsener malt
Alcohol/vol: 4.9 to 5.6%	1.5 lb (0.68 kg)	13%	pale crystal malt
Color: Bright amber	*Extract + Steeped Grain Recipe:*		
Bitterness: 49 IBU	5.75 lb (2.6 kg)	76%	pale dry extract
Yeast: Belgian Ale	1.0 lb (0.45 kg)	16%	medium crystal malt
Maturation: 6 to 8 weeks	*Hops:*		
	2.0 oz (57 g)	60 min	Liberty (4.5% AA)
	2.0 oz (57 g)	30 min	Saaz (3% AA)
	1.0 oz (57 g)	5 min	Saaz (3% AA)

RECIPE	**Jaggery Pale Ale**		
Yield: 5 gallons (19 liters)	*All-Grain Recipe:*		
Gravity: 1.076 (18 °P)	8.5 lb (3.9 kg)	70%	English pale ale malt
Alcohol/vol: 6.5 to 7.3%	2.0 lb (0.90 kg)	17%	jaggery, added to kettle
Color: Deep gold	1.5 lb (0.68 kg)	13%	malted wheat
Bitterness: 63 IBU	*Extract+ Mini-Mash Recipe:*		
Yeast: English ale	5.25 lb (2.4 kg)	60%	pale dry extract
Maturation: 8 to 12 weeks	2.0 lb (0.90 kg)	23%	jaggery, added to kettle
	1.5 lb (0.68 kg)	17%	malted wheat
	Hops & Spices:		
	2.25 oz (0.64 kg)	90 min	Northdown (5% AA)
	4.0 oz (113 g)	5 min	East Kent Goldings (7.5% AA)
	1.0 tsp (3 g)	5 min	fenugreek (ground)

Chinook or Ahtanum. You might get really perverse and use the Saaz for bittering and the U.S. hops for aroma. The twist—literally—in this recipe, is grapefruit peel, just the outer layer, shaved off a well-scrubbed grapefruit with a potato peeler. About half a grapefruit, prepared this way, should be added to the kettle at the end of the boil. Ferment with your favorite Belgian yeast, but keep the temperature on the low side to keep the Belgian character subdued.

Jaggery Pale Ale The East Indians treasure a beautifully creamy, partially refined sugar made from the fruits of certain palm trees. Golden in color and congealed into blocks the size and shape of a fez hat, *jaggery* resembles maple sugar in taste and aroma, except perhaps with some buttery accents. Once prohibition against the use of sugar in British beer was lifted in 1847, jaggery, as well as other semirefined "concrete" sugars from Jamaica, Cuba, and elsewhere, found their way into the commercial beers of the day, so there's some historical basis for this. As with all fully fermentable sugars, jaggery has the effect of lightening up the texture of a beer, and adds nice soft caramelly maple notes.

Here, 10 percent of the recipe is jaggery, which may be found at markets specializing in Indian foods. Just break it apart and add to the kettle. If you want to get really adventurous, add a teaspoon or two of crushed fenugreek to the secondary. This spice, popular in Indian cuisine, has a delicate maple character, and is, in fact, used in pancake syrup for that very purpose. Here it will accentuate the maple qualities of the jaggery and add a fruity depth to the beer.

India Cream Ale The cream ale style is a kind of amalgam of the English-derived American ale style, as brewed by German brewmasters in American lager breweries.

RECIPE	Hinky Dink India Cream Ale		

Yield: 5 gallons (19 liters)

Gravity: 1.062 (15 °P)

Alcohol/vol: 6 to 7%

Color: Ravishing blonde

Bitterness: 50 IBU

Yeast: American lager or German altbier

Maturation: 6 to 8 weeks

Fermentation should be warmer than normal lager temperatures, around 62 to 65° F (16.5–18° C), with an extended lagering period. Bottle or keg with fairly high carbonation.

All-Grain Recipe:

7.5 lb (3.4 kg)	74%	U.S. Pilsener malt
2.0 lb (0.09 kg)	19%	Munich malt
0.75 lb (0.34 kg)	7%	corn sugar, added to boil

Extract + Mini-Mash Recipe:

6.0 lb (2.7 kg)	80%	pale dry extract
2.0 lb (0.91 kg)	20%	pale crystal

Hops:

1.5 oz (43 g)	60 min	Spalt or Tettnang (4% AA)
2.0 oz (57 g)	30 min	Spalt or Tettnang (4% AA)
3.0 oz (85 g)	5 min	Spalt or Tettnang (4% AA)

It's my view that many of them simply applied their experience with German ales such as Kölschbier, and *voilà*, Cream Ale. Some of the early brewery advertising indicates that cream ales were often a blend of stock ale with lager, so this recipe has a certain historical resonance. Clusters would have been used, at least for bittering, and you can use them if you want, but I prefer the mix below, with a big load of them added at the end of the boil. Ten percent malted wheat will provide a creamy texture and lively head, and 10 percent corn sugar will lighten the body and keep the beer crisp and refreshing, as well as true to history.

R E C I P E	**Vatted Stale IPA**		
Yield: 5 gallons (19 liters)	*All-Grain Recipe*		
Gravity: 1.085 (20.5 °P)	14.0 lb (6.3 kg)	88%	Maris Otter pale ale malt
Alcohol/vol: 7.5 to 8.5%	2.0 lb (0.09 kg)	12%	biscuit/amber malt
Color: Deep gold	*Extract + Mini-Mash*		
Bitterness: 90 IBU	8.25 lb (3.7 kg)	85%	pale dry extract
Yeast: English ale	1.0 lb (0.45 kg)	10%	biscuit/amber malt
Maturation: 8 to 12 months	0.5 lb (227 g)	5%	pale crystal
	Hops:		
	3.0 oz (85 g)	60 min	East Kent Goldings (4% AA)
	1.5 oz (43 g)	30 min	East Kent Goldings (4% AA)
	5.0 oz (142 g)	5 min	East Kent Goldings (4% AA)

Vatted Stale IPA In the old days, strong beers were always aged in wooden vats, often for extended periods of time. Under these conditions, certain wild yeast and bacteria wiggle their way into the brew and make themselves at home in the crevices in the wood. This "contamination" can make a valuable contribution to the beer in the form of exotic musky, earthy, animal, and fruity aromas, and sometimes more than a hint of acidity. "Stale" was the term used for this aged character, without the negative connotations we have today. It's a virtual certainty that most of the original IPAs had some of this exotic character.

After fermenting through the primary with a conventional British ale yeast, add a package of either mixed lambic-style culture, or some pure *Brettanomyces* to the secondary. These are rather slow acting, and will take a few months to make a difference. Note that the mixed culture will give you a fair amount of sourness, while the bret alone will be less intense.

If you want to go the extra-authentic route and add some wood barrel character, a good way to go is with small oak "beans" sold to wineries to revive tired barrels. These are sold in several woods and degrees of toast by a company called Stavin

Oak "Beans" from Stavin
Available in several woods and toast levels, these are a convenient way to give your ale a dose of wood.

To this day, brown ale retains its anti-cachet as a somewhat backward and rustic product.

Engraved cobalt "rummer," c. 1850

A perfect half-pint for dark beers.

(www.stavin.com). Stay away from American oak, as it's very sharp and pungent and will overwhelm a beer pretty quickly. Just add a small handful of the beans during the extended secondary.

With or without oak, the beer will show more "wild" character as the months pass. It's up to you to decide when it's ready to carbonate and drink.

BROWN IS BEAUTIFUL

Poor unloved brown ale. This often ignored style is a victim of our love of the extreme, our need to be titillated, our contempt for the middle of the road. Once a mainstay, brown ales were eclipsed first by darkness, in the case of porter, then out-shone by light in the great rush to blondness that began with pale ale itself, and hit a wall one hundred and fifty years later with Miller's aborted introduction of that ultimate personification of pale—Clear Beer.

Part of it may be the name. Of all the sensuous descriptors applied to ales and beers, "brown" is perhaps the least appetizing. While one can find the occasional mention of the "nut-brown ales of old," beers have in the past been far more often described by their town of origin, strength, or even their effect on the drinker—clamber skull, for example. Even if color is used as a style descriptor, amber or red is the more common term. Perhaps there were so few beers that weren't some shade or another of brown, that the term seemed meaningless.

Even today, I find the commercial range of brown ales somewhat confusing. British examples are often just slightly darker, lightly hopped versions of pale ales. As a typically obtuse American, I am looking for something distinctively, unquestionably brown in my brown ale. I want toast!

What we want is a certain round toastiness right in the middle of the range of possible malt flavors, darker than pale or Munich malt, but much lighter than chocolate. These middle range malts—amber and brown—used to be among the most common malts in the brewer's flavor kit. Briess makes an amber malt called Victory. Continental maltsters tend to refer to it as "biscuit." A few British maltsters also make amber malt.

You can also easily roast your own. Start with uncrushed pale or Pilsener malt, and pop it into a 350° F (190° C) oven for thirty to forty-five minutes. Pull a few grains out and taste them; they will taste much darker than they look. You want a rosy pale copper color, although nutty, toasty flavors start to come in when the malt just starts to turn in color. By the time it is a deep copper, sharp roasty notes inappropriate to brown ale start to develop. Do this a couple of weeks in advance to allow harsh flavors to mellow before brewing. Dry roasting gives the toastiest flavors; moist-roasted malt tends to develop softer, more caramelly notes. See p. 224 for more on this.

How much to use? A quarter-pound of amber malt per gallon will start to get the toasty brown ale thing going, but you can use much more. I like about three-quarters of a pound per gallon for a rich toastiness and solid brown color. I have found lots of variation between commercial amber malts, and the home roasted ones are all over the map, so this is a fertile area for exploration.

Hopping should be for balance and little else. The traditional hops used in darker

RECIPE	**Old Nut Case Brown Ale**

To hell with watered down "session" pints, let's have a real beer!

Yield: 5 gallons (19 liters)

Gravity: 1.067 (16 °P)

Alcohol/vol: 5 to 5.8%

Color: Brownish amber

Bitterness: 26 IBU

Yeast: English ale

Maturation: 8 to12 weeks

For a wacky twist, add a cup of lightly toasted walnuts or pecans, finely ground, to the mash. Be sure to protect the beer from marauding squirrels.

All-Grain Recipe:

8.5 lb (3.9 kg)	65%	mild ale malt
4.0 lb (1.8 g)	12%	biscuit/amber malt
0.5 lb (227 g)	4%	brown ale malt

Extract+ Mini-Mash Recipe:

6.0 lb (2.7 kg)	67%	amber dry extract
2.0 lb (0.90 kg)	22%	biscuit/amber malt
1.0 lb (0.45 kg)	11%	medium crystal

Hops:

0.75 oz (21 g)	90 min	Northern Brewer (7% AA)
0.5 oz (14 g)	20 min	Northdown (6.5% AA)

Mash or extract brews: mash with 1 quart of water per pound of malt at 157° F (69.5° C) for 45 minutes, then raise immediately to 170° F (76.5° C) by heating or adding boiling water to stop conversion. Carbonation should be light, or serve as real draught ale.

beers were Fuggles, but any vaguely English hop is worth trying. Northdowns are nice, and I like WGV or Challenger here as well. Avoid anything overly resiny, and keep the hopping to the early and mid stages of the boil.

Yeast and fermentation also affect the flavor. I find the estery, woody, sulfury yeasts so fine for pale ales fall flat on browns. My choice is malt-accentuating yeasts such as Scottish ale or the Fuller's strain (Wyeast London ESB), especially at cooler temperatures.

PORTER

The story of porter is the chronicle of the Industrial Revolution as it applied to beer. The tale follows the rise of steam power, coal smoke, and the rapid expansion of eighteenth-century Imperial Britain. Although today Britain is better known for pale ale, it was porter that turned beer from a craft into an industry.

Porter never stayed the same thing for more than one generation. This is the difficulty one encounters when trying to pin down the style. To add confusion, porter actually died out completely in its home country in the late seventies, leaving its close relative, stout, to carry on the family name.

Contemporary porters vary hugely in color, bitterness, gravity, and flavor, and occupy every bit of the territory

Intire Butt Beer, or, a Taste of Real Porter

And what this flood of deeper brown,

Which a white foam does also crown,

Less white than snow, more white than mortar?

Oh, my soul! can this be Porter?

—The Dèjeuné

between brown ale and stout. The official judging categories have settled into a lighter brown porter and a heavier robust version, but from my reading of history, this is somewhat arbitrary.

Few products have such a definite beginning, even if it is a myth. Porter, the story goes, was created in the autumn of 1722, the brainchild of Ralph Harwood, who owned the Bell Brewery in Shoreditch, London. Patrons of London establishments had grown fond of a blended concoction called "three threads," formed from equal parts of mild (young) and stale (aged) brown ale, and a sweetish pale ale called twopenny, the last remnant of the old unhopped ale (although by this time it did have some hops in it). The new brew, originally named Mr. Harwood's Entire, or Entire Butt, quickly became a favorite of the porters who lugged vast amounts of goods about town, so the beer was eventually named after them. A full piercing of this bit of lore may be found in Martyn Cornell's excellent book, *Beer: the Story of the Pint* (Headline, London).

The real story starts earlier. In 1689, a war with France occasioned a rise in taxes affecting brewers: on malt, on hops, on coal, and on the beers themselves. As it shifted the economics from one sort of beer to another, it generated a churning of brewing styles, with a lot of competition as brewers sought an equilibrium in the form of a product that made sense all around. As the relative expense of hops came down, their use went up. And what else was going on in London about this time? Well, gee, the whole place burned down in 1666, so the place was a hive of activity while it tried to rebuild.

"...for we see no Men in England more healthy than the Country Farmer, who keeps a cup of good brown Ale and a Toast, and temperately will drink a Glass of Stout."

—Edward Whitaker, 1692

Around the same time, many of the gentry from the hinterlands were coming to London to live, bringing with them a taste for the highly hopped "October" beers brewed on their estates, and were having public brewers custom-brew this for their use. Commercial breweries were still small at this point—in 1740, a 30-barrel brew kettle was referred to as a "great copper."

One of the ancestors of porter was butt beer. Butts were large casks set upright rather than on their sides like hogsheads and other smaller casks. *"The butt is certainly a most noble cask for this use..."*

In his 1734 *London and Country Brewer*, William Ellis describes several of the beers then (and for some time before) brewed from brown malt. These were sold in several strengths:

Beer Type	Qty per qtr*	Price	Hopping	Homebrew equivalent
Stout Butt Beer	1 bbl/qtr	30'	Heavily hopped ≥ 3.5 lbs/Hogshead	6.5 oz/5 gal
Stitch	1.25 bbl/qtr	21'	Lightly hopped	1–2 oz/5 gal
Common Brown Ale	2.75 bbl/qtr	16'	1 lb/Hogshead**	2 oz/5 gal
Entire Small beer	5–6 bbl/qtr	7–8'	1/2 –1 lb/Hogshead	1–2 oz/5 gal

*Quarter of malt, equal to 336 lb ** Whitaker, 1700: "ordinary strong beer beer to be soon Drank out...'"

In addition to the various gravities, some of the beers were aged at the brewery for up to a year, acquiring a sharp, vinous mature taste. This was called "stale," without the pejorative connotation we now attach to the word. "Mild" beer was shipped to the pubs without extended aging.

In its early days, there were two innovations that made porter unique. First was the use of a type of specialty malt from Hertfordshire called brown malt, which became available in London after the construction of a network of canals in the seventeenth century. This brown malt was the key ingredient in a range of brown beers that became quite popular in London before the "official" birth of porter. The second innovation was the use of "entire" brewing. Previously, most beers had been brewed by mashing, then draining the mash for the first runnings, then mashing again with the same grains for second runnings and a second beer, then sometimes for a third time, which produced a small beer. The idea of mixing the runnings together was not new at this time, but porter was the first successful beer brewed this way. This method offered huge advantages in an industrial setting, and the brewers of eighteenth-century London were quick to realize this. Porter spread like wildfire.

The deep copper color of brown malt, 75 to 150 °Lovibond, is much lighter than our chocolate malt. It came in two varieties, one kilned conventionally, and another called "blown" that was torrefied by rapid heating, giving it a puffed appearance. The old books generally do not make a huge distinction between the two, but accord-

"The Stronger Beere is divided into two parts (viz.), mild and stale; the first may ease a man of a draught, but the latter is like water cast into a Smith's forge, and breeds more heart-burnings, as rust eates into Iron, so overstale Beere gnawes aulet holes into the entrales, or else my skill failes, and what I have written of it is to be held as a jest."

—The Water Poet (John Taylor), 1580–1654

RECIPE	Stout Butt Beer, 1720

Yield: 5 gallons (19 liters)
Gravity: 1.082 (19.5 °P)
Alcohol/vol: 6 to 7%
Color: Deep chestnut brown
Bitterness: 69 IBU
Yeast: English stout
Maturation: 6 to 12 months

All-Grain Recipe:

4.5 lbs (2.0 kg)	33%	English pale ale malt
4.5 lbs (2.0 kg)	33%	biscuit/amber malt
4.5 lbs (2.0 kg)	33%	brown malt

No Comparable Extract Recipe

Hops & Spices:

3-4 oz (85–113 g)	Fuggle or Golding hops (55-70 IBU), treated as below
0.25 oz (7 g)	licorice root, ground, added to kettle
0.25 oz (7 g)	brewers' licorice, added to kettle.

Mash fairly high at 154° F (68° C) for 90 minutes. This can be served relatively fresh, or allowed to age. Follow directions given for the Vatted Stale IPA recipe.

---

ing to Richardson (the brewmaster for Whitbread), the blown malt had a lower yield, which was the primary reason for its demise. Some brown malt was kilned over oak or hornbeam, although much of it was kilned with coal or coke. Although smoky flavors are delicious in porter, most of the early authors make it clear that they have no fondness for the rude tinge of "smoak," and were only too happy to leave it behind.

By the late eighteenth century, pale and amber became part of the mix along with colorants of various kinds, especially cooked sugar. The most common colorant was *"essentia bina,"* a dark sugar made from boiling down first wort (or sometimes sugar)

1850: "For brown or porter malt, the grain is placed to the depth of about half-an-inch on the floor of the kiln, which, in this case, usually consists of perforated iron or wire network, while a strong, blazing fire, produced by the ignition of faggots of wood, is applied below. During this process, the temperature rapidly rises to 180°F, or higher; a portion of the starch and sugar of the malt become carbonized, while, as some allege, the pyroligneous acid and other products evolved from the burning wood, impart to the malt that peculiar flavor so much esteemed by the porter drinker."

—William Loftus, 1850

until very dark. The legality of these colorants changed a couple of times, but the issue was moot when black patent malt was invented in 1817. This was the subject of passionate feelings among brewers and drinkers alike. The more conservative purists hold-

---

RECIPE — 1776 Porter

Yield: 5 gallons (19 liters)	*All-Grain Recipe:*		
Gravity: 1.062 (15 °P)	4.5 lb (2.0 kg)	33%	English pale ale malt
Alcohol/vol: 4.6 to 5.5%	4.5 lb (2.0 kg)	33%	biscuit/amber malt
Color: Deep chestnut brown	4.5 lb (2.0 kg)	33%	brown malt
Bitterness: 69 IBU	*No Comparable Extract Recipe*		
Yeast: English stout	*Hops & Spices:*		
Maturation: 6 to 8 weeks	3-4 oz (85–113g) Fuggle or Golding hops (55-70 IBU), treated as below		
	0.25 oz (7.0 g)	licorice root, ground, added to kettle	
	0.25 oz (7.0 g)	brewers' licorice, added to kettle.	

Start by soaking the hops in 160° F (71° C) water. Mash the malt at 156° F (69° C) for one hour, then sparge. Take a half-gallon of the first wort and put into your boil kettle without any hops. Boil vigorously until reduced to a thick syrup. Continue cooking slowly, watching very carefully, tasting the goo every couple of minutes (Be careful, it is very hot). You are trying to get it as dark as possible before it starts to burn. When you judge it to be done, turn the rest of the hot wort into the kettle, add the hop infusion, and boil for an hour and a half.

Fermentation in the large breweries was traditionally at very warm temperatures, up to 80 degrees or more, although home breweries were more likely to be in the 65 to 70° F (18.5 to 21° C) range. This beer was sold both fresh and stale. See the recipe for Vatted Stale IPA for the technique.

ing out for more traditional brews than the gigantic Whitbread, Barclay's, and Truman's had all switched to patent malt by 1826. John Tuck, in 1822, said, "*To say the truth, there is little left of porter but the name; and indeed the taste of the public is so changed, that very few would be found to fancy its original flavour.*"

Porter was always a bitter drink, and with a tax on hops, brewers (or their book-keepers) were always looking for a loophole. Even though bittering substances other than hops had been banned since 1710, this didn't stop the wacky common brewers of London, who put all manner of noxious chemicals in porter to either make it cheaper or to give it an unnatural kick. The government spent a lot of time tracking down and fining the offending brewers and druggists who sold to them, and by 1820 things were pretty well cleaned up.

One wholesome seasoning was licorice, in both the root form and in a material called "Spanish juice" (also called Italian juice), which was licorice root boiled down to the form of golden strings of syrup that were left to cool and harden. One book stated with great conviction that licorice was essential to the flavor of well-brewed porter, but there never was a time when this was condoned by the government.

LOFTUS THE BREWER: A Familiar Treatise on the ART OF BREWING, 1863:

London Porter Bottles, c. 1840

Even then, porter was a brisk transatlantic trade item.

"*The qualities which characterize what would be termed good porter or stout, in the present condition of the public taste, are—a light, brown color, fullness on the palate, pure and moderate bitterness, with a mixture of sweetness, a certain sharpness or acerbity without sourness or burnt flavor, and a close, creamy head, instantly closing in when blown aside, a tart and astringent flavor.*"

"*Porter and Stout are now prepared almost exclusively from pale and roasted malts, the use of brown and amber malt being confined to a few of the most extensive and best known porter breweries. But although on the score of economy and simplicity there is an advantage in brewing form pale and black malt only, it cannot be doubted, judging from the practice of the great porter-brewers, that to obtain the true porter flavor, a certain proportion of amber or slightly scorched malt should enter into the composition of the grist.*"

"*Porter, brewed for exportation, with 10 lbs. or 11 lbs. of hops per quarter of malt, has a density of from 1069 to 1089 [16.5–21 °P]. Prior to shipment, it ought to be vatted ten or twelve months; and as the motion of the ship and the heat are apt to set it at work again, it is necessary to flatten it before final racking, by leaving the man-hole open for three weeks.*"

The gravities (based on an efficiency of 80 percent) on the following page show the decline.

Brewing was accomplished in the form of an infusion mash, with three additions of water, which were mashed, drained, and boiled separately. My 1822 source lists tap heat (draining wort) at 150° F (65.5° C), so initial mash temperature must have been higher at 154 to 156° F (67 to 68° C).

Porter Gravities, 1725-1887

Year	Lb/5 g	OG	Hops oz/g per 5 gal
1725 (Stout Butt)	39	1100?	3.2/91 g
1725	19-29	1082-1096	1.2/34 g
1760	17-19	1069-1082	3.8/108 g
1780-1800	11-13	1054-1063	4-7/113–198 g
1800-1830	11	1054-1065*	3.4–5.4/96–153 g
1850 (London)	na	1056-1067	6.5–7.4/184–210 g
1850 (Export)	12–16	1069-1078	5.8–8.3/164–235 g
1887 (American)	na	1056-1075	3.2/91 g

*Higher number reflects improved yield from switch to patent + pale malt

Note that the hop data is a little jittery because there are a limited number of sources from which to draw. Hop use does seem to peak around 1850, though.

Hops were presoaked in 160° F (71° C) water during the mash before being added to the boil, to aid in extracting flavor and bitterness. This soaking was allowed to go on as long as four hours. A pint per ounce of hops was the recommended quantity of hot water. The whole thing was dumped into the kettle when the wort came to a boil.

RECIPE — 1850 Export Porter

Yield: 5 gallons (19 liters)

Gravity: 1.070 (16.5 °P)

Alcohol/vol: 5.5 to 6.5%

Color: Near black

Bitterness: 39 IBU

Yeast: English stout

Maturation: 8 to 12 weeks for mild; 6 to12 months for "stale"

All-Grain Recipe:

9.5 lb (4.3 kg)	73%	pale ale malt
2.0 lb (0.90 kg)	15%	biscuit/amber malt
1.0 lb (0.45 kg)	8%	black patent malt
0.5 lb (227 g)	4%	sour malt

No Comparable Extract Recipe

Hops:

1.0 oz (28 g)	90 min	Fuggles (5% AA)
1.0 oz (28 g)	20 min	Fuggles (5% AA)
1.25 oz (35 g)	5 min	Fuggles (5% AA)

English brewers of this era aged their strong porters up to a year before releasing, and the sour malt included in the recipe gives a hint of this tangy flavor. A more authentic touch would be to add some *Brettanomyces* and even some *Pediococcus* to your batch, to recreate the effects of extended aging in wooden barrels. Mixed lambic culture offers an easy way to do this. An option would be to ferment only a gallon or so with the wild stuff, and add it to the rest of the beer at bottling or kegging. This technique continues today with Guinness.

RECIPE	Modern British Mild or Brown Porter

Yield: 5 gallons (19 liters)
Gravity: 1.038 (9 °P)
Alcohol/vol: 3.5 to 4%
Color: Chestnut brown
Bitterness: 25 IBU
Yeast: English stout
Maturation: 3 to 5 weeks

All-Grain Recipe:

5.5 lb (2.5 kg)	81%	British pale ale malt
1.0 lb (0.45 kg)	13.5%	very dark (140°L) crystal malt
0.25 lb (113 g)	4%	wheat/wheat malt
2.5 oz (71 g)	2%	black patent malt

Extract+ Mini-Mash Recipe:

3.5 lb (1.6 kg)	72%	amber dry extract
1.0 lb (0.45 kg)	20%	very dark (140°L) crystal malt
0.25 lb (113 g)	5%	wheat/wheat malt
2.5 oz (71 g)	3%	black patent malt

Hops:

0.25 oz (7 g)	90 min	Northdown (6.5% AA)
0.5 oz (14 g)	5 min	Fuggles (5% AA)

This has much in common with the much discussed "first wort" hopping, which creates a more intense hop flavor than by simply adding hops to the boil.

Porter eventually died out completely in England. In various forms, it lived on in America and the Baltic region. Once hugely popular here, the U.S. versions eventually deteriorated into thin, brownish lagers. In Poland and nearby countries, a strong brown lager version exists today, perhaps offering a tantalizing hint of what the original beefy brown beer might have been like.

Wagner, 1877 (Handbuch der Bierbrauerei), Porter Formulas

Pale	Amber	Brown	Black
—	95%	—	5%
48%	24%	24%	4%
57%	15%	25%	3%
58%	10%	30%	2%
60%	—	34%	6%
91%	—	—	9%

You can see that there were (and still are) many ways to approach the creation of porter. He gives hop quantities at 6.7 ounces (190 grams) per 5 gallons (19 liters), which is in line with the sources above.

RECIPE — Modern American 'Robust' Porter

Yield: 5 gallons (19 liters)

Gravity: 1.055 (13 °P)

Alcohol/vol: 4.5 to 5.2%

Color: Dark brown, 37 °SRM

Bitterness: 28 IBU

Yeast: English stout or American ale

Maturation: 6 to 8 weeks

Although it's in the judging style guidelines, this is kind of an arbitrary, or at least historically unattached, style. Homebrew and commercial versions may be much more bitter than the recipe detailed here, so if you're a hophead, you can double the hop quantities.

All-Grain Recipe:

6.25 lb (2.8 kg)	64.5%	pale ale malt
2 .0 lb (0.90 kg)	20%	Munich malt
1.25 lb (0.56 kg)	12.5%	medium (40°L) crystal
6.0 oz (170 g)	3%	black patent malt

Extract+ Mini-Mash Recipe:

5.5 lb (2.5 kg)	72%	amber dry extract
1.25 lb (0.56 kg)	12.5%	medium (40°L) crystal
6.0 oz (170 g)	3%	black patent malt

Hops:

1.0 oz (28 g)	90 min	Fuggles (5% AA)
0.5 oz (14 g)	20 min	Fuggles (5% AA)
0.25 oz (7 g)	20 min	Goldings (5% AA)
1.0 oz (28 g)	5 min	Goldings (5% AA)

A Beer Called Cooper

"A favourite mixture of modern Londoners is known by the name of "Cooper," and consists of porter and stout in equal proportions. The best account of the origin of this name is one which attributes it to a publican by the name of Cooper, who kept a house in Broad Street, City, opposite to where the Excise Office stood. Cooper was a jolly, talkative host, and associated a good deal with his customers—principally officers of the Excise, bankers' and merchants' clerks, and men of that stamp. His guests found on bits of broken plates, pieces of beef steak and mutton chops already priced with paper labels. These they had but to choose, mark their name on the ticket, and carry to the cook at the grid-iron, which was in the room in which they dined. Cooper drank and recommended a mixture of porter and stout, the fame of which spread very rapidly. The combination became the fashion in the City, and finally it was brewed entire."

—John Bickerdyke, 1889

TWELVE WAYS TO IMPROVE A STOUT

I imagine we've all had the experience. We are offered a stout. A thick, beautiful head floats atop the inky juice, making an artful eyeful. We sniff, then sip, and the search for adjectives begins.

"Hmmm. Roasty. And dark. And, um roasty. Did I mention it was roasty?"

And so it often goes, even with our own homebrewed stouts. This popular style often lacks the depth and dimension it needs. Because it is so easy to get into the ball-park—just add a pound of black malt or roasted barley to any recipe—it is hard to know what to do to make our stouts stand out. Here are a few suggestions, some traditional, some fairly deranged.

1. Weird grain British brewers rely on what used to be called "head grains," to improve the head-forming abilities of their beers. In fact, those grains were used abundantly by brewers a few hundred years ago. In quantities of 5 to 10 percent they will indeed boost a head; in larger amounts they will contribute their own quality to a beer. Both wheat and oats tend to soften a beer's character, blunting the sharpness of the roasted grains. Oats seem to have a thickening effect, giving any beer a milkshake-like richness without sweetening it. I have used flaked, unmalted wheat from the health food store in amounts up to 40 percent without adverse effects on the sparge. Oatmeal will get gummy on you, so 10 percent or below is most manageable. If you're using these grains in a mini-mash, be sure to add equal amounts of pale, or better, six-row lager malt to convert the starches. A protein rest of thirty to sixty minutes at 122° F (50° C) seems to help, too. Other grains should contribute their own complexities, and everything has been used in beer at some time and place: millet, buckwheat, quinoa, spelt, rye, and wild rice.

2. Syrups In colonial America, brewers often made a substance called beer simply from molasses, oat bran, and hops. While this may have satisfied George Washington's servants, we can do better with the stuff. Molasses adds a unique sourish, rumlike character to stout that can be quite satisfying. Adding various sugar syrups is a good way to make a stronger beer that is dry enough to be drinkable, as is the case with abbey triples. Syrups may be added directly to the brew kettle, although delicate aromas may be best preserved by adding them to the secondary, as one would

RECIPE	Fundamental Stout—Base Recipe		
Yield: 5 gallons (19 liters)	*All-Grain Recipe:*		
Gravity: 1.060 (14.5 °P)	9.5 lb (4.3 kg)	84%	mild ale malt
Alcohol/vol: 4.9 to 5.6%	1.0 lb (0.45 kg)	8%	black patent malt
Color: Inky black	1.0 lb (0.45 kg)	8%	dark crystal
Bitterness: 39 IBU	*Extract+ Mini-Mash Recipe:*		
Yeast: English stout or American ale	5.5 lb (2.5 kg)	72%	amber dry extract
	1.0 lb (0.45 kg)	8%	black patent malt
Maturation: 6 to 8 weeks	1.0 lb (0.45 kg)	8%	dark crystal
	Hops:		
	1.5 oz (43 g)	90 min	Fuggles (5% AA)
	1.5 oz (43 g)	15 min	Fuggles (5% AA)
	1.5 oz (43 g)	15 min	Fuggles (5% AA)

fruit. I have not yet tasted a honey stout, but this may be a good opportunity to a stronger-tasting variety such as buckwheat.

3. Hop character   Although the yapping lapdogs of style appropriateness will tell you that hop character has no place in a proper stout, it is our job as homebrewers to thumb our beer-soaked noses at such dogma. Hop character can indeed be a good thing in a stout. Try the kind of hop schedule you might apply to an IPA—dry hopping, the whole works.

4. The 3 percent factor   Guinness uses a secret potion in their stouts that is made by deliberately souring some of their beer. When added in small amounts to the stout, it confers a lactic tanginess that makes their products absolutely unique. Technically, this is a difficult thing to do, although commercial cultures are available to homebrewers. Hold out a quart or three of beer and experiment. Hint: *lactobacillus* is happiest at higher temperatures, so incubate at 85° F (29.5° C) or so. You might try one of the commercially packaged lambic microbes such as *Pediococcus damnosis* or one of the *Brettanomyces* wild yeasts. It will probably be best to pasteurize these errant cultures before adding them back to the main brew. Or, simply add a tablespoon of 80 percent lactic acid, sometimes available at homebrew shops. A simpler approach would be to use a pound or two of sour malt, available from many German maltsters.

5. Smoked grain   The intensity of smoked grain is far less intrusive in stouts than in paler beers, and actually adds a nice complexity. These can be added in very small amounts, an ounce or two, just to add a subtle depth to the roast character. Or, you can add a pound or two for the full effect. Peat-smoked Scottish distiller's malt and beechwood-smoked German *rauchmalz* are available commercially, or you can smoke your own in a barbecue with the wood of your choice. See p. 189 for more detail.

6. Crystal malt   One of the most common deficiencies of stouts is not having enough malt character. Think of your stout as a paler beer that happens to have a load of dark malt in it. Try to add the richness that you might look for in a fine Oktoberfest. Even though you may not see it in your final beer, you sure will taste it! Crystal is the malt of choice if you're doing mini-mashes to add to extract beers. Its sugars are already in a converted and soluble form, so all you need to do is soak the cracked crystal malt in hot water to dissolve, then strain and add to the pot.

7. Oddball roasted grains   Fire up the oven! You can make all kinds of roasted grain you can't buy at the homebrew shop. Wheat, oats, buckwheat, and other grains can be toasted, and each can lend a unique twist to your stout. I especially love the taste of toasted oats, the same intoxicating aroma created by baking oatmeal cookies. This aroma carries through well into the fermented beer, lending an unforgettable richness to your stout. Toast at 350° F (177° C) until oats are starting to turn golden and the kitchen smells like cookies. One note on home-roasted grain: various harsh chemicals are created during roasting that make beer unpleasantly rough and slow to clear. Allow two weeks for these to waft away between roasting and brewing.

8. Amber and brown malt Traditionally, two types of grains were used to brew porter (stout's cousin) in the eighteenth century. These malts were the only legal source of color in black beers before the 1817 invention of black "patent" malt. These taste very different than modern malt types such as crystal, and can add tremendous complexity. You could use up to half a recipe of either one, or possibly even more.

9. Mild ale malt If you're mashing, this poor forgotten malt can do a lot for you. Mild is a slightly higher kilned malt than pale, and will brew an amber beer if used all by itself. Traditionally the highest grade of malt was reserved for making pale malt, and everything else was turned into mild and darker malts. Pale malt was used only to make pale ale where its clean flavor and extremely low protein were essential. Mild was used in the production of darker beers, where it lent a caramelly sweetness that played against the bitter intensity of the brown and black malts. It is still sometimes available; if you can't find it, Vienna or Munich malt might be a passable substitute.

10. Spices and herbs In past times all beers were herb beers. In stout, I like cloves, cassia, rosemary, black pepper, grains of paradise (an African cardamom relative), coriander, and orange peel. Quantities range from a quarter-teaspoon (rosemary, black pepper, grains of paradise) to 1 to 2 ounces (28 to 57 grams) of coriander. Cayenne pepper was also a common additive, as were ginger, cinnamon, and nutmeg. Cocoa can be used to add a chocolatey smoothness. Spices may be added at the end of the boil, to the secondary, or steeped in vodka before adding at bottling or kegging.

11. Coffee With a similar roasting process to black malt, coffee makes a nice change of pace in a stout. The best way to use it is with a cold extraction (see above). Four to 8 ounces (113 to 227 g) of coffee will season a batch.

12. Wood Aging This was the norm during the heyday of porter and stout, and has only been replaced by less troublesome methods in the last hundred years. Dealing with barrels is a little problematic. Small barrels have too much surface area, which tends to add too much wood character, and big barrels obviously require a lot of beer. Whiskey—specifically, used bourbon—barrels are the modern norm for wood-aged beers, and such a beer can be a great group project (see p. 280). Wood or even bourbon-wood character can be imparted through the use of chips or "beans" of oak added to the beer as it ages in the carboy. Winemakers have a range of products available (see p. 91). For bourbon character, you'll have to do a little prep work, but you'll be rewarded for your patience with a bottle of custom-aged bourbon. Oh, and yes, a great stout, too.

Buy a bottle of basic bourbon. Take two or three pieces of white oak about as big as your finger, and burn them with a torch until they are deeply charred. After removing (and drinking) a little of the whiskey in order to make room, plop the sticks into the bottle, put the cap back on, and allow it to sit for six months to a year. In the meantime you can brew a serious stout. Add the sticks to the secondary and let it age like this for a few more months. Then bottle or keg as usual.

(see p. 280); (see p. 91)

Coffee—Cold Extraction
This is a way of getting very smooth coffee flavor to add to your beer. Add 0.5 lb (0.45 kg) ground coffee to 24 ounces of cold filtered water in a sanitized container. Allow this to sit in the refrigerator for 24 hours, then run the mixture through a coffee filter. All or part of this extract (see below) may be added to your stout.

Chapter 8

Lager On!

Lager is one of the two great families of beer. Lower fermentation temperatures suppress much of the fruity and spicy chemicals yeast produces at warmer temperatures. This allows the pure, clean flavors of malt and hops to shine through. Since there is nothing to hide behind, lagers can require a little more brewing discipline, but there is no reason for them to be intimidating. Solid brewing practice combined with good temperature control can make this a deliciously rewarding range of beers to brew.

THE WISDOM OF A PERFECT PILSENER

If you love the convenience of a crisp, refreshing pale lager never being more than a pop-top away whether you're in Springfield or the Serengeti, you can thank the brewers of Plzen (Pilsen), who, in 1842, created what would go on to become the world's most popular beer style. If, on the other hand, you hate the tongue-numbing blandness that characterizes most of the tin-can lagers, well, technically the idea started in Plzen, but I think the blame lies with a combination of corporate hungers and consumer thirsts.

The real stuff—fresh from the tanks—is pure delight, and for the homebrewer, it's a true challenge of skills, senses, and attention to detail.

A Pilsener is simplicity itself: one kind of malt, one kind of hops, and pure water. Nothing to hide behind—an "itsy bitsy teenie weenie bikini" as far as showing off the faults and foibles that a rowdy amber ale wrapped in crystal and Cascades will utterly conceal. It's a terrifying thought, this nakedness—and it scares brewers more than it should.

Pilsener is brewed in a wide range of interpretations, and of course most of the industrial versions bear little resemblance to the golden nectar of Plzen. The best Czech versions have a burnished golden color, a soft maltiness, and just a hint of creamy caramel. Balancing that is the crisp, minty, herbal character of Saaz hops, with no trace of rough or resiny flavors despite considerable bitterness.

A few thoughts on what's important and what's not:

1. Use appropriate ingredients Pilsener malt from Europe is a must; ultra-authentic Moravian malt from the Czech Republic is available for the sticklers. Saaz hops have a unique spicy/herbal aroma, although the U.S.-grown variety Sterling is very similar (although higher in alpha acid) and makes a great Pils. A variety called Ultra is

lovely if you can find it. Tettnang hops are related to Saaz and have a similar flavor profile. Whole hops seem to have a cleaner flavor than pellets, as the pelletizing process smashes the plant's cells, spilling some green, chlorophyll-like flavors into the beers.

2. Water is a key element, not just marketing fodder Plzen's water is the softest in the brewing world, with few minerals of any kind. The lack of alkalinity (carbonates) means the hop bitterness is superbly clean and crisp, without the raspy aftertaste that accompanies bitter beers made with hard carbonate water. To be authentic you need to use distilled water. For those of you scientifically treating your water, the PPM levels of all the common water minerals in Plzen's water is in the mid- to high single digits.

3. Mashing plays a role in flavor development The traditional triple decoction Plzen mash is diabolically complicated—the most complex of any of the historical lager mash schedules. Three times, a portion is removed, boiled, and added back to the mash to increase its temperature. This process was developed long ago as a way of heating the mash in a wooden vessel, since a much smaller vessel is required for the decocted portion (one-third of the mash). The twenty-two-step mashing sequence was also needed to deal with the old, undermodified malt that needed much more vig-

---

R E C I P E — Polka Dot Pilsener

Yield: 5 gallons (19 liters)

Gravity: 1.048 (11.5 °P)

Alcohol/vol: 4.1 to 4.8%

Color: Straw gold

Bitterness: 43 IBU

Yeast: Czech lager

Maturation: 6 to 8 weeks

I suggest that you make a Pils style ale if you can't manage the kind of temperature control needed for true lager. Another nice variation is to up the ante and increase the quantities of everything. An extra 10 to 20 percent of malt will get you to 1.053 to 1.060 (12.51 to 14.5° P) which is export range, probably not out of line with nineteenth century versions.

All-Grain Recipe:

9.0 lb (4.02 kg)   Moravian Pilsener malt (fully modified)

Extract Recipe:

5.5 lb (2.5 kg)   pale dry extract (best quality you can find)

Thick mash (1.25 quarts of water per pound or .53 liters per kilogram). First rest at 131° F (55° C), 30 minutes. Immediately remove thick one-third of mash and slowly (30 minutes) raise to boiling, then boil 15 minutes. Add back to main mash, stabilize at 152° F (66.5° C), rest one hour. Raise to 165° F (74° C) (by adding boiling water if needed) and begin sparge.

Note: Those of you who want to skip the decoction thing, use the wort caramelization trick described above, or substitute 1 pound (0.45 kilograms) of Munich or 2 pounds (0.90 kilograms) of Vienna for an equal amount of Pilsener malt in the recipe.

Hops:

2.5 oz (71 g)	60 min	Saaz (3% AA)
2.5 oz (71 g)	15 min	Saaz (3% AA)
1.0 oz (28 g)	end of boil	Saaz (3% AA)

* Old-style undermodified malt requires the use of the classic three-decoction mash process and eight hours out of your life.

orous cooking to unleash all its sugar content and to reduce the larger proteins so they would not create haze in the beer later on. If you decide to use the lightly modified Moravian malt, you will need to read up on the triple-mash decoction procedure and follow it—a brew day to remember, for sure.

The other thing that happens in a decoction is that some caramelization of the wort and grain occurs while it is being boiled. This is a crucial element in old-time Pilseners, and is the reason you may want to include at least one decoction in your process. Simply take a thick third of your mash out during the protein rest, raise it up to saccharification temperatures of 148 to 154° F (64.5 to 68° C) and hold for fifteen minutes, then raise it to boiling. Boil this decoction for fifteen minutes, stirring vigorously to prevent scorching, then add it back, which should just about get the whole mash up to saccharification temperature. Another method that might develop similar flavors is to take a quart or two of the first runoff and boil it briskly until it is reduced to a syrup and begins to darken, just slightly. This technique can also be used with extract beers, but there is a danger of adding too much color in such a pale beer.

4. Cold fermentation is important You can make a delicious beer by following all

Is Lager Beer Intoxicating? An 1874 View

Media coverage of alcohol consumption issues is so intense today that we may tend to think of our era as one of wild, unbridled abuse. This is far more perception than reality. In 1874, the atmosphere was so different that, well, just read on:

"It is a debatable point whether lager beer will intoxicate, and the question came up regularly before the Kings county circuit court, at Brooklyn, New York, on a trial there of a charge for selling intoxicating liquors, in which the defendant made the plea, in a defense, that lager did not intoxicate. A synopsis of the testimony on this point follows:

"Valentine Eckfeldt swore that he had, on one occasion, drank fifteen glasses before breakfast, to give him an appetite.

"Bernhardt Miller had seen a man drink forty glasses in a short time, without being intoxicated. He himself had drunk that number in the space of about one hour.

"Joseph Siser—who weighs two hundred and twenty five pounds—drank an average of about forty glasses a day. It never hurt him any. He had drunk lager since he was six or seven years of age, and he was now over fifty."

Some lager beer glasses were sent for, and exhibited to the jury. They held a pint apiece.

"James White testified to drinking fifty-two glasses of lager in two hours, and a companion drank double the quantity in the same time. It had no intoxicating effect on either of them.

"Philip Kock testified to drinking a keg of lager on a bet, within the space of two hours. The keg contained seven and a half gallons, or thirty quarts. He felt comfortable afterward, and was not intoxicated. He would frequently drink from sixty to ninety glasses a day.

"Nicholas Haherny testified to seeing a man in Bavaria drink seventy-two glasses between nine and ten o'clock in the morning and not get drunk.

"Dr. Arning testified to the effect that he saw a man in Germany drink one hundred and sixty pint glasses in a sitting of three or four hours, and yet not show any appearance of intoxication.

"At St. Louis, Mo., on the 2nd March last, Frank Lauman, keeper of a lager beer saloon in that city, on a wager of twenthe guidelines here, then fermenting with an altbier yeast at coolish temperatures, but it won't exactly be a Pilsener. To get the real stuff you need to use lager yeast to its best advantage, and this requires a method of controlling fermentation temperature. Primary fermentation should be about 50° F; secondary should be in the 35 to 40° F range. A couple of days of elevated temperatures of 60 to 65° F (15.5 to 18.5° C) late in the lagering will be needed to reduce the buttery diacetyl that commonly rears its head. Authentically Czech yeast produces a dry, soft maltiness with an authentic touch of diacetyl, and is highly recommended. It's available as liquid yeast.

5. Use fresh extract If you're attempting to make an extract version, the freshness of your extract is of supreme importance. Liquid extract ages over time, producing thin, cardboardy, tangy, or even "ballpoint pen" aromas, and darkens as it gets older. For a beer this pale and delicate, dry malt extract is a better choice as it is more stable, although a brisk-selling bulk syrup may also be good. If you have doubts, ask your supplier.

ty-five dollars, drank one hundred and fifty glasses of lager. By the terms of the bet he was allowed from eight a.m. to twelve p.m. of the same day to perform this feat. He swallowed fifty glasses before ten o'clock, and by four p.m. he had finished seventy more, being eight hours of the allotted time, and leaving him eight more in which he might dispatch the remaining thirty at his leisure.

"It is hardly necessary to add any testimony of my own to this, but I can say freely, that I am knowing to the fact that Dr. Walcker, formerly of Volksbuhne, drank every day, for a series of years, five gallons of lager, which with a few pretzels constituted his entire sustenance. I learn also, on a respectable authority, that Professor Kern, of College Hall, drank at that place, six gallons at a sitting, which, it is true, lasted several hours. Some of these, doubtless, are extreme cases, but a gallon to an individual, at convivial parties, is a common allowance.

"James R. Chilton, the celebrated chemical analyst of New York City, ascertained by the usual tests, that lager contained three and three-fourths percent of alcohol...He says that lager beer will not intoxicate unless drunk in extraordinary quantities."

This amazing quote was taken from a book entitled *Cincinnati in 1874*. Obviously, as we know differently today, lager beer will indeed cause intoxication. The physiology of alcohol has remained the same in the last one hundred and seventeen years. It is interesting to try to grasp what they must have meant by "intoxicated."

When beer foams,
ditty is not far

Tankard, tankard,
I know I love to you

Son, learn be wise always
find moment to drinking

Don't drink beer by eyes

Good meal, good drink are
ground of all liverhood

Beer warms up,
but it does not dress

God saves the drunken

Where there is brewery, there is
not necessary baker will be

Good beer can be also
in ugly barrel

Drink beer which you have
boiled yourself

Good beer, pretty girl, they are
gifts of Czech country

Barley is not grown for donkeys

Malt and hops—divine cement

—Czech beer proverbs from an Iron Curtain era Pilsner Urquell promotional book.

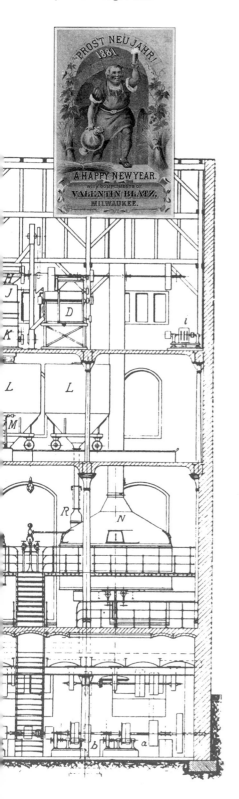

DECOCTIONS—ARE THEY WORTH THE BOTHER?

You may have heard spine-chilling tales, told by hard-core homebrewers, of arcane and sometimes gruesome mashing procedures, more resembling the opening scene in *Macbeth* than the profoundly rational hobby of homebrewing. They are true.

Toil and trouble notwithstanding, decoction mashes do have a place in the brewer's arsenal of techniques. It's an advanced technique, more complicated than most other types of mashes, but decoctions allow you to create rich, malty flavors unattainable any other way.

A decoction mash is a method of conducting a step mash by withdrawing a portion of the mash, heating it to boiling, then returning it to the main mash. This process may be repeated two or three times before the entire batch reaches the appropriate final temperature. There are numerous traditional procedures, each suited to a specific beer type, but all share the same idea.

Why did something so convoluted come about? Although it may seem illogical, decoctions are an adaptation to inferior implements and ingredients. If steam-heated stainless steel kettles were available five hundred years ago, we would have never heard of decoctions. They neatly solve the problem of how to heat a large vat of highly scorchable substance through a series of precise temperature changes, without a large metal vessel, thermometer, or gentle heat source such as steam. Additionally, decoctions help break down the flinty ends of poorly modified malt that used to be standard in Europe, for a much improved yield. And there is some caramelization of the sugars during the decoction boiling, which gives a decocted beer a caramelly sweet maltiness quite different from malts alone.

The main portion of the mash can be kept in a simple insulated tub, while the small decocted portion is boiled in a smaller pot on the fire. Controlling the mash temperature by heating part of the mash, then returning it to the main mash, takes advantage of water at its boiling point, which remains constant at any given altitude. When the mash temperature is indexed to this constant natural standard, a brewer can have precise control over the brewing process even without access to a thermometer. As with so many of the old time methods, decocting is a slick and well-thought-out procedure.

As you may have figured out by now, decoctions are a hassle.

Unlike an infusion mash, which you can walk away from for a while, decoctions require constant fussing. A decoction mash will take two to three times as long as an infusion mash, probably longer than a step mash with the same number of steps. Some brewers like this kind of intimate involvement with their brews, but others find it a chore. Fortunately, you needn't follow every step of the traditional three-mash decoction to get many of the benefits. A simplified decoction can be very effective in giving your Pils or dunkel a little malty kick.

All the traditional techniques share certain common elements. Typically, malt is doughed-in (mixed with water) at around 95° F (35° C) and allowed to stand for twenty minutes or so. This gets everything wet and allows the enzymes to become active, especially the low-temperature beta glucanase responsible for degrading the gummy beta glucans that can cause a slow runoff. At the end of this rest, about a third of the mash, usually the thick part, is removed, leaving thinner stuff in the mash tun. The withdrawn portion is put in a small kettle and heated through a series of rests at the optimal protein (122° F or 50° C) and saccharification (145 to 152° F or 62.5 to 66.5° C) temperatures. The decocted mash is then raised to the boiling point and allowed to boil for up to a half-hour. It is then added back to the main batch, where it serves to raise the temperature of the main mash up to its next rest step. After the first decoction, the mash comes up to protein rest temperatures; after the second, saccharification, and after the third, mash-off (165 to 170°F or 73 to 79° C). When two-mash decoctions are used, the first temperature rise is accomplished by adding hot water.

Decoctions are usually mashed a little thinner than infusion mashes: 1.5 to 2.1 quarts of water per pound of malt (0.64 to 0.88 liters per kilogram). This makes it easier to work with the mash, and allows much of the enzyme content to remain behind in the thin portion, leaving it unaffected by the boiling of the decocted portion. Sticking—and scorching—may be a problem, especially with a thin, stainless steel kettle. This scorched flavor is awful and can ruin a beer. Stir as often as necessary, which may be almost continuously. A heavier cooking pot will give better results. Dark beers are usually mashed at the thicker end of this range, while pale ones are usually mashed thinner.

There are several different traditional decoction routines used for producing beers in Germany and elsewhere in Central Europe. The *Zweimaischverfahren*, or two-mash decoction, is the simplest, and in the widest use. Traditionally reserved for the production of pale beers, it is suitable for dark beers as well, but will not produce effects as intense as the more complex mashes. Dilution of the two-mash is about 1.5 quarts per pound (0.64 liters per kilogram). The main saccharification rest takes place between 144 and 148° F (62 to 63° C). Use a slotted spoon or colander to allow the mash to drain somewhat before dumping it in the decoction pot. The second decoction, half of the mash, having already had some starch conversion, is removed without straining, so it is the same thickness as the rest of the mash. When it's returned to the mash, the whole thing comes up to a mash-out temperature of 164 to 167° F (73 to 75° C). For details of this and all the mashes discussed here, refer to the accompanying charts for specifics of time and temperature.

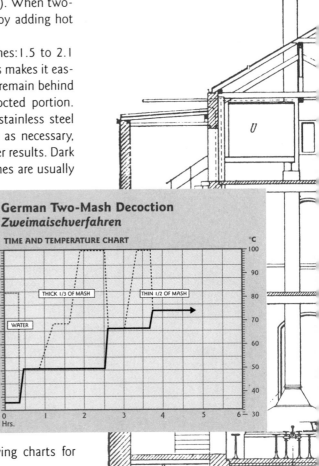

German Two-Mash Decoction
Zweimaischverfahren

TIME AND TEMPERATURE CHART

THICK 1/3 OF MASH THIN 1/2 OF MASH WATER

The *Dreimaischverfahren*, or three-mash decoction, is the historical mash-of-choice for darker beers, as it contributes the maximum amount of rich maltiness so prized in dark lagers. The longer boiling time may add too much color for some pale beers, but it was used for producing pale Munich lager, which can tolerate a golden color, and benefits greatly from the added maltiness. Dilution is 1.25 quarts per pound (0.53 liters per kilogram) for dark beers, and 1.75 quarts per pound (0.74 liters per kilogram) for Munich Helles. The thicker mash tends to produce more dextrinous worts, although this effect is slight. The main saccharification rest happens at the

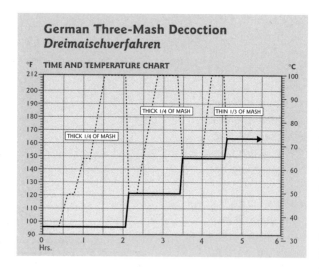

German Three-Mash Decoction
Dreimaischverfahren

TIME AND TEMPERATURE CHART

THICK 1/4 OF MASH

THIN 1/3 OF MASH

THICK 1/4 OF MASH

middle of the range, around 149° F (65° C). The first two decoctions are one-fourth of the volume of the mash each, and are thick in this mashing procedure. The third decoction is one-third of the mash and is thin.

The Pilsener mash is the most complex decoction of all, a grueling challenge involving twenty-two individual steps over nearly six hours. And, of course, it works properly only with very soft water. The dilution is quite loose, at 2.1 quarts per pound. The main saccharification rest happens at only 144.5° F (62.5° C), very low. All three decoctions are one-third of the mash each, and are thick.

You can get some of the benefits of this flavor-enhancing technique without losing your mind by doing streamlined decoctions. The simplest way is to just do a single decoction. You can dough-in at 95° F (35° C) and then raise to 131° F (55° C). The decoction can be taken off after the mash has had a fifteen-minute protein rest. Raise the decoction to 155° F and let it stand for twenty minutes before raising it up to boiling. This will saccharify the decocted portion before its few remaining enzymes are destroyed by boiling. Heating the decoction will probably require constant stirring, but try to do it as gently as possible as air has some undesirable effects on the mash include oxidative darkening and possible increases in viscosity.

Don't skip the 95° F (35° C) dough-in if you're doing a mash with a large proportion of Munich or other lightly roasted malt. These malts have had some of their enzymes deactivated due to the heat used in kilning, although they still will convert themselves. Beta glucanase is the enzyme most sensitive to destruction by heat. It operates at a very low temperature, below 100° F (38° C). If you start your mash out at 122° F (50° C) or higher, you run the risk of not letting the small amount of glucanase enzymes left do their job of degrading beta glucans. When these gummy materials are present they turn your mash into the proverbial bowl full of jelly. If you can imagine trying to sparge malt-flavored Jell-O, you get the picture. Dragsville.

Instead of doing your decoction between protein and saccharification rests, you could do it at the completion of saccharification, and use the temperature rise to bring the whole mash up to mash-off temperature of 165 to 169° F (74 to 76° C), an important step often neglected by homebrewers. Mashing-off inactivates the enzymes present, fixing the ratio of fermentables and unfermentables, and decreases the viscosity of the wort, making lautering easier. Doing a little decoction is an ideal way to accomplish it.

I recommend additional water (25 percent) to be added to the removed portion of the mash. This will make it easier to handle, and especially to heat it up to boiling without a lot of scorching. Be sure to use the same water you're using for your mash water.

You can adjust the length of the decoction boiling to correspond to the color of beer being brewed. Dark beer can handle up to half an hour, but you might want to limit pale beers to fifteen minutes.

If you just can't swing the time and effort of a real decoction, all is not lost. Some of decoction's effects can be had by faking it. Longer-than-usual boils will produce effects similar to decoctions. So you can, simply by adding an hour to the boil, get a beer that is darker, richer, and more caramelly than usual—similar to the effects produced by a decoction. This is effective with extract beers where there is nothing to decoct. With modified extract beers, you might raise your specialty grain side-mash up to boiling before straining it out to add to the extract in the kettle. So while there is no true substitute for tradition, there are workarounds.

So is it really worth the effort? Well, generations of German brewmasters would emphatically say "yes!" I guess it really depends upon how badly you want to get the creamy malt flavor and aroma so important to a Münchener dunkel. If you're going for the gold in the next competition, it may just give you the edge you're looking for—not to mention the respect you'll get from your beer geek friends as they whisper, "Decoctions? He is serious."

MUNICH DUNKEL

You can monkey around with crystal malt if you want to, but in my mind, there is only one way to make a dark Munich lager, and that's with large amounts of dark Munich malt. In the old days, a brewer had only a very small range of malts—sometimes just one—to work with. Pilsener was brewed with Pilsener malt; Dortmunder with Dortmund malt; Vienna with Vienna malt. Likewise with Munich.

Munich malt is kilned longer and at a higher temperature than other lager malts, resulting in a profoundly malty flavor with a hint of toastiness. It contains enough enzymes to convert itself, so a 100 percent Munich malt beer is possible. Even though Munich malt doesn't seem all that dark to look at it, it can produce a beer with a deep amber color. In the old days, it was the only malt employed in the production of

---

RECIPE	Monk-y Business Munich Dunkel		
Yield: 5 gallons (19 liters)	*All-Grain Recipe:*		
Gravity: 1.048 (11.5 °P)	9.5 lb (4.3 kg)	97%	Munich malt (fully modified)
Alcohol/vol: 3.7 to 4.4%	4.0 oz (114 g)	3%	Carafa II roast malt
Color: Ruby	*Extract + Mini-Mash Recipe:*		
Bitterness: 26 IBU	4.0 lb (1.8 kg)	85%	amber dry extract
Yeast: Bavarian lager	1.0 lb (0.45 kg)	9%	aromatic (dark Munich) malt
Maturation: 6 to 8 weeks	1 lb (0.45 kg)	6%	medium crystal malt
An infusion mash will work with modern malts—an hour at 154° F (68° C) should do.	*Hops:*		
	1.25 oz (35 g)	90 min	Hallertau (3.5% AA)

Köstritz and Kulmbach (Culmbach) are the two centers of schwarzbier in Germany.

Dunkel, and, when combined with carbonate water and an intensive three-mash decoction schedule, produced a suitably brown beer. Today a small amount of very dark roast malt is used to add a touch of color.

As mentioned previously, a complex decoction was the traditional method of choice. Today's malts no longer require it, although decocting does add a certain fatness and deep malty aroma. Cooking down some of the first wort (see p. 199) is a quick-and-dirty substitute for a real decoction.

Hopping is light in this style, there just to provide some balance. Hallertau is a good choice, although I like the chocolatey character of Northern Brewer. The hops are added only at the beginning of the boil for maximum bitterness and minimum aroma.

As with the Pilsener, a true lager yeast strain fermented at cool temperatures then stored cold is critical to the character of this style. An ale yeast will ferment the wort, of course, but the fruitiness created by ale yeasts at higher temperatures will mask all the lovely maltiness you've worked so hard to develop.

ALMOST PORTER—GERMAN SCHWARZBIER

The stereotype of Germany is of a country where everything fits into scrupulously tidy compartments, utterly regulated, suiting the tastes of the residents like a pair of custom-fitted *lederhosen*. I've heard brewers there bemoan the situation that brewing a beer outside of well-established styles is not only frowned upon, but in some cases simply not permitted.

This is belied by a strong interest in such Americana as free jazz and the artistic *oeuvre* of David Hasselhoff. And if you look carefully, you might see an eccentric beer that slips outside the carefully constructed framework of allowable brews. Black, roasty, caramelly schwarzbier is such a product.

Porter made such a big splash in the beer world that by the mid-nineteenth century brewers all over Europe were brewing it, not wanting to be left behind in case it really was the Next Big Thing. Of course these brews were adapted to local ingredients, techniques, and tastes—see the description of German porter, c. 1877, p. 260. As it happened, the Next Big Thing turned out to be Pilsener, and Continental porters got pushed to the margins, assimilated into local tradition or forgotten entirely.

One such dark beer survived in Kulmbach, near Nürnberg (Nuremberg) in Franconia, home of many interesting obscurities. A similar beer is still brewed in Bad Köstritz, a small town in the former East Germany. In centuries past, brewing towns were known either for white or red beer, and schwarzbier is clearly in the latter category. Bad Köstritz is situated near Leipzig, long famous for a dark beer called rastrum.

It should be noted that brewers in Central Bavaria use the term schwarzbier to describe their dark lagers, which are paler than even those from Munich. These amber beers, delicious as they are, don't quite do justice to the word "black."

Köstritzer schwarzbier is a mahogany-colored lager of above average strength. Its two-dimensional malt character is key: a mellow, malty base drawn from Munich malt, balanced by a soft roastiness provided by a de-bittered roast malt such as Carafa. On top of this, further balancing the malt, is a solid 40 IBU of hop bitterness. Lager fermentation smooths out the mix and prevents distracting flavors of fruit or spice that

RECIPE	Doktor Schnurrbart Schwarzbier

Yield: 5 gallons (19 liters)

Gravity: 1.061 (14.5 °P)

Alcohol/vol: 4.1 to 4.9%

Color: Ruby-brown

Bitterness: 26 IBU

Yeast: Bavarian lager

Maturation: 8 to 12 weeks

This is a lager, so lager yeast and cool fermenting temperatures are recommended, with a long (six weeks) cold lagering period.

All-Grain Recipe:

9.0 lb (4.1 kg)	74%	Munich malt
1.0 lb (0.45 kg)	21%	pale or Pilsener malt
8.0 oz (170 g)	3%	Carafa II roast malt

A decoction procedure would be traditional, and this indeed accentuates the rich maltiness here. If you have the time and inclination, by all means go for it (see p. 108), but you can make a fine beer with a stepped infusion. Use a glucanase rest at 95° F (35° C) for half an hour, then step up to 153° F (67° C)—a little on the high side, to emphasize unfermentables for a sweeter, fuller beer—and hold there for an hour before mashing out at 170° F (77° C) and sparging as usual.

Extract + Steeped Grain Recipe:

6.5 lb (2.9 kg)	78%	amber malt extract
1.5 lb (0.68 kg)	18%	dark crystal malt, crushed
6.0 oz (170 g)	4%	black patent malt

Hops:

2.0 oz (56 g)	90 min	Spalt (4% AA)

higher temperatures can bring. It's a cool-weather beer for sure, but one that is crisply drinkable thanks to its well-balanced personality—deeply malty but not cloying.

ALTERNATE BOCKS

Traditional bock beer is not much more than a stronger version of Munich dunkel, so you can take the recipe on p. 111 and multiply everything except the water by 1.25, which will bring it to 1.070 (16.4 °P) or so.

The idea of a strong lager brewed as a celebration of spring is an extremely simple concept, one that lends itself to embellishment in a number of ways. Here are a few to get you started:

Pilsenerbock Who can say they don't love the combination of light caramelly malt played against the spicy tang of fresh Czech Saaz hops? As Martha Stewart likes to say, "More is more." This is a pale bock with real personality. There's historical precedent too with a "Bohemian double beer" at 1.057 (13.5 °P) mentioned in some of the old books as late as the 1930s. It was described as golden in color, the result of a slightly higher kilning temperature for the malt.

Try to get ahold of the real thing: genuine Czech-grown Saaz hops. I would brew this one to about 1.068 OG (16 °P), about like a Maibock, which it resembles. About 8.5 pounds (3.9 kilograms) of syrup or 7.5 pounds (3.4 kilograms) of dry malt extract should get you there. Use the palest extract you can find. Pale dried extract may be paler than syrup. Bitterness should be about 45 to 60 IBU, a little higher than a normal Pilsener, to compensate for higher gravity and longer lagering time. An ounce of Saaz hops for the full boil, 2 ounces added twenty minutes from the end, and another 2 ounces in the last five minutes should give you the bitterness and delicious, spicy aroma you're looking for.

A two-hour boil will intensify the caramelization of the wort, simulating in part the effect of the traditional triple decoction mash. If you're mashing, do a decoction if you can manage it. See earlier in this chapter for more on decoctions.

R E C I P E — Festbock

There are pale bocks and dark bocks, but why no amber bocks? Just shoot right down the middle of those two styles and you have a lovely beer.

Yield: 5 gallons (19 liters)

Gravity: 1.070 (16.5 °P)

Alcohol/vol: 5.2 to 6.1%

Color: Ruby-brown

Bitterness: 30 IBU

Yeast: Bavarian lager

Maturation: 10 to 12 weeks

All-Grain Recipe:

12.0 lb (5.4 kg)	92%	Vienna malt
1.0 lb (0.45 kg)	8%	aromatic malt

Extract + Mini-Mash Recipe:

5.75 lb (2.6 kg)	62%	pale dry extract
2.0 lb (0.09 kg)	22%	Munich malt
1.0 lb (0.45 kg)	11%	aromatic malt
0.5 lb (227 g)	5%	U.S. six-row (U.S. two-row can substitute)

Mash-in at 90 to 95° F to allow for a beta-glucan rest, then step it up to the traditional 122° F and 153° F protein and saccharification rests. Of course, a decoction will intensify the caramel aromas in the finished beer.

Hops:

1.5 oz (43 g)	90 min	Spalt (4% AA)
1.0 oz (28 g)	90 min	U.S. Tettnang (4.5% AA)

Schwarzbock If you've ever had a decent Kulmbacher schwarzbier, you know what a delicious style this is. Again, why not "bockify" it?

The key to this beer is a subtle, three-way balance between malt sweetness, hop bitterness, and the roasty bitterness of black malt. The important thing when brewing is to get enough fat malty sweetness to counter the roast malt and hops. I would take the grist bill above and add an extra half-pound (227 grams) of Carafa II malt plus an additional pound (0.45 kilograms) of malt or extract.

All black malts are not created equal. Some maltsters "de-bitter" their deep-roasted malts, creating a softer, smoother roastiness appropriate for this style. Carafa is Weyermann's trade name for this type of malt. It comes in three shades and is available in a dehusked form for an even smoother flavor.

Bitter and finish this beer with Hallertau. Total bitterness should be moderate, maybe 30 to 35 IBU. About 1 ounce (28 grams) will do for the full one-and-a-half-hour boil. Add another half-ounce (14 grams) for the last twenty minutes of the boil, and a half-ounce (14 grams) for the last five minutes. This beer comes very close to the German porter described on p. 260.

Cherrybock Brewers in German cherry-growing regions did sometimes add cherries to their beers. Added to an already luscious ruby-colored bock, cherries turn into a dessert in a glass. Bock's a perfect platform for this kind of vamping, too. Round and smooth, with nothing sticking out. I would recommend between 5 and 10 pounds of frozen sour cherries, possibly augmented by some dark sweet ones. See Chapter 13 for more detail on adding fruit to beers.

BELGIANS ARE EASY

Tonnendragers,
Bruges c. 1900

We beer snobs worship Belgium. With its astonishing range of idiosyncratic beers from ancient, rustic lambic to heavenly monastic tripels, Belgian ale can be a literally religious experience. Many existing styles are living remnants of medieval brewing traditions. Some of the techniques and procedures sure make you feel like you're slogging through the Dark Ages.

Luckily, many Belgian beers are models of simplicity, as least as far as brewing technique is concerned. Most use the same basic infusion mash as any ordinary ale, so there's no need to fear. Belgian ales will test your ability to judge good materials and put a balanced, complex recipe together, but that's where the fun is.

Here's a smattering of easy-to-brew Belgian styles, and some suggestions for striking off on your own. It's important to keep in mind that half of all beers in Belgium don't really fit into any particular style, which makes the whole adventure very appealing to a beer artist like me. For those wanting greater challenges, the more technically complex Belgian styles will be covered in Chapter 15.

BELGIAN PALE ALES

Of modest strength and varying shades of amber, these pale ales retain enough wacky character to remind the drinker that something Belgian is being consumed. Not heavily hopped like their British cousins, they rely on a mix of subtle maltiness and offbeat yeast character to make their point. As a hophead, you may be disappointed. But if you love the intricacies of a well-malted beer, this could be your cup of beer.

The two best known examples are Palm Ale and De Koninck. Both are of medium strength, around 1.050 (12 °P), with hopping in the low 20 IBU range. De Koninck is a little paler and crisper, just a touch lighter on the palate, while Palm is a bit richer and darker. De Koninck is currently being imported to certain regions in the United States; I haven't seen Palm in a decade or more. If you have a chance to try either, don't pass it up.

As a brewer, I find Belgian-style pale ale a perfect launching pad for investigating the many facets of medium-colored malt. Vienna, Munich, and pale ale malts are all pretty subtle, and are best enjoyed in an uncomplicated beer. Added to a base of Belgian Pils or pale malt, they'll give you a range of flavors from purely malty to caramel, toffee, nutlike, even hints of toast.

On top of that you can sprinkle a little of the slightly darker malts the Belgians also use, like biscuit and aromatic, for even more malty fun. These apparent twins, identical in color, have very different personalities. The aromatic is roasted moist, for a full, sweet, caramel nuttiness. Dry kilning gives biscuit a crisp, toasty quality.

Brewing sugars can also add a little magic. Let me first say that I believe the gravel-sized rocks of "candi sugar" sold to homebrewers to be a complete rip-off. Sure, they look nice and cost a lot, but they are nearly pure refined sugar—that's what crystallizing does, remember? Get your hands on some unrefined sugar—rough, lumpy, tan stuff that actually has some flavor. Five to 10 percent in a recipe will add mysterioso flavors, as well as lighten the palate a tad. Just dump 'em into the brewpot.

And of course, it wouldn't be Belgian beer if you couldn't further liven it up with some Secret Spice. The orange peel/coriander combo blends so perfectly with amber malty beers, it is often impossible to sort the flavors out. Then there are zillions of other spices like star anise, licorice, and grains of paradise, which go even further. The

---

RECIPE — Yellow Diamond Belgian Pale Ale

Yield: 5 gallons (19 liters)

Gravity: 1.055 (13 °P)

Alcohol/vol: 5 to 5.6%

Color: Pale amber

Bitterness: 30 IBU

Yeast: Belgian ale

Maturation: 4 to 6 weeks

All-grain and mini mash: mash at 152° F (67° C) for an hour, then add boiling water to raise to 170° F (77° C), and sparge.

All-Grain Recipe:

4.0 lb (1.8 kg)	40.5%	Belgian pale ale malt
3.0 lb (1.4 kg)	30%	Belgian Munich malt
1.0 lb (0.45 kg)	10%	Belgian aromatic malt
6.0 oz (170 g)	0.5%	Belgian medium crystal
1.5 lb (0.68 kg)	15%	Piloncillo or other unrefined sugar, added to brew kettle

Extract + Mini-Mash Recipe:

3.0 lb (1.4 kg)	40%	pale dry extract
1.5 lb (0.68 g)	20%	pale dry extract

Plus: the aromatic and crystal malts, and the piloncillo

Hops:

1.0 oz (28 g)	90 min	Northern Brewer	(6.5% AA)
1.0 oz (28 g)	15 min	Saaz (3% AA)	
0.67 oz (19 g)	90 min	Saaz (3% AA)	

Add at end of boil:

1 to 2 oranges, zested

0.5 oz (14 g) coriander, crushed (variety from an Indian market for best flavor)

1 whole star anise, or 0.5 tsp (2 g) grains of paradise, or your secret spice of choice

---

sky's the limit—just keep it very subtle if you want to stay in the ballpark.

Use fresh orange peel. The best is Seville, which may be found in Caribbean or sometimes Latino markets described as "sour orange." Ordinary oranges or tangerines will do, but use two instead of one. Just peel the outer orange layer of the skin with a potato peeler (avoiding the bitter white pith), and add it to the brew kettle at the end of the boil.

Hops are there primarily for balance, which isn't to say any old cone will do. With their former ties to the Austrian Empire, Belgian brewers have a tradition of Czech (Saaz) hops. Styrian Goldings are another popular variety there; often both are used. Don't use high alpha hops unless you want to twist this style into something altogether different; grapefruit is for breakfast.

Yeast is a crucial flavor contributor, and there are plenty from which to choose. Employ one with Belgian character, such as a Trappist strain. These yeasts add complex spicy and fruity notes impossible to obtain anywhere else, yet don't swerve off-road like the wild yeasts and other fuzzy bugs in lambics. Trappist ales are traditionally fermented quite warm, even as high as 80° F (26.5° C), but this is overdoing it for the pale ale style. Normal ale brewing temperatures of 60 to 70° F (15.5 to 21° C) will give you the right amount of zing.

Mashing is pretty straightforward with the highly modified malts used here. A simple infusion mash will do, with a single conversion rest, then a bump-up to mash out before sparging. Note: you can also brew this beer with German or English pale and Munich malts.

BREWS OF BEELZEBUB—BELGIAN STRONG PALE ALES

You know the ones. Friendly little lawnmower beers, crisp and fruity, a light spicy tang on the finish, just gotta have one more. Then you find yourself on the floor, the Devil looking down at you, and she's leering menacingly as the pitchfork is coming down, hard. Welcome to the style, sucker!

Duvel is the archetype, of course, brewed originally as a dark beer then switched over to its current pale avatar only in 1970—twenty years after the Trappist brothers at Westmalle came up with their famous tripel.

The strong pale ales of Belgium represent an interesting intersection of four things: the drive toward pale beers in England (IPA) and the Continent (Pils) that really took off in the middle of the nineteenth century; a rebound from the catastrophically weak beers of the wartime years; a desire to compete with full-strength British beers imported after World War I; and a 1919 law that prohibited the on-premise sale of gin, which necessitated a suitably zippy replacement.

Here you have a beer that's part Pils, part IPA, and burly enough to stand in for gin. Not a hard beer to brew, in theory, but you have to get all the details right. There's nothing to hide behind.

Very high quality Pilsener malt is essential. To this is added pure corn sugar to keep the color and texture light. Saaz and Styrian hops are used. The brewery uses two different strains of yeast, originally cultured up out of a McEwans bottle by no less a beer god than Jean DeClerck himself.

Brewing is pretty straightforward. A step infusion with a protein rest is recommended, as it will reduce the amount of haze-forming proteins in the final beer. This is one we do want nice and clear. The brewery uses a long, cold conditioning period—lagering, really—and this is also recommended for the home version, as it really smooths out the flavors. A month at refrigerator temperatures ought to do it.

Bottled versions are highly carbonated, as is common with Belgian beers. I again recommend half as much priming sugar as normal. Such a beer bomb must be served

RECIPE	**Fallen Angel Strong Pale**		

Yield: 5 gallons (19 liters)
Gravity: 1.073 (17.5 °P)
Alcohol/vol: 7.1 to 8%
Color: Pale gold
Bitterness: 41 IBU
Yeast: Belgian ale
Maturation: 8 to 10 weeks

All-Grain Recipe:

10.5 lb (4.8 kg)	93%	Pilsener malt
1.75 lb (0.79 kg)	7%	corn sugar

Extract Recipe:

6.75 lb (3.1 kg)	93%	pale dry extract
1.0 lb (0.45 kg)	7%	corn sugar

Hops:

1.25 oz (35 g)	60 min	Northern Brewer (6.5% AA)
1.0 oz (28 g)	30 min	Saaz (3% AA)
1.0 oz (28 g)	30 min	Styrian Goldings (5.5% AA)
1.0 oz (28 g)	end of boil	Saaz (3% AA)

chilled, of course. It is difficult to serve a draft beer with that much pressure. I would carbonate it as highly, maybe around 15 psi (cold). When serving, turn the pressure down to about 5 psi, pour, then crank it back up to the storage pressure.

SAISON: BEER OF HEAVENLY BALANCE

When you get done mowing the lush green lawn that coats the cloud tops all over heaven, of course you're going to need a beer to drink. And one would think that in that ultimate luxury skybox a cool, golden, refreshing saison would always be within an easy reach. I know the song says heaven is bare of beer, but this seems to me an impossibility, given its reputation as the ultimate pleasure dome. I like to think the Vikings had the right idea along these lines. For them heaven didn't just have a beer hall. Heaven *was* a beer hall.

I can think of few beer styles that give me more pleasure here on earth. Crisp yet substantial, fragrantly hoppy, but underlain with a delicate maltiness, it maintains a hair's breadth balance among its many aspects. Hovering between weak and strong, hoppy and malty, spiced and straightforward, this beer is what you find in it, always adding up to a harmonious whole.

Saison is about as close to homebrew as a commercial product can get. The handful of remaining Belgian producers are all very small, and brew in a traditional, even rustic fashion. The beers are usually bottle-conditioned in 750-milliliter "champagne" type bottles, so there's really nothing about the style that's beyond the homebrewer's range of technique.

Saison is the product of francophone Belgium, specifically the western part of Hainault province. It has a long provenance as a farmhouse ale, brewed to serve as a fortifying—but not stupefying—thirst quencher for the labors of the summer field.

Coriander, Indian Variety

This larger, paler type has a softer, fruitier flavor and is better for beer than the ordinary kind, which can taste somewhat vegetal in beer.

Gravities used to be around 4° B (1.040 or 9.5 °P), but have crept up in the last half century; now they're at 1.048 to 1.062 (11.5 to 15 °P), with "speciale" versions going even higher, up to 1.085 (20 °P). Nothing would prevent you from doing a barley wine strength interpretation.

Pilsener malt is the main ingredient. A dab of specialty malt adds depth without tarnishing the lovely blond glow. Munich, Vienna, or even pale ale malt will round out the flavor. In small amounts—less than 20 percent—they won't add too much color. I find crystal malt a little too chewy for this style, but some very light crystal might be a good idea if you're trying to make a mostly extract version, and then, well, let the color be damned. A small amount of malted wheat—about 10 percent—adds a firm, creamy head. With stronger interpretations I like to use some sugar. Partially refined sugars such as turbinado, demerara, piloncillo, or jaggery are great for this purpose, as they contribute another layer of flavor and not just extra alcohol.

Hops should be assertive, but not overwhelming. Bitterness levels are usually in the 30 to 45 IBU range. All manner of European hops are used in Belgium; Kent Goldings are the signature aroma in at least one commercial saison. The spiciness of Saaz also goes well with this style. I would stay away from high-alpha hops of any kind, as their flavors are likely to be too intrusive.

Spices are a part of the mix, typically at a very subtle and self-effacing level. Orange and coriander are common; other "mystery" ingredients crop up as well, from black pepper to aniseed to "medicinal lichen" (Go to www.lichen.com/usetype.html and see if you can sort this one out). I especially like the crisp pepperiness added by grains of paradise, a once-popular culinary spice with a flavor that's a blend of white pepper and plywood, with citrusy overtones.

Much of the available coriander reeks strongly of celery seed, which I find very obtrusive in a beer. The type sold at Indian groceries is far superior, and I believe a nice variety is sold through some homebrew channels. Seville (usually sold as "sour") oranges are the best, although they're hard to find. A mix of regular orange and grapefruit peel can serve as a substitute. I find that the dried chunks add an awful lot of pithy bitterness and not enough orange. I just peel (with a potato peeler) the colored outer zest from fresh oranges and add them at the end of the boil.

Mashing is a straightforward infusion. The lower the gravity, the higher the main mash temperature. This will raise the percentage of unfermentables, in keeping with saison's pedigree as a beer of sustenance. Beers of 1.040 (9.5 °P) should be mashed at around 155° F (68° C), dropping down to 152° F (66.5° C) for beers higher than 1.065 (15.5 °P). An hour should be sufficient to convert.

Saison yeasts are some of Belgium's most ancient and earthy cultivated yeasts, often with unique personalities. Both Wyeast (3724) and White Labs (WLP 565) produce a saison strain for homebrewers, and I highly recommend them if you want an authentic taste. If you can't get your hands on either, try another Belgian strain. Yeast character is such a part of this style that I recommend you not even bother if you can't come up with a Belgian strain of some sort. Fermentation at the higher end of the temperature range (70 to 76° F or 21 to 24.5° C) will encourage the development of the rich fruity aromatic character we're after.

In the old days, these beers were often a blend of fresh beer with stale, resulting in a crisp lactic tang counterbalancing the sweet freshness of young beer. This is obviously a difficult thing to do successfully. Invite lactic acid bacteria into your brewery for a little snack, and the next thing you know they're hogging the couch and demanding more batteries for the remote, if you know what I mean. So exercise caution if you go this route. Less threatening solutions include blending in a bottle of lambic at bottling/kegging time or adding 5 to 20 milliliters of food grade lactic acid at any time in the process.

RECIPE   **Saisoon Buffoon**

Yield: 5 gallons (19 liters)
Gravity: 1.060 (14.5 °P)
Alcohol/vol: 5.3 to 6.1%
Color: Pale gold
Bitterness: 38 IBU
Yeast: Belgian ale
Maturation: 6 to 8 weeks

All-Grain Recipe:

5.5 lb (2.5 kg)	55%	Pilsener malt
2.5 lb (1.1 kg)	25%	Munich malt
1.0 lb (0.45 kg)	10%	malted wheat
1.0 lb (0.45 kg)	10%	piloncillo (or other partially-refined sugar)

Extract + Mini-Mash Recipe:

3.5 lb (1.6 kg)	44%	pale dry malt extract

Plus the Munich, wheat, and piloncillo, above.

Hops:

1.0 oz (28 g)	Northern Brewer (7% AA) 60 min
1.5 oz (43 g)	30 min (3% AA) 30 min *Saaz*
2.0 oz (57 g)	Kent Goldings (5% AA) 5 min

For last 5 minutes of boil, add:

0.67 oz (19 g) Indian coriander

Zest of 1 Seville/sour orange or 1 regular orange plus zest from one-fourth of a grapefruit

0.25 tsp (1 g) grains of paradise or black pepper, coarsely crushed

Other mystery spices as you like

Mash should be a simple infusion, with a one hour saccharification at 153° F (67° C) or thereabouts. Sparge as usual. Boil for one hour, add hops as noted by each addition, above. Spices are added for the last five minutes of the boil. Ferment with a Belgian Saison-type yeast, between 65 and 70° F (18.5 to 21° C).

Bottle or keg at higher than normal pressures for an authentic texture—5.5 ounces (156 grams) of corn sugar priming should get you there. If force carbonating, aim for a final pressure about 25 percent higher than you normally would use. This may require bleeding some of the pressure from the keg before serving to prevent over-foaming. Serve cool, not cold, and enjoy the taste of heaven.

THREE TIMES THE FUN—ABBEY-STYLE BEERS

Abbey and Trappist beers have a proud lineage that goes back at least a thousand years. Monks of the Cistercian order, founded in the twelfth century, place special emphasis on vocation as part of their religious observances, and the production of beer and other foods such as cheese has a central role. Today there are five monasteries producing beer in Belgium, and numerous other commercial breweries produce the abbey style, sometimes under license to a monastery. It is difficult to accurately define the style, as there is a lot of variation. A common feature is the designation of a series of ever stronger beers sometimes designated by single, double, triple, and even quadruple, although other means—cap color, for example—may be used to designate the individual beers. Not all abbey beers follow this practice, however. The term "Trappist" constitutes an appellation indicating the beer is brewed by the monastery itself, as opposed to being contracted. It's not a guarantee of quality per se, but as it happens, all the abbeys produce beers of the very highest order.

The single is the weakest beer, and rarest in this country, as it was the beer traditionally brewed for routine consumption at the monastery and is falling into obscurity. Generally, singles are about 1.050 OG (12 °P) and pale amber in color. Fresh and fruity, with spicy yeast aromas, they're a delightful session drink. Dubbels are stronger and usually darker. The classic double/dubbel is Chimay Red Cap. At 1.063 OG (15 °P), it is deep amber, softly malty, with spicy fruity aromas, and a very slightly toasty finish. Tripels may actually be dark, but the archetype for the triple/tripel style is Westmalle. Brilliant gold, 1.080 OG (19 °P), with a honeyed maltiness and a crisp hoppy finish, it pioneered the style for many other Belgian strong golden ales.

The above examples are considered classics, but there's a lot of individuality even among the six monastery breweries, so nothing really fits into neat little categories. The whole range of Rochefort is dark and chocolatey, very rich and deeply flavored. The Westvleteren beers are also deep amber, evocative of dried fruit and spice, without the chocolatey roast character of Rochefort. Orval produces just one beer, which is as much a saison as anything, but crisper and not so lush. It's 1.054 to 1.055 OG, tawny gold, with a massively dense head fueled by very high carbonation. Fermented with both ale and lager yeast (which is used for bottle-conditioning), it has a unique, earthy, *Brettanomyces* "horse" aroma, high bitterness and hop aroma due to dry-hopping, all of which makes for a very refreshing beer.

All of the Trappist beers are artisanal products, bottle conditioned and flat-out wonderful. The commercial abbey beers tend to be a little more mass-market, and are sometimes filtered before bottling, which tends to affect both flavor and texture.

Abbey-style beers are subtle and captivating beers to mas-

ter, but there's nothing difficult about the technique. As a group, they are masterpieces of depth and balance, which always takes a little work on the recipe side. Here are a few hints and tips for abbey style ales.

- Pay special attention to quality of the mid- and dark-colored malts. A dubbel can be a showcase for the darker sorts of crystal malts, and it's important to find one with a rich, complex flavor. The mid color malts such as aromatic and biscuit also come in very handy. There's not much use for very dark malts in the style. In tripel, the pale malt is of special importance as sugar forms part of the grain bill, and it's important to have a malt that has enough punch to handle this.

- Mashing is a straightforward affair, with a simple infusion mash. With the stronger styles, a slightly lower saccharification temperature (145° F or 63° C) as opposed to 150° F (65.5° C) should be used to produce a more fermentable wort.

- Hop aroma is rarely a big deal in this category. Nevertheless, you want to stick with good aroma varieties as the Belgian brewers do. Saaz is generally favored for paler beers, sometimes in combination with Styrian Goldings.

- Spices such as orange peel, coriander, and grains of paradise can be used to add complexity, but if you can pick them out, you're using too much.

- Use sugar. The stronger beers should never be thick or cloying. This is one of the truly magical things about the category. It's absolutely essential to add some

---

R E C I P E	**Hoosonfurst Abbey Singel**

Yield: 5 gallons (19 liters)
Gravity: 1.050 (12 °P)
Alcohol/vol: 4.4 to 4.9%
Color: Medium gold
Bitterness: 28 IBU
Yeast: Belgian abbey ale
Maturation: 4 to 6 weeks

All-Grain Recipe:

6.0 lb (2.7 kg)	63.5%	Pilsener malt
3.0 lb (1.4 kg)	31.5%	pale ale malt
0.5 lb (227 g0	5%	aromatic malt

Extract + Mini-Mash Recipe:

4.5 lb (2 kg)	69%	pale dry malt extract
1.0 lb (0.45 kg)	15.5%	pale crystal malt
1.0 lb (0.45 kg)	15.5%	aromatic malt

Hops:

0.75 oz (21 g)	60 min	Challenger (7.5% AA)
1.0 oz (28 g)	30 min	Saaz (3% AA)
0.5 oz (14 g)	5 min	Northdown (6.5% AA)
0.5 oz (14 g)	5 min	Saaz (3% AA)

Star Anise

This Asian spice can add a rich, complex anise character, and is especially valued in dark beers.

sugar to tripels, and I think it improves dubbels as well, as it keeps the crystal malt from making the beer too heavy and syrupy. The expensive candi sugar you find in homebrew shops is nothing more than pure sucrose and is a waste of money. I get better results from semirefined sugars such as jaggery, piloncillo, and others (see p. 196). The usual dosage is 5 to 15 percent.

- Use a proper Belgian yeast. Many of the available strains have pedigrees from actual Trappist breweries, which you can sort out with a little sleuthing. These strains add that extra layer of spicy, fruity subtleness that is so important here. These beers are traditionally fermented at high temperatures, up into the 80° F range. This may be overdoing it a bit, but don't ferment them below about 65° F or you'll miss all the wonderful complexity the yeast can offer. Note that stronger beers may require an alcohol-tolerant strain.

- Cooked sugar—caramel—syrup can add color and depth without adding heaviness. Belgian brewers use them, but I have not found any available to homebrewers here. See p. 198 for how to make your own.

- Tripel can be a very strong beer, so observe the suggestions in the following chapter regarding strong beer fermentation.

- Don't be afraid to brew outside the narrow confines of the few classic examples. Belgian beer is all about creativity and self-expression, even in monasteries of a very strict order.

R E C I P E	**Two Bits Abbey Dubbel**

Yield: 5 gallons (19 liters)

Gravity: 1.063 (15 °P)

Alcohol/vol: 5.5 to 6.4%

Color: Deep amber

Bitterness: 29 IBU

Yeast: Belgian abbey ale

Maturation: 8 to 10 weeks

All-Grain Recipe:

6.0 lb (2.7 kg)	63.5%	pale ale malt
3.0 lb (1.4 kg)	23%	Munich malt
1.0 lb (0.45 kg)	9%	Belgian medium-dark crystal
0.5 lb (227 g)	4.5%	aromatic malt
1.0 lb (0.45 kg)	9%	Piloncillo or other partially-refined sugar

Extract + Mini-Mash Recipe:

3.25 lb (1.5 kg)	41%	pale dry malt extract
1.75 lb (0.79 kg)	22%	amber dry malt extract

Plus: the crystal, aromatic, and piloncillo, above.

Hops:

1.25 oz (35 g)	90 min	Northern Brewer (7% AA)

R E C I P E	Three-Nipple Tripel		

Yield: 5 gallons (19 liters)
Gravity: 1.080 (19 °P)
Alcohol/vol: 7.6 to 8.6%
Color: Pale gold
Bitterness: 43 IBU
Yeast: Belgian abbey ale
Maturation: 3 to 4 months

All-Grain Recipe:

10.0 lb (4.5 kg)	72%	Pilsener malt
2.0 lb (0.90 kg)	14%	Munich malt
2.0 lb (0.90 kg)	14%	jaggery or demerara sugar

Extract + Steeped Grain Recipe:

8.0 lb (3.6 kg)	89%	pale dry malt extract
1.0 lb (0.45 kg)	11%	pale crystal malt
2.0 lb (0.90 kg)	14%	jaggery or demerara sugar

Hops:

2.0 oz (57 g)	60 min	Styrian Goldings (7% AA)
1.5 oz (43 g)	15 min	Saaz (3% AA)

Trappist beers offer an amazing
variety of flavors and colors.

BIG HONKIN' BREWS

Not even the brandy stashed beneath the drooling chin of the faithful Saint Bernard can warm the bone-deep chill of winter like a rich, strong ale. They require more effort and expense than the ordinary stuff, but the rewards can be worth it. Few pleasures are greater than cracking open a well-cared-for barley wine basking in the glow of its fifth year. Such beers are best savored slowly and with great respect, as their intensity and alcoholic strength can be overwhelming if treated like a lesser brew.

We're talking about ales of 1.085 (20 °P) and up. This will limit our discussion to a manageable number of truly big styles, beers with 8 percent alcohol or more. They take a little more preparation and a lot more patience, but they are worth the wait!

BIG WORT

Strong ales demand special production techniques. To produce high-gravity worts it is necessary to use a technique that will concentrate the sugars above the usual range of wort gravities.

With extract beers, the answer is to simply use a greater quantity of extract. The usual two 3.3-pound (1.5 kilogram) cans of syrup will produce a 1.054 (13 °P) wort; three cans will get you to 1.080 (19 °P); and if you use four cans, you'll get all the way up to 1.100 (24 °P). Be sure to use the freshest syrup you can find, or dried extract, which seems to hold up better.

Extracts may also be used to boost the gravity of mashed beers. Since the mashing process requires the mash be sparged, or rinsed, with hot water to recover all the fermentable sugars, it is difficult to *efficiently* obtain worts above 1.060 (14.5 °P). So adding a few pounds of malt extract to the kettle is the simplest way to boost the strength to the level we're talking about.

Another technique is to collect a normal gravity wort of about 1.060 (14.5 °P) and boil it until enough water has been vaporized to increase the gravity to the desired range. If a 1.060 (14.5 °P) wort is boiled down to two-thirds of its original volume, the remaining wort will be boosted up to 1.090 (21.5 °P). Remember to account for this decrease in volume, and make enough of the weaker wort to give you the proper batch size when reduced.

The most ancient technique is to do a split, or parti-gyle, brew. This involves using the strong first runnings only for the production of a strong beer, while boiling the second, weaker runnings separately to create a weaker beer. This makes formulation tricky—and requires a brewing system large enough to get a reasonable quantity of the strong wort—but it is very efficient. The key fact to remember is that the first third of the runnings will contain half the extract, making it twice as strong as the second two-thirds. For more on this technique, see p. 200.

Another method of producing strong wort is a double brew, used to brew strong beers at least as far back as Elizabethan times. A normal mash is conducted, then the wort collected from this is used to mash-in a second brew. The runoff from this will be exceedingly strong, way up over 1.100, resulting in beers with well over 10-percent alcohol.

Of course adding some type of sugar is a pretty easy way to get extra fermentables into your wort, and it has the added advantage of thinning out the body of the beer so it's a little more drinkable. Adding malt extract to an otherwise all-grain recipe is a technique used by many brewers of strong beers.

BIG HOPS

One important thing brewers of ultra-strong beers need to do is load them up with hops. There are three reasons for this: first, these intensely strong beers have an incredible amount of malt in them, and high hop rates are needed to balance this stickiness. Second, high-gravity worts assimilate hop bitterness rather poorly during the boil. Utilization rates of 35 percent may easily be achieved (1.5-hour boil, 1.040 and 9.5 °P wort) with normal strength beers, but this drops to 27 percent with a 1.090 (21.5 °P) wort, and goes down to just 22 percent at 1.110 (24 °P), so hop rates must be boosted to compensate for this poor utilization. The third factor is the long aging time required for strong beers. Over time, hop bitterness diminishes; my personal rule-of-thumb is that beer loses a quarter of its perceived bitterness every year it ages. This means at two years, that 70 IBU barley wine will taste like only 39 IBU.

What all this means is that you may use almost 5.5 ounces (156 grams) of 7 percent alpha bittering hops in a 5-gallon batch under the following scenario:

1.5 hr. boil	@ 25% utilization	90 IBU	= 3.3 oz (94 g)
30 min. boil	@ 15% utilization	35 IBU	= 2.1 oz (60 g)
	TOTALS:	125 IBU	= 5.4 oz (154 g)

This is probably far more hops than you might add simply by guessing. Aroma declines at least as quickly as bitterness, so the same adjustments need to be made to the quantity of finishing hops added at the end of the boil. One should also note that large quantities of hops in the wort may soak up a lot of that valuable wort, which might suggest that for very bitter strong beers, good quality high-alpha hops might be a better choice. Most hop-mad brewers end up brewing extra wort which will be left behind in the hops after the boil is finished. Or, you can centrifuge the wort out of them with a salad spinner!

"Men drink it thick, and piss it thin,
Mickle Faith by St. Elroy, what leaves it within?"

—Quoted by Edward Whitaker, 1700

BIG YEAST

This is the most difficult aspect of strong beer brewing. At high alcohol levels, yeast undergoes enormous stress, and conditions must be created to ensure this does not degrade beer quality.

First, it is important to use a yeast that will tolerate alcohol well. Most Belgian abbey ale yeasts pass this test, but British ale strains are much more variable in their alcohol tolerance. I have had good experience with the old Ballantine's ale yeast (Wyeast 1056 or White Labs WLP 001), the strain used to ferment Bigfoot Barleywine.

Yeast may be cultured from some commercial beers, but samples from high-gravity brews may be over-stressed, even mutated, so culture your yeast from the lowest-gravity beer in the family—the pale ale, for example.

You need to have enough yeast. The use of a starter is imperative, even when packets of commercial yeast—dry or liquid—are used. Four times the amount of yeast for a normal batch is the rule of thumb. A pint of thick slurry would not be too much. There is no need to worry about creating a yeasty-tasting beer. The ideal way to get this quantity of yeast is to save it from a past batch. Pour the lees from a recent secondary into a sterile mason jar and allow it to settle in the refrigerator. The smooth creamy layer in the middle contains the freshest, most active yeast. This will keep for a few weeks under refrigeration. Before using, it is a good idea to bring the yeast up to pitching temperature and feed it with some sterile wort a day or two before adding it to your beer.

Adequately aerating your wort is of supreme importance with high-gravity beers. Yeast requires oxygen to reproduce, and as noted above, it is crucial to get as much yeast going as possible. See p. 67 for the options.

Sometimes multiple strains of yeast are used. A normal ale yeast, chosen for its flavor characteristics, is used to ferment during the primary, then a second, alcohol-tolerant yeast is added to the secondary. Champagne yeasts will tolerate alcohol up to 15 to 17 percent, but produce bone-dry, neutral-tasting beers when used as the sole yeast.

BIG TIME

Once brewed, Grasshopper, you must learn patience. It takes a long time for the yeast to hack its way through all that sugar under the high-alcohol conditions that quickly develop. Six months in the carboy in the secondary is not an unusually long time. It's best to buy an extra carboy if you plan to brew this style regularly.

It's a good idea to prime barley wines lightly, as there is usually some residual sugar that will eventually ferment, plus they're traditionally just barely sparkling. I recommend priming with a half-cup of corn sugar at bottling. If the beer has spent an extended time in the secondary (more than four months), it may be advisable to add some fresh yeast when bottling. Note that introducing a vigorously fermenting yeast at this time can spur more fermentation in the bottle than you really want. It may be better to add new yeast during the secondary, and allow a few weeks for it to ferment out before adding to the bottles. Carbonation will take longer with this style than with ordinary-strength beers, perhaps up to a couple of months.

Most inexperienced brewers follow the maxim, "The beer is ready when you've drunk the last bottle." If you're patient, your barley wine will reward you with a gold star. I recommend stashing a quantity in the basement of a non-drinking relative, and just forgetting it exists for a year or two. When you remember to retrieve it and sample it in its most elevated state, your surprise and pleasure will be twice as great.

BIG STYLES

Scottish Wee Heavy The "wee" refers to a small bottle, the traditional package for the style. The Scots like their beers a touch darker and less bitter than their English counterparts, and also slightly sweeter. This is accomplished by using a dark base malt such as mild ale malt along with other dark malts, fewer hops, and lower fermentation temperatures. A good amount of kettle caramelization adds malty flavors, so a long, vigorous boil is recommended for this style. Also, during mashing, starch conversion should take place at a high temperature (154 to 158° F or 68 to 70° C) to produce a less-fermentable wort.

Barley wine This designation was invented by Bass in 1903, but now is applied to most English-style ales of 1.075 (18 °P) strength and over (in Britain, even weaker beers will sometimes wear this label). There are few defining characteristics to the style, other than top fermentation and blinding strength. Color and hop rates vary widely, but a typical example will be a deep shimmering amber, sweet when young, and balanced by a large quantity of hops.

Imperial Stout This was a style once sold by the English to the Imperial Czarist court of Russia. It is just what you might expect of an ultra-strong stout: jet-black, thick, rich, and blisteringly hoppy at 70 to 125 IBU (normal beers are in the 20 to 40 IBU range), although some modern interpretations are much milder. Gravities start at 1.075 (18 °P) and go as high as beer can go, up to 1.120 (29 °P)!

DRAGON'S MILK: ENGLISH OCTOBER BEER

It's the stuff of legend, the muse of poets, the nectar of the gents. Strong beer, brilliant as topaz, sweet as dew, and dripping with the perfume of hops, was for centuries a revered icon of English culture. In typical language-loving English style these beers were nicknamed angel's-food, clamber-skull, huffcap, and more.

October beer was the most laudable product of country brewing, specifically country house brewing. Beer wasn't a readily transportable product in the oxcart era, so the maintenance of an estate, large or small, required beer to be brewed on the premises.

Dwarf Ale Glass, c. 1800
Strong October beers were drunk from tiny glasses like this. Shown actual size.

Edwardian Pub Sign for McMullen's Ales in London.

The country always had a reputation for better strong ales than the city.

From about 1600 to 1900, there were four classes of beers brewed on estates, although not all kinds were brewed by every brewer. On the bottom was weak and watery small beer, usually the last runnings of whatever was being brewed, although occasionally brewed on its own in summer months. Next up the scale in strength was "table" beer, what we today would regard as ordinary strength, roughly in the 1.050 (12 °P) (4.5-percent alcohol) range. Next was March and October beer at about 1.080 (19 °P), followed by rarely brewed "double" beers, well over 1.100 (24 °P) (9-percent plus), and reserved for special occasions (see p. 135).

Beer was allotted according to employment or familial status on the estates. Everyone was allowed liberal access to the weak, small beer as a means of providing a safe form of water. The table beer was doled out as part of employment contracts, as was the stronger beer—although, as you would expect, much less liberally. It was a point of civility that the family drank the same small beer as everyone else, and no upgraded version was made strictly for their use. Of course, they had access to the stronger stuff whenever they wanted it.

Before the invention of refrigeration, brewing was much more strictly tied to the whims of the seasons, both on the brewing and consuming sides of the tun. The summer heat, availability of ingredients, and the need for large amounts of quenching—but not too intoxicating—brews in the summer, and warming ones in the winter, all played a part.

October was generally regarded as the best month to brew. The barley harvest was in, so new malt was available and was widely believed to contribute to a beer that kept very well. Fresh hops added their own special charms, although they were usually mixed with the last of the old crop. Cooler fermentation temperatures made long-aged beers less vulnerable to frets and souring than March beers. And by October, the strong beer made in the previous year was starting to be tapped, so the necessity of brewing its replacement became obvious.

October and March beers are identical, except for the use of last year's malt and hops, and the warm summertime fermentations that gave March beer a lesser reputation for quality than October. The old recipes vary a bit, but generally agree that only the very top grade of ingredients should be used. Malt is invariably of the pale "white" variety, and contemporary diatribes about the evil noxiousness of "smoak" make it clear that there would have been little of it evident in a well-made beer. Hops, too, were of the best quality, which in England has long meant East Kent Goldings. An instructive commercial example is J.W. Lee's Harvest Ale, made solely from the two aforementioned ingredients. Considering its utterly simplistic recipe, it is a beer of startling depth, and an object lesson for a brewer at any level. Of course its name bears directly on our subject here.

These English strong beers were well-aged. William Harrison observed in 1587, "The beer that is used at noblemen's tables in their fixed and standing houses is commonly of a year old, or peradventure of two year's running or more, but this is not general." This pattern continued as long as the house-breweries did. Typically the beer was brewed in October, fermented for a month or so, then transferred into barrels where it was stoppered loosely, then closed up tight when activity ceased. Often the bung had to be loosened the next summer as fermentation restarted in the warm weather.

In the late seventeenth century, as England and France tangled again, taxes on hops, malt, and other aspects of brewing were rearranged, which had the effect of reducing the relative cost of hops, up to that time fairly high. This put the final nail in the coffin of the old style sweetish "ales," sparking a rage for hoppy beers.

Every imaginable scheme for using hops was employed, and it is clear that there was a lot of variation in resulting bitterness. If we're going to use the high hop quantities called for in the old recipes, it is a good idea to use them in a less efficient way, like charging a hop back or adding a healthy portion of them at the end of the boil.

All the old texts stress the importance of cleanliness, no mean task when everything is made of wood. Scrubbing and scalding seem to have been the primary weapons in their fight. Any English ale yeast will serve, as long as it has the ability to handle a relatively high gravity wort. I would recommend making up as large a starter as you can manage.

Beer fermented in wood will inevitably show some wild character from microorganisms living therein, but it is clear from numerous references that sour beer was not a thing of beauty. Harrison, again: "...each one coveting to have the [beer] stale as he may, so that it not be sour, and his bread new as possible, so that it not be hot." A taste of Gale's Prize Old Ale or Greene King Strong Suffolk Ale will reveal hints of the "horsey" *Brettanomyces* character that usually accompanies wood aging of beer.

There are a couple of ways to achieve the wood-aged character. One is to add a *Brettanomyces* or mixed lambic starter after you rack to the secondary, or some months before bottling. These are slow-moving organisms and take a few months to make an impact, but they will continue to get stronger as the months and years go by. Another method would be to inoculate a gallon or so of beer with the wild stuff, wait a few months, then pasteurize by heating to 150° F (65.5° C) for half an hour, then allow it to cool and add to the beer before bottling. The easiest solution would be to add a bottle or two of a beer such as Rodenbach, which will contribute a slight tang and a noseful of wild, wood-aged character, but that is definitely cheating.

The earliest real recipe I have is from Gervaise Markham, *The English Housewife*, published in 1615:

> "Now for the brewing of the best March beer you shall allow to a hogshead thereof a quarter of the best malt well ground: then you shall take a peck of pease, half a peck of wheat, and half a peck of oats and grind them all very well together, and mix them with your malt: which done, you shall in all points brew this beer as you did the former ordinary beer; only you shall allow a pound and a half of hops to this one hogshead: and whereas before you drew but two sorts of beer, so now shall you draw three; that is a hogshead of the best, and a hogshead of the second, and half a hogshead of small beer without any augmentation of hops or malt."

In a 5-gallon batch, this works out to 19 pounds (8.6 kilograms) of pale malt, plus 10 ounces (283 grams) each of unmalted wheat, oats, and split peas. Hops comes to 1.75 ounces (50 grams) for the batch.

I have a number of later recipes that have certain similarities, but rather than aver-

Remedies for Soured Beer in 18th Century England

Chalk
Beechwood ashes
Ivory shavings
Crab eyes
Deer horn
Calcined tortoise shells
Alkalized coral
Ground oyster shells

RECIPE   Dragon's Milk October Beer

Yield: 5 gallons (19 liters)

Gravity: 1.088 (21 °P)

Alcohol/vol: 7.3 to 8.4%

Color: Golden amber

Bitterness: 74 IBU

Yeast: Alcohol-tolerant English ale

Maturation: 6 to 12 months

All-Grain Recipe:

10.0 lb (4.53 kg)	72%		Maris Otter pale malt

No Equivalent Extract Recipe

Hops:

3.0 oz (85 g)	90 min	East Kent Goldings (5% AA)
2.0 oz (57 g)	30 min	East Kent Goldings (5% AA)
2.0 oz (57 g)	end of boil	East Kent Goldings (5% AA)

RECIPE   My Old Flame Barley Wine

Thanks to my original brewing partner, Ray Spangler, for allowing me to share this recipe with you.

Yield: 5 gallons (19 liters)

Gravity: 1.091 (22 °P)

Alcohol/vol: 7.3 to 8.4%

Color: Deep copper, 18 SRM

Bitterness: 107 IBU

Yeast: Alcohol-tolerant English ale

Maturation: 8 to 12 months

Mash with infusion technique, one-hour rest at 152 to 154° F (66.5 to 68° C). Collect 6 to 7 gallons of wort and boil down to 5 gallons. Add the malt extract during the boil.

All-Grain Recipe:

6.0 lb (2.7 kg)	41%	mild ale or Vienna malt
4.0 lb (1.8 kg)	28%	pale ale malt
3.0 lb (1.4 kg)	21%	pale dried malt extract
1.0 lb (0.45 kg)	7%	40-60°L (medium) crystal malt, preferably imported
0.5 lb (227 g)	3%	biscuit/amber malt

Extract + Mini Mash Recipe:

6.0 lb (2.7 kg)	65%	pale dried malt extract
2.0 lb (0.90 kg)	20%	mild ale or Vienna malt
1.0 lb (0.45 kg)	10%	medium (40-60°L) crystal malt, preferably imported
0.5 lb (227g)	5%	Biscuit (or pale malt, home-roasted 20 min @ 350° F)

Hops:

1.5 oz (46 g)	90 min	Northern Brewer (7% AA)
1.0 oz (28g)	90 min	East Kent Goldings (5% AA)
1.0 oz (28g)	30 min	Northern Brewer (7% AA)
2.5 oz (71 g)	30 min	East Kent Goldings (5% AA)
0.5 oz (14 g)	30 min	Cascade (6% AA)
1.5 oz (46 g)	end of boil	East Kent Goldings (5% AA)
0.5 oz (14 g)	end of boil	Cascade (6% AA)

age them into a detailed October beer recipe, I'm going to give you a little chart of the recipes and their dates and let you select exactly where you want to take this yourself.

"Best quality" malt these days means Maris Otter, a much-prized barley variety cultivated in small quantities in England. Use that if you can get it.

These malt numbers are reduced by about 25 percent from the original recipes to account for the increased yield of modern malt. Mash-in relatively thick, at 1 quart per pound, and try to get a rest temperature of about 153° F (67° C). After an hour, add boiling water to mash out at around 168° F (75.5° C).

October Beer Ingredient Quantities (per 5 gallons)

Date	Author	Lb/kg Malt	Oz/g Hops
1727	Bradley	29/13.2	3.7/105
1748	Bradshaw	29/13.2	9.8/278
1783	Poole	26/11.7	7.4/210

ONE MAJESTIC BEER: IMPERIAL PALE ALE

"Imperial" is a term normally applied to beers that were brewed in Britain, then shipped to the court—the *Imperial* court—of the Russian Empire during the nineteenth century. This obscure but delicious style has nothing to do with that bit of history.

Imperial Pale Ale is a testament to the genius of American brewers of old, and also to American beer marketers, who, like it or not, are the most successful in the world. This willingness to inventively bend beer recipes and names to fit the times continues to this day, evidenced by the vitality of the craft beer scene

I became intrigued by the style from an old book I picked up recently, a privately published paean to Albany, New York brewer John Taylor, printed shortly after his death in 1863. One section, entitled *A Runlet of Ale*, is a long-winded rhyme about the joys of Taylor's ale. Here's a snippet:

> *"Among the ales most famed in story,*
> * From Adam's down—or old or new—*
> *There's none possessing half the glory,*
> * Or half the life of Taylor's brew.*
> *Their 'amber' brand is light and cheery,*
> * Their "XX" is strong though pale,*
> *But give to me, when dull and weary,*
> * Their cream, imperial "Astor" ale."*

Imperial pale ale is a variation of an American ale style called stock ale—strong, hoppy beers designed to be stored some time before drinking. The Wahl Henius *American Handy Book* (1901) lists these at somewhere between 16 and 19 °P, or 1.066 to 1.079 O.G. Hopping was high at 2 to 3 pounds per barrel, or 1 to 1.5 ounces per gallon, not including the dry hops. This calculates out at about 70 to 100 IBU—lip-peelingly bitter. As a warped point of reference, British Burton ales of the day were hoppier still, at an astonishing 3.5 to 4 pounds per barrel!

The addition of up to 25 percent sugar was the rule with stock ales. Dumped in the kettle with the last hop addition, sugar reduced the flavor intensity as well as the

Brewery Trade Card, c. 1900

The term "Imperial" was frequently applied to a brewery's more luxurious products.

RECIPE — Running Dog Imperial Pale Ale

Yield: 5 gallons (19 liters)

Gravity: 1.076 (18 °P)

Alcohol/vol: 6 to 7%

Color: Tawny gold

Bitterness: 85 IBU

Yeast: Alcohol-tolerant English ale

Maturation: 4 to 6 months

Ferment at 65 to 70° F (18.5 to 21° C) with your favorite British-style yeast, and add the dry hops when you rack to the secondary, or into your keg. If at all possible, try to age this beer for six months or more before consuming. A beer like this will age very gracefully, turning into something genuinely royal by about its fifth birthday. Dosing it with a *Brettanomyces* culture would lend an authentic touch if you plan on aging it for more than six months.

All-Grain Recipe:

7.5 lb (3.4 kg)	58%	American two-row Pilsener malt
4.0 lb (1.8 kg)	31%	British pale ale malt
1.5 lb (0.68 kg)	11%	turbinado or demerara sugar, added to the kettle

Extract + Steeped Grain Recipe:

6.25 lb (2.8 kg)	69%	pale dry malt extract
1.0 lb (0.45 kg)	11%	Cara-Pils malt
0.75 lb (340 g)	8%	Pale crystal malt
1.0 lb (0.45 kg)	11%	turbinado or demerara sugar, added to the kettle

Hops:

1.5 oz (43 g)	90 min	Cluster (7% AA)
0.75 oz (22 g)	30 min	Cluster (7% AA)
1.0 oz (28 g)	30 min	Goldings (U.S.-grown) (4.5% AA)
1.25 oz (35 g)	10 min	Goldings (U.S.-grown) (4.5% AA)
0.75 oz (22 g)	in secondary	Goldings (U.S. or East Kent)

bottom line. This is a good thing, as some sugar in the recipe keeps strong beers from being overwhelmingly rich and malty, making them lighter on the palate and reasonably quaffable.

Fermentation of stock ale was with ale yeast, at a fairly high 70° F (21° C), which would have produced a beer with some seriously fruity aromatics.

Of late, this style has been re-crafted by at least a couple of small breweries in this country. Rogue, in Salem, Oregon brews an Imperial India Pale Ale. Big, at 1.083 (20 °P), and satisfyingly hoppy at 53 IBU, it's aged nine months before leaving the brewery. Their "I2PA" is brewed with two-row Pipkin pale malt, Saaz, Cascade, and Northwest Golding hops. Three Floyds Brewery of Munster, Indiana brews another pretty satisfying one, with a blast of hops just about countered by a massive malt profile. It's an experience.

DOBLE-DOBLE

This is a technique used as early as Elizabethan times (and possibly earlier) for the production of strong beers. At times brewers were forbidden to brew them, as they were considered wasteful of malt and men alike. The process is straightforward. A mash is made as for a normal beer, then the runoff wort, instead of being boiled, is heated to strike temperature and then used as the liquor for a second mash. This concentrates the wort in a way no single mash can, and the resulting worts were usually over 1.010 (24 °P) in gravity.

During the eighteenth and nineteenth centuries, strong brews were produced in private house breweries to celebrate special events. A double beer might be brewed at the birth of a son, then saved and savored when he reached his majority.

"Now Double Ale or Beer is the two first Worts, used in the place of Liquor, to Mash again on Fresh Malt, and then doth it only extract the Sweet, the Friendly, Balsamick Qualities there-from, its Hunger being partly satisfied before, whereby its Particles are rendered globical, so as to defend themselves from Corruption, for being thus being brewed it may be transported to the Indies, retaining its full Goodness…"

—William Worth, 1692

RECIPE — Ignoble Doble-Doble

Yield: 5 gallons (19 liters)

Gravity: 1.120 (29 °P)

Alcohol/vol: 9 to 10.5%

Color: Pale gold

Bitterness: 72 IBU

Yeast: Alcohol-tolerant English ale

Maturation: 8 to 12 months

All-Grain Recipe:

20.0 lb (9.1 kg)	90%	Maris Otter pale malt
2.0 lb (0.90 kg)	9%	biscuit/Amber malt

No equivalent extract recipe, but 13 lb (5.9 kg) of dry extract will get you up to the same strength

Hops:

4.0 oz (113 g)	90 min	East Kent Goldings (5% AA)
3.0 oz (85 g)	30 min	East Kent Goldings (5% AA)
2.0 oz (57 g)	end of boil	East Kent Goldings (5% AA)
2.0 oz (57 g)	end of boil	East Kent Goldings (5% AA)

Divide the grain into two equal parts, and load one half into the mash tun. Mash in with 1.5 quarts of hot water per pound (0.64 liters per kilogram) for a mash temperature of 152° F (66.5° C). Mash for one hour. After recirculating the cloudy wort until it runs clear, run off the wort. Sparge with just enough hot water to collect 4 gallons and run it into the kettle. Heat back up to strike temperature. In the meantime, clean out the mash tun and recharge it with the remaining half of the grist. Repeat the mashing procedure, and sparge to collect 6 gallons of wort.

There will still be some recoverable extract in the grain. The English would typically "cap" the mash with more (2 pounds, or 0.90 kilograms) biscuit malt and run off a normal session ale, and you can do this if you like.

TOWARD A PORTLIKE BEER

Some of the old brewing books mention a skin-forming *kamm* yeast, especially in regard to the *dictbiers* (thick beers) such as *danziger jopenbier* (see p. 254), although I can't find a normal drinking beer that employed it. The word kamm literally means "comb," as Bosco's brewer Fred Scheer told me, because it may be skimmed off the surface with a combing motion. The word also means "crest," as in the comb on a rooster, and these yeasts do indeed form a film on the surface.

Some of the more adventurous beers being made are almost port-like—Cuvée de Tomme from Pizza Port's Tomme Arthur comes to mind. Why not close the loop and introduce yeasts that will add the wonderful nutlike aroma found in port and sherry? Well, here we give it a shot. Just so you know, this recipe is strictly experimental, and if complicated beers turn you off, you might as well turn the page right now.

We're going to brew a strong ruby-colored wort using an old Kulmbach mashing technique that will produce a rather under-attenuated beer. Because we're going to expose the beer to oxidative conditions later, and because dark malt melanoidins can be involved in these oxidation reactions, potentially producing cardboardy flavors, we're going to get much of our color from cooked sugar, perfectly traditional for beers such as the sour Flanders red ales. We'll be adjusting the acidity and alcohol levels and finally fermenting with sherry yeast and warm-aging it with a large amount of headspace, then bottling it uncarbonated, like wine. Goofy enough for you?

This will be a 2.5-gallon (9.5-liter) recipe.

Let's start with the cooked sugar. Take a pound of ordinary refined white sugar and place it in a heavy saucepan or skillet with one-fourth cup (60 milliliters) of water over medium heat. Allow the sugar to melt. At a certain point the water will boil away and the temperature of the sugar will start to rise. If you must stir, do so gently to avoid recrystallizing the sugar. After several minutes you will notice the color start to change. At this point, keep a careful watch on it, as the color change will happen more rapidly. The sugar will start to smoke as it darkens, but keep going. When it reaches the color of light molasses, you're done. It will have a taste like toasted marshmallows. At this point you can either dump it into your brew pot or into a pan lined with nonstick foil to let it harden for later use. It will keep indefinitely.

If you're using extract, try to find a brand that has a low proportion of fermentables—under 70 percent. And as always, freshness is very important in liquid extract. You'll need 11 pounds (5 kilometers) of liquid, or 9.5 pounds (4.3 kilograms) of dry. At the start of the boil, there should be 3 gallons (11.4 liters) in the kettle.

For the mashed version:

6.0 lb (2.7 kg)	Pils malt
6.0 lb (2.7 kg)	Munich malt

The mash procedure is one that was used to produce very full, rich-tasting beers. The malt is mashed in with 122° F (50° C) water—let's say 1.25 quarts per pounds (0.53 liters per kilogram). A little (0.5 to 1 gallon, or 2 to 4 liters) boiling water is added to bring the temperature up to 130 to 132° F (54.5° C), and then the mash is allowed to rest for half an hour. At this point, a couple of gallons (8 liters) of liquid from the mash is run off into the kettle and given a fifteen-minute boil, and then returned to the kettle, where it should bring the mash up to 162° F (72° C), the high end of the mashing range. After another half an hour, the mash is drained normally, and 3 gallons of wort is run off into the kettle and boiled. Because of the small batch size and desired high gravity, we will not be sparging.

To the kettle add the cooked sugar and 1.5 ounces (43 grams) of Northern Brewer hops (figured as whole; use 1 ounce or 28 grams if pellets). We are strictly looking for bitterness here and not a lot of aroma character. Boil for an hour, then cool and pitch the sherry yeast. I recommend you use Vierka liquid sherry yeast. If your shop doesn't carry this obscure item, just do a search and you'll come up with an Internet supplier. Dried sherry yeasts are also available.

Conduct the primary at room temperature, between 68 and 72° F (20 to 22° C). When it settles down, rack it into another carboy, and add the following ingredients for adjustment:

2.0 oz (118 ml) food grade lactic acid (80 percent) or equivalent

Alcohol, your choice of:

> 16.0 oz (473 ml) 90 proof spirits
> 35.0 oz (1.0 L) 90 proof vodka, unflavored schnapps
>   or Irish whiskey
> 40.0 oz (1.2 L) 80 proof, ditto

These adjustments should give the yeast conditions suitable for the sherry *flor* to form on the surface, which helps with the development of the nutty, pleasantly oxidized flavors we're looking for. At this time you can add a small handful of toasted French or Hungarian oak cubes (www.stavin.com) if you like. Move the carboy to a warm place—an attic or a furnace room, because contrary to normal practice, we're trying to oxidize the wine. Aging under these conditions should take from six months to a year. If you want to get your acidity naturally, you can use whatever Belgian wild yeast mix strikes your fancy instead of the lactic acid, but I would expect this would add six months or more to the whole process.

After this time, it should be bottled without carbonation. A beer of this complexity and strength should be a candidate for long aging, and just like homebrewers and fine port, only improves with age.

Beyond Barley (STICKY STUFF AND HOW TO DEAL WITH IT)

A waiter pours a highly carbonated weissbier into an immense glass in nineteenth-century Berlin.

One needn't brew by barley alone. Any starchy grain or tuber will serve as an ingredient in beer, even if it would produce a pretty strange brew on its own. Throughout history brewers have used whatever cereals they could lay their hands on: maize in the New World; millet in Africa; rice in Asia; rye and oats in the North; and, of course, all of the various grasses from the Fertile Crescent—barley, wheat, spelt, and others.

In the modern world, barley is what we've settled on, and it does have a lot going for it. But adjuncts can give you some additional tricks in your bag. Most may be used in small quantities to lend a little texture and improve the head, and for such uses, they can be simply tossed into the mash tun.

In larger proportions, adjunct grains require special brewing techniques. Most adjunct grains are not readily available in malted form, which means unless you want to malt them yourself, you'll have to deal with them unmalted. This means a more intensive cooking process, often with some boiling of the grain, and careful formulation of the rest of the grain bill to make sure there are sufficient enzymes to convert all the starch in the mash tun, as the unmalted grains won't be helping with this. Additionally, most adjunct grains are threshed free of their protective husks, which means that a filtering aid such as rice hulls will be needed.

Most have less assertive flavors than barley malt. Corn and rice are particularly bland, but in large amounts they do lend a certain character—consider the difference between Bud (rice) and Miller (corn). Rye is particularly zippy, with a peppery spiciness. Oats are pretty bland unless toasted lightly, when a lovely cookie-like aroma develops, although in either state they contribute an oily viscosity that's hard to miss.

All of the grains with a decent protein level—everything but rice and maize—also aid in head retention, and this is one of the more common uses for them. A typical proportion for this is 2 to 5 percent of a recipe.

WHEAT

Wheat is the most important grain next to barley, at least in the Western tradition. Three forms existed in the ancient world: emmer, einkorn, and spelt. Emmer gave rise to durum wheat, mostly used in pasta; the bread wheat we know today derives from a cross between spelt and einkorn. Einkorn is an ancient variety cultivated widely beginning about 7600 B.C.E. in Asia Minor before spreading quickly through Europe. In its ancient form, einkorn, like barley, did not thresh free of its hulls and had a weaker form of gluten than emmer or spelt, making it less suitable for bread. Both of these characteristics would have been likely to make it a better ingredient for brewing. It was soon displaced from the mainstream by the better-yielding wheats, but has been cultivated by peasants in the backwaters right up to the present.

Wheat has a more limited growing range than barley, and at times in history there has been tension between the two grains, with the brewing of wheat beer being restricted so as not to limit the supplies available for baking bread. Or, as in Bavaria,

American Adjunct Mash Procedure

This was developed in the late nineteenth century as a way of using corn and rice as inexpensive adjuncts for mainstream American lager beer. The process is still used today by industrial brewers around the world.

This mash will work with recipes of up to about 60-percent unmalted adjuncts, which can be corn, rice, wheat, oats, rye, or anything else, the remainder being barley malt. At higher adjunct levels (40 percent and over), you should consider using some—or all—six-row malt, as it has higher enzyme levels than two-row.

In addition to your mash tun, you will need a vessel large enough to cook all of your unmalted grain plus a pound or two of malted barley. Since this stuff wants to stick and burn, you are better off with an aluminum pot rather than a stainless one. Or you might go for a sort of brewer's "flame tamer" and place a thick sheet (1/8" to 1/4") of aluminum, brass, or copper on the burner beneath your pot to distribute the heat. This works like a dream with flat-bottomed pots. Keeping the adjunct mash fairly liquid (2 to 3 quarts per pound) also helps to avoid scorching.

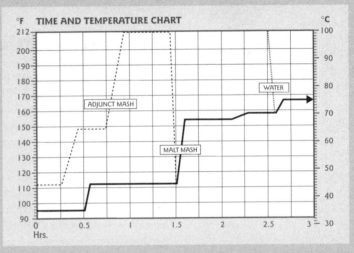

The process involves raising up the unmalted grain through the normal series of temperature rests to do whatever sort of conversions are possible on the way to boiling. See the chart for specifics. This should be done on a stove and monitored closely. Frequent, gentle stirring is advised. Once the various rests are finished, the mash should be brought to a gentle boil that should be held for about fifteen minutes. This adjunct mash is then glorped into the malt mash, which should be waiting at protein rest temperature—122° F. You might want to mix in no more than two-thirds of your adjunct mash at first, then stir it up and see what the rest temperature will be. You will be shooting for a saccharification temperature that will vary according to your recipe. If it looks like adding the whole boiling adjunct portion will overshoot the temperature, then add as much as you can and allow the rest to cool, or force it down with some cool water.

At the end of saccharification, add the rice hulls or wheat husks, mash out by adding hot water until you hit 170 to 180° F, and finally sparge as you would any mash.

it was held as the exclusive privilege of royalty, limiting its consumption through a monopoly.

The qualities that make it so great for baking bread—naked kernels and lots of gluten—make wheat a challenge to deal with in the brewery. Wheat may be malted just like barley, and contains everything you need to make a fine beer on its own. There are many classic styles showcasing this grain.

In the glass, wheat's abundant protein gives beer a soft, creamy texture without the sweetness added by barley malt. As a result, wheat beers can be both substantial

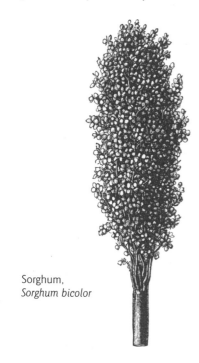

Sorghum,
Sorghum bicolor

Rye,
Secale cereale

and refreshing. These qualities have been exploited by brewers of low-gravity styles like Berliner weisse for a quenching beer that can be quaffed in large quantities without tasting thin and watery.

Wheat beers can be made in any strength including wheat wine, but I find that wheat ages quickly and doesn't have the staying power of barley-based beers. It tastes good—just don't let it sit around too long.

Malted wheat is available through the usual homebrewing channels, and unmalted soft wheat is sold at your local hippie food market. There are two types suitable for brewing: a red, rolled variety, usually with small corrugations pressed into it; and a large, soft, white whole-kernel variety. Both work fine, and may also be identified by a low protein content (under 13 percent). Often this is posted at the shop, but is also indicated by a chalky opacity, as opposed to a flinty or waxy translucency found in higher-protein types.

ADJUNCT GRAINS FOR BREWING

Unmalted grain yields relatively little character when mashed with a standard infusion mash. Something a little more vigorous is needed to coax out the wheatiness, and the classic American adjunct mash (see sidebar) seems to do the trick nicely. It's a little more complex than an infusion, but well worth the effort if you want to use raw grains in any quantity over about 10 percent. If you are short on time, you can skip the preliminary ramp-up and just go right to boiling the grain. It's still better than adding raw wheat to an infusion mash.

All unmalted grains should be ground to a kind of grits texture, as there's no fear of mincing the husks as with barley malt. I use a separate mill for this, a pin-mill coffee grinder from an old grocery store. It does an abominable job on malt, but it's great for this when screwed down to the tightest setting.

Two other things will make your life as an adjunct brewer bearable. First, use rice hulls as a filter aid when sparging. These can be stirred into your mash at the beginning or the end, and they make a huge difference. One pound of hulls for every 5 pounds of adjunct is about right. Wheat husks or other similar materials will work just as well if you come across them. Second, be sure to keep the mash nice and hot while sparging—above 165° F, (but below 180° F or 82° C). This will help keep things liquefied and flowing; the bed can start to gel at lower temperatures making sparging tortuously slow. Add boiling water at the end of saccharification to mash out at 170° F.

Also be aware that the high levels of protein in most unmalted adjuncts will form a haze in your beer, most noticeably when chilled. It's not a big deal for most homebrewers, and after a few weeks in the fridge it will settle out. But if you want a cold yet crystal clear beer, you'd best leave out the wheat, or plan on filtering the beer.

CLASSIC BAVARIAN WEIZEN

Few pleasures can top a luminous vase of weissbier, quaffed amidst the hop-dappled light of a quiet beer garden. And if it's a weissbier you have brewed yourself, the pleasure is doubled.

Adjunct Grains Used in Brewing

GRAIN	COMMENTS & DESCRIPTION
AMARANTH *Amaranthus caudatus*	A New World grain, sacred to the Maya, Aztec, and Inca. Made up of 15 to 17 percent protein, 7 percent oil, and gluten-free. Strong, nutty herb taste, a little like buckwheat. Three times more fiber than wheat, which generally spells trouble when sparging.
BARLEY (unmalted) *Hordeum species*	Nearly flavorless grain used as a cheap adjunct at times in Britain. Also can function as an aid to head retention (5 percent of batch).
BUCKWHEAT (kasha) *Fagopyrum esculentum*	Central Asian origin, but brought to America by Dutch settlers. Not related to wheat, but to sorrel and rhubarb. Made up of 12 percent protein. Gluten-free. Buckwheat has a fairly strong aroma due in some part to the presence of capric and capryllic acids that can contribute sweaty or goaty aromas. It's also relatively high in fat that may eventually become rancid, so long storage should be avoided. Available in health food stores and ethnic markets specializing in eastern European or Jewish products as both roasted and unroasted *kasha*. A few hundred years ago it was a key ingredient in a popular Dutch black beer. Included in small quantities in some interpretations of white beer. Occasionally added to *kvass* (see p. 247). Not available in malted form.
KAMUT *Triticum turgidum*	Closely related to durum wheat, which means lots of protein and very hard, flinty texture. Not very well suited for beer brewing. It is consumable by people with wheat allergies, so there may be some use along these lines.
MAIZE (corn) *Zea mays*	Originated and domesticated in Mexico or Central America. *Tesgüino*, made from malted corn, and *chicha*, made from unmalted corn and saccharified through the addition of human saliva, usually by chewing the grains before brewing.
MILLET Various species	Several plants fall under this name, the most common of which, *Pennisetum*, or pearl millet, comprises three species: *P. typhoides, P. typhideum,* and *P. americanum.* Millet is the small, round grain familiar to us as parakeet food. It's a hardy crop, more tolerant of heat, drought, and poor soil than most other grains. Other types include: finger millet (*Eleusine coracana*); Proso or common millet (*Panicum miliaceum*); foxtail millet (*Setaria italica*); tef (*Eragosis tef*, a small Ethiopian form sometimes seen in specialty stores); white and black fonio (*Digitaria exilis* and *D. iburia*); and guinea millet (*Brachiaria deflexa*). There are others of lesser importance. Overall, flavor is pretty delicate. Millets have a long-standing role in beer brewing, especially in eastern and southern Africa. *Pombe* (Swahili, meaning "beer") contains an unusual yeast, *Schizosaccharomyces pombe*, used to ferment this indigenous brew. It is reported to product a strong, sulfury nose along with a lot of other disagreeable aromas. *S. pombe* diverged from brewing yeast 1.1 billion years ago. A convenience product made from red millet called King's Brew Beer Powder is sold in South Africa by King Food Corporation, and is used just like our powdered malt extract. Pearl millet averages around 11 percent protein.
OATS *Avena sativa* (less commonly *A. byzania*)	Used in unmalted form as an adjunct to barley malt beers, where it adds a thick, somewhat oily texture, and as an aid in head retention. May contribute some chill haze so not a good choice for beers that will be served cold. Comprised of 16 percent protein and lots of gums, so sparging can be difficult. For most recipes oats are used as 5 to 10 percent of the grist. The "instant" product is precooked and has the smallest flakes; rolled and old fashioned are also pre-cooked. All may be added directly to the mash. Other forms need precooking.

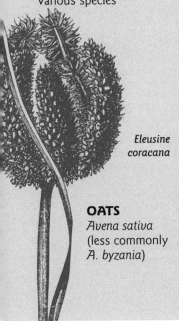

Eleusine coracana

Adjunct Grains Used in Brewing

NAME	COMMENTS & DESCRIPTION
OAT MALT *Avena sativa*	An antique sort of product. Widely used in pre-industrial Britain, oat malt is used to make oatmeal stout, and as a head-improving adjunct in paler beers. Less intense in character than raw oats, it is also much easier to deal with in the brewery. Protein levels are lower (10.5 percent), and malting does deal with some of the goopy stuff. Oat malt diastase contains mostly beta amylase, which means it will produce more fermentable worts than barley malt. Oat malt has the husk attached, making the use of rice hulls unnecessary. Oats were usually used to brew weak beers that were consumed quickly. Edinborough and Yorkshire were noted for their oat ales in the eighteenth and nineteenth centuries.
QUINOA *Chenopodium quinoa*	Played an important role in the diet of the Incas—who called it the "mother grain"—and other Andean people. Not a grass as are many other grains, quinoa is related to spinach and beets. At 13-percent protein, which is present in a highly complete form, quinoa is a highly nutritious food, and is quite delicious. It is free of gluten, and some recent efforts have been focused on its use as the basis of a commercial beer for that special dietetic market. There is some traditional use in beermaking, especially as an adjunct to *chicha*, which is largely made from various types of maize.
RICE *Oryza sativa*	Familiar wet-cultivated grain crop, the solid base of the food pyramid in Asia. Long tradition of rice beer (saké) and spirits in east Asia. Use in beer began in the United States and Britain in the nineteenth century as an inexpensive adjunct. American varieties have been bred largely for the beer industry, and thus have almost no flavor or aroma. Many other more interesting culinary varieties may be found in specialty stores. Basmati has a delicate nutty aroma, almost popcorn-like; Jasmine hints at the flower of the same name; Chinese black is a short grain rice with a deep purple outer layer that retains its color when cooled, and might make for a lovely lavender pils. The North American "wild rice" is not rice at all, as noted later in the chapter.
RICE HULLS	Not an adjunct per se, but the inert outer husks of rice that are used as a lautering aid for sticky or huskless grains such as wheat, rye, or others. One pound of hulls per 5 pounds of adjunct is about right, although you could use more with no harm.
RYE *Secale cereale*	Hardy northern grain capable of growing in regions where few others will. Long association with beer in Russia and Scandinavia, as a grain to turn to in hard times. Sharp, peppery, spicy aromas, with an oily texture due to plenty of sticky glucans, which make lautering a chore. This usually restricts its use to no more than 20 percent of the grist. Malted versions are available in both pale and chocolate roasted (200 to 300 °SRM) versions. Unmalted rye must be cooked before using, and a thirty-minute glucan rest at 95 to 100° F is advisable at the start of the mash to help break down the sticky stuff. Rice hulls as a filtering aid are a must when sparging either type. Be patient.
SORGHUM *Sorghum bicolor*	No fewer than twenty-five species, of which only one, *Sorghum bicolor*, is cultivated. In the United States, the juice is pressed from the cane, then boiled down and sold as a Southern culinary specialty. Sorghum beer is a traditional drink in parts of Africa, such as the *shakparo* beer of Benin. Such beers are widespread in southern Africa, and are made from the malted kernels of the plant rather than the juice of the stalk. Often maize or other ingredients are used as well.

Adjunct Grains Used in Brewing

NAME	COMMENTS & DESCRIPTION
SPELT *Triticum spelta*	Closely related to durum wheat, spelt dates back five thousand years or more. It was mentioned by Saint Hildegard in the twelfth century: "The spelt is the best of grains. It is rich and nourishing and milder than other grain," a fact likely backed by its whopping 16 to 19 percent protein content. In Europe, slightly unripe kernels are harvested and then roasted. Called *Grunkern*, the kernels are used in soups and bread, and are sometimes referred to as "German rice." Spelt does not thresh free like most wheats; it shares this trait with barley. It has been used to brew beer right from the beginning, with a tradition of spelt beer as a commercial product in Holland a few hundred years ago. Revival versions have been made more recently in Holland and Germany. In the mid-nineteenth century in Liège, Belgium (known as the home of the saison style) a beer was brewed from 42 percent malted spelt and 58 percent raw wheat. This would undoubtedly be a goopy beer to brew, and immensely cloudy, but such is the way of tradition. Weyermann produces a chocolate spelt malt at 450 to 700 °EBC (175 to 250 °L) but it may be hard to find. Otherwise, if you want spelt malt, you'll have to make it yourself. It should malt very much like barley.
TRITICALE *Triticum secale*	A cross between durum wheat and rye developed in the 1930s to combine the hardiness of rye with the yield and quality of wheat. Made up of 10 to 13 percent protein. Widely cultivated in Western Canada, and primarily used for animal feed. Malted triticale flakes are sold industrially by Edme, although they are not generally available as malt. A recent study showed that triticale is actually well suited as a brewing adjunct, with an insignificant increase in wort viscosity at up to 30 percent triticale in a recipe, which means it won't make you crazy-outta-your-mind trying to sparge it as rye is guaranteed to do. Flaked triticale is available through health food channels.
WHEAT (unmalted) *Triticum aestivus*	Common wheat is the adjunct of choice for making witbiers and lambics, but is not central to any other styles. More intense in wheat character than malted wheat, it is also more difficult to lauter, but can be useful in adding a sense of firm body and as an aid in head retention, qualities often sought in very lightweight beers. If used in quantities over 10 percent, raw wheat should be mashed with an adjunct mash procedure, or at the very least cooked until tender before adding to the mash, and rice hulls really help. Two sorts are generally available at health food stores: a flaked red type; and a large, soft white in whole kernel form.
WHEAT MALT	The most familiar high-quality brewing adjunct, the use of wheat in brewing is quite ancient. Readily malted, wheat adds a certain firm texture—which can be quite milkshake-like in large quantities—without the kind of heavy sweetness that barley malt adds. Malted wheat does contain enough enzymes to convert itself, making 100 percent wheat beer a theoretical possibility. The lack of husk and abundance of sticky gluten make sparging difficult, but this can be dealt with by using good lautering technique and plenty of rice hulls. Very low in aroma compared to barley malt.
WHEAT (torrified)	Unmalted wheat that has been rapidly heated until the kernels puff up like popcorn. This gelatinizes the starch and eliminates the need for pre-cooking. Most varieties are very pale in color, but I have seen amber-colored versions.
WILD RICE *Zizania aquatica*	Not a rice, but a native annual grass that thrives in marshy northern regions of North America. Very dense and slow cooking, it has a pleasant walnut flavor. Protein is high at about 14 percent, but it doesn't seem to have a lot of glucans or other complex carbohy-

Adjunct Grains Used in Brewing

NAME	COMMENTS & DESCRIPTION
WILD RICE (continued)	drates that cause slow or stuck sparges. Grind to grits and cook before brewing. Broken grain sells for a much lower price than whole because of its cosmetically challenged state, but since you're just going to grind it up anyway, it's the better choice for brewing. Wild rice is a good mystery grain for an English-style bitter, as it can add a subtle nuttiness that's hard to achieve otherwise.

W H E A T   T Y P E S

Hard Red Winter Wheat High in protein and strong in gluten, mainly used for bread. Widely grown in western states.

Hard Red Spring Wheat High in protein, similar to winter wheat, but suited to different agricultural conditions, especially the short growing season in northern states. Mainly used for bread, but also made into brewers malt.

Hard White Wheat Hard White Wheat has been grown in Kansas, California, and Montana. In recent years, much more research has been invested in hard white wheat so look for an increase in the production of this class of wheat. Sometimes available as brewers malt.

Soft Red Winter Wheat The most commonly grown wheat east of the Mississippi. Low in protein, it is used in cakes, crackers, pastries, and makes a fine material for brewing.

Soft White Wheat Mainly grown in the Pacific Northwest, but also in the upper Midwest. Similar protein levels and uses as soft red. Also good for brewing.

Durum Wheat The hardest wheat, mainly used to make pasta. Too much protein for brewing.

Einkorn Primitive wheat form from ancient times. A little more protein than modern wheat, but weak gluten. Being investigated for suitability as organic crop in Europe, but not widely available.

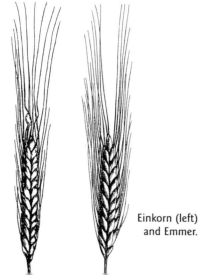

Einkorn (left)
and Emmer.

Weizen is not the easiest beer in the world to brew. During the long, slow process, it often picks up additional descriptors, as in "I brewed a *damn* wheat beer last weekend." Soft and subtle enough to amplify all flaws, the brewing challenge is provided by the naked, glutinous, enzyme-poor kernels. But if you go into it prepared, with eyes wide open and perhaps a magic ingredient in your bag of tricks, that refreshing glass of homebrewed wheat beer can be easily within your grasp.

Wheat beer has as long and glorious history as beer itself, and there isn't space to do it justice here. In the late medieval era, wheat beers were popular along the North Sea coast, and were exported widely. In the seventeenth century, a taste for wheat beer spread south to Bavaria and caught like wildfire among the royalty there, and it is this interpretation that is the most widespread today.

A well-made *Suddeutsche weizen*, more frequently referred to as a *weissbier*, is a pale, top-fermented beer of ordinary strength, made with between 50 and 60 percent malted wheat, lightly hopped, and usually unfiltered. Variations include a deep amber dunkelweizen and a tawny, intense-yet-quaffable weizenbock—one of the loveliest ways to overdo it that has ever been invented. A unique yeast strain is used for all, imparting a clove-like phenolic aroma often tinged with bubblegum, banana, and/or vanilla notes. This yeast is absolutely critical to achieving an authentic Bavarian weissbier taste.

For extract brewers, dealing with wheat is as simple as opening a package of wheat extract, but for grain brewers it is more complicated. A wheat beer recipe is a complex balancing act of flavors, enzymes, proteins, and inert husks needed for successful lautering. My life took a dramatic turn for the better due to the availability of rice hulls at my local homebrew store. These little slivers of joy might as well be called "Sparge Magic." They turn wheat brewing from sheer drudgery to total delight, and actually make *any* mash easier to sparge.

Weissbier was very popular in this country in the late 1800s.

Wheat doesn't possess an overabundance of starch-converting enzymes, but it does have enough to convert itself. The barley malt that makes up the other half should be of a pale color, and should be chosen for the quality of its flavor. I usually do as the Germans do and use a German Pils malt.

Start with a glucan rest at 95 to 100° F (which should make sparging easier), then step up to a protein rest for thirty to sixty minutes at about 122° F. Some brewers replace that with a rest at 111 to 113° F (44 to 45° C) to emphasize production of ferulic acid, a precursor to the signature clove-scented chemical 4-vinyl guiacol. A single or double decoction mash is traditional for weizen production, and as usual, it heightens malty grain-derived flavors. If you are using a basic infusion mash, near-

---

RECIPE	Garden of Wheat'n Bavarian Weizen

Yield: 5 gallons (19 liters)

Gravity: 1.053 (13 °P)

Alcohol/vol: 4.2 to 4.9%

Color: Pale gold

Bitterness: 14 IBU

Yeast: Bavarian Weizen

Maturation: 4 to 6 weeks

The beer may be served cloudy, or as the Germans say "Mit hefe" (that's "hay-fuh" to you). Or, you can filter or let it settle naturally for a nice *kristal*. Either way, it's heaven in a glass.

All-Grain Recipe:

4.75 lb (2.2 kg)	49%	wheat malt
3.75 lb (1.7 kg)	35%	six-row lager malt
1 lb (0.45 kg)	16%	Munich malt
1 lb (0.45 kg)	—	rice hulls

Extract + Steeped Grain Recipe:

6.25 lb (2.84 kg)	93%	liquid wheat malt extract
1.5 lb (0.68 kg)	7%	dry pale malt extract

Hops:

0.5 oz (14 g)	60 min	Tettnang (4% AA)
1.0 oz (28 g)	30 min	Tettnang hops (4% AA)
0.5 oz (14 g)	end of boil	Tettnang hops (4% AA)

Try to maintain fermentation temperature between 60 and 67° F. It can go warmer, but the yeast may produce excessive amounts of fruitiness and other intrusive flavors. Carbonation should be on the high side; I recommend 6 ounces per 5 gallons of corn sugar, or just shy (nine-tenths) of a full cup. If you're gassing up the draft, get as much carbonation as you can without excessive foaming. Somewhere around 15 psi is probably about right.

Marketers are always looking to class up their products, this time with an...uh...elf?

A distinct style of weissbier with aspirations to the famous bubbly was once popular in Germany.

Brewery Sign, c. 1910

This shows the pale color and the improbably long-necked traditional bottle.

boiling water can be added after the glucan and protein rests to raise the mash temperature up to the next step.

I usually hold off adding the rice hulls until I'm ready to set the bed for sparging.

Tettnangs are usually my hop of choice, as their delicate spiciness comes through without imparting any heavy, resiny tastes to the beer. The newer variety Santiam would also be appropriate, although its higher alpha acid content means lower quantities should be used. Any German-style hop would be an authentic choice, but remember, this is not a beer built upon hops. Just a little spice, a little balance.

I have specified dry malt extracts for this recipe, because they give you the best chance of creating a pale beer. Liquid extracts may be used in 20 to 25 percent greater quantities (to account for the added water), but be sure they are fresh, as malt syrup darkens considerably with age. Domestic extracts seem to be fresher than imported. Ask your homebrew supplier.

GOSEBIER OF JENA

Gose is German white beer that almost disappeared. It has been revived, and at this writing, is even available in the United States. It is a hazy, sourish beer similar to Belgian (Louvain) witbier, brewed from barley and wheat malts plus a small amount of oats. And like witbier, it is lightly hopped and seasoned with coriander. A unique addition is salt, and at certain taverns around Leipzig, Germany, the beer can be ordered at different salt levels. Salt isn't as strange an ingredient as it sounds; it can add a subtle richness or palate-fullness to an otherwise weak or watery beer.

Air-dried malt was the traditional base; this was replaced by kilned Pilsener malt by the mid- to late nineteenth century. Spontaneous fermentation was updated to more reliable pure cultures during the same time period.

Like many weissbiers, gose was primarily a bottled beer, as this works better for highly carbonated beers. As you can see in the picture, the bottle was a highly unusual form with a very long neck. This was the so-called "open gose," in which no attempt to seal the bottle was made, and the bacteria present in the brew actually built up a plug-like mass that rose in the neck and formed a gas-tight seal! Toward 1900 this quaint tradition was replaced by the more modern bail-top closures.

Like Berliner weisse, it is frequently adulterated at serving with raspberry or woodruff syrups, or with Curaçao, cherry, or even caraway (kümmel) liqueurs.

Traditional Beers Using Alternate Grains

Bitter
Corn or rice as cheap filler. Wheat (various forms) as head retention improver.

Berliner Weisse
Sour, lactic beer made from barley malt and between 30 and 40 percent malted wheat plus 60 to 70 percent barley malt.

Chicha
Indigenous maize beer of South America, made from malted maize.

Chang
Indigenous rice beer of Himalayan region.

Gose
White beer from near Leipzig, made with barley (40 percent) and wheat malts (60 percent), and seasoned with coriander and salt. See p. 146.

Kvass
Russian small beer traditionally made from rye bread and lemons, and sold by street vendors. Very low-gravity product with a very short fermentation. Modern, soda-like, no-alcohol versions in large plastic bottles can be found at some ethnic markets. (See p. 247)

Mazamorro
A beer, or more properly a braggot, made from honey and ground corn, brewed by the Nicaro and Chorotega peoples of Nicaragua.

Peetermann
Variant of Leuven witbier, and made dark with the addition of slaked lime (calcium hydroxide). (See p. 208)

Pissionia
A native beer of the Yuma people who lived along the California/Arizona border. It was made by roasting wheat to a light brown color over a charcoal fire, then crushing the kernels and fermenting the mash.

Pombe
East African beer made from millet and fermented with a "fission" yeast, *Schizosaccharomyces pombe*, which is capable of breaking down starch into sugar.

Roggenbier
German specialty beer; made like dunkelweizen, but with some rye instead of wheat.

Sahti
Finnish traditional beer made from barley malt and rye, flavored with juniper. (See p. 244)

Tesgüino
From an Aztec word meaning "heartbeat," this slurry-like beverage is made from malted corn saccharified using the bark or leaves of a large range of plants indigenous to the north and northwest of Mexico where it is prepared.

Weizen
Bavarian beer made from wheat malt (60 percent) and barley malt (40 percent), and fermented with special ale yeast that produces a fruity, clove-like character.

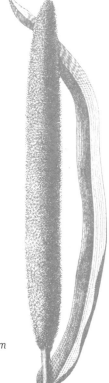

Pearl millet,
Panicum typhoides

Common millet,
Panicum miliaceum

RECIPE   Hose Your Nose Gose

Yield: 5 gallons (19 liters)

Gravity: 1.036 (9 °P)

Alcohol/vol: 3.2%

Color: Pale straw

Bitterness: 10 IBU

Yeast: Bavarian Weizen

Maturation: 3 to 4 weeks

At end of boil, add 0.25 teaspoon salt plus 1 ounce (28 grams) coriander. Ferment with a German weissbier yeast, a little on the cool side, at 62 to 67° F (16.5 to 19.5° C).

All-Grain Recipe:

1.5 lb (0.68 kg)	23%	Pilsener malt
1.0 lb (0.45 kg)	15%	sour malt
3.5 lb (1.59 kg)	54%	wheat malt
0.5 lb (227 g)	8%	unmalted oats (oatmeal)
1.0 lb (0.45 k g)	—	rice hulls

No Equivalent Extract Recipe

Step mash, with rests at 113° F (45° C) and 153° F (67° C). Dilution of 2 quarts per pound. Note that the first batch of hops goes into the mash rather than the boil. Mash-out at 170° F (76.5° C). This gets only a short 45-minute boil.

Hops:

1.0 oz (28 g)	add to mash	Spalt	(4% AA)
0.5 oz (14 g)	45 min	Spalt	(4% AA)

At end of boil, add 0.25 teaspoon salt plus 1 ounce (28 grams) coriander.

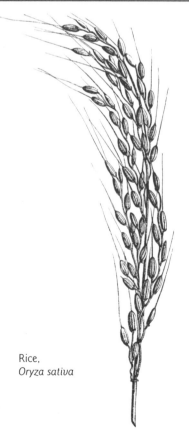

Rice,
Oryza sativa

Indian Popcorn Ale Puffing, or torrefying, grain goes very far back in history, as a way of making hard, flinty grains more palatable. Rapid heating causes an expansion of water within the grain, and the starches are instantly gelatinized and made soluble. There is sometimes a bit of Maillard browning going on as well, which helps add flavor to an otherwise insipid grain. In this recipe, the popcorn is used to thin out and add a dry, crisp texture to an IPA, which might be a little too dense otherwise. An air popper should be used, as the normal popping method with oil would cause problems in the final beer.

Wild Rizen Follow the recipe for Bavarian weizen, but swap out 2 pounds of the malted wheat for 2 pounds of wild rice. Grind the wild rice into grits, then cook it in plain water for thirty to forty-five minutes or until tender. Be aware that the rice will expand greatly as it cooks, so start with a large pot. After it's cooked, add it to the mash. A pint of maple syrup added to the secondary completes the Northern taste.

Wild Rice ESB Many British bitters display a sort of walnut complexity, a result of careful malting of certain varieties of barley. Wild rice here adds a similar nutty depth. Simply substitute 1 pound of cooked wild rice grits for a pound of the pale ale malt in the recipe on p. 79, or simply add it for a slightly stronger beer. Mash an extra half hour. Northdown or some other not-too-pungent hop would be my choice here. Lean toward a dry, high-attenuating English ale yeast for this one.

Triticale Tripel Start with the tripel recipe on p. 125, and substitute 2.5 pounds (1.1 kg) triticale, ground to grits and then precooked. This plays the spiciness of this wheat/rye hybrid right along with the same qualities from the yeast and spices in this strong pale Belgian style beer.

Roggenbier By simply substituting rye malt (unmalted will work if you boil it until tender first) for half the wheat in the weizen recipe (p. 145), and tossing in a half pound of crystal malt of your choosing, you can make a delightfully spicy rye beer. If you want to push the limits a little more, add one-fourth teaspoon of coarsely cracked black pepper or grains of paradise at the very end of the boil. Ferment with a traditional weizen yeast, or an ale yeast of your choosing. A bock version can be made by simply scaling everything up an additional 25 to 50 percent.

Chicago was a lot more than hog butcher to the world. It remains a trading and transport center for grain.

Oatmeal Cookie Ale This is a traditional English brown ale enlivened by the addition of toasted oats, and kept from becoming too thick by the use of a little brown sugar. Use the brown ale recipe on p. 92, and substitute 1 pound (0.45 kg) of rolled oats toasted at 300° F (149° C) until they start to smell like cookies for 1 pound (0.45 kg) of the amber malt. Also add 1 pound (0.45 kg) of dark brown sugar to the kettle. Use the standard infusion mash and fermentation instructions given for the brown ale recipe. If you like, a tiny dash of vanilla and a teaspoon of cinnamon will extend the cookie illusion. This would be a good base if you wanted to experiment with nut flavors like hazelnut, pecan, toasted coconut, or others.

This was concocted by my original brewing partner, Ray Spangler, and me. Wheat softens this burly brew, giving it a chocolate milkshake flavor and texture.

RECIPE	Electric Aunt Jemima Maple Buckwheat Ale		
Yield: 5 gallons (19 liters)	*All-Grain Recipe:*		
Gravity: 1.067 (16 °P)	8.0 lb (3.6 kg)	57%	pale ale malt
Alcohol/vol: 6.3 to 7.1%	1.5 lb (0.68 kg)	10.5%	toasted buckwheat (kasha)*
Color: Tawny amber	1.0 lb (0.45 kg)	7%	biscuit/amber malt
Bitterness: 34 IBU	1.0 lb (0.45 kg)	7%	dark crystal
Yeast: American ale	0.5 lb (227 g)	—	rice hulls
Maturation: 6 to 8 weeks	2.6 lb (1.2 kg)	18.5%	grade "B" maple syrup, added to kettle
Kasha is available at Jewish/Russian grocery stores; toast your own, 20 min at 300°F (149°C).	*No Equivalent Extract recipe*		
	Hops:		
	1.5 oz (43 g)	90 min	Fuggle (5% AA)
	0.75 oz (21 g)	30 min	Fuggle (5% AA)
	0.5 oz (14 g)	end of boil	Saaz (3% AA)
	0.2 oz (4 g)	end of boil	fenugreek seeds, crushed or ground

RECIPE — Amazing Daze American Wheat Ale

This is a cool refresher, with a little more crispness and bite than its German counterpart.

Yield: 5 gallons (19 liters)

Gravity: 1.049 (12 °P)

Alcohol/vol: 4.1 to 4.7%

Color: Pale gold

Bitterness: 23 IBU

Yeast: American ale

Maturation: 4 to 6 weeks

All-Grain Recipe

4.0 lb (1.8 kg)	44.5%	Pilsener malt
4.0 lb (1.8 kg)	44.5%	wheat malt
1.0 lb (0.45 kg)	11%	Munich malt
1.0 lb (0.45 kg)	—	rice hulls

Extract Plus Steeped Grain Recipe:

4.0 lb (1.8 kg)	92%	liquid wheat extract
0.5 lb (227g)	8%	Munich malt

Hops:

0.75 oz (21 g)	60 min	Cascade (6% AA)
1.0 oz (28 g)	15 min	US Tettnang (4.5% AA)

RECIPE — Pink Menace Red Rice Pils

Red rice is a short-grain rice with a deep burgundy hull and a nutty flavor. If you can't find it at your local hippie market, try www.indian-harvest.com.

Yield: 5 gallons (19 liters)

Gravity: 1.046 (11 °P)

Alcohol/vol: 4.3 to 5%

Color: Pinkish gold

Bitterness: 33 IBU

Yeast: American lager

Maturation: 6 to 8 weeks

All-Grain Recipe:

7.5 lb (3.4 kg)	86%	Pils malt
1.25 lb (0.6 kg)	14%	red rice, ground to grits consistency
0.5 lb (227 g)	—	rice hulls

Extract + Mini-Mash Recipe:

3.0 lb (1.4 kg)	48%	pale dry malt extract 1028
2.0 lb (0.90 kg)	32%	U.S. six-row Pils malt
1.25 lb (0.6 kg)	20%	Red rice, ground to grits consistency
0.5 lb (227 g)	—	rice hulls

Hops:

0.75 oz (21 g)	60 min	Mt Hood (7% AA)
1.0 oz (28 g)	20 min	Mt Hood (7% AA)
1.0 oz (28 g)	5 min	Saaz (3% AA)

For both all-grain and mini-mash recipes, grind rice to fine grits consistency, then cook as per package directions (as for eating). Add cooked rice to malt, and use an infusion mash at 150° F (65.5° C). Sparge as usual.

Dick's Elixir Wheat Porter

Yield: 5 gallons (19 liters)

Gravity: 1.073 (17.5 °P)

Alcohol/vol: 5.5 to 6.4%

Color: Ruby brown

Bitterness: 23 IBU

Yeast: English or Scottish ale

Maturation: 8 to 12 weeks

This was concocted by my original brewing partner, Ray Spangler, and me. Wheat softens this burly brew, giving it a chocolate milkshake flavor and texture.

As with all wheat-based beers, it does not bear long aging. Use caution when drinking; this is one seductive beer.

All-Grain Recipe:

5.0 lb (2.3 kg)	35%	wheat malt
4.0 lb (1.8 kg)	28%	Munich malt
3.0 lb (1.4 kg)	21%	six-row lager malt
1.5 lb (0.7 kg)	10%	medium crystal malt
0.5 lb (227 g)	3.5%	flaked oats, toasted @ 300°F/150°C until a light golden brown, and smelling like cookies
6.0 oz (170 g)	3.5%	black patent malt
1.0 lb (0.45 kg)	—	rice hulls

No Equivalent Extract Recipe

Hops:

0.5 oz (14 g)	90 min	Northern Brewer (7% AA)
0.5 oz (14 g)	10 min	Northern Brewer (7% AA)
0.35 oz (10 g)	10 min	Santiam (6.5% AA)

A standard infusion mash (one hour at 152° F or 66.5° C) will work, but you may get more creaminess if you do a protein rest at 122 to 131° F (50 to 55° C) for twenty to thirty minutes. A ninety-minute boil is recommended. For the smoothest taste, use debittered black malt if you can find it.

Use your favorite yeast, but avoid anything too wacky so the simple flavors can shine through the darkness. I like the Fuller's strain of ale yeast for its malt-accentuating qualities. Lager yeast would also do nicely with this one.

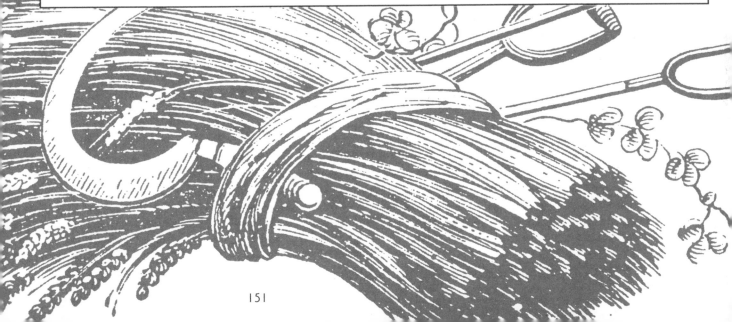

Chapter 12

Hops are Just Another Herb, Mon

Malt, hops, water, yeast, blah, blah, blah. The Bavarians have been pushing their notion of the supposed purity of beer for almost five hundred years now, but by this point in the book it should be clear that there are plenty of legitimate alternatives.

But if we were to be suddenly transported back to the dank, dark days of the Middle Ages, we might be hard pressed to recognize the sour, smoky herbal concoctions served up as beer.

"When we add to this list all the surrogates used in lieu of hops by ancient peoples, such as the konyce of the Sythians, the sorbum acidum of the Thracians, the tamarisk buds of the Tartars, and pine buds by all the Northern folk, and when we consider that dozens of other substitutes, spices, herbs, barks, etc., could be added here, it will be found that the definition of beer as it existed in 'ye good old times' would read somewhat different from what most people, even those more-or-less versed in these matters, would imagine them to be. And these were the ingredients which the fermentarius of mediaeval times and the apothecary of the mediaeval brewer, mingled and jumbled together according to his own sweet will, when preparing his beer. It is from that time, then, the time of official and authoritative control over this drugging campaign in beer, that dates the era of beer sophistication, lasting all through the Middle Ages and well into modern time, the time which neglected no herb or drug, no matter whether harmless or poisonous, in an endeavor to lend some new property or savor to the brew."

—John P. Arnold, 1911

Although this may not be the most appetizing way to describe these ancient brews, a glance into the past can serve as a starting point for a number of interesting and quite delicious beers.

In the long, broad history of beer, the hop is a relative newcomer. Hops began to be used in beer about 1100 C.E. in Europe, and much later in the British Isles. For a few centuries, herbed beers existed side-by-side with hopped beers before they were superseded by more modern fashion and banned by edicts such as the *Reinheitsgebot*.

Many lingered on until fairly recently. During the nineteenth century, spiced beers still lived, albeit in the margins. Heather ale was being brewed in the hills of Scotland; an anise beer called "swankey" was made in Pennsylvania; rustic spiced country brews were slowly winking out in England.

Some survive to this day. A cloudy, delicately spiced Belgian wheat beer called "wit" vanished for a few decades, then was resurrected. In Berlin, the local wheat beer, a light, yogurty brew called weisse, is still commonly served with a dash of syrup made from an herb called woodruff, while in the same region other spiced white ales such as *gose* and *kotbuss* still linger. North into Scandinavia, strong, juniper-tinged beers provide a delicious link to the past for the enthusiastic caretakers of the style.

With the rebirth of craft brewing in the United States and Europe, such exotic beers are again available to the beer aficionado. Anchor Brewing pioneered the renaissance of spiced holiday beers, and now they are brewed by many microbreweries. Pierre Celis single-handedly rescued the witbier style from oblivion. Bruce Williams in Scotland has resurrected a number of Bronze Age-inspired beers with pine, elderberry, and kelp flavorings. A mustard beer is being produced in Belgium.

USING HERBS AND SPICES

You can boil, "dry hop," make hop tea, or use herbal potions to season your brew. If you do boil, throw them in at the very end, or "...it will be just for the neighbors," as Pierre Celis says. Five minutes ought to do it. Hop teas and potions give you the option of controlling the exact dosage of spice to be added to the beer. For hop tea, steep the herbs in water that has just been boiled, then run through a coffee filter. Potions are made by soaking the herbs and spices in vodka for a week or two, dissolving out the essential flavors, then filtering. These last two options really give you much more control over the mix and strength of the spicing. Just add the tea or potion to the beer at bottling, having first conducted a small-scale experiment with a pipette or syringe and a small sample of beer, to test how much of the mixture needs to be added for the best flavor. Scale up this small test to the rest of the batch.

Don't add spices or herbs to the primary fermenter—the vigorous outgassing takes the delicate volatile oils with the CO_2 as the beer ferments.

The following recipes should serve as a starting point, but if you've got a garden full of bog myrtle, by all means make some beer with it. Don't overlook spices like black pepper, which are especially good at enhancing other tastes.

Strive for a mysterious blending of flavors. These beers are best when the individual flavors don't jump out at you. Even with simpler mixtures like coriander and orange in witbier, you can use other spices to add depth and complexity. Watch out for aggressive spices such as ginger and rosemary, which have a tendency to take over a beer unless regulated or counterbalanced by other flavors.

Hop lightly. You may still want to add hops, but they may or may not work with the mixture of spices you have planned. You must consider them as part of the mix.

Boiling spices can be tossed into the boil. Sanitary and safe, but some aromatics may be lost. Right at the end is the best time to add them to preserve aroma and avoid extracting harsh tannic substances that are sometimes present.

Dry hop spices can be added to the beer after primary fermentation has subsided. They may be put into a hop bag if you like.

POTIONS

This technique uses a solvent—alcohol—to solubilize and sterilize the aromatic components of spices and herbs. Many of these are more soluble in alcohol than in water, so this is a highly effective way to add spice, herb flavor, and aroma to a beer. It's easy, it's sanitary, and it's controllable.

- Mix spices with vodka or liqueur and allow to sit for a few weeks or longer.
- Add this to the batch at bottling.
- Test smallest quantities, then increase until taste level seems right.
- Liqueur contains sugar—about 4 to 6 ounces per 750-milliliter bottle.

Stoneware Bottle, c. 1890

These "botanic" brews were more like soda than beer.

Sassafras Extract

Some seasonings are best purchased in a prepared form. This one has the potentially harmful safrole removed.

Walk into your local liquor store and buy a big jug of the cheapest rotgut vodka you can lay your hands on. Not feeling shameful is actually the most difficult part of this flavoring method. More expensive brands may make you feel better (and your wallet lighter), but add nothing in terms of quality. Claiming that it is needed for your child's science project does not seem to take the sting away, either.

Once obtained, with curtains drawn, you can now put this cheap-yet-magical substance to work in the service of brewing. Put the herbs and spices you wish to use into a beaker or wide-mouthed jar. Use a little more than you think you'll actually need for the batch of beer. Measure the quantities of herbs and spices you add so you can repeat the recipe in case you win Best of Show. A gram scale works best, but dry measures will serve just as well. Pour a quantity of vodka over the spices, about double the volume of the seasonings. Cover and allow this to soak for a week or two. After that it doesn't change much.

After a week, taste it, or better yet, add a few drops to a beer. Scrutinize the mixture for balance, flavor, and depth. Now is the time to add more of whatever you think it will take to finesse the mixture. Allow it to sit for a few more days.

The next step is filtration. Pouring through a coffee filter removes nearly all of the spices, leaving just a bit of dusty stuff that settles right out with the yeast in the bottle. I recommend using a funnel with shallow ribs on the inside, designed for use with filters. The ribs keep the paper off the glass and allow the liquid to flow more freely than in a smooth funnel.

Once you have the filtered potion, you can do a test to determine how much of the potion to add for the best flavor. Small changes in quantity can translate into large changes in taste. I have found that there is a sharp transition between "not enough" and "too much," with only a very small range of "just right" in the middle.

Get a pipette or small syringe graduated in some small amount, like one-tenth of a milliliter, and a small measure such as a shot glass. Calibrate with a line indicating 1 ounce (this assumes you are keeping track of your batches by gallons; if you are using liters, use a similar metric quantity—25 or 50 milliliters).

Use a small amount of the intended beer for the test, or one that's similar. I have done it both ways with good results. Pour an ounce of the beer into the shot glass. Withdraw a small amount of the potion into the pipette, take a wild guess as to how much to start with, and add it to the shot glass. Stir well and taste. Too much? Not enough? You just have to tinker with it until you get it right.

Once you have determined the one-tenth milliliter per ounce ratio, all that remains is to scale it up. Get out the pocket calculator and do the arithmetic:

Scaling Up Small-Scale Flavoring Potion Tests—1 Ounce to 5 Gallons

1 oz x 128 (per gallon) x 5 (gallons in batch) = 640 ounces/batch

If the dosing test determined that 0.2 ml was the correct amount for 1 ounce, then multiply:

.2 ml x 640 = 128 ml of potion that must be added to match the small-scale test

If the beer is a strong one intended for long aging, you might bump up the quantity a bit to compensate for the inevitable fading of flavor that comes with extended time in the cellar.

I usually add the potion to the beer at bottling, although you can just as well add it toward the end of secondary fermentation. If the beer is to be kegged rather than bottled, add it when you rack into the keg.

So, how much extra alcohol gets into the beer with this method? It depends on the quantity and alcoholic strength of the spirit added, but really doesn't amount to much. In a 5-gallon batch, 16 ounces of 80-proof vodka will add 1 percent of alcohol. Some alcohol evaporates during the soaking period, so it may end up being a little less. This shouldn't affect things too much, but be aware that in beers over 8 percent, with some yeasts, this may slow priming a bit. If in doubt, you can always add champagne yeast when you bottle.

In addition to homemade potions, commercial liqueurs may be used as a source for exotic flavorings in beer. I have had very good results with Triple Sec (orange liqueur) and crème de cacao (chocolate). Spices may be added to these, using the same method as the vodka. Fruit-flavored brandies often have rather elegant fruit character and also work well, especially when some real fruit is used along with the brandy. I have used as much as a full 750-milliliter bottle of liqueur in a 5-gallon batch of beer. Benedictine, Chambord, Chartreuse, Frangelico, and many others offer sleek, sophisticated flavors in an easy-to-use form—for a price.

There are also a number of commercially prepared flavoring extracts meant for making homemade liqueurs. Home wine and beer shops often carry these products, which are available in all common liqueur flavors. Many of these, like hazelnut and crème de cacao, are difficult to extract on your own and are well worth using. Some

Henbane *Hyoscyamus niger*

Called *bilsenkraut* in German, this dangerous herb containing atropine was once used as a brewing ingredient. According to Christian Rätsch (*Urbock*, Verlag 1996) this plant may have given its name to the Pilsener style.

Calculating the Sugar Content of Liqueurs

Liqueurs contain a certain amount of fermentable sugar, so this may be unsuitable for kegging unless you plan on naturally carbonating in the keg. For bottling, the sugar in liqueur must be considered as priming material. You can determine the quantity of sugar present by measuring the specific gravity of the liqueur. By subtracting the effect of the alcohol, which is a known quantity (specific gravity of 0.789), you can determine the precise amount of sugar present. For every 10° proof, add 1.06 °Plato to the measured gravity. Once you've added the appropriate number of degrees Plato to compensate for the alcohol, it is simple to calculate the amount of sugar present. Since degrees Plato are a measure of the percentage of sugar, just multiply the °P (as a decimal: 10 °P = 0.10, etc.) times the weight of the liqueur. Add to this as much sugar as you need to bring the total up to the appropriate range for the beer you're bottling. For reference, a cup of corn sugar weighs roughly 6.7 ounces (190 grams).

Example:

> Frangelico: 21.6 °P, 56 proof (28% alcohol/volume)
>
> 56 (proof) x 1.06 °P = 5.91 °P (correction for alcohol)

Add for alcohol: 21.6 + 5.91 °P = 27.5 °P (% sugar)

Liqueur quantity: 6 oz (by weight) x 27.5% (sugar, as °P) = 1.65 oz sugar

This amount—1.65 oz of sugar can be included as part of your priming.

liqueurs contain oil that may cause problems with head retention. Be sure to check out the one you plan to use with a small-scale test. Watch carefully for deleterious effects on the head, especially with orange flavored varieties.

SPICY SMOKE

This obviously transforms the spices into something very different, but can be used to create unusual flavors. Simply build a small charcoal fire on your barbecue, then place soaked spices directly on the coals a small handful at a time. Whole malt can be placed in a small basket made out of bronze window-screen, less than one-inch deep, and put into the barbecue off to the side, not directly over the coals. Turn every few minutes. Twenty minutes to an hour is the usual time for smoking malts. Heavier spices such as clove, cinnamon, allspice, and star anise are best for this technique. More pungent herbs such as thyme or rosemary might make use of this technique. As long as we're talking fire, you might consider lightly toasting certain spices before using. This would alter the flavor, and perhaps knock off the raw, rough edges.

Smoked spice beers to ponder:

Jerked Island Gold A strong (1.055) export style lager—Pils malt with 10 percent Munich malt that has been smoked with all-spice. Add a habañero for some painful joy, mon.

Smoked Five Spice Porter This uses the standard Chinese culinary mix of cinnamon, red flower (Szechuan) pepper, cloves, fennel seed, and star anise. Either buy the mix or concoct your own, then soak and smoke. Add to a somewhat strong (1.060 to 1.070) brown porter made with lots of amber malt. Should be great with duck.

Smoked Wassail Take the spice proportions from one of the Christmas beer recipes later in this chapter, and use maybe five times the quantity. Add a few ounces of juniper to the mix, and start smoking.

GRAINS OF PARADISE

This is an exotic ingredient from the great Age of Spice, a time when black pepper was more costly than gold. Today it is seldom used except in its native West Africa, but it once was popular in many parts of Europe.

It goes by many names. *Aframonium melegueta* is its official scientific name. It is also called paradise seed, guinea pepper, and melegueta pepper.

The spice is the seeds of a reedlike plant of the *Zingiberaceae* (ginger) family, and is native to tropical western Africa. It is related to cardamom, and indeed it does share some cardamom-like aromatic qualities. The people of West Africa chew the peppery seeds along with cola nuts, providing a mildly stimulating caffeine break.

The seeds themselves are brownish in color, irregularly shaped, and about half the size of black peppercorns.

The flavor is intense and complex. It may be described as an intensely hot, white pepper taste with a spruce/juniper aroma. Like pepper, it seems to be a spice that enhances other flavors. It seems to not have the lemony/minty flavor of common cardamom. It has been used recently as a high-class pepper alternative in the grinders of some pricey restaurants.

Grains of paradise were part of the vast brewing herbarium, and like many other spices, persisted long after hops had established domination as the herb of beer. More recently, grains of paradise have been used in certain Belgian styles: white beers, strong pale ales, and also in Faro—sweetened, diluted lambic.

RECIPE	**Pudgy McBuck's Celebrated Cocoa Porter**

Yield: 5 gallons (19 liters)

Gravity: 1.068 (16 °P)

Alcohol/vol: 5.7 to 6.6%

Color: Chestnut brown

Bitterness: 32 IBU

Yeast: London ale

Maturation: 6 to 10 weeks

This celebrates the time when chocolate was being introduced to Europe. It's a bit of a fantasy, as chocolate was always competition for beer, rather than an ingredient in it.

All-Grain Recipe:

8.0 lb (3.6 kg)	52%	mild ale malt
3.5 lb (1.1 kg)	21%	amber/biscuit
1.0 lb (0.45 kg)	6.5%	wheat malt
1.0 lb (0.45 kg)	6.5%	lightly toasted
1.0 lb (0.45 kg)	6.5%	black patent malt
12.0 oz (340 g)	4%	dark molasses
6.0 oz (170g)	2.5%	creme de cacao liqueur (added to secondary)

No Equivalent Extract Recipe

Hops:

0.5 oz (14 g)	90 min	Bullion (8.5% AA)
0.5 oz (14 g)	45 min	Fuggles (5% AA)
1.0 oz (28 g)	5 min	Bullion (8.5% AA)
0.5 oz (14 g)	5 min	Fuggles (5% AA)

Spices, added at the end of the boil, or made into a potion and added at priming:

1.0 oz (28 g) cocoa, 2 tsp (9.5 g) cassia cinnamon, 0.5 tsp (2 g) allspice, 0.25 tsp (1 g) rosemary, 0.25 tsp (1 g) nutmeg, 0.25 tsp (1 g) ground cloves, 2 whole star anise, 1.0 tsp (4 g) orange peel

One Belgian brewer uses it in the last five minutes of the boil to keep the delicate aroma from boiling away. As far as quantities go, it is best used in small amounts. Old recipes show rates between .07 ounces (2.1 grams) and .2 ounces (5.6 grams) per 5-gallon batch.

Pirate Stout Think about these crusty guys traveling around the Spice Islands. Make a big, dark stout with molasses, then add ancho chile, black pepper, allspice, clove, nutmeg, orange peel, and whatever else strikes yer fancy, maytee, har, har, har!

Springtime Herbed Ale Start with delicate pale ale or lager. Appropriate herbs include woodruff, basil, heather, mint, pennyroyal, and yarrow. Try about 1 tablespoon (14 g) each as a starting point. Hop lightly. A pound or so of honey added to the secondary is a worthwhile addition.

Sources for Spices:

Penzey's Spices
www.penzeys.com
414/741-7787

The Spice House
www.thespicehouse.com

RECIPE — Chocolate Mint Stout

Yield: 5 gallons (19 liters)

Gravity: 1.065 (15.5 °P)

Alcohol/vol: 5.3 to 6.2%

Color: Chestnut brown

Bitterness: 32 IBU

Yeast: London ale

Maturation: 4 to 6 weeks

My inspiration for this one came from a brew at the Southern California Homebrew Fest (see p. 282). This beer was getting a lot of attention—and refills. And although there's no actual chocolate in it, the roast malt profile is formulated to give that bittersweet flavor we love so well. You could easily add cocoa if you want to try a variation.

All-Grain Recipe:

8.0 lb (3.6 kg)	76%	pale ale malt
2.0 lb (0.90 kg)	16%	biscuit/amber malt
0.5 lb (227 g)	4%	roast barley
0.5 lb (227 g)	4%	black patent malt

For extract + mini-mash recipe, substitute lbs of amber dry malt extract for the pale ale malt.

Hops and Spices:

0.5 oz (14 g)	60 min	Northern Brewer (7% AA)
1.0 oz (28 g)	20 min	Northern Brewer (7% AA)
1.0 oz (28g)	end of boil	fresh spearmint
0.12 oz (4 g)	end of boil	dried peppermint mint (or one Life Saver mint candy)

A straightforward infusion works great for this brew: an hour at 152° F (66.5° C), then sparge and boil one hour. Use your favorite British ale yeast with this one. For a smoother variation lager yeast might be used instead.

Herbs & Spices for Brewing (B) indicates bitterness.

NAME	COMMENTS & DESCRIPTION
ALECOST	See Costmary.
ALEHOOF	See Ground Ivy.
ALLSPICE *Pimenta dioica*	Seeds of a Caribbean plant with a taste between cloves and cinnamon. The flavoring used in spiced gumdrops, European spiced baked goods, and Jamaican cuisine.
ANGELICA *Angelica archangelica*	The root, stem, and leaves of a plant in the umbelliferae family, with a firm bitterness and a heady, perfumey quality. Much employed in liqueurs, but not a lot of history with beer. Once employed as an ingredient in hop bitters. (B)
ANISE, STAR *Illicium verum*	The star-shaped seed pods of an Asian evergreen tree. Complex, soft anise flavor. Less likely to dominate, flavorwise, than aniseed.
ANISEED *Pimpinella anisum*	Small seeds with intense, one-dimensional anise taste. Used in the brown Pennsylvania specialty beer, swankey.
AVENS *Geum urbanum*	A dried root with a clove-like aroma, once used to flavor an ale made in the German city of Augsburg.

Herbs & Spices for Brewing (B) indicates bitterness.

NAME	COMMENTS & DESCRIPTION
BALM *Melisa officinalis*	A lemon-tasting herb used in England as a fining agent as well as a seasoning.
BASIL *Ocimum basilicum*	Leaves of annual herb, with a delicate minty/anise aroma. Fresh leaves far superior to dried. There are numerous varieties from which to choose.
BAYBERRY *Myrica cerifera*	Also known as myrtle. Has resiny, slightly menthol flavor. Bayberry flowers are edible and were once used to make a beverage.
BAY *Lauris nobilis*	The leaves of a perennial shrub. Delicate herbal/resiny taste; enhances other tastes. Best quality product comes from Turkey. Stores poorly.
BIRCH BARK *Betula lenta*	The bark of the sweet birch tree, which has a strong wintergreen aroma. Available as essential oil, which is incredibly potent, and is used as the flavoring in birch beer, a soda pop. Important in Gottlandsdricka, where bark-covered wood is used to smoke malt prior to brewing.
BITTER BEAN *Ignatia amara*	Known in the old recipes as *Faba amara*. The beanlike seeds of a woody climbing shrub native to the Phillipines. Used commercially—illegally—in Britain as a cheap hop substitute. Toxic, as it contains strychnine—do not use! (B)
BLESSED THISTLE *Cnicus benedictus*	Referred to in old books as *Carduus benedictus*. Scorchingly bitter flowers sometimes used in beer, and especially known as an ingredient in mumme, which was described as "bitter as gall." Little flavor other than the ferocious bitterness. Use cautiously. (B)
BOG-BEAN/BUCK-BEAN *Menyanthes trifoliata*	A widely distributed northern bog plant. The stem is bitter, and has tonic and fever-reducing medicinal properties. One ounce was held to be the equivalent of a half pound of hops. (B)
BOG MYRTLE *Myrica gale*	One of the three main herbs used in gruitbeer. Also known as sweet gale, or *porst* in German, this herb is still used in some Swedish baked goods. Generally considered safe, but should not be consumed by pregnant women.
BROOM *Cytisus scoparius*	A heath plant found from England to Asia. Used as a bittering agent in Britain in the seventeenth and eighteenth centuries, one of the few legally allowed besides hops. The tips of young branches are used. (B)
CARAWAY *Carum carvi*	The seed often used in German cooking, most notably in rye bread. Unique, deep rounded flavor. Used in a liqueur called Kümmel. A common component of gruit.
CARDAMOM *Elettaria cardamomum* and *Amomum sublatum* (black cardamom)	Pods containing numerous aromatic seeds. Has bright, resiny, astringent taste, a bit citrusy. At least four varieties: green and white, which are pretty similar; black, which has much larger pods, a smoky, old leather/tobacco kind of character, lots of astringency, and will add a considerable drying quality to beer; and Chinese, which has a strong menthol or camphor aroma. White and green are the most common and the most useful, and both have a sweetish quality that blends well with fruit. The green is the more prized of the two, as the white has been chemically bleached. If you get the whole pods, crack them open and crush the seeds inside before using. Very nice in raspberry beer.

Herbs & Spices for Brewing (B) indicates bitterness.

NAME	COMMENTS & DESCRIPTION
CASSIA *Cinnamomum cassia*	Closely related to cinnamon, and more often than not passes for it. With a deeper, richer taste than true cinnamon, cassia bark gives the familiar cinnamon toast flavor. Vietnamese is the highest grade. Cassia buds look a bit like cloves, and taste like Dentyne gum. The buds may be difficult to find, but are worth searching out. Nice in Christmas ales.
CHAMOMILE *Anthemis nobilis*	The flowers of a perennial herb. Fragrant, sweet aroma reminiscent of Juicy Fruit chewing gum. Used as a "secret ingredient" in witbiers, where it adds fruitiness.
CHILE *Capsicum species*	Pods of a New World plant characterized by varying degrees of spicy head, chiles can make a wonderful seasoning for beers. In addition to heat, chile may also add layers of deep, rich taste. The best chile beers balance heat, chile flavor, and malt, not always an easy thing to do.
CINNAMON *Cinnamomum zeylanicum*	The bark of an Asian tree. Ceylon cinnamon is the only "true" cinnamon, which has a dry, woody, delicate aroma much prized in Mexican cooking and British baked goods. Grocery-store cinnamon is usually cassia rather than true cinnamon.
CLOVES *Eugenia aromatica*	The dried flower buds of a tropical plant. Deep, rich flavor, very good in beer, especially Christmas ales with a number of different spices in the mix.
COCOA *Theobroma cacao*	The de-fatted material derived from roasted fermented cocoa pods. Best added to boil. Pretty delicate flavor, takes quite a bit to be noticeable. Crème de Cacao or extracts for making it can also be useful for adding chocolate flavor to beer.
COFFEE *Coffea arabica*	The roasted, ground beans of a shrub originating in Ethiopia, good for adding complexity to stouts or strong porters. Blends in very well. Instant espresso is also good. Although they may be a bit strong, flavored coffees (e.g. hazelnut) can be used, imparting their flavors to the beers. Cold extract added to the secondary gives the cleanest flavor, as coffee becomes very harsh when boiled.
CORIANDER *Coriandrum sativum*	The seeds of a plant long used in brewing. The leaves are known as cilantro. Complex lemon-resin flavor, essential for Belgian style witbiers. Two kinds available: the regular type, with round seeds and a resin, often vegetal or celeryseed aroma; and a paler, rugby-ball-shaped East Indian variety, with a softer, sweeter aroma.
COSTMARY *Chrysenthemum balsamita*	A strongly scented herb once used as an ale flavoring.
CUBEB PEPPER *Piper cubeba*	A little-used African spice regarded as inferior in flavor to either black or long pepper.
ELDER FLOWERS *Sambucus canadensis*	A medicinal substance with sophisticated fruity/floral sweet aromas. Use toward the end of the boil; all parts of this plant must be cooked—it is toxic when raw.
FENNEL *Foeniculum vulgare*	The seeds of a plant with a complex, anise-like aroma. A cousin to caraway. The spice of Italian sausage.
FENUGREEK *Trigonellum foenum*	The small, hard, kidney-shaped seeds of a plant with a distinct, maple syrup flavor, so much so that it's used as a base for imitation maple flavoring. Useful as a flavor booster in maple flavored beers. Traditional use is in Indian cuisine.

Herbs & Spices for Brewing (B) indicates bitterness.

NAME	COMMENTS & DESCRIPTION
GALINGAL ALPINA *officinarum*	The root of a plant related to ginger; used in Thai cooking. Has a sharp, pungent, peppery character. Stronger than ginger, but also inclined to be less earthy. Available fresh or dried at Thai or other Asian markets.
GENTIAN ROOT *Gentiana lutea*	The slightly aromatic, very bitter roots once commonly used as a hop substitute. Clean, bitter flavor. Used in a German beer from Merseburg. Available as chunks of root or extract. Main ingredient in bitters such as Underberg. (B)
GINGER *Zingiber officinale*	The rhizome of a low spreading plant, available fresh or dried. Jamaican is the best of the dried varieties. It has a sharp, peppery, yet earthy flavor that can dominate a beer easily, so use restraint. Most fresh ginger sold here is woody and somewhat earthy. Fresh young roots have a pinkish tinge to the flesh and a superior flavor. May be available in Thai or other Asian markets. Candied ginger seems to be of much better quality, milder and purer-tasting than fresh. Ginger "tea" concentrate (available at Asian markets) has a nice, clean ginger flavor.
GINSENG *Panax species* *Eleutherococcus senticosus,* or Siberian ginseng	There are two types, from completely unrelated species, *Panax* species, and *Eleutherococcus senticosus,* or Siberian ginseng. Long history of medicinal or tonic uses in wine, but not present in the European beer tradition.
GRAINS OF PARADISE *Aframonium melegueta*	A West African spice, a relative of cardamom. Once common in England as a beer seasoning as well as a culinary one. Very potent, with a sharp, white pepper taste with sprucy plywood aroma. A mild stimulant, too.
GROUND-IVY *Glechoma hederacea*	Also called alehoof or alecost. Formerly used as a substitute for hops. Mildly bitter, with a balsamic fragrance; otherwise pretty delicate. (B)
HEATHER *Calluna vulgaris,* others; several *Erica* species.	Tiny purple blooms of Scottish shrub. Has a delicate, buttery/honey-like taste. Traditionally used in making Scottish liqueur Drambuie. Particularly good in honey beers.
ITALIAN JUICE	See Licorice.
JUNIPER BERRIES *Juniperus communis*	The dried berries of a shrubby evergreen, with the unmistakable aroma of gin. Relatively weak in flavor compared to other seasonings, so large amounts are needed. In making Finnish sahti, whole berry-covered branches are boiled in the mash liquor, and are also used in the bottom of the lauter tun. The traditional form, called a *kuurna,* is a hollowed out log half.
LICORICE, LIQUORICE *Glycerrhiza glabra*	A unique seasoning derived from the woody roots, and having a unique persistent sweetness. Extracted juice is commonly boiled into a solid (called Spanish or Italian juice) and used as a flavoring ingredient. Was once widely used as a colorant in porter, at the rate of about 1 ounce per 5 gallons. Used in some dark Belgian ales.
MEADOWSWEET *Filipendula ulmaria*	An aromatic herb that has a traditional association with honey. Widely used in Bronze Age beers such as Scottish heather ale. Does have certain preservative effects similar to hops, but not as effective. (B)
MACE *Myristica fragrans*	The outer seed covering of nutmeg, with a similar taste, but sweeter and less pungent than nutmeg.

Herbs & Spices for Brewing (B) indicates bitterness.

NAME	COMMENTS & DESCRIPTION
MUGWORT *Artemesia vulgaris*	A close relative of wormwood, which was once used as a beer-bittering herb, mostly in Central Europe. There seem to be no well-recognized toxicity issues. (B)
MYRTLE *Myrtis communis*	Subdued resiny, slightly menthol aroma, a little astringency. A bit like bay leaves.
NUTMEG *Myristica fragrans*	The seed of a tropical plant. Has complex, rich taste, enhances other flavors. Very potent! A classic in Christmas beers.
OAK CHIPS *Quercus species*	Sometimes used to simulate barrel aging in wines. In beer, oak may impart a musty, astringent character, and it takes a pretty strong beer and a lot of time to make good use of it. In time, lignin in wood degrades to vanillin, which can be very nice. Best forms to use are winemaking "beans," small cubes of pedigreed oak used to refresh tired wine barrels, available in a variety of toast levels. French or Hungarian oak is milder and much preferred over American white oak.
OAK EXTRACT	Available from winemaking shops. Much more subtle and vanilla-tinged than new chips. Still, be cautious.
ORANGE BLOSSOMS	Petals of orange blossoms, dried. Has a delicate, perfumey orange aroma. Adds complexity to orange-tinged beers like wit. Available at Middle Eastern markets.
ORANGE PEEL	Fresh or dried, adds citric aroma to beers. Important in Belgian witbiers. See p. 178.
ORANGE WATER	A dilute extract of orange flowers. Adds perfumey tinge to citrus-flavored beers. A little goes a long way.
PENNYROYAL *Mentha puligium*	A close relative of spearmint, once quite popular. Nice flavor, but sadly not recommended for consumption.
PEPPER, BLACK *Piper nigrum*	Adds depth and complexity to beer, especially dark ones. Enhances other flavors. Use in small quantities, less than a teaspoon per 5-gallon batch.
PEPPER, CHILE	See Chile.
PEPPER, CHINESE FLOWER *Xanthoxylum piperitum*	A relative of black pepper, used in Chinese cooking. Also calles Szechuan red pepper. No heat, much less pungent. Very aromatic, complex aroma enhances other tastes. Available at Chinese markets.
PEPPER, INDIAN LONG *Piper longum*	A seasoning much favored centuries ago in Europe, but largely superseded by black pepper. Contains a little more piperene (6 percent) than black pepper, but missing its aromatic resiny terpenes. It has a kind of sweet/hot flavor. In Roman times, it was valued at thrice the price of black pepper.
PEPPERMINT *Mentha piperata*	Leaves with the familiar aroma and cooling spicy taste. Note that the fresh mint sometimes found in groceries is actually spearmint rather than peppermint. Very aggressive aroma, use sparingly.
PINKS *Dianthus armeria*	An edible flower in the chrysanthemum family. Mentioned in some old European mead recipes.
QUASSIA *Quassia excelsia*	The wood or bark of a tropical New World tree, once a common bittering agent for porter, and considered fairly wholesome for that purpose. Used in tonic water. (B)

Herbs & Spices for Brewing (B) indicates bitterness.

NAME	COMMENTS & DESCRIPTION
PUMPKIN PIE SPICE	A mixture of cloves, cinnamon, nutmeg, and the like. Will make any beer taste just like pumpkin pie.
ROSEMARY *Rosmarin officinalus*	Needlelike leaves of evergreen perennial shrub. Has minty, resinous aroma. Very potent aromatic!
SPANISH JUICE	See Licorice.
SAGE *Salviae folium*	Leaves of a common culinary herb more often used for mead than beer, although sage ale existed in pre-industrial Britain.
SASSAFRAS *Sassafras albidum*	Roots and inner bark of a shrubby tree native to the eastern U.S. No real history as a beer ingredient, but rather with root beer and other sodas. Contains a carcinogen, safrole, which has been removed from commercial extracts.
SPEARMINT *Mentha spicata*	Leaves of a perennial plant with a fresh, complex minty aroma. This is the variety sold as fresh "mint" in grocery stores. Exotic varieties such as lemon and chocolate mints are sometimes seen at farmers' markets or garden stores.
SPRUCE *Picea albies (and others)*	New-growth tips are traditionally used, which produce a refreshing resiny flavor. A historic American beer flavoring.
SWEET GALE	See Bog Myrtle.
SWEET FLAG *Acorus calamus*	Dried root of a reed-like marsh plant, used for its aroma and in bitters. Mentioned in recipes for purl, a spiced beer popular in the seventeenth and eighteenth centuries in Britain. (B)
VANILLA *Vanilla planifolia*	The fermented bean-like seed pod of a tropical orchid, most commonly available as an extract. Soft, enveloping taste and mouthfeel. Able to mask other flavors, and in a pinch is useful for covering up unwanted fermentation characteristics such as lactic sourness.
WILD CARROT *Daucus carota*	Seeds of a plant used since ancient times for their pungent, slightly bitter flavor. Said to add a flavor reminiscent of peaches or apricots when added to the secondary. Contains Vitamin C, and was once valued for its tonic effect against scurvy. A common adulterant in eighteenth-century London beers.
WILD ROSEMARY *Ledum palustre*	A low-growing marsh plant with a strong resiny and astringent taste. In German, *porst*. Used in the traditional gruit mixture. Very hard to find in the United States, although it does grow in Alaska and similar northern climes. Contains a substance, andromedotoxin, that is quite harmful if consumed in large quantities. Now often considered dangerous for internal use; not recommended as an ingredient in beer.
WOOD SAGE *Teucrium canadense* *or T. occidentale*	Part of a group known collectively as germander, these native North American shrubs were once used as hop substitutes. Because of possible problems with liver toxicity, this herb cannot be recommended. (B)
WOODRUFF *Asperula odorata*	A delicate herb used as a flavoring in May wine. Similar to tarragon, but sweeter. The fresh herb is flavorless; the aroma develops only upon drying. Blends well with basil, honey, and heather. Called *waldmeister* in Germany, it is used to flavor a syrup that is added to Berliner weisse. A beautiful ornamental plant.

Herbs & Spices for Brewing (B) indicates bitterness.	
NAME	**COMMENTS & DESCRIPTION**
WORMWOOD *Artemesia absinthum*	A very bitter herb once widely used in herbed beverages (like absinthe) and tonics, and as a bittering agent in beer. Containing the toxic material Thujone, wormwood is classified by the FDA as dangerous, and so cannot be recommended. But, it does appear as if both the toxicity and the mind-affecting abilities of thujone may have been overstated by both sides of the debate. A related species, *A. maritima* or sea wormwood, was used to flavor a beer in England and Ireland around 1700, and is sometimes sold as a garden plant. See also *Artemesia vulgaris* (mugwort).
YARROW *Achillea millefolium*	A moderately bitter herb, long used in beer. One of the three classic gruit herbs. Dried leaves and stems used. Mildly toxic, said to exacerbate headaches.

"As we gaze back on these old scenes of fun and frolic, their rougher outlines perchance softened by distance, their true-heartiness and geniality shining through the golden mist of time, which of us will be found to deny that in some respects the old was better?"

— John Bickerdyke, 1889

WASSAIL!

The industrial mindset has squeezed nearly every drop of cultural significance out of beer, but if you read between the lines of nursery rhymes and Christmas carols, you can still find scraps of our ancient heritage peeking out from the cracks.

"Wassailing." The specific meaning is rather foggy for most of us. But even so, the sound of it conjures up some special bond of community, a closeness unique to the winter festival season, apple-cheeked folks in jolly old England singing and making merry by the fire. Wouldn't you know it had something to do with beer?

The tradition of festivities at the winter solstice is widespread and ancient. The Roman festival of Saturnalia, with its twelve days of feasting and gift giving, formed the model for our Christmas revelries. As Christianity spread into northern lands inhabited by beer-brewing Barbarians, this winter bash dovetailed neatly into existing midwinter Yule festivals.

The word wassail was originally "*waes hael*," to "be whole" or "be well," and was connected to the concept of toasting from a large bowl of spiced ale. The same sentiment of "to your health!" is expressed by most common toasts even today. Wassailing survived as an activity until modern times, and involved a ceremonial bowl garnished with rosemary, holly, and evergreens. In Devonshire it was the custom to wassail the apple orchards, pouring ale or cider over the roots of the trees as a rhyming toast was recited.

Such sacrificial customs have long been a means for honoring the gods. As the finest lamb or the fruit of the fields was given up as a gift to the heavens, so it was with drink. King Haakon the Good (died 961 C.E., somewhere in the frosty North), decreed that Yuletide should be kept at the time of Christian Christmastime, and that every man should use in brewing for this festival at least one-third of a tun of malt, and that he should celebrate until the beer was gone. Woo-hoo!

King Haakon's merry brewsters were most likely not using hops for this special ale. The bitter, spicy qualities needed to balance the sweet stickiness of malt were supplied by any number of culinary or medicinal plants. "Bitter herbs" are mentioned frequently in the Bible. Traditions varied from place to place, with each region's brewers making best use of the locally available plants.

Unlike beer, mead (honey wine) never became industrialized, and so retains its rustic charm to this day. The word used to denote a spiced mead, "metheglin," is cognate with the word "medicine," an illustration of the serious regard held for the power of herbs and drink long ago.

| R E C I P E | **Christmas Ale** |

This is a modestly hopped Belgian-inflected beer with a complex malt character and a brown color. The spice flavor is very soft and round, with nothing sticking out.

Yield: 5 gallons (19 liters)

Gravity: 1.083 (19.5 °P)

Alcohol/vol: 6.8 to 7.8%

Color: Tawny amber

Bitterness: 45 IBU

Yeast: Altbier or Belgian abbey

Maturation: 3 to 5 months

All-Grain Recipe:

8.5 lb (3.2 kg)	45%	U.S. two-row lager malt
4.0 lb (1.8 kg)	21%	wheat malt
2.5 lb (1.1 kg)	13%	oatmeal (toasting optional: 15 min @ 300° F (150° C)
1.5 lb (0.68 kg)	8%	German Munich malt
1.5 lb (0.68 kg)	8%	brown malt
1.0 lb (0.45 kg)	5%	dark crystal malt
1.0 oz (28 g)	—	carafa malt

For an extract + steeped grain recipe, replace the lager and wheat malts with 4.5 lb (2 kg) amber dry malt extract and 3 lb (1.4 kg) liquid or dry wheat malt extract.

Hops:

1.0 oz (28 g)	90 min	Northern Brewer (7% AA)
0.5 oz (14 g)	30 min	Northern Brewer (7% AA)
1.0 oz (28 g)	30 min	Fuggle (5% AA)
1.0 oz (28 g)	30 min	Coriander, crushed
0.5 oz (14 g)	10 min	East Kent Golding

Spices added to liqueur potion, 12.5 oz (370 ml) of this mixture added at bottling:

250 ml	Creme de Cacao liqueur
600 ml	Orange Curaçao/Triple Sec liqueur
50 ml	Benedictine liqueur (optional)
0.25 tsp (1 g)	black pepper, crushed
1.0 tsp (5 ml)	vanilla extract
2.0 tsp (9.5 g)	cassia buds, ground
1.0 tsp (5 ml)	orange blossom water
0.25 tsp (1 g)	aniseed
3.0 oz (85 g)	coriander, cracked

Scandinavian Jul Öl labels, c. 1900

Holiday brews have long been a big tradition in the chilly North.

The British still uphold the tradition with unspiced strong ales called winter warmers. In Continental Europe, especially in Belgium and Scandinavia, winter holiday beers persist. Spiced holiday ales have made a revival in America, as brewers are seeking their roots wherever they can find them. Interest in all kinds of seasonal brewing naturally led to a special beer for the holiday season. Anchor Brewing in San Francisco started the renaissance with a spiced strong brown beer made for the 1984 holiday season. According to those at the brewery, Fritz Maytag is "a great admirer of British beer tradition" and always interested in doing something unique.

Certain characteristics define the style. Most are strong, with gravities from 1.050 to 1.070 and up. They tend to be deep amber to brown, with thick, cream-colored heads. Generally, 100 percent malt is used, with crystal malts playing an important role in the flavor profile. For stronger beers, semi-refined sugars may be used to thin out the texture, even as they add a layer of flavor. Hops usually play second fiddle to the spices, but they may be fairly bitter just the same.

TWELVE BEERS OF CHRISTMAS

Holiday icons seem to settle into the same old routine; beers are not immune. And while I enjoy the wassail-inspired brown brews, much of the fun of homebrewing lies in the surprising, the fun, and the new.

So, in that spirit, I present a brewer's dozen, minus the accompanying song, plus a bonus—my interpretation of the classic wassail-spiced brew. These are just outlines; I promised earlier not to spoon-feed you every little thing. If you've brewed a few batches, you should able to fill in the gaps quite nicely.

1. Caramel Quadrupel Start with the tripel recipe on p. 125, but add 4 pounds of amber malt, and use the following toffee sugar recipe instead of the sugar of the original recipe. Sugar and malt caramelized together will impart a lingering toffee-like quality. Mix a pound each of light malt extract and white sugar in a heavy saucepan. Heat until it melts; stir only enough to mix together, and continue until it starts to darken. Use your judgment about when to stop. Once it starts to brown, things happen quickly, but it can get fairly dark before it will make the beer taste burnt. When done, remove from the stove and scrape it directly into your brew kettle or cool it by lowering the pan into a larger pan of water. Once cooled, add brewing water and reheat to dissolve the caramel, then add to your brew in progress. Gravity: 1.100 (24 °P). Color: deep reddish-brown.

2. Spiced Cherry Dubbel Start with a good rich dubbel (p. 124), toss in an additional pound of piloncillo or turbinado sugar, and use a combination of sweet (black) and sour (Montmorency) cherries, which should ferment in the beer for a month or so. A pound per gallon is a minimum. Two is better. One teaspoon of ceylon (true) cinnamon added at the end of the boil will enhance the natural spiciness of the sour cherries. Add one drop (no more!) of almond extract for added depth. Gravity: 1.070 to 1.078 (17 to 18.5 °P). Color: deep ruby-amber.

RECIPE	3. Spiced Dunkel Weizenbock

Yield: 5 gallons (19 liters)

Gravity: 1.083 (19.5 °P)

Alcohol/vol: 6.7 to 7.7%

Color: Deep amber

Bitterness: 28 IBU

Yeast: Altbier or Belgian abbey

Maturation: 3 to 5 months

All-Grain Recipe:

5.0 lb (2.3 kg)	38%	wheat malt
4.0 lb (1.8 kg)	31%	Munich malt
2.0 lb (0.90 kg)	15%	two-row Pilsener malt
1.0 lb (0.45 kg)	8%	wheat malt, toasted 30 min. @ 350° F
1.0 lb (0.45 kg)	8%	medium crystal malt

No Equivalent Extract Recipe

Hops:

1.75 oz (50 g)	90 min	Tettnang (4.5% AA)
0.5 oz (14 g)	30 min	Tettnang (4.5% AA)

Spices, 1.0 tsp (4.7 g) each, added at end of boil:

allspice, star anise, caraway; plus 0.5 oz (14 g) of orange peel; 2.0 oz (57 g) of candied ginger may be chopped coarsely and tossed into the secondary.

RECIPE	4. Juniper Rye Bock

This beer is a hybrid between the rustic Finnish sahti and classic German brews.

Yield: 5 gallons (19 liters)

Gravity: 1.080 (19 °P)

Alcohol/vol: 6.4 to 7.2%

Color: Deep amber

Bitterness: 24 IBU

Yeast: Danish lager

Maturation: 4 to 6 months

All-Grain Recipe:

9.5 lb (4.3 kg)	62%	Munich malt
3.0 lb (1.4 kg)	19%	two-row Pilsener malt
2.0 lb (0.90 kg)	13%	malted rye or flaked rye, precooked
1.0 lb (0.45 kg)	6%	dark crystal malt
1.0 lb (0.45 kg)	—	rice hulls
4.0 oz (113 g)	—	crushed juniper berries, in the mash

Hops & Spices:

2.0 oz (57 g)	90 min	Hallertau (3.5% AA)
2.0 oz (57 g)	90 min	juniper berries, crushed
2.0 oz (57 g)	end of boil	juniper berries, crushed

A standard infusion mash will suffice, although you may want to follow the traditional sahti stepped infusion procedure (p. 244).

RECIPE **5. Fruitcake Old Ale**

However leaden the cake, the dried fruits in this "delicacy" can be delicious in beer. Brew an old ale, not too hoppy, and ferment through the primary.

Yield: 5 gallons (19 liters)

Gravity: 1.075 (18° P)

Alcohol/vol: 6.5 to 7.5%

Color: Deep reddish amber

Bitterness: 31 IBU

Yeast: Scottish ale

Maturation: 6 to 9 months

All-Grain Recipe:

8.75 lb (4.0 kg)	62%	Munich malt
3.0 lb (1.4 kg)	22%	amber malt
1.0 lb (0.45 kg)	13%	Special B (very dark crystal)
4.0 oz (113 g)	6%	Carafa II malt

For an extract recipe, substitute: 6.5 lb (3 kg) of amber dry malt extract for the Munich and amber malts, and add 1.0 lb (0.45 kg) medium crystal malt.

Hops:

1.5 oz (43 g)	90 min	Liberty (4.5% AA)
0.5 oz (14 g)	15 min	Saaz (3% AA)
0.5 oz (14 g)	15 min	Liberty (4.5% AA)

Add at end of boil:

0.25 tsp (1.0 g) nutmeg, allspice; 2.0 tsp (8.0 g) Ceylon cinnamon; 1.0 tsp (4.0 g) powdered ginger and vanilla extract.

After primary fermentation, assemble 3 lb (1.4 kg) of dried fruit: raisins, apricots, cherries, blueberries—whatever—plus the zest of two of oranges and two whole cloves. Pour boiling water over it to rehydrate; allow to stand for an hour or two to cool and plump, then mix with the beer which has been racked into a vessel with some headspace. Allow this to ferment for two weeks, then rack off the fruit to another carboy, allow to settle, then bottle or keg as usual. This beer will benefit from several months of aging.

6. Saffron Tripel Pick your favorite Belgian tripel recipe as a start. If there's no sugar in it, substitute 20 percent of the base malt for some unrefined sugar—turbinado or piloncillo, for example. Jaggery (Indian palm sugar) is also lovely. Add the zest of one orange at the end of the boil, along with a pinch of crushed grains of paradise or black pepper. Ferment with Belgian ale yeast, and add a half-teaspoon (2 g) of saffron threads after transferring to the secondary. Gravity: 1.090 (21.5 °P). Color: orange-gold

7. Christmas Gruit This is a throwback to the days before hopped beers were the norm. I have included some hops here, largely for their preservative value. Note that the "gruit" component of this is only partially authentic (bog myrtle), as yarrow and wild rosemary can't in good conscience be recommended for internal consumption. The rosemary and California bay laurel provide a safe approximation. Start with the dunkel weizenbock recipe (number 4) but substitute the following spices, which may be added at the end of the boil: 4 oz (113 g) juniper, crushed; 1.0 tsp (4 g) ceylon cinnamon; 0.5 tsp (2 g) bog myrtle/sweet gale; 0.25 tsp (1 g) rosemary; 0.12 tsp (0.5 g) mace, two California bay laurel leaves. Add one pound of heather or dark wildflower honey to the secondary and allow it to ferment out before bottling or kegging. Saison or other characterful Belgian yeast is recommended. As an option, a package of mixed lambic culture, added after the primary, will add wild aromas and a bit of sourness after a few months. Substituting a bit of smoked malt will impart a suitably medieval funkiness. Gravity: 1.091 (22 °P). Color: hazy amber.

8. Honey Ginger IPA Ginger was a popular ingredient in British beers prior to 1850, and here we're pairing it with a dab of honey. Start with an IPA, and brew and ferment as normal. Once transferred to the secondary, add 2 pounds (0.90 kg) of honey, plus 2 ounces (57 g) of candied ginger, coarsely chopped. This is a higher-quality ginger than the stuff in the produce section, less pungent and less earthy. I would use British East Kent Goldings exclusively. Gravity: 1.065 (15.5 °P). Color: pale amber.

9. Crabapple Lambicky Ale Crabapples add not only a festive touch, but tannins and acidity as well, which makes it easier to get that tart, champagny character without extended aging. Brew a simple pale wheat ale like the Amazing Daze recipe on p. 150. If mashing, go low (145° F) and long (two hours). Ferment with ale yeast, Belgian or otherwise. Obtain 3 to 4 pounds (1.4 to 1.8 kg) of crabapples (cranberries work also), wash well, then freeze. Thaw and add to the beer when it is transferred to the secondary, along with a package of mixed lambic culture. Allow to age on the fruit for two months, then rack, allow to clear (which may take a month or two), and bottle. Lambic character will continue to increase with time. Gravity: 1.050 (12 °P) Color: pale pink.

10. Gingerbread Ale Liquid cake! One of our Chicago Beer Society homebrewers hit me with this one a few years ago, and the flavor was quite striking. The base brew should be a soft brown ale, lightly hopped, with no pronounced hop aroma. The gingerbread flavor depends on a specific balance of spices used in the common dessert: 1 tsp (4 g) cinnamon; 0.5 tsp (2 g) ground ginger; 0.25 tsp (1 g) allspice; 0.25 tsp (1 g) cloves. Just add them at the end of the boil. Gravity: 1.055 (13 °P). Color: pale brown.

11. Spiced Bourbon Stout Take your favorite stout recipe and dose it with spices. Into 6 ounces (177 ml) of vodka and 2 ounces (59 ml) of bourbon (more if you wish), add: 0.5 tsp (2 g) vanilla extract; 0.25 tsp (1 g) allspice; 0.5 tsp (2 g) cinnamon; 0.25 oz (7 g) crushed coriander; 1 whole star anise (or 0.25 tsp ground); 0.5 oz (14 g) crushed juniper; pinch of black pepper. Gravity: 1.050 (12 °P) Color: India ink.

12. Abbey Weizen This one's easy. Take a classic Bavarian Weizen recipe and ferment it with a Belgian abbey yeast. For a little more zip, add a little citrus peel—try a tangelo or a handful of kumquats for a fairly close approximation of the Seville/curacao orange. Coriander and chamomile (.25 ounce, or 7 g) added at the end of the boil provide even more depth. You could brew this same recipe at much higher gravities if desired. Gravity: 1.045 (11 °P). Color: hazy deep gold.

AND MORE...

The possibilities are endless. As noted in the Arnold quote that opens this chapter, the spice cabinet of all human history is open to us. Ther are the individual herbs and spices, of course, as well as combinations in unlimited variety. Culinary practices can be of great help in coming to grips with the mixes. Most of all don't be afraid to experiment and try something unexpected. You never know when that weird idea will turn out to be the next great thing.

Here are a couple of recipes that came to me through homebrewer Gordon Strong. His recipe is based on a Indian spiced tea mixture called chai. The other one is just pure homebrew fun—although black pepper was occasionally used as a beer ingredient a few centuries ago.

| RECIPE | Gordon Strong's Chai Brown Ale |

Yield: 5 gallons (19 liters)

Gravity: 1.046 (10.5 °P)

Alcohol/vol: 4.4 to 4.7%

Color: Deep amber

Bitterness: 18 IBU

Yeast: British ale yeast

Maturation: 6 to 8 weeks

"The general concept is to make a sweet-ish, slightly creamy northern English-style brown ale and then blend in a spiced tea to taste. This one is different since it's a lighter beer that's enjoyable in the summer."

All-Grain Recipe:

4.0 lb (1.8 kg)	46%	Maris Otter pale malt
2.0 lb (0.90 kg)	23%	Vienna malt
1.0 lb (0.45 kg)	11.5%	Munich malt
0.75 lb (kg)	8.5%	CaraVienne (pale crystal) malt
0.5 lb (227 g)	6%	UK Crystal 80
0.25 lb (kg)	2.5%	UK chocolate malt
0.25 lb (kg)	2.5%	rolled oats

No Equivalent Extract Recipe

Hops:

| 1.25 oz (35 g) | 60 min | Saaz (4% AA) |

Mash at 147 °F for 1 hour. Mash out at 170 °F. Boil 90 min. Ferment at 67 °F.

Post-fermentation, blend in chai spiced tea to taste:

1 vanilla bean, split and scraped	2 cinnamon sticks
2" ginger, peeled, sliced	5 whole cloves
1 star anise	18 green cardamom pods, split
1 black cardamom pod, split	2 tsp black peppercorns
1/2 whole nutmeg, roughly chopped	0.25 tsp fennel seeds

"Bring about 1 quart filtered water to a boil, then pour over spices and cover in a separate container. Let steep for 15 minutes, then strain to remove spices. Cover tea and keep chilled until used. I think I blended in about 2 cups of this liquid in the 5-gallon batch. But you want to do it slowly, mix it well, and taste it."

RECIPE — Bat Bateman's Black Pepper Porter

Yield: 5 gallons (19 liters)

Gravity: 1.060 (15.3 °P)

Alcohol/vol: 4.9 to 5.7%

Color: Deep brown

Bitterness: 66 IBU

Yeast: British ale yeast

Maturation: 8 to 12 weeks

"The idea for Pepper Porter came from a brew called Back Biter" by Paul Williams of Foundry Ale Works. Tim Steininger and I used the concept, modified to use our basic porter recipe as a starting point. It is a well-hopped beer, and the pepper was added to provide character. Notes of pepper could be picked up, but the pepper heat was masked by the high BUs, and the aroma by the hop fragrance. It would be difficult to over-hop this beer."

All-Grain Recipe:

6 lb (2.7 kg)	50%	Munich malt 300
3.5 lb (1.6 kg)	29%	2 row malt grains (Light)
1.5 lb (0.7 kg)	12%	dark crystal malt (120 L)
0.75 lb (0.3 kg)	6%	chocolate malt (350 L)
0.4 lb (0.2 kg)	3%	black patent malt

For an extract + mini-mash recipe, substitute 3.3 lb (1.5 kg) dry amber malt extract for the Munich malt

Hops & Spices:

1.5 oz (43 g)	30 min	Target (9% AA)
0.75 oz (21g)	30 min	Perle (8% AA)
0.75 oz (21g)	5 min	Crystal (3.5% AA)
0.4 oz (11 g)	end of boil	freshly ground black pepper
0.4 oz (11 g)	in chilled wort	freshly ground black pepper

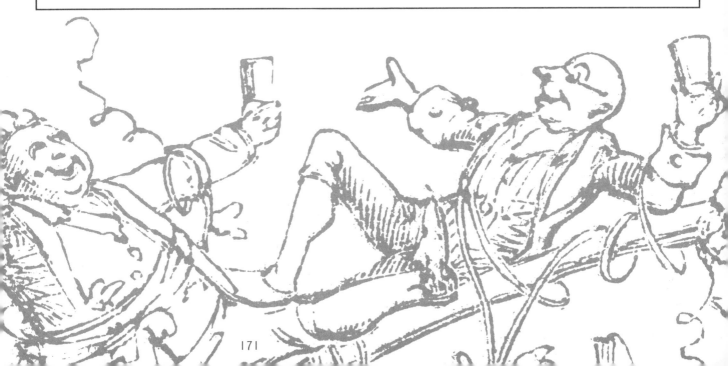

Chapter 13

Tooting Your Fruit

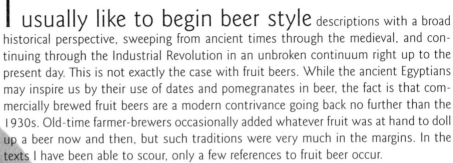

I usually like to begin beer style descriptions with a broad historical perspective, sweeping from ancient times through the medieval, and continuing through the Industrial Revolution in an unbroken continuum right up to the present day. This is not exactly the case with fruit beers. While the ancient Egyptians may inspire us by their use of dates and pomegranates in beer, the fact is that commercially brewed fruit beers are a modern contrivance going back no further than the 1930s. Old-time farmer-brewers occasionally added whatever fruit was at hand to doll up a beer now and then, but such traditions were very much in the margins. In the texts I have been able to scour, only a few references to fruit beer occur.

Outside of the teasing references to ancient Egyptian beers, the earliest fruit beer reference I can find comes from Heinrich Knaus, in 1614 Germany, who refers to a beer made with cherries—pits included. A French brewing book dating to 1828 lists a couple of basic recipes to which the reader is advised to add raspberries, gooseberries, strawberries, apricots, peaches, wild or cultivated cherries, plums, or currants. Oddly, in a book about beer, these recipes recommend using sugar, honey, or maple syrup rather than malt! One recipe, *Bière framboisée dite bière des dames* (raspberry beer called Beer of Ladies), uses pure white sugar to create a 8 to 10° "wort," topped off with "eight or ten small baskets" of raspberries in a 300-liter *barrique* barrel. So wine coolers are nothing new. Bear in mind that this book also advises us on how to fabricate beer from beets, potatoes, and carrots.

Seventeenth- and eighteenth-century German books list beers made with raspberries, cherries, and sloe, which is a type of plum. German-born brewmaster Fred Scheer describes seeing dark cherries added to lagering beer during his youth, but says that it was only at small village breweries.

Many old British brewing books from the same period describe a beer called *ebulum*, which was fermented with elderberries and has since been revived by a Scottish brewery. Dark and pale versions were brewed using purple and white elderberries, which were placed in a muslin bag and hung in a barrel of aging beer.

The tradition of commercial fruit beers in Belgium extends back only to the 1930s. The cherry lambic, *Kriek*, originated at this time, raspberry *framboise* lambic wasn't made until the 1950s, and the peach flavored variety, *pêche*, is a very recent invention. Even more recent interpretations include banana, strawberry, muscat grape, and pineapple lambic.

Cherries played an important role in lambic brewing for centuries without ever finding their way into a beer. Cherry orchards in the Senne Valley outside of Brussels served as the primary habitat for the famous "wild" yeast of that region. Lambic brewers lament that so many of the orchards have been cut down to accommodate encroaching urban sprawl that sufficient microbes to inoculate their beer may no longer exist in the night air. Each brewery building now houses its own complex ecosystem, so much so that old brewery walls are cut out and installed in new buildings in an attempt to infect the structures with the proper mix of brewing bugs.

The traditional method of brewing kriek is so costly and time consuming that only the smallest and least commercial lambic breweries can manage it on any kind of commercial scale. First a lambic is made, by itself no easy task. After the beer has gone through a year of its complex fermentation cycle, whole fresh cherries are added to the casks and allowed to remain for two to three months, pits and all. The beer is then racked off the lees and allowed to clear. The beer is bottled and allowed to condition for up to six months before release. The preferred cherry variety is the Schaarbeek, a small, dark sour cherry that has no counterpart in America. Sometimes these cherries are allowed to dry somewhat on the tree, concentrating the flavor further, much like late-harvest wines. Fermenting the beer on the pit gives the beer a woody, almond character instantly familiar to anyone who has ever tasted kirsch.

Today, many kriek brewers cut this process somewhat short. Various degrees of expediency result in beers that are, at best, less complex, to beers that are sugary and soda pop-like. The usual shortcut is to use some form of processed fruit concentrate or extract, which shortens the fermentation time at the expense of depth. The resulting beers, though they may be tasty enough, lack the wine-like profundity of the traditional versions.

Raspberry lambics, called framboise or frambozen, are made in the same way, although a lesser quantity of fruit may be required, owing to the more intense flavor of raspberries. Cherry and raspberry beers are also made in Belgium using a sour brown ale as a base rather than the lambic.

In America, the microbrew revolution has brought upon us a number of new fruit beers. Foremost among them in popularity is the fruit wheat beer, a frothy concoction typically made with fruit extracts and aimed at the "beginner" segment of the market. With a fresh fruity nose, a thin, slightly acidic palate, and a relatively quick finish, this style is the perfect summer refresher. Raspberries and apricots do well in this style. Their intensity allows them to just lightly perfume the beer. Fruit quantities are low, shortening production time and lowering cost. More delicate fruits such as cherries require greater quantities to achieve a recognizable taste, making it difficult for commercial producers, although some are starting to come through with extremely fruity beers.

The quality of homebrewed fruit beers can be high because the cost and time factors are not a big issue. Also, there is a greater range of fermentable fruits and fruit products available for very small-scale fermentations. Passion fruit, plum, thimbleberry, and other unusual fruits can be had from time to time, and the price to pay for a failed experiment is a beer that is less than wonderful—but when one is drinking nearly for free, who can complain?

While the following list covers most of the fruits commonly used in beer, there are hundreds of exotic possibilities. Wild cherries, currants, and gooseberries all make fine beers. There are lots of wild fruits hanging out there in the woods, just waiting for someone to brew with them. Some of them—chokecherries, for example—are too intense to be eaten, but their concentrated flavor, acidity, and color mean that they can be great for brewing beer or mead.

Belgian label, c. 1950

German Encyclopedia plate, c. 1895
There are far fewer choices now.

Dates have an ancient brewing pedigree, and are sometimes available as canned syrup at Middle Eastern markets. Pomegranate juice, concentrated or normal strength, may also be found at such markets, and adds a bright acidity and tannic bite to beer and mead. A number of tropical juices may be found at Latin American markets—tamarind, guanabana, mango, guava, and papaya. Each has its own unique flavor, and it's up to us to find out which ones make the best beer!

Fruits for Brewing

NAME	COMMENTS & DESCRIPTION
BLACKBERRIES 1 to 4 pounds per gallon (quantity of whole fruit per gallon of beer)	Similar to raspberries, but with a considerably less specific aromatically intense flavor. Quantities on the order of cherries—1 to 4 pounds per gallon—are about right. They have a beautiful purple color, and may be used in other fruit beers for that effect alone.
BLUEBERRIES 1 to 3 pounds per gallon	Blueberries are another fruit that does not hold up well in fermentation. The fresh blueberry character is so delicate that it often gets lost in the context of a beer, even a light one. In beer, their color is not blue; it's more of a purplish pink. Cooking may actually enhance the flavor of blueberries, so you may be able to use a couple jars of jam in a beer like a wit or a weizen, where the pectin haze won't be a problem. Wild berries have much more aroma than cultivated.
CHERRIES 1 to 4 pounds per gallon	Of all fruits, cherries are the most traditional, as well as one of the most elegant. The subtle flavor of the cherry blends well with the tastes of malt, without completely overtaking it. Not all cherries are well suited to making beer, and it requires at least a pound per gallon to make a worthwhile beer. Sour cherries are best; sweet ones just don't have the guts to do the job. If you want to make a beer that tastes just like cherry pie, use the Montmorency cherry. It will send you back to your childhood. Other sour cherries have a less specific point of view. Remember, it may take a blend of different cherries to make the best beer—some for color, some for intensity, and some for acidity.
PEACHES 1.5 to 5 pounds per gallon	Peaches have been, in my experience, a terrible disappointment. The taste of the finished beer is rather flat and somewhat gummy, very different from the intense bouquet of fresh peaches. Apparently, some of the crucial flavor components of the peaches are transformed during fermentation. Apricots produce a much better beer; in fact, they make a fine peach beer! I have had good experience with the apricot extract being sold for brewing purposes these days. If one insisted on trying a peach beer, it might be wise to have a bottle of apricot extract sitting around to beef up the flavor at the end of fermentation.
 **RASPBERRIES** 0.25 to 3 pounds per gallon	The easiest fruit from which to make beer. Their intense, single-minded character hangs in there forever and cuts through almost any other flavor present. As little as 0.25 pound per gallon will give a pleasant flavor in lighter, frothy beers, but 0.5 to 1 pound per gallon is a better rate for serious brews. Usually the fruit provides enough acidity, but taste before bottling and add acid if the fruit tastes dull. Red raspberries seem to have a better flavor in beer than black.

Fruits for Brewing

NAME	COMMENTS & DESCRIPTION
STRAWBERRIES 1 to 5 pounds per gallon	Strawberries rarely live up to their promise. The familiar flavor fades quickly along with the color, leaving an orange-hued, vaguely fruity beer behind. The best strawberry beers are those made in a light style, to be drunk in their youth. Absolutely ripe fruit is essential, which means you won't be able to use grocery store berries. Strawberries refuse to ripen further once they're picked, so commercial berries, harvested when young and rocklike to prevent rotting in transit, aren't worth bothering with. Unless you can get out in the fields and pick them yourselves, frozen strawberries are your best bet. Use 2 pounds of fruit per gallon or more, and keep the underlying beer light. Serve it as soon as it's ready, and drink it all up when it's young; strawberry beer lives best in one's memory.

NAME	COMMENTS & DESCRIPTION
APPLE	Mild aroma, acidic. Improves head. Best for mead, cider.
APRICOT	Similar to peaches, but better (see Peaches).
BANANA	Used in a lambic, but not too common.
DATES	Lots of sugar, not much aroma.
FIG	Soluble fiber keeps you regular. Not much aroma.
GRAPE	Huge variety available. Best in meads (pyment). Aromatic varieties like Muscat are good.
GUANABANA	Whitish tropical fruit. Subtle perfumey aroma. Low acidity.
GUAVA	Tropical fruit. Mild aroma and flavor.
MAMEY	Delicious tropical fruit with carob-like flavors. Low acidity.
MANGO	Complex and attractive aroma. Modest acidity.
PAPAYA	Tropical fruit with protein-dissolving enzymes. Low acidity.
PASSIONFRUIT	Small tropical fruit with intensely aromatic pulp. Beautiful!
PEAR	Soft and subtle aromas add depth to ciders or meads.
PINEAPPLE	Familiar tropical fruit. May be best as a hat decoration, or in mead.
PLUM	Large variety available. Ripeness critical. Elusive aroma.
POMEGRANATE	Delicate acidic fruit with some tannic character. Best in mead, cider.
TAMARIND	Gummy pods with tart, thirst-quenching pulp. Great for mead.

ENBÄR DRICKA

A.-B. AXVALLS ÅNGBRYGGERI
AXVALL. Tel. 8

Fruit Beers to Ponder

Raisin Abbey Dubbel	Kiwi Pils	Blackcurrant doppelbock
Raspberry Vanilla Porter	Mango Tripel	Guanabana Weizen
Passionfruit Witbier	Sapote Bock	Muscat (Grape) Old Ale

Tropical fruit offers a whole range of exotic flavors to explore.

BREWING WITH FRUIT

The underlying beer is important. While homebrew competition judges like to be able to detect "a beer in there somewhere," drinkers of commercial fruit beers make no such demand. Lighter-bodied beers do work better with most fruits, but assertive beers can work as well if carefully considered. Excessively bitter beers seem to fight the sweet and sour character of most fruit. In general, sharp roasty flavors from malts like chocolate fight with the fruit, but as the cherry stout example points out, there are exceptions. Lighter beers meld easily with fruit. Caramelly notes from Munich, Vienna, and pale crystal will usually blend beautifully, though they may up the ante in terms of fruit quality, which in turn extends the maturation time. Very little work has been done, even on a homebrew scale, with very strong fruit beer, although I feel this is an area worth exploring.

Fruit beers require a modified concept of beer balance. We usually think of the big players as malt sweetness versus hop bitterness. Balance in fruit beers is more of a sweet/acid thing, with bitterness and sometimes tannin supplying a bit of toothy background. The crucial point is that without enough acidity, fruit loses its luster, a condition wine experts refer to as "flabbiness." This is easily adjusted, right up to bottling time, by the careful addition of various acids. Citric and malic acids are often used in wine and meadmaking, and work well in beer, malic (the acid of apples) being the softer of the two. Lactic acid may also be used for a yogurty tang. I recommend testing various quantities using a shot glass and syringe or pipette to dose beer with acid until the right quantity is determined by taste, then scaling up to full batch size. Once this is done for a particular recipe, the acid may be added to the fermenter without having to repeat the dosing test.

The perfect fruit, perfectly ripe, added in sufficient quantity will produce a profoundly complex beer. But unfortunately, these conditions rarely exist for any brewer, large or small. It is therefore necessary to find ways of getting the best, most complex flavor from the ingredients at hand. For example, since sour, dark cherries are just about impossible to find in this country, a mixture of sour pale cherries and dark sweet ones may be used to create a reasonable facsimile of a kriek. When fruit syrups or extracts are used, a small amount of real fruit may add a fresh fruit taste without a lot of fuss. If real fruit is not an option, then at least blend a couple of different extracts for a better taste than either alone. Sometimes a small quantity of a different fruit altogether may add depth—cherries added to raspberry beer, for example. Fruits may be added strictly for color; the Belgians add the inky purple elderberry to cherry beer to intensify color without adding any detectable flavor.

Occasionally, fruits ferment into a very different flavor than they have when fresh. Peach is a prime example. In fact, you can make much better peach beer with apricots than peaches. Blueberries seem to fade to nothingness, although someone recently suggested to me that cooked blueberries have more of a recognizable "blueberry" flavor than fresh, a notion I have not yet verified. Strawberries are almost hopeless, losing all their color and much of their flavor within a month or two. The only solution is to use lots of very ripe fruit (and remember strawberries don't ripen after they are

picked), and brew the kind of light summer beer that doesn't take long to mature.

Fruit also contains some strange carbohydrates that complicate the brewing process. Pectins can form a kind of permanent starchy haze, especially if the fruit is cooked prior to adding it to the beer. Pectinase enzymes are available, and do work, if somewhat slowly. The other complication is the presence of a bunch of oddball sugars that ferment very slowly. This causes problems for bottle conditioned beers. The only exploding bottles I ever had were of a cherry brown ale. Champagne bottle time bombs tucked away in innocent closets are not the greatest way to endear yourselves to your friends, I can tell you. Allow your beer to mellow in the secondary as long as you can, and cut back the priming by one-fourth to one-half, depending on the strength of the beer and the estimated completeness of fermentation.

The best way to incorporate fruit into your beer is to add it to the secondary fermenter. By this time the crop of yeast should be strong, and conditions should be acidic, alcoholic, and nutrient-depleted enough to keep invading microbes at bay. When using whole fruit, I like to freeze it first. Outside of the obvious benefit of keeping it stable until I'm ready to brew, freezing ruptures the cell walls, and allows the fruit to mush up and release its flavors into the beer more rapidly. Freezing does not kill the microflora on the fruit's surface, though it may reduce it a bit. Thaw the fruit in a sanitized container before adding to avoid shocking the yeast from a sudden drop in temperature.

A covered open container is the preferred vessel for this. Avoid glass carboys. If you must use them, be sure to leave at least a couple of gallons of headspace to avoid clogging the outlet and blowing up the whole jug, which can be an unforgettably unpleasant, not to mention dangerous, event. I have acquired an 8-gallon stainless steel milk can from my local junkyard, and am now brewing 5 gallons of cherry beer in it. Try to maintain a blanket of CO_2 gas over the fruit at all times to avoid encouraging mold and vinegar-causing acetobacter. Purging the empty container with CO_2 before racking should help, as well as a tight-fitting (but not airtight) lid. And remember, the more you open it to look, the less secure the gas blanket will be.

Fruit concentrates must be treated in the same manner as fresh or frozen fruit, but they are stronger on a weight basis. Usually, the packaging for a concentrate will state what the fresh fruit equivalent is. As with fresh fruit, adding to the secondary fermentation is the preferred method.

Concentrated juice is available for some fruits, and when available, it can be an excellent way to add a lot of fruit flavor with zero fuss. I have had especially good experience with black cherry juice concentrate, available at health food stores. As with all concentrates, the flavor can be a little one-dimensional, so the beer may need a little something else—a different extract, fresh fruit, fruit extract—to deepen and richen the flavor. As always, taste your fruit beer before kegging or bottling, and add acid if you think you need it.

Fruit extracts, lacking fermentable sugars, can be added directly to the serving tanks, or just prior to bottling. This allows for trial-dosing of a small sample using a pipette or syringe. Once the optimum quantity and mixture is decided upon, the test can be scaled up to full batch size by simple multiplication. Extracts can give very intense flavors, but may be somewhat flat in taste. Acids, especially, are missing, and

R E C I P E	**Mister Boing Boing Cherry Barley Wine**		

Yield: 5 gallons (19 liters)

Gravity: 1.095 (23 °P)

Alcohol/vol: 8.4 to 9.5%

Color: Pale amber

Bitterness: 43 IBU

Yeast: Alcohol-tolerant English ale

Maturation: 6 to 8 months

All-Grain Recipe:

14.0 lb (6.4 kg)	77%	Maris Otter or other high quality British pale ale malt
2.0 lb (0.9 kg)	11%	aromatic/melanoidin malt
0.25 lb (115 g)	1%	Carafa II malt (preferably huskless)
2.0 lb (0.9 kg)	11%	Barbados or other semi-refined sugar, added to kettle

Mash with single infusion at about 153° F for an hour.

For an Extract + Steeped Grain Recipe, replace the pale malt with 8.5 lb (3.9 kg) of pale dry malt extract

Hops:

2.0 oz (57 g)	90 min	Northdown (6.5% AA)
2.0 oz (57 g)	end of boil	East Kent Goldings (5% AA)

Ferment through the primary, then transfer into a 10-gallon fermenter. Add 8 pounds of sour cherries, plus 4 pounds of sweet dark cherries. Both should be previously frozen, then warmed to room temperature before adding. If you have CO_2, add a blanket of gas after you add the cherries. Allow to sit on beer for two to eight weeks—longer if you like. Rack beer back into a carboy and allow a couple months to settle out before bottling or kegging. Carbonate lightly!

beers flavored with fruit extracts almost always need some acid to bring out the fruit character. However, fruit extracts are also a good way to turn up the volume on a beer fermented with real fruit—a little extra fruity kick.

ORANGES AND OTHER CITRUS

Of the myriad seasonings used in beers over the millennia, few have such a prized role as the orange. From the subtlest nuances to the brightest starring role, oranges have been used to enliven countless mugs of ale through the ages.

There are two species of oranges. *Citrus sinensis*, the sweet orange, has a number of varieties: Valencia, blood, and navel. All have a thin, easily peeled skin and a large, juicy interior. *Citrus aurantium* is the bitter orange, also called Seville or sour orange, originally native to southern Vietnam. This is the type most useful to brewers and marmalade makers, prized for the oil in its intensely flavored rind.

Curaçao oranges are a specially harvested bitter orange, picked when still small, gray-green, and unripe, and are sometimes called "orange peas." These go to distillers and flavor manufacturers, and are extremely hard to find in the consumer marketplace.

My local Caribbean market stocks bitter oranges, which they call "sour oranges." The season is from September to May. They're ugly, unappetizing things. Bumpy and dull, they don't look like something you want to put in your prized homebrew, but scratch the skin and they come alive with a beautiful marmalade aroma.

Originating in China and treasured for their aroma, oranges were familiar in

Greece, India, and Rome two thousand years ago. Bitter oranges, native to southern Vietnam, reached Europe around 1100 through Sicily and Seville, thanks to an expanding Arab empire. Sweet oranges appeared in Europe several hundred years later, probably through Italy.

It is hard to say precisely when oranges were first used in beer, but brewers adopted every exotic spice as soon as it appeared. Oranges may have been part of the brewers' cupboard by the Renaissance. Hugh Platt (English) mentions oranges in a 1609 recipe, and by 1700 they're in all kinds of meads, possetts, syllabubs, and the like, as well as beer. England outlawed the use of such seasonings in commercial beer in the early eighteenth century, but spiced beers containing orange lived on in private breweries until about the end of the nineteenth century.

The only part of the orange you want is the oil contained in the colored outer rind of the peel. Wash it well, then take off the outer rind with a grater (a MicroPlane grater works wonders), zester, or potato peeler. The white inner rind, or pith, is unpleasantly bitter and should be avoided if possible.

The zest may be dropped into the kettle at the end of the boil, added to the secondary, or soaked in vodka for a few days and dosed into the beer at bottling or kegging. I find that one bitter orange is about right for 5 gallons of beer. I helped a brewer at a local brewpub concoct a 10-barrel batch of a Grand Cru-style ale. In that larger batch, the peels of two dozen bitter oranges added at the end of the boil gave the beer a lovely orange nose.

I have had good results with Triple Sec liqueur, which can be added to the secondary or used as priming for bottling. There are approximately 5 to 6 ounces (142 to 170 grams) of sugar in a 750-milliliter bottle, more than enough to prime a batch of beer. Sugar content varies considerably, so see the method of calculation in Chapter 12. One 750-milliliter bottle of liqueur will add around 1 percent alcohol to your beer. You can also use the liqueur as a solvent to extract flavor out of coriander or other spices. Just grind them up and let them soak in the liqueur a few days before straining through a coffee filter.

The dried tangerine peel available at Chinese markets has the bitter white pith as well as the aromatic oils. I haven't figured out a way to get one without the other, so I can't recommend them. The same goes for the dried peel sold in homebrew shops.

Marmalade is just chock full of good bitter/Seville orange flavor. It also contains a starchy substance, pectin, that may impart a haze to the finished beer—desirable in a white beer. Try a tablespoon or two as a starting point.

Nineteenth Century Flute Glass

Nothing shows off the elegant color of a fruit beer like a tall, slim glass.

Seville, aka Sour or Bitter Orange

These are best for brewing if you can find them. Note the rough skin and thick rind.

Citrus Beers to Ponder

Grapefruit American IPA

Lime Prickly Pear Weizen

Tangerine Chipotle Märzen

Kumquat Brown Ale

Lemon Honey Cream Ale

Marmalade Imperial Stout

Blood Orange Winter Warmer

For some reason, the oils present in oranges do not seem to interfere with beer head formation, at least in my own brewing experience.

If you can't find bitter/sour/Seville oranges, sweet varieties may be used, although

More Citrus Fruits for Brewing

Bergamot Orange A small citrus fruit (*Citrus aurantium* subsp. *bergamia*) cultivated in southern Italy. The flavoring used in Earl Grey tea.

Blood Orange Reddish skin and deep red juice with some tannins.

Grapefruit Pungent aroma blends well with American hops.

Key Lime The true lime, golf ball size. Milder, more complex than large limes.

Kumquat Tiny oblong orange fruits eaten skin and all. Sharp, clear aroma. A suitable substitute for Seville oranges. Use them whole.

Lemon Bright sunny aroma, very familiar.

Lime Common limes are related to lemons. Strong, single-minded aroma.

Mandarin Small tangerine variety. Delicate, mellow aroma.

Pomelo Giant grapefruit-like fruit popular in Middle East.

Tangelo Mandarin and orange cross. Nice complex aroma.

Tangerine Soft, rich aroma, especially nice with medium to darker malt flavors.

R E C I P E — 'London Ale' Adapted from John Tuck's *Private Brewer's Guide*, 1822

This recipe is typical of the rustic country recipes containing spices and seasonings. Such beers, invariably named for a region or a city, were brewed in the private brewhouses of manor houses. This tradition had pretty much died out by 1900. The amber malt adds a unique nutty/toasty edge to this beer.

Yield: 5 gallons (19 liters)

Gravity: 1.058 (14 °P)

Alcohol/vol: 4.2 to 5%

Color: Pale amber

Bitterness: 45 IBU

Yeast: London ale

Maturation: 2 to 4 months

All-Grain Recipe:

9.0 lb (4.1 kg)	86%	pale ale malt
1.0 lb (0.45 kg)	14%	biscuit amber malt

Mash with single infusion at about 153° F for an hour. Sparge and collect wort normally.

Extract + Steeped Grain Recipe:

6.0 lb (3.2 kg)	86%	amber dry malt extract
1.0 lb (0.45 kg)	14%	medium crystal malt

Hops:

2.0 oz (57 g)	120 min Fuggle (5% AA)

At end of boil, add: the peel of one bitter/Seville/sour orange or three regular oranges; 0.25 oz (7 g) coriander seed, freshly ground. Add to secondary: 2 tsp (9.5 g) powdered ginger; 0.25 tsp (1 g) salt.

*Amber malt can be made by roasting pale malt for 20 minutes at 350° F. Allow to mellow a week or two before brewing. See p. 224 for more information on malt roasting.

RECIPE — **Dark Night Tangerine Porter**

This was created to answer the question: "How dark can a beer be and still have some witbier character?" Well, it turns out, if you keep the roastiness under control and use a very mellow citrus, the answer is "fairly dark." You will notice a rich milkshake texture to this beer, and the net result is a little like a chocolate Orange Creamsicle.

Yield: 5 gallons (19 liters)

Gravity: 1.058 (14 °P)

Alcohol/vol: 4.7 to 5.5%

Color: Chocolate brown

Bitterness: 31 IBU

Yeast: Belgian ale

Maturation: 2 to 4 months

All-Grain Recipe:

4.0 lb (1.8 kg)	35%	Munich malt
3.0 lb (1.4 kg)	26%	mild ale or Vienna malt
2.0 lb (0.90 kg)	17%	unmalted soft red wheat flakes
1.0 lb (0.45 kg)	8.5%	oatmeal
0.75 lb (340 g)	6.5%	Cara Munich (medium crystal)
0.5 lb (227 g)	4%	black patent malt
0.25 lb (113 g)	2%	Special B (dark crystal)
0.25 lb (227 g)	—	rice hulls, added to mash

The unmalted grains take some special treatment. Mix them, finely ground, with a pound of the six-row, and mash in for 15 minutes at 150° F (65.5° C), then raise to a boil and maintain for 10 minutes. Have the rest of the goods at protein rest, and raise to mash at 154° F (68° C) when you add the boiling unmalted grain to the main mash. Continue for 30-40 minutes, then mash out at 170° F (77° F), and maintain at least 165° F (74° C) during sparging to keep the starch liquified.

Extract + Steeped Grain Recipe:

3.0 lb (1.4 kg)	36%	amber dry malt extract
2.5 lb (1.1 kg)	30%	liquid wheat extract

Plus: all of the specialty grains from the all-grain recipe, from the oatmeal on down.

Hops:

0.5 oz (14g)	90 min	Northern Brewer hops (7% AA)
0.25 oz (7 g)	30 min	Styrian Golding hops (5.5% AA)
0.5 oz (14 g)	30 min	Northern Brewer hops (7% AA)
0.5 oz (14 g)	15 min	Styrian Golding hops (5.5% AA)

Add at end of boil, add: zest of 1 tangerine; 1 oz (28 g) coriander; 0.5 tsp (2 g) ground star anise. Ferment with your favorite Belgian ale yeast.

with a different flavor. Using two parts sweet orange peel plus one part of grapefruit peel comes a little closer to the Seville taste. I'd recommend two to three times the total quantity of sweet orange peel substituted for bitter orange for the same intensity. Tangelos have a nice, deep aroma, and blood oranges are complex. I have also used tangerines to good effect, especially with richer, darker beers. Sweet oranges are coated with a wax that is often laced with antifungal agents. While I couldn't come up with anything definitively dangerous about them, it seems prudent to use organic oranges for this purpose, since they are coated solely with food-grade materials like carnauba and beeswax.

DRINK YOUR VEGETABLES

At most times and places vegetables have been added to beer only during desperate—usually wartime— shortages. Slices of sugar beets tossed into the kettle may not be your idea of delicious, but there are a few vegetables that actually make fine beer ingredients.

Pumpkin Ale Brewing with pumpkins—or *pompions* as they were then called—was one of the privations endured during colonial times, and must have been one more reason for the overwhelming popularity of rum in many places. Typically the old recipes called for dried pumpkin, which must have been rather leathery and required a lot of cooking to soften up.

Pumpkin itself is rather bland, but will make its presence known in a beer if you know to look for it. The best way I have found to use it is to start with small "pie" pumpkins bred for flavor rather than gigantism, hack them in half, then bake pulp side down in a 300° F oven for one to two hours until they're slumping, tender, and well caramelized on the bottom. It's best not to grease the pan, as you don't want that stuff in your brew. Line the pan with a sheet of heavy-duty foil. Allow to cool, then scoop out the pulp, which can be added to the mash. Pumpkins contain about 6.5

RECIPE	**Ray Spangler's Pumpkin Spice Beer**		

Yield: 5 gallons (19 liters)

Gravity: 1.079

Alcohol/vol: 7.5 to 8.7%

Color: Pale amber

Bitterness: 27 IBU

Yeast: American ale

Maturation: 3 to 6 months

All-Grain Recipe:

8.0 lb (3.6 kg)	55%	six-row lager malt
4.0 lb (1.8 kg)	14.5%	pumpkin, baked 90 min @ 350° F, smash up, add to mash
2.0 lb (0.90 kg)	14%	pale crystal malt
1.5 lb (0.68 kg)	10%	wheat malt
1.0 lb (0.45 kg)	7%	dextrine malt
2.0 lb (0.90 kg)	14%	mild-flavored honey, added to brew kettle
0.5 lb (227 g)	—	rice hulls

No Equivalent Extract Recipe

Hops:

0.5 oz (14 g)	60 min	Cascade (6% AA)
0.5 oz (14 g)	60 min	Kent Golding (5% AA)
0.5 oz (14 g)	10 min	Cascade (6% AA)
0.5 oz (14 g)	10 min	Fuggle (4.4% AA)

Add at end of boil: 0.5 oz (14 g) coriander, crushed; 0.25 oz (7 g) allspice; 0.5 tsp (2 g) each of pumpkin pie spice, cinnamon, and nutmeg; 0.25 tsp (1 g) nutmeg. Add 0.5 oz (14 g) of whole coriander to the secondary for a little extra flavor.

percent carbohydrates. At an 80-percent utilization rate, that comes to the paltry gravity contribution of 1.005 per pound (0.45 kg) in a 5-gallon (19-liter) batch.

Any variety of winter squash can be prepared in the same way, with the same effect. Hubbard, butternut, and turban are all good varieties for this purpose.

Headless Horseman Pumpkin Barley Wine This uses fresh-roasted pumpkin to add flavor. Split a 5- to 7-pound pumpkin horizontally, discard seeds, place cut side down, and roast in the oven until soft and somewhat caramelized. Brew a barley wine recipe (see *My Old Flame*, p. 132), but cut the hops by one-third. Add the roast pumpkin, mushed up, skin removed, right into the mash. If you want to do an extract version, do a mini-mash of Pilsener malt with an amount equal to the pumpkin, then add to the rest of the extract recipe. A pound of rice hulls will hasten the sparge. Mash as you normally would, and complete the brew as any other barley wine. Dose your secondary with a tiny amount of pumpkin pie spice—0.125 to 0.25 tsp (0.5 to 1 g). Ferment with an alcohol-tolerant ale yeast, and allow plenty of time for aging. Hopping can be high or moderate. Let the pumpkin shine by avoiding large amounts of rough-tasting, high-alpha hops. Gravity: 1.098 (23.5 °P). Color: Deep orange-amber.

HOLY CHIHUAHUA, IT'S CHILE BEER!

The pepper is one of the New World's great gifts to the planet. It's a rare homebrewer who doesn't crave the delicious heat of various types of chilies, although not always in beer. In brewing chile beers, they are treated more as a spice than a vegetable, typically being added at the end of the boil or during secondary fermentation.

Holy Mole Bock Start with a classic bock recipe (p. 113), then at the end of the boil,

Ancho, left, and Pasilla

Two chiles with deep raisiny flavors. Pasilla is the hotter of the two.

Chiles for Brewing

Variety	Heat (Scoville)	Description
Anaheim	1,200	Dried or green, clean peppery flavor.
Ancho	1,000	Dried version of poblano. Deep rich chocolatey flavor.
Cayenne	35,000	Very sharp, crisp, and neutral.
Chipotle	4,000	Smoke-dried ripe jalapeño. Elegant but zippy.
Guajillo	5,000	Dark fruity chile with medium heat. Dried version of chilaca.
Habañero	300,000	Complex, fruit-scented. Blistering heat.
Jalapeño	4,000	Sharp green pepper flavor. Plenty of heat.
Paprika	0 to 2,000	Very nice bright pepper flavor; hot or mild varieties.
Pasilla	2,500	Intense dried chile flavor: dark, winelike, raisiny.
Poblano	1,000	Deep complex green tastes. Heat varies considerably.

RECIPE	**Smoked Habañero Amber Lager**

Yield: 5 gallons (19 liters)

Gravity: 1.053 (12.5° P)

Alcohol/vol: 4.3–5%

Color: Tawny amber

Bitterness: 24 IBU

Yeast: Bavarian lager

Maturation: 2 to 3 months

You can smoke your own grain easily on a covered grill, with half a dozen briquettes off to the side (see p. 191), with chips of oak, hickory or other smoke wood on top. I usually do an hour on the smoke.

Smoked malt requires no special treatment beyond a step infusion mash, rest an hour at 150° F (65.5° C). Be sure to age it at below 45° F (7° C) for true lager character.

All-Grain Recipe:

4.0 lb (1.8 kg)	40%	pale ale malt
4.0 lb (1.8 kg)	40%	Munich malt
1.0 lb (0.45 kg)	10%	pale crystal malt
1.0 lb (0.45 g)	10%	smoked malt

Extract +Steeped Grain Recipe:

2.5 lb (1.1 kg)	36%	pale dry malt extract
2.5 lb (1.1 kg)	36%	amber dry malt extract
1.0 lb (0.45 kg)	14%	pale crystal malt
1 lb (0.45 kg)	14%	smoked malt

Hops:

1.0 oz (28 g)	90 min	Hallertau or Crystal hops (3.5% AA)
1.0 oz (28 g)	30 min	Hallertau or Crystal hops (3.5% AA)
1.0 oz (28 g)	5 min	Hallertau or Crystal hops (3.5% AA)

1-3 (according to your heat-tolerance) Habañero or Scotch Bonnet peppers, chopped, seeded, and deveined.

Scotch Bonnet Chile

Blow-your-head-off heat!

add 0.5 ounce of coriander, 4 ounces of low-fat cocoa, and 1 ounce of ancho chile—or guajillo if you want to push the heat envelope a little.

Chipotle Parched Corn Amber Ale If you can get your hands on 2 pounds of field or Indian corn kernels, you can toast them over charcoal on your grill (see the setup on p. 191). You want an amber kind of toast level, and it isn't important if the toasting is even. An alternate to dried corn is to fire-roast sweet corn. Get a small amount of charcoal going on your grill, then roast four dehusked ears of sweet corn until they're light brown. Strip the kernels off and add them to a mash consisting of half six-row and half Munich. This one can be hopped aggressively if you like. Use 0.25 to 1 ounce of chipotle, depending on your desire for heat.

SHROOMS, MAN!

People have put all kinds of crazy stuff into their beer. This includes dangerous psychotropic drugs, hideously bitter herbs like blessed thistle, toxic heavy metals like cobalt (improved head retention), and animal parts such as Rocky Mountain oysters, not to mention the real oceanic shellfish of the same name. So a few culinary mushrooms don't seem so odd. Another thing to keep in mind is that beer is largely the product of a fungus—yeast—so some of the tastes have certain similarities.

Most mushrooms do have a certain earthiness—not often welcome in a beer—so the choice of which mushroom to use is very important. I started all this mucking with mushrooms in beer after reading about a rustic German schnapps infused with chanterelle mushrooms. I'd long been a fan of these beautiful, apricot-perfumed shrooms, and it turns out that they blend in quite well with pale and amber beers, if the hop aroma is held back to allow the subtlety of the chanterelles to shine through.

The mushroom kingdom offers a huge variety of flavors, although in many cases you'll have to go tromping through the woods to get them. This is a fun and engaging hobby on its own, of course, and there are lots of books available if you're interested. Fortunately, supermarkets and specialty stores are stocking a fair number of different mushrooms in fresh and dried form these days, and many of them work as seasonings in beer.

Please note that if you do go foraging in the woods, get a good field guide and pay very close attention to both the pictures and *especially to the written descriptions*, as there are sometimes toxic look-alike species. Wild mushrooms are quite safe to eat—or brew with—but only if you pay attention. You should be aware that many species must be cooked before eating; this is noted in the field guides.

A Truffle Hunter and His Trained Pig
Looks like he's got a pretty good haul!

In addition to food and flavor value, many mushrooms have important medicinal qualities as well. Common properties are along tonic lines, with immune and circulatory system benefits. This is another interesting area of study, and fits with the long, historical tradition of using beer as a base for delivering medically useful ingredients.

There are several easy ways to get mushroom flavors into your beer, along the same lines as using any other spice or seasoning. Chopped mushrooms can be tossed in during the boil, which cooks them and extracts flavor as well as the complex carbohydrate materials bearing the medicinal properties of certain species. More delicate mushrooms may be made into tea, then filtered, cooled, and added in the secondary or at bottling or kegging. Species like chanterelles or truffles that don't require cooking can be finely chopped and soaked for a few days in vodka, strained through a coffee filter, then added in the same manner as a tea.

Reishi Sumo Stout Reishi mushrooms, or Ling Chi in Chinese (*Ganoderma lucidum*), are a prized ingredient in Chinese traditional medicine, holding the esteemed place of "superior." They are a shelf fungus with a glossy, lacquered top surface, and grow on hardwood trees. They have a delicate but rich, warm flavor, and some specimens have a slight bitterness. They can be found occasionally in the wild, or at any Chinatown herb shop. Health food stores will often carry capsules or other preparations, but they may be inconvenient and/or expensive.

Ling Zhi/Reishi

One of the ten superior ingredients of traditional Chinese medicine.

Chaga, *Inonotus obliquus*

This lumpy fungus is a Siberian tonic.

Chaga Sahti Chaga (*Inonotus obliquus*) grows on birch trees in northern climes, and resembles nothing so much as chunks of asphalt stuck at eye level to the sides of the trees. It has a long history in Siberia as a folk tonic, and is drunk in a tea as an immune system booster. I've never seen the stuff for sale, so you're going to have to find it on your own. I once collected several bags near Lake Superior, so that's the kind of environment we're talking about. Chaga is quite woody, and may be a challenge to grate. Fresh off the tree it's a little softer, but after it's dried out, get the hammer!

Chaga has a soft earthy/shroomy flavor, with some bitterness. I thought it fitting to put this into a northern-style beer, so a Scandinavian sahti forms the base. Note that this wheat- and rye-based beer can be difficult to lauter, so do not skip the rice hulls. Reishi would be an acceptable substitute for the Chaga if you can't get up north. See p. 244 for more detailed instructions on sahti.

A Thousand Saints Truffle Tripel Start with the tripel recipe on p. 125, and make the following modifications:
- Use 1 additional pound of jaggery (or other partially refined sugar)
- Cut the spice quantities in half
- Ferment at a somewhat cooler temperature
- Add 1.0 oz (28 g) sliced truffles to the secondary

Irish Moss, *Cetraria islandica*

This lichen is used in beer brewing to help coagulate proteins in the boiling wort. It is added about ten minutes before the end of the boil.

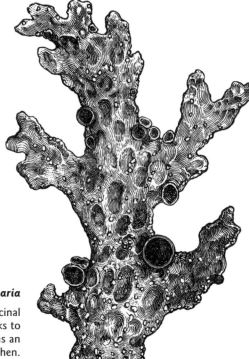

Lobaria pulmonaria

Half fungus, half algae, this medicinal lichen was once used by Siberian monks to bitter an ale. Saison de Pipaix contains an undisclosed "medicinal" lichen.

RECIPE — Nirvana Chanterelle Ale

This is one of my regular house beers. The chanterelles add an ethereal fruitiness, very delicate and complex. It was inspired by a reference to a German schnapps made from chanterelles.

Yield: 5 gallons (19 liters)

Gravity: 1.083 (20.5 °P)

Alcohol/vol: 5.7 to 6.7%

Color: Amber

Bitterness: 27 IBU

Yeast: Belgian abbey

Maturation: 2 to 3 months

All-Grain Recipe:

9.5 lb (4.3 kg)	64%	U.S. two-row lager malt
2.0 lb (0.90 kg)	13%	British two-row pale ale malt
1.5 lb (0.68 kg)	9.5%	Munich malt
1.5 lb (0.68 kg)	9.5%	wheat malt
0.5 lb (227 g)	3%	aromatic/melanoidin (dark Munich)

Extract + Steeped Grain Recipe:

8.0 lb (3.6 kg)	80%	pale dry malt extract
1.0 lb (0.45 kg)	10%	dextrine malt
0.5 lb (227 g)	5%	pale crystal malt
0.5 lb (227 g)	5%	medium crystal malt

Step mash: mash in at 113° F (45° C), hold for half hour, raise to 145° F (63° C), hold for half hour, raise to 156° F (69° C), hold for 45 minutes. Mash out at 170° F (78° C) and sparge until 6.5 gallons are collected. Note: Single infusion mash will work for this beer. Try 154° F for one hour. Add hot water to mash out.

Hops:

0.75 oz (21 g)	90 min	Saaz (3% AA)
1.5 oz (43 g)	30 min	Saaz (3% AA)
1.5 oz (43g)	10 min	Saaz (3% AA)
0.5 oz (14 g)	end of boil	Cascade (3% AA)

Chanterelles
My choice for the perfect beer mushroom.

Chapter 14

BENT BEERS

I have a conflicted view on beer styles. As historical artifacts, they're endlessly fascinating to study. And I think that they generally represent confluences—and compromises—of technology, agriculture, cuisine, and geology that make the most of what a region has to offer. That means existing styles are usually quite wonderful to drink, and I'm all for that.

But as a brewer who approaches the craft from an artistic point of view, I'm not always interested in precisely reproducing a particular style, challenging as that may be. I do it, of course, but it's more for the experience of getting inside and finding out what makes a style tick. More importantly, I like to use the basic style as a springboard, a starting point for brewing beers that go beyond style and shine as unique personal expressions.

Beer styles exist for a variety of reasons, some of which make sense. Shaped by geology, climate, agriculture, religion, tax policy, and many other factors, styles offer a comfortable handle for drinkers and brewers alike. In most countries, style are pretty clear cut, evolving over decades—even centuries, leaving little room for experimentation. In Germany it is disreputable, if not illegal, to brew off-style. Belgium is the exception, with half the beers there fitting no clear classification except "other." The ones that do claim a style often take ferocious liberties with them. It's a country of artists, to be sure.

Invariably, the mix of characteristics in a successful style reaches a flavorful equilibrium. Where limited to hard water, brewers settle on malty beers, avoiding the harshness that would result if hoppier brews were attempted. Where hops are inexpensive, brewers figure out a way to use a lot of them. With ice unavailable to early West Coast brewers, they used their lager yeast at higher-than-normal temperatures, and steam beer was the happy result. There are lots of interrelated factors. Studying them brings one to the very core of brewing science and history.

There's much more to be done. If you're not interested in winning contests with these style pariahs, you can amaze and astound your friends and even yourself (to be fair, there is usually a category or two in competitions reserved for beers outside the mainstream styles). Such beers can vary from expectations in color or bitterness by more subtle means, using a non-traditional malt bill to achieve the expected color, for example.

When playing this dangerous game, you should be ever alert to the basics of balance, water chemistry, aromatics, and all the rest. Charging off into the unknown is a true test of your brewing knowledge and skill. *Not every combination is a winner.*

To get the juices flowing, here a few musings along these iconoclastic lines.

Hoppy Amber Wit Cross a pale ale with a classic Leuven wit, and you'll get a beer that will satisfy the cravings of hopheads and Belgomaniacs alike. Try a 70/20/10 mix of pale, Munich, and Belgian crystal malts. Shoot for about 1.065 (15.5 °P). Hops can be up to about 50 IBU before they get ragged. I like the classic blend of Styrian Goldings and Saaz, usually starting with the first, finishing with the latter. And you'll want to spice it up with the zest of one orange (just use a potato peeler), plus a half-ounce of freshly crushed coriander seed, both added in last five minutes of the boil.

Abbey Weiss Use your favorite weizen recipe (40 percent wheat malt, 60 percent Pilsener malt, 22 IBU), bump up the gravity to 1.060 (14.5 °P), then ferment with your favorite Belgian yeast at 65 to 70° F (18 to 21° C). This is what the monks would drink if they were allowed to hang out in the beer garden all summer. I like Tettnanger or Saaz for this concoction. Spice it up with a dash (0.25 oz or 7 g each, at the end of the boil) of coriander and chamomile. Garnish with a slice of orange or a tiny kumquat slice, if you dare.

Pilsener Wine What would happen if you brewed a classic American adjunct mash beer (70 percent malt, 30 percent rice), but at a vastly higher gravity? This is not as silly as it sounds, as high-gravity beers often benefit from the addition of tasteless adjuncts such as corn, rice, or sugar to make them drinkably crisp. Those who have tasted the hi-grav brews made to maximize production in big industrial breweries report ambrosia. I'd go about 1.090 (21 °P), 50 IBU, no colored malt of any kind. You can bypass the complex adjunct mash needed for corn or rice, and just go with corn sugar if you like. Noble German or Czech hops are the ticket here, although (yuck!) Cluster hops would be considered classic. If you ferment with Belgian yeast, I bet it'll taste a lot like Duvel!

Wheat Wine This non-traditional beer is a high-strength ale brewed from at least 30 percent wheat. The wheat seems to lighten the beer and make it more drinkable. Normal wheat beers are lightly hopped, but with this wildcat style, you may do as you please. Be aware that this will age much more quickly than barley wine.

SMOKIN': BEERS, THAT IS

I had tasted smoked beers a couple of times without great enjoyment or horror, regarding them as novelty beers, just an offbeat curiosity. My thunderclap conversion to a card-carrying smoked beer lover occurred in a hospitality suite at the 1988 American Homebrew Association convention. Rogue brewer John Maier, then of the Alaskan Brewery, was greeting visitors with a bathtub of earthly delights: a cool quarter barrel of smoked porter, and its natural soul mate, a big plastic bag of smoke-cured salmon belly strips. It was one of the defining food and beer moments of my life, a true *Beer Experience*. The delicate alder smoke gave the rich, slightly sweet porter a per-

French Label, c. 1900
This was a nutritious malt beverage rather than a beer.

Polish beer label, c. 1930

This was the Polish name for Grätzer, the final incarnation of this once-popular Prussian smoked wheat beer.

fectly deranged finish of dry smokiness, and the savoriness of the salmon played off this beverage perfectly. This was a *real beer*!

In the way-old days, of course, most beers were smoked. Prior to the Industrial Revolution, malt was cured with the common fuel of the region. In Europe, this meant wood. Out on the north part of the boggy islands of Britain and Ireland, ancient, compressed peat was burned, as was straw, which gave a less smoky taste.

In the desert, where beer was born, trees were scarce and a natural energy source—the sun—was available in abundance. Consequently, very pale sun-dried malt could be easily produced if needed. Malt was also shaped into conical cakes like big muffins, and baked in bread ovens that would have been powered by some local fuel—I'm guessing dried ox dung or something equally pungent. Red and black beers are mentioned in ancient Sumeria. In kilning, the beer would have picked up some smoky flavors.

In medieval Europe, malt was dried in whole kernel form for brewing, as it is now. Oak and beech, then as now, were the preferred woods for fire-kilning malts because of their high energy density and clean-burning manners. But as far back as the seventeenth century brewers were railing against "smoaky" flavors in beer. Coal- and later coke-fired kilns made this switch to cleaner malt flavors possible. Hard Welsh coal was particularly prized.

Progress reigned supreme, and the trend toward lighter, clearer, crisper (is it beer or is it mouthwash?) flavors meant the end of smoky beers nearly everywhere.

Everywhere, that is, except Germany. From lederhosen to precision machinery like cuckoo clocks and BMWs, this tradition-obsessed country has held onto much of its cultural heritage, and in the Franconian region of Bavaria, smoked beers are a part of the package. This brewery-rich area produces smoked beers in a variety of styles. The most typical versions are amber lagers—Märzens—overlaid with the pungent, woody tang of beechwood-smoked malt. Smoked versions of other Bavarian favorites are also brewed.

Another smoked beer that was once quite popular has now died out. This is Grätzer beer, a low-gravity ale brewed with oak-smoked wheat malt that survived until recently in Poland under the name *Grodzisk*. Grätzer was once very popular in West Prussia (now Poland; then part of Germany), and is part of the family of white beers that includes Berliner weisse and Belgian witbiers. Ranging from 1.028 to 1.057 (6.5 to 13.5) in gravity, with low to moderate alcohol at 2.0 to 5.5 percent by volume, these smoky, highly carbonated beers would have been enjoyed in quantity as an everyday thirst-quencher. Grätzer would have been amber in color due to a proportion of well-kilned wheat malt similar to the "aromatic" malt. Perhaps this intriguing and delicious beer will be revived for our enjoyment sometime soon, but in the meantime, you can make your own.

From the Fischer/Pecheur Brewery in France we get a peat-smoked beer called Adelscott. It is pale amber in color, and relatively strong at 1.065 (15.5 °P) original gravity. Its hint of Scotch whiskey smokiness comes from Scottish distillers' malt. It has a full caramel body nicely set off by the smoky malt.

Another emerging trend is to use peated distillers' malt in Scottish ales. Although breweries in Scotland have not done this for about three hundred years, the idea seems workable enough. If done with restraint, the peaty malt lends a touch of dryness to an otherwise sweetish beer. I should point out that this is in no way authentic. Scottish brewers were only too happy to get away from the coarseness of smoked malt, so as soon as an alternative was available, they jumped ship.

The homebrewers, as usual, are leading the charge with the really wacky stuff, and no doubt such brews as pecan-smoked altbier, smoked imperial stout, smoked habañero ale, and even Jamaican allspice-smoked jerked beer may be showing up, first at homebrew meetings, and then at brewpubs across the country.

Two sorts of smoked malt are available commercially: German oak-smoked malt, and Scottish peat-smoked malt. The German malt is made to brew Bamberg Rauchbier, and the peated malt is used to make Scotch whiskey. Both are quite pungent, and a pound or two will add a noticeably smoky note in a beer's aroma and finish, although German rauchmalts are often used for 100 percent of the batch in Bamberg.

SMOKING MALT ON THE BARBECUE

You can smoke your own malt on a kettle-type grill or any kind of smoker. You need a very small fire and some sort of open-bottomed basket for holding the malt. A simple wooden frame made from 1 x 2 wood, with bronze window screen stapled to the bottom, wrapped up the sides, and stapled some more, works great. If you're using a kettle grill, make the basket so it doesn't cover the whole area, because you don't want the malt directly over the charcoal.

Build a very small fire (eight briquettes or equivalent of lump charcoal) off to one side of the grill, or in the regular place in the smoker. Place a small handful of soaked wood chips or equivalent in larger pieces on top of the coals. Fill the basket about an inch deep, then place it in the smoker or grill and close the lid, making sure the vent holes are open to allow a draft for the fire. You can make additional baskets and stack them if you like; just shuffle them as smoking proceeds. Maintain this status for between thirty minutes and two hours or longer, turning the malt and adding more charcoal and wood chips occasionally. When done, allow to cool and use when you like.

GRÄTZER

Once again, an odd beer reminds us of the incredible richness of beer's past, and of the narrowness of our own view of beer today. I hardly know which chapter to put this in. It's wheat, it's smoked, it's historical. Well, here goes.

Grätzer is a light, highly hopped wheat beer made entirely from smoked wheat malt, and usually described as having

Smoking Setup

A kettle-type grill and a shallow screen basket are all that's needed. Smoking wood rests on small pile of charcoal. Lid should be closed while smoking.

Malt Smoking Woods

Alder Sweet woodiness, very neutral, delicate

Apple Sweet, spicy, extremely mellow

Beech Dry, woody, neutral, with hint of pungency

Birch Spicy, hints of wintergreen, especially in bark

Cherry A dry, complex, almondy fruitiness

Grapevine Intensely dry, herbal, and woody

Hickory Dry, mellow, mild

Maple Sweet, spicy, buttery, mild

Mesquite Delicate, slightly spicy

Peach Fruity and delicate

Pear Slightly sweet and spicy, very mellow

Peat Phenolic, sharp, oily, creosote-like

Pecan Massively spicy, pungent, intense!

Red oak Somewhat sharp, but softer than white oak

White oak Intensely pungent, acidic, musty

an apple-scented aroma. Originating as early as the fifteenth century in the Grätz district in the province of Posnan in West Prussia, Grätzer was hugely popular in the North of Germany in the late nineteenth century.

To brew an absolutely authentic 1884 version, you would make a 1.057 (13.5 °P) wort from 93 percent pale, oak-smoked wheat malt, plus 7 percent of the same stuff

RECIPE — Grätzer, Real Version

Yield: 5 gallons (19 liters)
Gravity: 1.057 (13.5°P)
Alcohol/vol: 5.0 to 5.7%
Color: Hazy gold
Bitterness: 44 IBU
Yeast: German ale
Maturation: 6 to 8 weeks

All-Grain Recipe:

9.0 lb (4.1 kg)	93%	smoked malted wheat
0.75 lb (0.68 kg)	7%	smoked malted wheat, toasted*
1.0 lb (0.45 kg)	—	rice hulls

The traditional mash procedure was described simply as "infusion," with rests at 50° C (122° F), 64° C (148° F), then a mash out at 79° C (175° F).

Hops: as below

RECIPE — Grätzer, Cheaters Version

Yield: 5 gallons (19 liters)
Gravity: 1.057/13.5°P
Alcohol/vol: 5.0 to 5.7%
Color: Hazy gold
Bitterness: 44 IBU
Yeast: German ale
Maturation: 6 to 8 weeks

Ferment at 50-60°F (10 to 15.5 °C) for primary, then drop to 40-45°F for 4-week cold-conditioning. Prime with 1 cup of corn sugar or dry malt extract.

All-Grain Recipe:

7.25 lb (3.3 kg)	69%	malted wheat, smoked 1 hour on oak (see p. 191)
2.5 lb (1.1 kg)	24%	U.S. six-row lager malt
0.75 lb (0.68 kg)	7%	aromatic/melanoidin malt
1.0 lb (0.45 kg)	—	rice hulls (to aid sparging)

Mash all ingredients at 148° F (64° C) for one hour. If you can swing it, do a protein rest first, one hour at 122° F (50° C).

Extract + Mini-Mash Recipe:

6.0 lb (2.7 kg)	67%	liquid wheat extract
1.0 lb (0.45 kg)	11%	U.S. six-row lager malt
1.0 lb (0.45 kg)	11%	malted wheat
1.0 lb (0.45 kg)	11%	medium crystal malt

Smoke all the specialty grains two hours over oak (see p. 191). Crush all grains and combine with 165° F (74° C) water to mash at 150 to 155° F (65.5 to 68° C) for one hour. Drain, rinse with hot water, and add all liquid to brew pot.

Hops:

1.0 oz (28 g)	60 min	Saaz (3% AA)
2.0 oz (57 g)	20 min	Saaz (3% AA)
3.0 oz (85g)	5 min	Saaz (3% AA)

that has been slow-roasted to a copper color. At about the turn of the century the tax laws were changed in Germany to favor production of *schankbier*, or very low-gravity beer. After this time Grätzer slipped into this category, at about 1.032 (7.5 °P) original gravity. Grätzer has been extinct in Germany since the 1930s, and the one brewed until recently in Poland under the name *Grodzisk* is no longer in production.

Hopping was heavy, at 1 ounce per gallon (8 grams per liter) of traditional Czech hops. A variety called *Lublin*, very similar to Saaz, is widely grown in Poland, including the Posnan region. Top-fermenting yeast was used, and like most wheat beer of the day, it was highly carbonated and packaged in heavy crockery bottles.

LICHTENHAINER

This beer is sort of halfway in character between a Berliner weisse and a grätzer. It was a pale, top-fermenting beer with a slightly sour taste and a smoky character. It was traditionally produced solely from smoked barley malt, although by the 1930s, it was composed of one-third wheat and two-thirds barley malt. Unlike Berliner weisse, the wort of which was not boiled, and which was soured by lactobacillus present in the grain, Lichtenhainer was fermented with a conventional ale yeast, then placed in inoculated barrels, which induced a slight souring.

In 1880, gravity was reported at 1.045 (11°P); in 1886, a different source gives it as 1.037 (9 °P); by 1898, it was 1.031 (7.5 °P). Slightly earlier (1877) gravity is given at about 1.044. Although this is just three data points, it does fit with the general trend of these small beers weakening up to about World War I. For all, lactic acid content was about 0.2 percent. I can't find any hard facts about hopping. For the purpose of the recipe, I'm guessing about 23 IBU.

RECIPE	Dingelheimer's Lichtenhainer		
Yield: 5 gallons (19 liters)	*All-Grain Recipe:*		
Gravity: 1.040 (9.5 °P)	5.5 lb (2.5 kg)	73%	German rauchmalt
Alcohol/vol: 3.2 to 3.7%	2.0 lb (0.90 kg)	27%	German sour malt
Color: Hazy straw	*No Equivalent Extract Recipe*		
Bitterness: 23 IBU	*Hops:*		
Yeast: German ale	1.5 oz (43 g)	90 min	Hallertau (3.5% AA)
Maturation: 4 to 6 weeks			

This Icelandic label sets the mood for archaic Scandinavian brews.

This detail from a Swedish label. c.1910, shows a characteristic Scandinavian wooden tankard.

GOTLANDSDRICKA

Many believe that Gotlandsdricka was the everyday drink of the Vikings, with mead being reserved for more important occasions. Gotland is an island off the southeast coast of Sweden, and the name means "good land." Its remoteness from the Swedish mainland has helped preserve this quaint old brew. *Dricka* simply means "drink."

Like its relative, sahti (see p. 244), Gotlandsdricka is a farmhouse ale made primarily from barley malt, with additions of other grains: rye and wheat heavily laced with birch-smoke, which has a faint wintergreen tang. In its traditional form it is unhopped, bittered instead with bog bean, *carduus* (blessed thistle), and/or wood sage (*Teucrium sp.*). Like all the Scandinavian folk brews, it reeks of juniper.

Gotlandsdricka is made in a number of styles: fresh, still, and sweet; aged still, aged sparkling; strong, sour, aged, sparkling; and blends of aged still and sparkling. Contemporary versions are pale to amber. Older recipes seem to indicate that the beer used to be much darker, a truly brown beer. There's a lot of variation in the gravity, too, but mostly it tends to be made as a strong beer.

Unlike Finnish sahti, Gotlandsdricka is not produced commercially at present. But if you live in Gotland, it's possible to buy wort and ferment it yourself.

Traditional Gotland malt is quite smoky, due to six to seven days over birch fires. This malt is produced commercially on the island, but if you want to try your hand at this beer, you'll have to smoke your own malt. When smoking with birch, use the bark as well as the wood, as that's where the wintergreen character resides. If you don't have a week, two to four hours on the smoker ought to do it. The malt is described as "about as smoky" as German rauchmalt.

Juniper gets into the brew in the mash liquor, preboiled for an hour with berry-laden branches; and as a filtering base in the bottom of the combination mash/lauter tun called a *rostbunn*. At the bottom is a cross made of juniper wood, which forms the base of the filter bed.

"There are brewers who use very old sticks, used by generations, and believe there is some magic force in them." —Håkan Lundgren

A simple infusion mash is used, a little on the warm side at 154° F. After an hour, the wort is drained, and additional juniper-infused liquor is ladled on top of the goods.

Historically, Gotlandsdricka was fermented in oak vessels, so if you want to be authentic, oak chips or cubes should be used. Stay away from new American oak, as it's way too pungent, even for this odoriferous brew. French or Hungarian would be a better choice (see p. 91 for more on barrel wood). Some of the stronger, longer-aged versions develop an aromatic sourness, which is what you'll get with an oak-aged beer.

RECIPE	Gotlandsdrickå

Yield: 5 gallons (19 liters)

Gravity: 1.075 (18° P)

Alcohol/vol: 5.8 to 6.8%

Color: Hazy gold

Bitterness: 44 IBU

Yeast: Baker's yeast

Maturation: 4 to 6 weeks

As noted, these rustic beers are often fermented with baker's (pressed cake) yeast. Because the stuff is kind of hyperactive, use a piece no bigger than the size of a sugar cube, dissolved in water before adding to the wort.

All-Grain Recipe:

6.0 lb (2.7 kg)	43%	pale malt*
4.0 lb (1.8 kg)	29%	biscuit/amber malt*
1.0 lb (0.45 kg)	7%	flaked rye, ground to grits and precooked
1.0 lb (0.45 kg)	7%	wheat malt

*Smoked several hours over birch logs, preferably with the bark still on.

2.0 lb (0.90 kg)	(14%)	honey (preferably a Northern variety), added to secondary

Boil juniper branches with berries in brewing liquor. A simple infusion mash is used, a little on the warm side at 154° F. After an hour, the wort is drained, then additional juniper-infused liquor is ladled on top of the goods to sparge.

No Equivalent Extract Recipe

Hops:

1.0 oz (28 g)	60 min	Saaz (3% AA) or other low-alpha hop
0.1 oz (3 g)	60 min	bog bean (equivalent: 50% AA) or blessed thistle
0.25 oz (7 g)	end of boil	bog myrtle (Myrica gale)

A number of different spices and herbs can be used to season the finished drink right in the mug: mace, clove, mugwort (*Artemesia vulgaris*), and/or woodruff.

ESTONIAN KODOULU

Kodoulu is yet another iteration of the family of Scandinavian folk-brews. The name means literally "homebrew," and it is pale in color, made from malt that may or may not be smoked. Hops provide bitterness, and baker's yeast is used to ferment the brew.

The mash takes about three hours, and as in all these beers, the lauter tun is lined with juniper branches. The first wort is simply run off rather than being sparged, resulting in a strong wort between 1.080 and 1.120. The wort is not boiled, although in traditional versions, the hops are boiled in water and the hopped water is added to the wort, and the quantities suggest bittering rates between 40 and 60 IBU.

Bronze Age carved stone, Gotland

SUGAR, SUGAR

In violation of one of the most sacred principles of quality homebrewing, I'm going to recommend that you add that evil, dreaded bogeyman—sugar—to your beer. Not just any sugar. *High-performance sugar*. This is the dark, gooey crystallized sweetener that bears as much resemblance to the white stuff as homebrew does to industrial beer—the *other* purified white stuff. Specialty sugars with a variety of ethnic origins are available these days, and contrary to what you might have been taught, they really can add to a beer.

Sugar has been used as an adjunct to cheaply add gravity since the days of wooden ships, to substitute for scarce and expensive malt, and sometimes just for its own properties. Sugar can lighten the body of strong beers, making them more drinkable. Abbey tripels owe much of their devastating quaffability to the addition of up to 20 percent or so of sugar. Without it, these modestly hopped beers would be cloying and unbalanced, so sugar is an integral part of the style.

Sugar is harvested from a number of plants: sugar cane, beets, sorghum, palm, and maple. By slicing, crushing, or drilling a hole, a dilute, impure syrup is produced. This juice is usually treated so as to precipitate proteinaceous material, then boiled down to a syrup. At a certain point the sugar begins to crystallize, a process often aided by "seeding" the solution with granulated sugar. The result is a slushy mass of crystals in a surrounding matrix of molasses. The whole mess is put into a centrifuge, and much of the molasses is spun off. Lather, rinse, repeat—two more times. What remains is unrefined sugar, about 96 to 98 percent pure sucrose, the rest being dark, highly flavored material. White sugar undergoes further refinement: dilution, diatomaceous earth and carbon filtration, and final crystallization. The aim is to strip out any flavoring or coloring material.

Some sugars don't get quite this far in the refining process, and are simply poured into molds after the concentration process and allowed to cool into bricks, blocks, cones, or other shapes. These don't have the intense cooked tarriness of molasses, and are much milder and complex in flavor, and therefore more versatile in beer.

Unrefined sugars work in all colors of beers. With Pilsener malt, it can be hard to get a lot of character in a strong blonde beer without adding too much color. An unrefined sugar like jaggery can add a crisp drinkability as well as a unique creamy aroma. In stouts, the dominant roasted malts can sometimes be a little one-dimensional, and the addition of molasses or other dark sugar can be just the tonic needed to make your black beer stand out in a crowd, perfectly in line with tradition as well. Belgian brewers make extensive use of sugar, both white and cooked.

In a 5-gallon batch, a pound of sugar contributes 1.0094 original gravity. I would place the top limit at about 20 percent of the total batch, with 5 to 15 percent being more typical amounts. Using specialty sugars couldn't be easier. Equally useful to extract and all-grain brewers, they may be dumped directly into the brew kettle; the only precaution is to stir well to make sure it doesn't stick and scorch. Remember that sugar will ferment completely, lightening the body and drying out any beer to which it's added.

So let's talk variety. For a long time, I was fascinated by the oddly shaped cones,

Panela

Partially-refined Latin American sugar called "*piloncillo*," or "*panela*" comes in a variety of forms, including this Salvadoran pair of cones wrapped in a corn husk. This form is particularly dark and flavorful.

Jaggery

A 5-kilo block comes wrapped in burlap and purple twine. This Indian palm sugar is pale, rich, and creamy, great for light and dark beers alike.

Sugar Varieties for Brewing

NAME	COMMENTS & DESCRIPTION

CRYSTALLIZED "CANDY" SUGAR

This is sugar that has been decoratively crystallized by dipping cotton string into super-saturated vats of sucrose derived from sugar beets. It is available in white, golden, and light amber varieties, and is exquisitely beautiful, with huge, sparkling crystals. The flavor is identical to ordinary cane sugar, and for four to five bucks a pound, isn't much of a bargain as far as I'm concerned. But if you're going for sheer monastic traditionalism, this is the stuff to use in your tripel. Candy sugar may be found in homebrew shops or by mail order sources, and also in Middle Eastern markets, where it is sold as a decorative sweetener for tea.

DEMERARA, TURBINADO, MUSCOVADO, BARBADOS SUGARS

These are all cane sugars with varying degrees of molasses character. Demerara is the most delicate, and is usually available at natural foods markets. Turbinado is similar, but a bit darker. Barbados is a dark sugar made from specially cultivated cane from the island of the same name. It has a profound "rummy" flavor, very smooth and rich.

MOLASSES

This is what most sugar refiners are trying to get rid of: the dark, pungent material so delicious in cookies and dark beers. There are light and dark varieties produced at progressive stages of the sugar refining process, with flavor intensity (and tarriness) commensurate with color. Molasses was a popular beer ingredient in colonial times; George Washington's famous recipe for small beer actually uses molasses in place of malt! I find it enjoyable in darker beers such as stouts, as in the recipe for Pirate Stout. Treacle is a confusing term. In Victorian times it was a further refined molasses syrup, paler than light molasses. Today the term is somewhat generic for molasses, with black treacle referring to blackstrap molasses. Molasses weighs 11.7 pounds per gallon, 1.4 kilograms per liter.

Type	Color	Flavor	% Sucrose	OG lb/5 gal
Light molasses	lt. brown	full, rummy, medium heaviness	65	1.0061
Dark molasses	dk. brown	very full, a little tarry	60	1.0056
Blackstrap	blackvery	heavy, tarry; may be astringent	55	1.0052

GOLDEN SYRUP (Lyles)

This is a proprietary product with a light golden color and a delicate taste. It is composed mainly of invert sugar in water, and is an excellent material to use for stovetop caramelization.

PILONCILLO

This is a medium to dark brown cane sugar which, after partial refining, is poured into cone-shaped molds and allowed to harden. Usually made in Colombia, it is popular throughout Mexico and Central America, where it is used for a variety of sweetening purposes. Taste varies by color, from a light caramel nuttiness to a deep rumminess. It is a staple in Mexican *supermercados*, and is also known by the name *panela*. I have used the lighter-colored version to thin down an otherwise chewy saison; see p.119. Darker ones are a nice touch for brown ales or porters, and perfect for purging that abbey dubbel of its cloying sweetness.

JAGGERY

Also known as *gur*, this creamy palm sugar is a seasonal product with such a following that Indian grocery owners display signs enthusiastically trumpeting the appearance of the new crop. Jaggery is somewhat soft, with a creamy texture and a light golden color.

Sugar Varieties for Brewing

NAME	COMMENTS & DESCRIPTION
JAGGERY (Continued)	Flavor is delicate but complex, with buttery, nutty, and fruity aspects. This sugar has a history in British brewing beginning in the early nineteenth century when it was used to make up for some disastrous barley harvests. In Indian markets a 5-kilogram fez-shaped block is standard, but smaller sizes are also available. It is also popular in parts of Southeast Asia. I found a 1-pound, leaf-wrapped, button-shaped lump of it, called *kaong*, in a Philippino market. With a creaminess similar to maple, palm sugar can simultaneously soften and add dryness to a beer. A small amount in a weizenbock would be an elegant touch.
DATE SYRUP	Dates have been used as a fermentable sugar since Babylonian times at least. The date has a relatively bland flavor, with not much fruit character of its own, which is why it's here rather than listed with the rest of the fruits. About the same density of honey, it should substitute pound-for-pound. Date syrup is usually available canned in Middle Eastern markets.
MAPLE SYRUP	The high cost of this "Yankee gold" makes it expensive to use in beer, but the result can be a special treat. It has a unique taste that makes it more of a seasoning than anything else. Like honey, maple syrup is best added to the secondary, avoiding the early vigorous part of the fermentation, which scrubs away much of the precious aroma. The chewy nuttiness of the maple rounds off the roasty stuff and adds its own unique character. Maple syrup is available in two grades, A and B, the C grade having been upgraded and incorporated into B. Use the B if you can get it. It is usually less expensive, and has more flavor. One helpful hint if you want to cheat: the spice, fenugreek, has such a "maply" taste that it is a frequent substitute for real maple in syrups and other food products. It would be a useful additive in maple beers, to extend and enhance the maple flavor. Some homebrewers use the undiluted sap, which has a lot of the aromatics that otherwise get boiled away in the syrup-making process, as a base for their brew. This gives plenty of nice maple flavor, but obviously requires proximity to the right trees at the right time.

crystals, and blobs of sugars offered in the ethnic groceries in my Chicago neighborhood. Eventually it dawned on me that these might be good for brewing, and I began experimenting. I was amazed at the intensity and sheer deliciousness of them, and was hooked. They may take some searching out in your area, but as America's taste becomes more adventurous, these exotic products should become easier to find.

COOKED SUGARS

Commercial brewers have long relied on cooked sugar syrups as colorants, unless prohibited by purity laws. An early coloring material for porter was made by cooking first wort or molasses until it thickened and turned black, at which point it was *set on fire* and allowed to burn for five or six minutes, then mixed with water and saved for use as a colorant. *Essentia bina* was a black syrup made by cooking sugar, and was used in porter production at the rate of 2 pounds per barrel. It was legally allowed only between 1811 and 1817. After that time it was superseded by the newly patented black malt.

These syrups today have a lot more subtlety, and are available in a number of shades. They have commercial application as color adjusters in mainstream beers, where exacting standards are needed to match finely honed consumer expectations. They are also used in a more creative way in Belgium. The Chouffe brewery uses them to provide much of the character for their amber and dark beers. One should be aware that dark sugars lack the kind of melanoidins present in dark grains that have certain protective effects against oxidation, so beers colored exclusively with sugars may age poorly. Colored sugars also figure heavily in the flavor and appearance of Flanders red sour beers. The Belgians love this stuff. When the old recipes mention "candi" sugar, this is usually what they were talking about, not the expensive crystallized stuff sold to homebrewers under that name. It is commonly used in sour red beers, and was an important ingredient in the blended beer called *faro*.

Unfortunately, these sugar syrups are not available in the homebrew market. The good news is that you can make them yourself by cooking sugar until the desired color is reached. Use a heavy saucepan or skillet for this. Mix white sugar with a small amount of water, and apply medium heat. Once a smooth syrup has been formed, do not stir, as this encourages crystallization, which you do not want. The water will slowly boil away and the sugar will start to darken. Once the color change happens, it goes fast, so be prepared to pull it off the heat quickly. You can add cold water carefully (watch for spattering) to stop the browning process and redissolve the sugar, or just pour it right into your kettle of wort.

There are four chemical classes of caramel, and they are produced industrially for use in food, soft drinks, beer, and other uses. The different classes react differently to pH, proteins, and other factors, and not all of them are stable in beer. Some types may throw a haze or lose color as the beer ages. Class III caramels, which are made from invert sugar cooked together with an inorganic source of nitrogen, are the type used in beer.

Homemade Caramel

By simply cooking sugar until it darkens, a range of flavorful caramels can be produced.

Malt extract may be cooked down until it darkens, with equally delicious but different results. You get a big load of Maillard reaction products (see p. 42) that are different from cooked sugar flavors. There is historical precedence for this in England and the Continent. Darkly cooked wort was used as a colorant in porter around 1800, after brown malt was abandoned due to its inefficiency and high cost, but before the method of roasting malt to a palatable black was worked out in 1817. A similar cooked sugar product called Porterine was used to brew porter in nineteenth century America.

In Germany, a brewmaster's trick sometimes employed was to preheat the brew kettle before the first wort was run in, causing caramelization—a sort of instant decoction as far as the flavor goes. This can be done in the home brewery, but you are better off putting a pint or so of the thick first runnings in the kettle and boiling it down until it becomes thick and begins to develop some color. Then you can flood additional wort on top of it and stop the process.

RECIPE	Black Ship Pirate Stout

Yield: 5 gallons (19 liters)

Gravity: 1.070 (17 °P)

Alcohol/vol: 5.4 to 6.2 %

Color: Inky black

Bitterness: 46 IBU

Yeast: British ale

Maturation: 4 to 6 weeks

Mash at 152° F for an hour. Sparge as usual. Add molasses to kettle and boil for 90 minutes. Ferment with your favorite ale yeast at moderate temperatures of 60 to 65° F. Rack to secondary, allow to clear, and bottle or keg as usual. If additional spice flavor is desired, add the above mix of crushed spices to some vodka, allow to stand a week or two, then run through a coffee filter and add to your beer at bottling.

All Grain Recipe:

6.0 lb (2.7 kg)	46%	pale ale malt
4.0 lb (1.8 kg)	31%	German/Belgian Munich malt
1.5 lb (0.68 kg)	11.5%	black patent malt
1.5 lb (0.68 kg)	11.5%	dark (blackstrap) molasses

Extract+ Steeped Grain Recipe:

5.5 lb (2.5 kg)	58%	amber dry malt extract
1.5 lb (0.68 kg)	16%	black patent malt
1.5 lb (0.68 kg)	16%	dark (blackstrap) molasses
1.0 lb (0.45 kg)	10%	dark crystal malt

Hops:

1.0 oz (28 g)	90 min	Willamette (5% AA)
1.25 oz (35g)	90 min	Willamette (5% AA)
2.0 oz (57 g)	30 min	Styrian Golding (5.5% AA)

At end of boil, add: 1.0 oz (28 g) of crushed coriander; 1.0 tsp (4 g) allspice; 0.5 tsp (2 g) black pepper. Post-fermentation: zest of one orange or tangerine, soaked in vodka to cover, then added at bottling.

"Ale and Beef" Tonic, c. 1890

Sure, it's a great combination, but in the same bottle?

Toffee Ale Put a few ounces of liquid malt extract in a heavy saucepan and start cooking it until color starts to turn. Once the color starts to change, it will happen quickly. When you pull it off the heat, you can scrape it out of the pan and into your brew kettle, then use a little hot water or wort to rinse the remainder out of the pan.

A SMATTERING OF RADICAL TECHNIQUES

Parti-Gyle Brewing Several hundred years ago, beers were mashed in two, or more often three, mashings, with successive infusions resulting in weaker and weaker beers. Each beer was run off to its own fermenting vat, or gyle. This served the private or small commercial brewer well, producing a range of two or three different products with a single day's brewing. This is obviously a cumbersome system, and was abandoned as soon as brewing became industrialized, starting about 1700. The Scots were pioneers in this, and became famous for their "Scotch system" of brewing, which included the then-radical concept of sparging. By 1900, parti-gyle brewing was abandoned.

It takes a bit of calculating and recipe-twiddling to come up with one grain bill that makes two equally wonderful beers. If you're trying to brew a barley wine, it may be the way to go, because the only way to get a really high wort gravity is to use only the heavy first runnings. This is a way to get something useful out of the considerable extract that remains behind, rather than simply throwing it away.

The crucial tidbit of information here is that the first third of your wort will contain half of your extract. To put it another way, the first third will be twice as strong as the second two-thirds. This is the perfect ratio for brewing, say, a barley wine at 1.090 and a bitter at 1.045, a ratio of 2:1. If you use the same amount of grain, but choose to split the batch half and half, the difference in strength will be more pronounced—for 1.083 and 1.037, a ratio of about 2.2:1. For both of these examples, the master batch was 1.060, if it were all mixed together, entire, as they say.

Capping This is a simple technique traditionally employed to boost the gravity of the third, small beer runnings of a parti-gyle batch. The malt of choice was traditionally amber (biscuit), which works well. Crystal malt works very well for this purpose, as it contains sugars in a soluble form, and requires no further mashing. The "cap" malt is crushed as normal, then either strewn on the surface or stirred into the upper layer of the mash, allowed to rest fifteen minutes, then run off. This is a good tool for manipulating the character of the smaller beer by adding dark or other colored malts. Crystal works especially well in this situation as it needs no further mashing and can boost the body, useful for second-running beers.

Satz Mashing This is a traditional mashing process used in southern Germany—Augsburg, Ulm, Nürnberg, Bamberg, Kulmbach—up until the late nineteenth centu-

RECIPE — Big Stinky & Little Stinky: a Basic Parti-Gyle Recipe

Yield: 2.5 gallons barley wine + 5 gallons of bitter

Gravity: 1.090 (21.5 °P) + 1.045 (11°P)

Alcohol/vol: 7.3 to 8.5% + 3.7 to 4.3%

Color: Medium amber + light amber

Bitterness: 46 IBU

Yeast: British ale

Maturation: 6 to 12 months (barley wine), 4 to 6 weeks (bitter)

All-Grain Master Recipe:

7.5 lb (3.4 kg)	64%	Maris Otter pale ale malt
1.5 lb (0.68 kg)	13%	biscuit malt
1.5 lb (0.68 kg)	13%	aromatic malt
1.0 lb (0.45 kg)	9%	dark crystal malt

Mash with a simple infusion at 150 to 152° F (65.5 to 66.5° C). Dough-in should be fairly thick, at 1 to 1.25 quarts per pound. Be sure to mash out by adding hot water at 190° F (88° C) to arrive at a final mash temperature of 170° F (76.5° C). The first third of the runoff will be the barley wine, so collect a little over 2.5 gallons (9.5 liters) and boil this separately. The remaining two-thirds will be half the strength, and will be the bitter. Sparge as normal. If a darker second beer is desired, add some fresh dark malt to the top of the goods after you've run off the barley wine.

For hopping, see the barley wines (p. 132) and bitter (p. 79) recipes elsewhere in this book.

Who know where further experimentation will take us?

ry. It's a somewhat cumbersome process, but its advocates claimed a clearer beer and a "more harmonious" taste. This technique was primarily used with dark malt.

The malt is infused with room temperature water, then allowed to stand for two to five hours. This cold mash is then drained, and the runoff—called "satz"—is split; a portion of it is mixed with mash liquor in the kettle and boiled for thirty minutes, while the rest is run into an underback. The boiled kettle liquid is reinfused into the mash, raising the temperature to 140 to 144.5° F (60 to 62.5° C); this is then held for fifteen to thirty minutes. The remainder of the cold satz is added to the boil kettle. Immediately, some of the first wort is run off into the underback and some into the cool ship, where it is allowed to cool (This gets added later to the kettle to boil with the hops).

About two thirds of the first wort in the underback is run into the kettle and brought slowly to boiling, then underlet into the mash tun, bringing the temperature of the mash to 144.5 to 149° F (62.5 to 65° C) after stirring. Now the thick portion of the mash is taken from the tun and placed into the kettle, boiled approximately forty five minutes, then returned back into the tun, bringing the mash temperature to approximately 158° F (70° C). The kettle is cleaned, then the satz that has been idling on the cool ship is run into it, and immediately the hops are added. After sixty to ninety minutes of mashing the wort is drawn off the mash tun into the kettle and boiled with the hops. It is likely that brewers using this process were trying to cope with poorly modified malts. A long stand in cold water would have ensured adequate hydration and would also have allowed proteolytic and glucanase enzymes plenty of time to do their thing, which could have resulted in clearer beers. The early mixing of hops with the satz in the brew kettle constitutes first wort hopping, which results in better hop flavor. This mashing technique has some similarities to Belgian "slijm" mashing (see p. 219), one result of which was to produce a poorly fermentable wort. Note the very short first saccharification rest before the liquid is run off, which probably keeps all of the enzymes from being removed from the mash and destroyed in the kettle.

Blinking This was a technique practiced by brewers in the North of England a few centuries ago. Their reputation at the time was for luminously clear, strong October beers. The technique was for wort clarification. Rather than running off the mash directly into the kettle, the wort was directed into a vessel where the solids were allowed to settle out. In modern times, recirculating the wort until it runs clear achieves the same result.

JUST PLAIN CRAZY

Sometimes, radical brews can be brewed from quite ordinary ingredients—in stupefying quantities. Nashville homebrewer Tom Vista has anointed himself the Hop God and if divinity were based on quantity alone, he would surely qualify. If you were wondering how hoppy a beer can be, well, then just brew this one. Although the wort won't absorb much more than 100 IBU of bitterness, this calculates out at 473 IBU! And that's without hops in the mash or in the sparge water.

RECIPE — Thomas Vista's Hop God Ale

Yield: 5 gallons (19 liters)

Gravity: 1.070 (17° P)

Color: Inky black

Bitterness: 100 IBU

Yeast: American or British ale

Maturation: 8 to 12 weeks

Note: these extract figures are calculated for 7 gallons, not 5, as lots of wort remains trapped in the giant pile of hops.

"I have been known to dry hop in as many as three stages, but lately have been avoiding as final addition seems to be enough for both flavor and aroma. But if I do dry hop, I have switched to using pellets and will use the same variety as my main flavor hop."

All-Grain Recipe:

8.0 lb (3.6 kg)	49%	Maris Otter or Golden Promise pale malt	410
4.0 lb (1.8 kg)	24%	Moravian Pilsener malt	130
2.0 lb (0.90 kg)	12%	biscuit/amber malt	69
1.5 lb (0.68 kg)	9%	torrefied wheat	62
0.5 lb (227 g)	3%	pale crystal (20°L)	17
0.5 lb (227 g)	3%	pale crystal (20°L)	17

The Hop God speaks: *"This is mashed in at between 156° F and 158° F (God I love dextrins!) at between 1.15 and 1.25qts/lb. Hops can be added as early as the mash (pellets are preferred just for ease of use). I have hopped the sparge water before and will again. As I have refined the effort I now try to feature a flavor variety; however I just can never get enough... "*

First Wort Hopping (see p. 53):

4.0 oz (114 g)	Columbus (15% AA)	52
4.0 oz (114 g)	flavor hop: Cascades, Liberty, Crystal or Willamette	108

Standard Hopping:

4.0 oz (114 g)	60 min	Centennial (10% AA)
2.0 oz (57 g)	45 min	Centiannial or Columbus (10% AA)
2.0 oz (57 g)	30 min	Centennial or Cascades (10% AA)
8.0 oz (228 g)	15 min	aroma hops, your choice (Cascade—6% AA)
8.0 oz (228 g)	end of boil	aroma hops, your choice (Cascade—6% AA)

The Hop God's Kettle, post-boil

Two pounds of hops in the boil sucks up so much wort that the recipe must be adjusted to replace the missing wort.

Photo: Thomas Vista

THE MYSTERIES OF BELGIUM

By now I would think you'd be forming a picture of Belgium as the land that time forgot, at least when it comes to beer styles. These messy remnants of the past are always fascinating, and they create an atmosphere in which nearly anything is possible—great from an artist's point of view. Sometimes these archaic beers are pretty straightforward to brew, but sometimes the elaborate techniques employed can leave you feeling as if you've stepped off the time machine into the Dark Ages of brewing. Welcome to Chapter 15.

If you look at the old brewing books, there's no end to the crazy schemes: eight-hour boils, hops boiled separately from the mash, grain soaked in cold water, and on and on. Before the nineteenth century, brewers knew *how* to brew the way they did, but usually not *why*. Science, in the service of industrial efficiency, got a lot of these old procedures converted into more sensible practices, leaving only a few quirky beers that needed special techniques to produce the desired qualities.

Some of these techniques are certainly more challenging and time-consuming for the brewer, but produce results that can't be obtained any other way. Besides, what kind of pursuit is it that has no challenges?

A PERFECTLY WHITE BEER

Pick your adjective: elusive, sublime, luscious, mysterious, maddening. White beer is all of these and more. When perfectly brewed, it is a lovely combination of grain and seasoning, a billowing, frothy, yet satisfying quencher. Yet I must say that I am more frequently disappointed by this style—in both commercially brewed and homebrewed versions—than any other.

The standards are high. The beers of his youth recreated so wonderfully by Pierre Celis make the many poor renditions all the more painful to taste. But with the right approach, truly fine white beer is within the reach of almost every homebrewer.

As a bit of background, the beers repopularized by Celis are but one regional variation of a broad and ancient style that stretched from the Baltic to Cornwall, and nearly vanished only within this century. References to white beer brewers' guilds—distinct from red beer brewers—appear by the late Middle Ages. Interestingly, white beers were found in places such as Hamburg and Nuremburg, also known as the earliest trading centers for hops.

Wheat, oats, spelt, and other grains were often, but not always, a feature of these white beers. They are invariably low-to-medium-strength everyday beers, fermented quickly and consumed young and cloudy.

The style might still be dead if Celis had not revived it in his native Hoegaarde, Belgium, which was known for witbier, although the style we know is more famously referred to as Louvain/Leuven white (after the university town southeast of Brussels,

home to Belgium's famous brewing school). During the seventeenth century, there were forty-two breweries in Leuven making witbier and its darker cousin, peetermann. Much of the production was exported to Brussels, Antwerp, and the Netherlands. Jean DeClerck (1957) mentions the then-abandoned Hoegaarde beer in passing, saying only that it "…had a very acid palate."

Witbier features a modest gravity, light hopping, pale color, permanent haze, delicate spiciness, a slight lactic tang, and a firm, milkshake sort of body that comes from a thorough mashing of unmalted wheat and oats.

Malt for witbier was traditionally "wind malt" that was dried in the rafters without using any source of heat. This would suggest we use the palest variety available, Pilsener malt. For the unmalted wheat, you want the lowest protein content you can find—a soft wheat. I get very good results from the flaked soft red wheat that comes from my local hippie market. The whole-kernel soft white variety will work just as well.

Regular "old-fashioned" oatmeal is the norm, although if you're doing the infusion version, instant oatmeal is preferred.

All of your raw, huskless grains should be ground to a fine grits consistency. This is essential to getting a good yield, and may require something other than your regular malt mill. I use an old grocery-store coffee mill.

Many of these early white beers fermented unboiled wort, or had a portion of unboiled wort added to the batch, either of which will cause a lactic souring of the beer. This requires that the beer be consumed quickly, usually within a couple of weeks, as the increasing sourness will make the beer unpalatable in time. The easiest and lowest-risk way to get a true lactic character is to include some acidified malt in your mash. Many German maltsters make this *Reinheitsgebot*-certified product by naturally souring the malt with lactic bacteria, giving the same yogurt-like tang you'd get with a sour side fermentation. One to 3 percent will do—perhaps more if you wish to go with an older historical style.

While you can brew a white beer with an infusion mash, I find it impossible to get the right kind of texture this way. Unmalted wheat and oats are difficult materials to brew with, and need to be boiled during the process in order to get much out of them. After a lot of trial and error, I have settled on the classic American adjunct-mash as the best process. And in fact, this is just about identical with a procedure detailed in Belgium around 1900 for this style.

In this method, a small amount (5 to 10 percent of the total batch) of six-row malt is added to the wheat and oats. This is stewed at 122° F (50° C) for fifteen minutes, then raised to 150° F (65.5° C) and held for another fifteen minutes. This goo is then heated further and

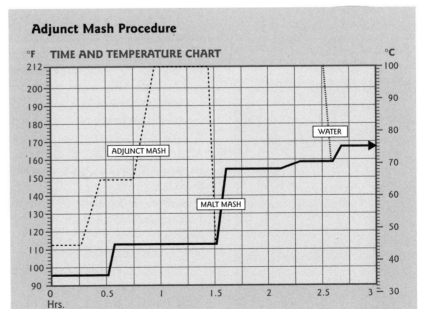

Adjunct Mash Procedure

boiled for fifteen minutes. At this point, you should have your malt mash at the protein-rest stage (150° F), and the boiled grains, when added to it, will bring the whole mash up to 155° F (68.5° C). This fairly high mash temperature is used to produce a wort with large amounts of unfermentables, which helps contribute to its texture. After forty-five minutes of mashing, the mash is raised to 170° F (76.5° C) to stop enzyme activity and help liquefy the whole thing. Traditionally, the wheat chaff removed at threshing was added back to help provide a filter bed. Rice hulls, about 1 pound per 5 gallons (0.45 kilograms per 19 liters), will do the same thing. Be sure not to let the bed drop below 160° F (71° C) during sparging or runoff will become very difficult.

If all of this seems a bit overwhelming to you, there's a workaround. With a high proportion of malted wheat (70 percent is about right), you can achieve a similar thick, lubricious body. Use instant oats rather than the old-fashioned kind, as they require no precooking.

If you're an adventurous extract brewer, I would urge you to attempt a smaller-scale version of this, using the formula that follows. It is an excellent opportunity to observe all kinds of mash chemistry at close range.

Boiling can be as long or short as you like. Leuven wit employed a boil of one to two hours. Its darker sibling, peetermann, was usually boiled for about six hours to develop color.

One cheap trick for creating a permanent haze or "shine" is to add a tablespoon of ordinary flour to the kettle. Unlike a protein haze, this won't go away as the beer warms up in your glass.

SEASONING

This has been the subject of much speculation. Orange peel and coriander are universally mentioned in old recipes for the style. I have had good results with every kind of orange peel *except* the dried chunks of *Curaçao* found in homebrew shops, which I feel impart too much pithy bitterness and not enough orange aroma. Any sort of orange-colored citrus will work: navel oranges, tangerines, mandarins, or kumquats. I have had the best results with Seville oranges, from which marmalade is made. These are sold as "sour oranges" in Caribbean markets, and are dull, gnarly blemished fruits with juice as sour as lemons and an intensely aromatic peel. Use a zester or a potato peeler to carve off all the orange-colored outer peel. Since we're trying to produce a hazy beer, there's no problem with using marmalade, whose starchy pectin normally precludes its use in beer.

Grocery store coriander is too vegetal and celery-like to give good results. Buy your coriander at an Indian market if possible. This variety can be distinguished by its larger size, more oblong shape, and paler color. The aroma is sweeter, more delicate, less "piney," and more citrusy.

Now for the mystery spice. Although I have personally been told by a Belgian brewmaster that he uses cumin, I think this may just be a trick to throw us off the track. I like chamomile, a small flower with a soft, Juicyfruit aroma. I have brewed these beers with and without, and the beer tastes more like Celis with the chamomile.

| R E C I P E | **Wit Guy White Ale** |

Yield: 5 gallons (19 liters)
Gravity: 1.052 (12.5 °P)
Alcohol/vol: 3.6 to 4.2%
Color: Hazy straw
Bitterness: 28 IBU
Yeast: Belgian wit or wheat ale
Maturation: 4 to 6 weeks

All-Grain Traditional Adjunct-Mash Recipe:

For adjunct mash:

3.0 lb (1.4 kg)	30%	unmalted wheat (see text)
2.0 lb (0.90 kg)	20%	U.S. six-row malt
1.0 lb (0.45 kg)	10%	oatmeal (make sure it's fresh)

For malt mash:

3.0 lb (1.4 kg)	30%	two-row Pils malt
1.0 lb (0.45 kg)	10%	Munich malt
1.0 lb (0.45 kg)	—	rice hulls (may be stirred in at end of mash)

Create two separate mashes and follow the schedule as outlined previously in text.

All-Grain Infusion Mash Recipe (Cheater's Version):

5.5 lb (2.5 kg)	58%	malted wheat
2.0 lb (0.90 kg)	21%	U.S. six-row malt
1.0 lb (0.45 kg)	10.5%	Munich malt
1.0 lb (0.45 kg)	10.5%	oatmeal (make sure it's fresh)
1.0 lb (0.45 kg)	—	rice hulls

This uses a normal single infusion mash, with saccharification at 148° F (64.5° C).

Extract + Mini-Mash Recipe:

6.0 lb (2.7 g)	75%	wheat extract syrup
1.0 lb (0.45 kg)	12.5%	U.S. six-row malt
1.0 lb (0.45 kg)	12.5%	oatmeal (make sure it's fresh)
0.5 lb (227 g)	—	rice hulls

Give this an hour rest at 148 to 150° F (64.5 to 65.5° C).

Hops:

0.5 oz (14 g)	Northern Brewer (7% AA) 90 min
1.0 oz (28 g)	Tettnang or Saaz (7% AA) 30 min
1.0 oz (28 g)	Tettnang or Saaz (7% AA) 5 min
zest of 1 to 2	oranges (see text) 5 min
0.5 oz (14 g)	Indian coriander, crushed, 5 min
0.25 oz (7 g)	chamomile, 5 min

Other spices are possibilities: grains of paradise, with its peppery spruciness, is great for stronger versions; juniper adds a soft, wintry aroma; star anise adds warmth and roundness, especially suitable for stronger, amber variations. A touch of sage might add a dry earthiness.

Spices can be added to the last five minutes of the boil. Otherwise, "It is just for the neighbors," as Pierre Celis says. I also like to use vodka extraction of spices, which can be added to the beer at bottling or kegging (see p. 153).

Hops should be mild ones. I like Saaz, Sterling, or Tettnang—their spiciness builds on the other seasonings very nicely. Although hopping is traditionally light, I have found that the style works well with fairly high hop rates, as long as you stay away from the higher-alpha types that obscure the delicate spicing.

Most Belgian yeasts will add a spicy/fruity overlay, but be aware that their flavor profiles are especially sensitive to temperature, pumping out more spiciness at higher temperatures. Generally, fermentation temperatures between 68 to 75° F (20 to 24° C) are best.

Peetermann This is another form of witbier associated with Leuven/Louvain; it was at one time more celebrated than wit. Darker, a bit stronger at 1.045 (11 °P) instead of the 1.036 to 1.042 of wit, and with double the hop rate (0.7 to 0.9 ounces or 20 to 26 grams per 5 gallons), it is brewed in much the same manner, but without the oats and with the addition of a small amount of slaked lime (calcium hydroxide) in the kettle. This makes the beer a little darker—especially when combined with a six-hour boil. It is described in the old books as a brown beer.

L'Orge d'Anvers—the Barley Beer of Antwerp Antwerp was famous for a barley-malt beer brewed from pale malt and a little wheat (4 to 12 percent) and oats (3 percent). Typically, it used the same Byzantine mashing procedure as witbier, where the first mash is removed and boiled while the grist is remashed with boiling water. The effect of this is to kill off the enzymes, so the resulting beer ferments fairly poorly—a plus in weaker beers.

Three mashes were performed, and the third would go to produce a small beer. The wort was boiled—the first runnings for three to four hours, which added some color, although sometimes slaked lime was added to artificially darken it as in *peetermann*. The various runnings were either fermented separately or blended together to produce beers of various strengths. At around 1.075 to 1.080 (18 to 19 °P), the full-strength beer would keep for a year if brewed in the winter. Hopping was reported (in the 1880s) at 2 to 2.7 ounces (57 to 77 grams) per 5 gallons, which would have put it around 30 to 40 IBU.

A "white" variation was brewed in a similar manner, but with an unspecified amount of buckwheat added, and a shorter boil to keep the color down. This was a weak beer, using just 4.7 pounds (2.1 kilograms) for 5 gallons, resulting in a wort of about 1.025 to 1.030 (6 to 7 °P), depending on efficiency. Hopping rate was about an ounce "of old hops."

STRANGE BELGIAN BREWS

Alsembier A wormwood-infused beer in eastern Belgium, documented in 1674, but likely brewed for a very long time. It was flavored by either wormwood, *artemesia absinthium*, or mugwort, *artemesia vulgaris*.

Caves (Kaves) or Liers Bier Around 1820, two kinds were brewed in Liers, in the province of Liège in eastern Belgium: one for local consumption and another called *Ghentse Caves* that was exported primarily to Ghent. The *Lierse* caves was stronger, drawing 25 barrels from the grist, and using only the first runnings. The Ghentse added the second runnings and drew 35 barrels off the same amount of grist. Proportions were 69 percent malt, 22 percent unmalted wheat, and 9 percent oats. A five- to six-hour boil was used. Hops were used at the rate of 0.75 to 1 ounce (21 to 28 grams) per 5 gallons (19 liters). The flavor is said to be refreshing, and it was drunk mainly in the summer. Brouwerij Goetze brews a 5.8 percent a/v version commercially.

Diest Soft and very dark, this was a sweet porterish brew, very popular in Brussels before the mid-nineteenth century. The older recipes incorporated brown malt, although newer recipes use caramel malt instead. Sources give the following proportions: 30 percent each of wheat, pale malt, and brown (or dark caramel) malt, plus about 10 percent oats. Diest was very lightly hopped, and the fermentation was arrested by adding lime, leaving the beer sweet and low in alcohol. It is very nutritive (511 calories per liter versus 400 for other beers), and for this reason it was recommended for nursing mothers. A related style, *Gildenbier*, was a much beefier product that could be as strong as 1.140 (33 °P), although versions around 1.070 (16.6 °P) were more common. In later days, diest was a non-alcoholic malt extract drink or tonic.

Belgian Malt-Beer Technique

For all (or mostly) malt beers, this procedure was followed: The grain was sometimes mashed-in cold, but more often at about 108° F (42° C), and was held for half an hour as a protein/acidification rest. This mash was thick, at 0.6 quarts per pound. Then, 0.4 to 0.8 quarts per pound of water at 158 to 167° F (70 to 75° C) was underlet, raising the mash temperature to 122 to 131° F (50 to 55° C). At this point, the mast taps were opened, allowing the cloudy liquid, enzyme-rich portion to run off. This turbid wort was transferred to the "chain copper," a boiling kettle fitted with rotating chains designed to keep particles from settling on the floor of the kettle where they would be subject to scorching. This wort was heated rapidly to boiling, with only a short rest (fifteen to thirty minutes, I would guess) for starch conversion along the way.

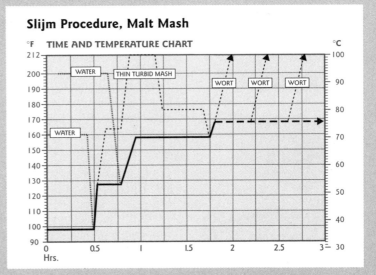

Slijm Procedure, Malt Mash

During this time, water near the boiling point is added to the mash, bringing the temperature of the goods up to 158° F (70° C). Since most of the diastatic enzymes are drained away along with the cloudy wort, conversion is relatively slow. After forty-five minutes, taps are opened, and the bright wort is run off into the conventional boiling copper. The boiled turbid wort is then added back at either boiling temperature, or to assure more complete conversion, at 176° F (80° C). Typically, the resting temperature of this stage was about 167° F (75° C), favoring the production of dextrins. Once the wort runs clear, it is pumped up to the copper, joining the clear wort from the earlier mash, which has been maintained at about 167° F (75° C) to facilitate conversion of any undigested starch still remaining in it by the infinitesimal amounts of enzymes still present in the later, clear wort.

The range of historic Belgian styles is even more dazzling than the current offerings.

Mars/Meerts A rather generic term for a small beer made from second runnings. This product is obviously very light at 1.035 (8.5° P) or less. The names—in French and Flemish—mean March, the last month it was allowed to be brewed before summer. Mars is perhaps best known as the diluting beer that is mixed with lambic, along with some dark cooked sugar, to make the blended beer called *faro*, although faro was also drawn directly from the second runnings of lambic wort. Mars came from the third runnings of the same mash and so would have the same raw wheat and malt proportions as lambic. The term Mars was used to describe similarly light beers in Poland. Note that there is a French beer called *"bière de Mars,"* which is altogether different.

Seef A very ancient beer from Antwerp, little is known of it except that it was spiced with coriander, cloves, and cinnamon, according to a 1793 reference.

Uitzet Brewed in the same manner as l'Orge d'Anvers (see p. 208), but from barley malt, wheat, and oats. Said to have been invented in 1730 by an innkeeper in Wetteren, it was widely popular in Ghent and Bruges during the nineteenth century. Like the Antwerp (Anvers) beers, uitzet featured a five- to six-hour boil. Ordinary, double, and triple versions were brewed from combinations of multiple mashings.

Zoeg A pale, lightly hopped, and very sweet ale popular in the sugar-producing towns of Tirlemont, Tienen, and others. The name means "sow," although it was also called *strieep*. It was fairly weak—only about 1.035 (8.5 °P)—and had a reputation as a healthful, nourishing drink, probably due to the 2.5 pounds (1.1 kilograms) of sugar per hectoliter added before it was shipped out.

OFF-WHITE

With the traditional product so well defined, one would expect that to deviate from tradition would be to invite the whole glorious creation to fall apart into muddled chaos, but the spirit of Belgian witbier endures. It's a pretty good platform for vamping. You can make it stronger, darker, or hoppier, and the essence of it still shines through.

If you think about it, this makes sense. Historically, white beers were brewed all across Northern Europe, from about 1400 on. It stands to reason that brewers in different cities would evolve different interpretations.

This is a great framework within which to experiment. I was drawn into this years ago in an attempt to recreate Hogaarden's Verboden Vrucht, which I hadn't tasted but knew to be stronger, darker, and maltier, with similar orange and coriander spicing as the wit. After a few experiments the beer got to be pretty good, but an error in hop calculation in one brew led to a doubling of hop bitterness. This turned out to be a delicious mistake and opened up the style to further rearrangement.

Stronger versions exist in the real world, too. There's a beer restaurant in Bruges called Den Dyver which has an 8 percent alc/vol version brewed for it by Brouerij de Gouden Boom, and as one would expect, it is absolutely fabulous with food. In this country, Tim Rastetter and Ray Spangler cooked up a barley wine-strength version

RECIPE			Nit-Wit Strong Wit

Yield: 5 gallons (19 liters)

Gravity: 1.080 (21.5 °P)

Alcohol/vol: 6.5 to 7.5%

Color: Medium gold

Bitterness: 27 IBU

Yeast: Belgian wit or wheat ale

Maturation: 8 to 12 weeks

All-Grain Recipe:

7.0 lb (3.2 kg)	47%	Pilsener malt
5.0 lb (2.3 kg)	33%	malted wheat
2.0 lb (0.90 kg)	13%	Vienna malt
1.0 lb (0.45 kg)	7%	oatmeal
0.5 lb (227 g)	—	rice hulls

Standard infusion mash: 1 hour at 150° F (65.5° C).

Extract + Mini-Mash Recipe:

5.0 lb (2.3 kg)	48%	wheat extract syrup
4.0 lb (1.8 kg)	38%	pale dry malt extract
1.0 lb (0.45 kg)	13%	pale crystal malt
0.5 lb (227 g)	7%	instant oatmeal, precooked
0.25 lb (113 g)	—	rice hulls

Hops & Spices:

1.0 T (14 g)	60 min	white flour (added to create a starch haze)
1.0 oz (28 g)	60 min	Styrian Golding (5.5% AA)
0.75 oz (21 g)	5 min	Styrian Golding (5.5% AA)
0.5 oz (14 g)	5 min	Saaz (3% AA)
2.0 T (28 g)	5 min	marmalade
1.0 oz (28 g)	5 min	coriander, crushed
0.25 tsp (1 g)	5 min	grains of paradise, crushed

called Wit Lightning at the short-lived BrewWorks in northern Kentucky a few years back (whoooeee!). So there are plenty of options.

The same notes on procedures, especially the need for an intense adjunct mash, apply to these beers as well.

The recipes that follow use lower proportions of wheat and oats than a normal wit because for the higher gravity beers, smaller proportions are needed to give an adequate amount of character. All of these recipes are formulated for a standard infusion mash; rest temperature is indicated in the recipes. Yield is calculated at 75 percent—your mileage may vary. A pound or two of rice hulls will aid in sparging. If you want to brew these with extract, I would suggest replacing all the pale malts (wheat and barley) with a good wheat extract (pound-for-pound for liquid extract; 25 percent less for dry), then using a mini-mash for the colored malts. Hop rates are calculated for whole hops; for pellets, use 25 percent less. Be sure to scrub citrus fruit thoroughly before zesting. All the spices should be added for the last five minutes of the boil. Use a not-too-extreme Belgian yeast strain, at temperatures in the high 60s if you can manage it. Carbonation for all of these should be on the high side.

RECIPE **Claude of Zeply Amber Strong Wit**

Yield: 5 gallons (19 liters)
Gravity: 1.070 (17 °P)
Alcohol/vol: 5.2 to 6.2%
Color: Tawny amber
Bitterness: 25 IBU
Yeast: Belgian wit or wheat ale
Maturation: 6 to 10 weeks

All-Grain Recipe:

6.0 lb (2.7 kg)	45%	Munich malt
5.0 lb (2.3 kg)	37%	malted wheat
1.0 lb (0.45 kg)	7.5%	medium crystal (40°L) malt
1.0 lb (0.45 kg)	7.5%	oatmeal, toasted for 20 minutes @ 300° F, or until it smells like cookies
0.5 lb (227 g)	4%	dark crystal (80°L) malt
0.5 lb (227 g)	—	rice hulls

Mash at 154° F (68° C).

Extract + Steeped Grain Recipe:

5.0 lb (2.3 kg)	53%	malted wheat liquid extract
2.0 lb (0.90 kg)	21%	amber dry malt extract

Plus: the same quantities of the three specialty grains, above.

Hops & Spices:

1.0 oz (28 g)	60 min	Northdown (6.5% AA)
0.5 oz (14 g)	5 min	Northdown (6.5% AA)
zest of 2	5 min	tangerines (outer zest only)
1.5 oz (43 g)	5 min	coriander, crushed
2 whole	5 min	star anise or 0.25 tsp (1 g) ground

OUD BRUIN: FLANDERS SOUR BROWN ALE

Sometimes, a single sip of a beer can transport you back through the centuries, a sort of liquid time machine. The sour beer of Flanders, with its unique tangy, fruity aroma, magical ruby color, and refreshing yet earthy taste, can do just that.

There was a time when stainless steel was just a twinkle in an alchemist's eye, when wood was the only practical material for constructing fermenting vessels. In addition to a high load of maintenance obligations, wood fermenters come with a whole zoo of little creatures that snuggle in and use the beer as their own personal picnic grounds. This can be a nightmare if it goes wrong, but such microbes can be extremely elegant, adding a profound, earthy perfume to the brew, topped off with lac-

RECIPE	Major Blankety-Blank India Wit Ale

Yield: 5 gallons (19 liters)

Gravity: 1.061 (14.5 °P)

Alcohol/vol: 5.4 to 6.2%

Color: Gold

Bitterness: 48 IBU

Yeast: Belgian ale

Maturation: 4 to 6 weeks

This beer would benefit from a little dry hopping, maybe half an ounce of East Kent Goldings added to the secondary or the serving cask.

All-Grain Recipe:

5.0 lb (2.3 kg)	50%	British pale ale malt
4.0 lb (1.8 kg)	40%	malted wheat
1.0 lb (0.45 kg)	10%	medium crystal (40°L)
0.5 lb (227 g)	—	rice hulls

Conventional infusion mash at 148° F (64.5° C).

Extract + Steeped Grain Recipe:

4.0 lb (1.8 kg)	44%	pale dry malt extract
4.0 lb (1.8 kg)	44%	wheat extract syrup
1.0 lb (0.45 kg)	12%	medium crystal (40°L)

Hops & Spices:

1.5 oz (43 g)	60 min	East Kent Golding (5% AA)
2.0 oz (57 g)	20 min	East Kent Golding (5% AA)
1.0 oz (28 g)	5 min	East Kent Golding (5% AA)
Peel of 1	5 min	sweet orange (outer zest only)
Peel of 1/2	5 min	grapefruit (outer zest only)
1.0 oz (28 g)	5 min	coriander, crushed,

tic and acetic acids, which add a quenching tartness.

Present commercial versions are made with a small proportion—less than 25 percent—of soured beer, blended into a batch fresh from a few weeks fermentation. This dilutes the overwhelming sourness of the aged beer, and of course adds complexity.

Some sources draw a distinction between the East and West Flanders versions of this beer type, the West Flanders variant generally the sharper tasting. But to me, the differences seem less important than the similarities. Once such beers were plentiful in Flanders; today only a few remain. In such a situation where the number of producers is greatly reduced, the big picture gets distorted, and the idiosyncrasies of those that remain get magnified beyond their importance as far as the original style is concerned.

Gravity is modest at 1.045 to 1.050 (11 to 12 °P), although stronger versions are brewed. Color should be a rich, reddish brown. Hopping is light, as with most types of sour beers, with no detectable hop aroma. The palate should be dry, with a very soft chocolatey richness balanced against the acidity.

Because of its simple malt/hop profile and bright acidity, these beers make great bases for fruit beers, with cherries and raspberries preferred.

Brewing is straightforward; a simple infusion mash is adequate. Relatively low

RECIPE	**Wyse Foole Wit Wine**

Yield: 5 gallons (19 liters)
Gravity: 1.095 (22.5° P)
Alcohol/vol: 9–10.2%
Color: Deep gold
Bitterness: 41 IBU
Yeast: Belgian ale
Maturation: 4–8 months

Maple syrup would add an interesting twist. This is by no means all that can be done with (or to) the wit style. If you want something really extreme, take that wit wine recipe and make an ice beer out of it!

All-Grain Recipe:

3.0 lb (1.4 kg)	19%	Pilsener malt
4.0 lb (1.8 kg)	25%	Vienna or pale ale malt
7.0 lb (3.2 kg)	47%	malted wheat
0.5 lb (227 g)	—	rice hulls
2.0 lb (0.90 kg)	12%	jaggery (Indian palm sugar) or other partially refined sugar such as piloncillo, demerara or turbinado.

Standard infusion mash at 148° F (64.5° C)

Extract + Steeped Grain Recipe:

5.0 lb (2.3 kg)	44%	wheat malt syrup
3.5 lb (1.6 kg)	30%	pale dry malt extract
1.0 lb (0.45 kg)	9%	pale crystal malt
0.5 lb (227 g)	—	rice hulls
2.0 lb (0.90 g)	17%	jaggery (Indian palm sugar) or other partially refined sugar

Hops & Spices:

1.5 oz (43 g)	60 min	Styrian Golding (5.5% AA)
2.0 oz (57 g)	20 min	Saaz (3% AA)
3.0 oz (85 g)	5 min	Saaz (3% AA)
6-10	5 min	kumquats, whole
2.0 oz (57 g)	5 min	coriander, crushed
0.5 tsp (2 g)	5 min	grains of paradise, crushed

mash temperatures should be used, as this promotes the kind of enzymatic activity that creates a highly fermentable wort, which in turn creates a crisp, dryish beer. This is a good beer to brew from extract, with augmentation from some crystal malt or cooked sugar. This beer was often brewed from pale or Vienna malt only, and then colored with cooked sugar syrup. This gives sufficient color and a creamy caramel flavor, without a lot of toasted brown flavors to interfere with the vinous character of the style. Instructions for making cooked sugar are on p. 198. It's easy to do.

A normal top-fermenting yeast is used, and I think it makes sense to use a Belgian one. Temperatures on the coolish side (57 to 67° F or 14 to 19° C) will keep the beer from developing too much spiciness that might interfere with the fruitiness from the wild yeast.

So this leaves only one detail: how to get it to turn sour. I have had good results from the liquid mixed lambic cultures, added after primary fermentation is complete.

These critters are rather slow in the chow line, so expect to wait a few months before you get much effect from them. I would let them have at it for three months, then have a taste.

As mentioned before, oak vessels are traditional. And at Rodenbach, at least, they are scraped to expose fresh wood between every brew. In addition to being a good home for critters, especially acetobacteria, oak eventually imparts a soft vanilla character from the metamorphosis of lignins in the wood into vanillin.

Wood in the homebrewery can be difficult to manage, but there are some short-cuts. Fortunately, it isn't absolutely essential to get you into the ballpark with this style of beer.

If you want to dive into wood, the most manageable solution is to use small oak cubes manufactured for the wine industry by a company called StaVin (www.stavin.com). They produce French, Hungarian, and American oak cubes, about 3/8" (1 cm) on a side. These are intended to refresh tired wine barrels, but will suit our purposes perfectly. They come in several degrees of toastiness, and are pre-sanitized in foil packs. A small handful will suffice. American oak will be far too pungent for beer use, except for massive and very long-aged brews.

On the other hand, you can go to extremes. I know an amazingly dedicated home-brewer who keeps a 50-gallon barrel of the stuff going, withdrawing some when he has fresh beer to add, in much the same manner as a sherry *solera*. This is beyond the reach of most of us individually, but it's a rocking good idea for a club (see p. 280).

If you choose to use this as a base for fruit beer, ferment through the primary, then rack into a secondary onto plenty of fruit, at least a pound per gallon of cherries, half that for raspberries. You could easily double those quantities and not have too much. I like to use fruit that has been frozen, as this lightens the microbial load a bit, but more importantly breaks down the cell walls to make sugars more accessible to the yeast. I also prefer cherries with pits, as they add a certain almond/kirsch complexity. Sour pie cherries are generally better than the eating type (such as Bing) for intensity of flavor.

My own method is to do the secondary in a glass carboy, filling it with beer and fruit up to just below where the jug necks into the narrowest part. I find this reduces the surface exposed to air, and thereby reduces the likelihood of mold developing, but still leaves enough headroom to prevent a piece of fruit from blocking the stopper hole, which can develop enough pressure to explode the carboy (it has happened!). Just as a precaution, don't fit the stopper too tightly into the carboy. Let the beer sit on the fruit for one to four months, rack into a carboy, and allow it to settle clear before bottling or kegging.

R E C I P E	This Old Barrel Flanders Sour Brown Ale		

Yield: 5 gallons (19 liters)

Gravity: 1.057 (13.5 °P)

Alcohol/vol: 5.3 to 6.2%

Color: Ruby amber

Bitterness: 31 IBU

Yeast: Belgian Flanders ale, plus mixed lambic culture, added after primary.

Maturation: 6 to 18 months

When primary is finished, rack into the secondary and add a package of mixed Lambic culture.

All-Grain Recipe:

3.0 lb (1.4 kg)	28%	Pilsener malt
6.0 lb (2.7 kg)	57%	Munich malt
0.75 lb (340 g)	8%	aromatic/melanoidin malt (around 20 °L)
0.25 lb (112 g)	2%	dark crystal
2.0 oz (57 g)	1%	black malt—preferably European, de-bittered
0.5 lb (227 g)	4%	unrefined brown sugar, such as piloncillo, demerara, etc.

Mash 1.5 hrs at 145° F (63° C), then mash out and sparge normally.

Extract + Steeped Grain Recipe:

5.5 lb (2.5 kg)	4%	amber dry malt extract
1.0 lb (0.45 kg)	4%	dark crystal
2.0 oz (57 g)	4%	Carafa II (German roast malt)
0.5 lb (227 g)	4%	unrefined brown sugar, such as piloncillo, demerara, etc.

Hops:

1.0 oz (28 g)	90 min	Northern Brewer (7% AA)

SOUR BROWN BEER OBSCURITIES

Brune d'Aarschot Similar in style to Jack-Op, but a little lighter at 1.045 (11 °P). The recipe is reported to be 50 percent pale malt; 30 percent aromatic malt; and 20 percent wheat. It was lightly hopped. Huyghe, in Melle, still produces one.

Jack-Op A brown, half-sour beer, known especially as a student favorite during its heyday, 1910 to 1925. Belle Vue brews a version that weighs in at 1.050 (12 °P).

Zottegem An amber to brown beer made from pale and caramelized malts, using an infusion mash, and brewed as an "entire" beer of 1.060 (14.5 °P) gravity. Top fermentation was used, and the beer reportedly had some serious acidity in the old days, due to lactic acid fermentation in the casks and vats. It was generally sold as a draft beer, but more recently bottle-conditioned.

Maastrichts Oud From the Limburg province of the Netherlands, one would expect this to share traits with Belgian brews. I can find nothing about it but these labels.

LAMBIC

Well, here we've come to the holy grail of geekdom, the very core of radical brewing. With a strange mashing procedure, years-long wild fermentation, stale hops, blending, and many other unusual and archaic techniques, lambic is one of the most fascinating beers in the universe, as well as a challenge to brew. As a subject, it richly deserves far more space than I'm going to be able to devote to it.

The basic form of lambic is a pale sour beer between 1.050 to 1.065 (12.5 to 15.5 °P) currently; one hundred and fifty years ago it was as high as 1.084 (20 °P), but more commonly 1.060 (14.5 °P). The mash is made from a blend that is usually 60 to 70 percent malted barley and 30 to 40 percent unmalted red winter wheat. In times past, the mashing procedure was typical of many other Belgian beers of old, and featured the removal and boiling of the enzyme-laden turbid wort, which had the effect of producing a wort with a high percentage of dextrins or unfermentable sugars important as food for the pediococcus that will get to work later on and produce lactic acid. These old processes were designed to work with old-fashioned malts, in this case very steely and poorly modified ones. Romantic as they are, they're not necessarily the best tools for the job today.

Modern lambic mashing practice follows a more familiar decoction and/or stepped infusion schedule. Mash is struck with hot water at 144° F (62° C), bringing the goods up to 115 to 120° F (16 to 19° C) for a ten-minute rest. Boiling water is underlet, raising the temperature to 136° F (58° C). Immediately 20 percent of the mash is removed and given a short boil, then added back to the main mash, raising its temperature to 149° F (65° C), adjusted with boiling water if needed. Another 20 percent

Lambic Sub Styles	
Lambic	The basic style, served straight after aging, or blended to make gueuze or faro.
Jonge Lambic	Young lambic, also known as "fox."
Gueuze	A blend of young and old lambics, which are bottled and aged further.
Faro	Typically a blend of lambic and mars, sweetened with sugar and colored with dark caramel sugar. Sometimes brewed entire rather than using a blend. Hugely popular a hundred years ago. Gravity is around 1.040 (9.5 °P).
Mars*	Weak beer made from the last runnings of a lambic mashing.

*Not to be confused with bière de Mars, an amber springtime seasonal specialty, brewed from spring barley mainly by French breweries.

decoction is removed, boiled, and added back, bringing the next rest to 162° F (73° C). After a short rest, a final infusion of boiling water is added, bringing the goods up to mash-out temperature of 170° F (76.5° C). This is allowed to settle a few minutes before runoff is begun. By the end of all this activity, the water to grain ratio may be as high as 4.5 quarts of water per pound of grain, double that of a normal mash.

An alternate technique is to perform a stepped infusion mash, with fifteen-minute rests at 95° F (35° C), 113° F (45° C), 131° F (55° C), and 149° F (65° C), then mash-out at 162 to 164° F (72 to 73.5° C). The entire mash is pumped into the kettle and boiled for a short time, then added back

to the lauter tun to settle before being run off.

Very hot sparge water—around 200° F (93.5° C)— is used, as this will remove the maximum amount of sugars, and more importantly starches, from the grains. Since the mash is so dilute, a relatively small volume needs to be run through the goods during the sparge.

The boil may last five to six hours; modern practice sometimes gets this down to less than four. The hop rate is high, at 3.5 to 4 ounces per 5 gallons, and was about a third higher in the 1800s. The hops used to come from the Poperinghe hop fields in Belgium, and had a very low alpha content (2 to 3 percent AA). In addition, hops aged three years were used, and the brewers wanted no bitterness, just the preservative present in the cones. It is important to note that aged hops often display obnoxious cheesy or spoiled butter aromas, and it takes a long boil to expel them from the wort.

"The intoxication of the faro drinker only shows itself at first by an increase in noise which is only deafening, and finally by a silent deterioration of the mind."

— Gerard de Nerval, c. 1842

The cooling process is part of beer legend. The hot wort is pumped upstairs to coolships under the eaves, and doors are opened, allowing the local microflora to waft in. Because of the increasingly suburban character of the neighborhood—cherry orchards replaced by shopping centers—brewers are preserving the structures of their brewery buildings in such a way as to make use of its magic dust as a fermentation starter. And fortunately, a lot of the tiny creatures live in the wood of the barrels used as fermenters. On a parallel track, much research has been done to try to tease apart the complex ecology of lambic in case it becomes necessary to augment nature with a little pure culture here and there. This is good news for us, as lambic organisms are available as single or mixed cultures that are quite easy to use.

Blending is a critical aspect of the lambic tradition. The general gist is that hard, sour, complex, expensive beers get mixed with softer, fresher, mellower, less expensive beers, resulting in a drinkable, affordable beer combining the best qualities of both. Oddly, the most famous lambic sub-style, gueuze, was invented only as recently as 1860 or so, although with beers occasionally turning out so sour they're only good for polishing copper, it's hard to imagine that nobody thought of blending them with a younger beer before—but such is beer mythology.

Faro was at one time the most popular forms of lambic. The *'pure sucre candi'* refers to caramel syrup, and was the only coloring material in the brew.

Since lambic depends on the set of conditions that existed in centuries past on the outskirts of Brussels, it is impossible for us to brew a completely accurate copy in our own breweries. However, the available commercial products are quite good, and if you are of a microbiological bent, lambic offers challenges and rewards like no other beer.

In commercial breweries, fermentation takes place in wooden barrels similar to wine casks. The ale yeast goes first, as many of the other microbes work very slowly.

I am the Slijm—Traditional Lambic Production, P. Boulin, approx 1880:

The goods being in the tun, one underlets a certain quantity of water, between 114° F (40° C) and 122° F (50° C) and then of almost boiling water until the tun is full, then one highly brews. When the mixture is quite homogeneous [at 117° F (45° C)], one covers surface with the mash tub with a light layer of wheat and then at once plunges into the mash large baskets of wicker as high as the mash tun and 60 to 70 cm diameter. With the assistance of copper scoops, one withdraws all the liquid that compression makes flow to the interior of the baskets.

When all the liquid which it is possible to extract is removed, one drains the false bottoms and the whole is poured in the kettle.

In Brussels brewing terms, this wort having undergone the first boiling is called the slijm. After a second mashing [with hot water], the wort is again run off and mixed with the slijm. The slijm is poured on the goods and stirred again gently, after which the mash tub is left to rest half an hour and tapped from the bottom of the tun, slowly and with precaution, to make sure the wort runs clear. When, despite all this care, the first part of the runoff is not sufficiently clear, it is rejected into the tank to be filtered again.

The purpose of the boiling undergone by the first two runnings is to achieve saccharification of the starch that the liquid contains, then to achieve clarification by coagulating the dissolved albuminous matter. As soon as boiling approaches, a multitude of small flakes are formed and the liquid, formerly turbid and milky, becomes transparent by the dissolution of the starch and the precipitation of albumin.

With the clarification of the slijm finished, one does two new mashings with hot water, performed in the same way but more quickly. Wort from this mashing it is used to prepare mars. When all mashings are mixed, faro is obtained; for the lambic, one uses only the slijm.

At home, generally ale yeast is pitched, and a conventional fermentation completed before the wild stuff is added. It is possible to nurture the many strains of microorganisms individually—if you have access to some pretty sophisticated equipment and knowledge. For most of us, pitching a conventional belgian ale yeast, and then adding a packet of a commercially-prepared mixed lambic culture at the end of the primary fermentation gives pretty good results. Sometimes good results can be achieved by transferring some sludge from one successful beer into the next batch or even using the dregs of a bottle as a starter for the wild things.

Lambic Microflora Oversimplified

Saccharomyces cerevisiae	Top-fermenting yeast consumes sugars, produces alcohol + CO_2
Enteric bacteria *E. coli and others*	Feeds on glucose; produces fruity to fecal "outhouse" aromas (nice in small doses)
Kloeckera apiculata	Ferments glucose; winey and cidery flavors
Brettanomyces species	Wild yeast that produces the characteristic "horsey" aroma
Pediococcus species (also *lactobacillus*)	Bacteria that metabolizes dextrins and produces lactic acid and aroma
Oxidative yeasts *Candida, Pichia,* **and others**	Film-forming yeasts; adds some fruity esters, esp. ethyl acetate

As a fermenting vessel, glass works fine, although you may feel you are more authentic if you toss in a few cubes of French or Hungarian oak (see p. 91). It will take at least a year before the beer really starts to taste like lambic. Two years and it's ready

for bottling, although this was considered "young" lambic in the past, although it tastes pretty good at that point. After another year or two it will develop that stinging acidity and ethereal aroma that only an old lambic has. With this kind of extended aging, the yeast will be pretty much shot. If you plan on bottling, adding some fresh yeast with the priming sugar will assure proper carbonation (which should be high).

Clearly, this is an intense beer style, and brewing it can be daunting. But lighter and quicker versions were enjoyed as everyday beers in the past, so there's nothing that says you have to make the heavy-duty stuff all the time. This recipe will get you started on the long and twisted road to Lambicville.

WINE BARREL LAMBICS

Used wine barrels make pretty good aging vessels for lambic-style beers. They come on the market when they get to the point where they're not adding anything to the wine. This toned-down taste is exactly what we want, since a fresh barrel can be gawdawful rough on a beer. Get one directly from a winery if you can so you can find out what kind of wine was in it. Heavier reds might be best for such intense fruit beers as raspberry, while lighter reds might be suitable for cherries or for a non-fruit beer such as a Flemish sour brown. Whites might go for peaches or for straight lambics. Wine barrels come in different sizes, but 50 gallons is the most common size. Smaller barrels have a higher surface area to volume ratio, which means the potential for too much wood and too much evaporative loss.

A homebrewer in northern Wisconsin maintains two barrels, one for lambics and one for sour browns. He uses them in *solera* fashion, in which a quantity of beer is periodically removed to make way for a new brew. The whole barrel is never emptied, avoiding the really difficult problem of how to deal with an empty barrel. This also means the beer is always a blend of old and new, a desirable characteristic of many antique beers. Such a barrel can be maintained as a "club beer," which can be bottled or kegged for group use, or bottled a few gallons at a time and dispersed. Brewers can contribute on a rotating basis, or get together periodically for group brews.

RECIPE — Lambic

Yield: 5 gallons (19 liters)

Gravity: 1.058 (14 °P)

Alcohol/vol: 6 to 7%

Color: Pale straw

Bitterness: 10 IBU (or less)

Yeast: Belgian ale for primary, then mixed lambic culture

Maturation: 6 months to 2 years

Wait until the primary fermentation has finished, then rack into secondary, and pitch a package of mixed lambic starter, sit back, and and be patient. It will take several months before the effects will be noticeable, and it may take a year or two for the flavors to develop to a decent level.

All-Grain Traditional Adjunct-Mash Recipe:

For the adjunct mash:

3.0 lb (1.4 kg)	30%	unmalted wheat
2.0 lb (0.90 kg)	20%	U.S. six-row malt
1.0 lb (0.45 kg)	10%	oatmeal

For the malt mash:

4.0 lb (1.8 kg)	30%	two-row Pils malt
1.0 lb (0.45 kg)	10%	Munich malt
1.0 lb (0.45 kg)	—	rice hulls (may be stirred in at end of mash)

Create two separate mashes and follow the schedule as outlined in the witbier text, p 205.

Hops:

4 0z (113 g)	5 hrs	Old low alpha acid hops (3 years is ideal). Lesser quantities (1 to 2 oz) should be used for fruit beers.

Brune Gueuze?

I've only seen it mentioned on this label.

ROLLING YOUR OWN

*"Make beer,
not war."*

—Kate Geiser, Homebrewer

GOING ORGANIC

Concerns about the healthfulness of what we put into our mouths, as well as issues such as sustainability, pollution, and genetic diversity, are increasingly on people's minds—brewers and consumers alike. And while brewing organic ale might not be the most obvious place to start, this "living right" thing is the kind of program that, once you start, you have to make an effort to make changes all around and not leave some big, uncool thing hanging out there, whether it's a giant SUV or just a batch of beer.

Not so long ago the selection of organic ingredients was so pitiful that you really did have to raise your own if you wanted to have anything beyond the basics. Today the situation is much different. With green living becoming very popular in Europe, growers in Germany are producing a pretty decent variety of malt and hop types. There have been organic hops from New Zealand for years now, and there are also limited varieties of hops and malt coming from English and U.S. producers. Selection, at least as far as some of the more obscure specialty grains, is a little restrictive, but it's a pretty simple deal to toast or roast your own (see p. 224).

Briess Malting in Chilton, Wisconsin offers a range of organic liquid malt extracts, plus its DME (diastatic) extract in a spray-dried form. There are even Internet-based homebrew shops specializing in organic ingredients.

Because the amount of hop matter extracted into the beer is quite small (2 percent of the weight of the hops; 20 to 90 ppm in the finished beer) compared to the other ingredients, you may choose to live dangerously and add conventionally grown hops to an otherwise organic beer. German growers go to extreme measures—warning sirens for peronospora, for example—to avoid chemically treating their hop plants, so this might be something to keep in mind in your search for the most healthful ingredients.

Growing your own hops is an even better possibility, as they seem to be much less disease-prone when grown in widely scattered gardens rather than acre-upon-acre in a commercial agricultural setting. See p. 226 for details.

Whether your yeast is organic or not shouldn't be an issue, as yeast is more a process than an ingredient. At any rate, nobody sells a specifically "organic" yeast.

Since there's more water in your beer than any other ingredient, it bears some consideration. Sound brewing practices would guide you to use clean, healthful water, stripped of any chlorine, heavy metals, or toxic organics. A good drinking water filter will accomplish this for you, and there's no need to go to any further lengths for organic homebrew. I should note here that while distilled water may seem like a good choice, it actually lacks the minerals necessary for proper brewing chemistry for most beer types. Spring water is okay, but you should get a mineral analysis. See the section on water chemistry, p. 54.

MALTING YOUR OWN BARLEY

I'm going to be perfectly honest and tell you I have not done this. For most of us, the huge variety of available malt types fills just about any conceivable grain bill. Considering the time, equipment, and expertise involved in malting grain, it's not something to be taken up on a lark. You've got to really want to do it.

That said, it is possible to produce perfectly fine malt at home. Remember, in the old days they just threw a sack of barley in the creek, waited for it to sprout, and dried it over anything that would burn, so it isn't exactly astrophysics. The accompanying sidebar outlines the process.

The Stages of Malting

Steeping	The grain is soaked in *dechlorinated* water for between sixty and eighty hours at temperatures around 60° F (15.5° C), never higher than 70° F (21° C). A change of water twice a day is made to keep things clean and to ensure that plenty of oxygen is available for the seeds to germinate. The quantity of water needed is about a gallon per pound. Calcium hydroxide (lime) is sometimes added to the steep water to counteract mold and to help leach bitter, astringent materials from the husk (0.1 to 0.2 grams per liter). Hydrogen peroxide is sometimes used for this purpose, and this has the benefit of adding free oxygen.
Couching	This is the seven-day period during which sprouting occurs. Since this process generates heat, careful management of the thickness of the pile of grain is needed to keep things at the desired 59 to 65° F (15 to 18.5° C), although malt destined for dark beer may be germinated a little higher, up to 77° F (25° C). Warmer temperatures result in faster malting, which results in poorer quality malt, more noticeable in the palate of pale beers. It is important to aerate the grain during germination, to introduce oxygen and to remove carbon dioxide generated by the sprouting plants. Proper modification is indicated by an *acrospire* (shoot) equal in length to the kernel, which grows underneath the protective husk.
Kilning	This drying process reduces moisture levels in the malt from 45 percent to below 5 percent. This stops the germination process and stabilizes the enzymes and other components of the malt, allowing it to be stored for future use. In general, a two- or more stage kilning is used: first, a low-temperature one to dry out the grains, which lasts about forty-eight hours, during which time the malt must not get above 112° F (44.5° C), or else enzymes may be destroyed. This is followed by one or more high-temperature steps to "cure" the malt, first at 176° F (80° C) for five hours (pale malt); darker malts are cured five hours at 230° F (110° C). Darker colors are reached by further kilning at higher temperatures, but above this, enzymes are destroyed, limiting the malt's use to specialty purposes.
Mellowing	This a period of a couple of weeks or more after kilning during which the malt just sits, allowing some of the harsher compounds developed during kilning to waft away, especially important with darker malts.

Obtaining the proper grade of barley may be the most difficult part of home malting. Generally, malting grade is the highest quality available, as the criteria is a high count of live, viable seeds. But it is normally sold in railcar-sized lots, as there's not a lot of call for small amounts. Seed barley or other grains should be avoided because it often is treated with fungicides or other chemicals to protect it when it's in the earth, and these are not such nice things to have in a beer.

Of course, if you have a couple of acres to spare and live in the proper sort of climate, you can grow your own. It's admirable, of course, but this is only for the deeply committed.

Wheat, oats, rye, and other grains may also be malted, and each has a time schedule different from barley, generally shorter. If you're planning on malting alternative grains, you would be well advised to research the specifics.

ROASTING YOUR OWN

These days, the wide variety of available commercial malt serves the homebrewer fairly well. But it can be interesting and rewarding to do a little home-roasting, and you can come up with some colors and flavors not available any other way. Amber rye, brown wheat, and toasted oats are all products you can make—but not buy.

Kilning malt involves complex chemistry collectively known as the Maillard reaction, which is covered elsewhere (p. 42). Maillard chemistry is the source of nearly all malt flavor and aroma. Each different combination of time, temperature, moisture, and raw ingredients creates a different set of flavors, which means there's tremendous room for exploration.

It couldn't be easier. A cookie sheet or a cake pan and a standard oven are all that's needed, although an accurate thermometer will be helpful if you want to be able to calibrate your oven and thereby repeat your successes. If your oven has convection capability, this will make a more evenly kilned product in a shorter time. Spread the grain out thinly, not more than an inch deep.

The temperature range for kilning is between 200 and 400° F (93 and 204° C), and although it may seem obvious, higher temperatures are generally used for darker malts. Time ranges from twenty minutes to a little over an hour. We're normally working with malted barley, but any grain can be roasted. This brings out the unique character of each kind of grain, sometimes dramatically.

Here are a few hints and tips on malt toasting at home:

- Use whole, uncrushed grain, as it roasts more evenly.

- Kilned grain will brew darker than it looks. A golden-looking kernel will brew a pretty toasty-tasting beer, and is suitable for brown ales. A copper-colored grain tastes sharply roasty. Sometimes it's best to just go by the aroma, and take the grain out of the oven as soon as it smells right.

- Darker roasts should be done at a higher temperature; lighter roasts at lower ones.

- Smaller or thinner grains will develop color more quickly than fatter ones, and may require more frequent turning.

- Malts kilned moist will taste richer and, well, maltier than those roasted dry, which lean toward sharper, dryer flavors. A two-hour soak will be enough to make the difference.

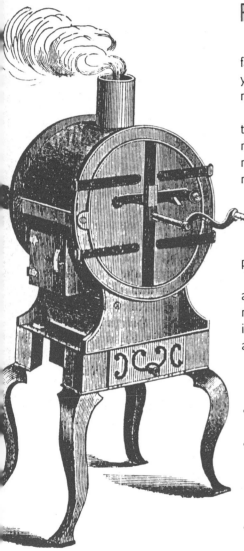

Drum Malt Roaster, 1877

This method of kilning black malt was patented in 1817 by Daniel Wheeler. Simpler equipment can be used at home.

- Freshly kilned malts need a couple of weeks to mellow out. If you brew with them right away, you'll get harsh, burnt aromas along with the good stuff. This is not like coffee.

- There is a zone of harshness around 200 to 300° SRM, which coincides with copper-to-chocolate malts. At even darker roasts, the roughness seems to soften into a cocoa roastiness. There's a place for this very sharp roastiness, but you need to use it in a way that doesn't overpower everything else in the beer.

- It is pretty much impossible to produce black malt without special equipment, and you can end up with something that, if not actually on fire, tastes as if it were. Most maltsters also take extra steps to "debitterize" their darkest malts, further knocking the rough edges off of them.

- Experiment with other grains for unique flavors; everything can be toasted. Many adjuncts are bland and lifeless without a little kilning. Think of the difference between a bowl of oatmeal and cookies made from the same stuff. It's a magical transformation, and oh, that cookie flavor is delightful in a brown ale or porter. Toasting corn gives you a nice tortilla chip flavor, a suitable accent for a chile ale (see p. 184). Malted wheat can be turned into crystal malt (see sidebar), and this creates different flavors than barley malt crystal.

Time and Temperatures for Several Malt Types

Minutes	° F	(° C)	Color (°L)	Flavor
20	250	(121)	Pale Gold (10)	Nutty; not toasty
25	300	(149)	Gold (20)	Malty, caramelly, rich; not toasty
30	350	(177)	Amber (35)	Nutty, malty; lightly toasty
40	375	(191)	Deep Amber (65)	Nutty, toffee-like; crisp toastiness
30	400	(204)	Copper (100)	Strong toasted flavor; some nutlike notes
40	400	(204)	Deep Copper (125)	Roasted, not toasted; like porter or coffee
50	400	(204)	Brown (175)	Strong roasted flavor

Both brown and amber malts may be approximated in the homebrewery. You can simply roast the grains in the kitchen oven, or over wood on a barbecue. For amber, first wet the malt by soaking for fifteen minutes or so, then toast at 300° F (149° C) for about half an hour. You are looking for a light orange color and a nutty, toasty taste. Brown malt can be made by roasting dry at 350° F (177° C) for one-and-a-half to two hours. You want a medium ruby-brown color with a sharp, roasty taste. It should not be anywhere near as dark as chocolate malt. Always keep in mind that malt brews darker than it looks. And don't forget to let it mellow for a couple of weeks.

Homemade Crystal Malt

Get 2 pounds of whole, uncrushed pale malt and soak it for twenty-four hours in dechlorinated tap water. The grain will absorb water and become quite soft. Place it in a colander and drain it well, then put it in a cake pan, about 2 inches deep. Put this into a low oven at 160° F (71° C), which you should confirm using a thermometer of known accuracy. Let it stew like this for two to three hours, during which time the enzymes in the malt will convert the malt starches into sugars.

At the end of this time, take half the malt and remove it to another cake pan or cookie sheet, so it's an inch thick or less. Crank up the oven to 200 to 220° F (93 to 104° C), and put the pan of malt back in. Turn every half-hour or so until the malt is dry and crispy when bit through. This will take some time. At this point, you can stop the process and use it as a pale crystal, or crank up the heat to 300° F (149° C) and allow it to kiln until it's anywhere from pale gold to deep amber. Taste as you go, and be aware that the malt will always taste darker than it looks, and brews darker still. So, err on the pale side.

And remember that each different combination of time, temperature, and moisture will produce a different flavor, even if the resulting grains are the same color. Hotter, drier roasting tends to produce harsher, roastier flavors. If you want more rounded, caramelly flavors, you might raise the heat before the grain is completely dry, roast to the desired color, then lower the heat until it's nice and dry.

Once it's done roasting, pull it out of the oven and let it cool off, turning a time or two. The malt should be allowed to mellow for a week or two to allow the harsher components of the roasting process to waft away.

This process is most commonly used on barley malt, but you can also make crystal from malted wheat, rye, oats, or any other malted grain.

GROWING HOPS

Hops do well in the northern United States, and make a lovely—if scary—ornamental plant as well as a homegrown brewing ingredient. Because they require a certain day-length to trigger the production of cones, cultivation is restricted to between the thirtieth and fiftieth parallels. Luckily, this includes the continental United States, except for southern Texas and the peninsula of Florida. Because heat and humidity seem to encourage pests and disease, the commercial hop crop has largely been in the North—New York and Wisconsin in earlier times, now primarily in Washington and Oregon. In large-scale cultivation they're susceptible to a number of pests, but this seems to be less of a problem for the individual grower, whose little garden presents a less tempting target.

To grow hops, one obtains rhizomes, which are tuberous, stubby, root-like things. They are planted about four feet apart (allow a couple of extra space between different varieties) in the spring. Rhizomes should be planted so the bud end is one inch below the soil surface. Light-textured rich soil with good drainage is ideal, which is similar to what tomatoes like. As with many plants, the old maxim of "a five-dollar hole for a one-dollar plant" applies, and the surrounding soil can be enriched with composted manure or similar fertilizer. It's a good idea to apply a slow-release garden fertilizer every spring. Mulching is recommended as well.

Soil type and climate do have an effect on varietal character, but they generally do come somewhat true regardless of where they've been planted. Many varieties of rhizomes are available. Often homebrew shops will pre-order them when they're available in April or May, so check with your local retailer.

The traditional saying about hop growth is, "First year, creep; second year, leap." So it will take a little time, but that second year, oh boy! One plant can yield 0.5 to 2 pounds of dried cones.

Since hops are a climbing plant, a trellis or something vertical for them to climb is mandatory unless you want them sprawled all over your yard. Strings or wires will do. They will easily grow 20 feet or more, and put out cones late

August through September, depending on location. In commercial harvesting, the bines are cut down and the cones are then stripped off mechanically. You can just pluck off the cones, leaving the plant to build reserves before it dies back after the weather gets cold.

As hops ripen, the cones dry out and get papery, while the small yellow-orange lupulin glands swell and get sticky with resins. Pull off a cone and rub it briskly between your palms and have a good sniff. If the cone releases sticky aromatic stuff onto your hands, the hops are ready to harvest.

The cones can be used fresh, dried in a food dehydrator, or air-dried in a dry shady spot. A convection oven set at a low (150° F or 65.5° C) temperature can work as well. The hops are fully dried when the *strig* (the stick through the middle of the cone) is brittle and snaps rather than bending.

Sheet Music Title, *London Illustrated News,* 1851

There has always been a sort of romantic quality about the hop.

THE BARLEY AND THE HOP.

Forward Into the Past

The march of progress has made the accountants giddy and turned corporate brewers into respectable technocrats, but as homebrewers we know that beer *must* have been better in earlier, simpler days. Of course there was always crappy beer available, and in some cases—like America's colonial past—the beer was often pretty horrendous. One of the pleasures of homebrewing is the ability to strip away the technological "improvements" that nearly extinguished interesting beer, and let the past inspire us to brew with the daring and wisdom of people through the ages.

Often the old brewing books contain brewing sequences of bewildering complexity. Frequently in books before 1750, it appears as if some of the authors never brewed a drop themselves—sometimes boastful of the fact—and clearly misunderstood what was happening with the process. Even in mid-nineteenth century texts you find seemingly senseless techniques, often quite long and elaborate, for what seemed to be quite ordinary beers.

Some of these techniques may be the remnants of an earlier day when limited technology dictated a certain way of brewing. Early ingredients also required specific techniques. Decoction was developed both as a way to mash steely, undermodified malt, and as a way to raise the temperature of a mash in a wooden vessel that couldn't be heated with fire. There also were some strange taxation systems, such as in nineteenth-century Belgium, where different rates assessed on mash tuns for malted and unmalted grains led to the present recipes for witbiers and lambics.

Weights and measures are another headache. Before things were reorganized rationally in the eighteenth and nineteenth centuries, these were often a local thing varying from place to place.

Unraveling these mysteries can be tough, especially in an archaic dialect of a language you don't know all that well. It might be worth the effort, but you have to use your judgment as to whether the seemingly senseless procedures in some of these old books will really affect the beer in any meaningful way. It is likely that some of these arcane procedures are the best way the old-timers had to cope with limitations on ingredients, equipment, energy sources, and other factors, but as a practical matter, you just have to try to sort out what the end result would have been, and find a more straightforward way to get there.

In general, English beers before 1850 were brewed by infusing and draining the mash two or three times. In pre-industrial brewing, these different worts or *gyles* were destined for separate beers of different strengths. Porter was the first industrial beer in the world, and was the first beer to routinely combine the several different runnings into a single brew, hence the term "entire" that was applied to it. Starting around 1800, you see reference to the "Scotch system" of brewing, whereby after the first mash, water is sprinkled on top of the goods to rinse out the remaining sugars. Of course we recognize this as the preferred system today.

The hydrometer was first documented in brewing by the groundbreaking work of Richardson in 1777. Prior to that time, strength of beer had been entirely guesswork, and brewers were quite shocked to find out how little fermentable extract was yielded by the darker malts, particularly blown (torrefied) brown malt, then the very soul of porter. This led to a complete turnaround in the formulation of porter and stout from the less efficient brown and amber malts to a mix of pale and black, or patent malt.

We have more varieties of malt available to us than at any time in history. In most times and places, brewers had to make do with just a few malts—often just one or two. If you are striving for authenticity when you're recreating old beers, try to avoid the anachronistic use of colored malts. See the chart for a little malt history.

Of course legislation and taxation have always had a big impact on this highly regulated product. The 1516 Purity law, the *Reinheitsgebot* of Bavaria, is the most famous, but it's important to know that it applied only to Bavaria—and not the whole of Germany—until 1877, after Bavaria had been incorporated into the German union. It also made an exception for wheat and other top-fermenting beers. For this reason you will find an interesting tradition of "outlaw" beers in the north of Germany that lingered well into the last century.

England, too, had purity laws. A tax was placed on malt in 1697, and this law also forbade the use of wheat, which remained untaxed. In the early eighteenth century, brewers were adding ingredients that not only diluted the flavor of malt or substituted for the bitterness of hops, but were actually dangerous drugs—opium, and more commonly *cocculus Indicus*, for example—that were added to increase the intoxicating power of the brews.

A Timeline of Malt History

Ancient Middle East	Air-dried and kilned malts, plus malts baked into cakes, which would have added caramelized flavors and color.
Ancient to Medieval Northern Europe	Some air-dried malt, but wood-kilned malt quite common. Straw—regarded as a premium fuel for paler malts because of its less smoky taste—or peat were also used.
1516	Reinheitsgebot instituted in Bavaria.
1600s Europe	Smoke-free malt, dried in coal-or coke-fired kilns, is enthusiastically adopted almost everywhere.
1817	Black malt patented and quickly adopted.
1842	Sugar and grain adjuncts allowed in British ales.
Approx. 1870	Crystal/caramel malt developed in Germany.
1877	Reinheitsgebot enforced in greater Germany.

Something had to be done, and in 1710 a law was passed forbidding the use of bittering agents other than hops. As these restrictions applied only to commercial brewers, a quaint tradition of spiced beers lingered on in the country house breweries of large estates up until about 1900, when house-brewing largely ceased.

After several disastrous barley harvests in the early part of the nineteenth century, the laws were relaxed in 1847 to allow for the addition of sugar, and further in

Brewing Measures and Weights

Aam — Cask size:

Germany	155 liters
Netherlands	155.2 liters

Amber — Old British measure of 4 bushels; 140 liters

Ankare — Scandinavian barrel measure:

Swedish	39.256 liters
Danish (ankre)	38.645 liters
Norwegian	38.51 liters

Anker — A highly variable barrel measure:

Dutch	466 liters
English	37.85 liters; 10 U.S. gallons
Scottish	34 liters; 20 Scots pints

Artaba — Ancient Persian measure, 17.44 U.S. gallons; 66 liters

Barrel, British — Beer cask holding 31.5 British gallons; 43.2 U.S. gallons; 163.53 liters

Barrel, Dutch — (1715) 80 liters; 21.25 gallons

Barrel, U.S. — 31 U.S. gallons; 117.35 liters (derived from old British "ale" barrel)

Bole, Boll — Scottish dry volume measure equivalent to four U.S. (originally Winchester) bushels, 38.432 U.S. gallons, or approximately 145 liters; 136 pounds of malt. Morrice (London, 1819) mentions a Welsh bole as equaling 6 British bushels, or 240 pounds of malt.

Brente — A Swiss measure of 50 liters (half hectoliter); 13.25 gallons

Brewer's lbs/bbl — British term for original gravity. One BP/bbl = 1.0028 OG

Bushel — Dry measure of varying capacity:

British (modern): 8 British gallons; 9.608 U.S. gallons; 36.37 liters

British (in 1496): 6.68 U.S. gallons; 25.29 liters

U.S.: 8 U.S. gallons; 30.28 liters

For malt: British 40 pounds; 18.14 kilograms; U.S. 34 pounds; 15.42 kilograms

For barley: British 50 pounds; 22.68 kilograms; U.S. 48 pounds; 21.8 kilograms

U.S. grain: wheat 60 pounds; 27.22 kilograms; oats 32 pounds; 14.52 kilograms rye 56 pounds; 25.4 kilograms

Butt — British cask or vat of 126 U.S. gallons; 477 liters; usually placed vertically rather than horizontally

Brewing Measures and Weights

Chopine   Old French measure of about half a liter; 16.9 fluid ounces

Choppin   Scottish term, equal to 1.8 U.S. pints; 852 milliters

Collothun   Ancient Persian liquid measure, equal to 8.25 liters or 2.18 U.S. gallons or 1/8 artaba.

CWT   Abbreviation for hundredweight 112 pounds; 50.8 kilograms

Eimer   European measure (often used for barley) which varied widely:

Swiss	37.5 liters; 9.9 gallons
Viennese	56.58 liters; 15 gallons
Württemberg	293.92 liters; 77.6 gallons

Firkin   British quarter-barrel cask containing 10.8 U.S. gallons, 9 imperial gallons; 39 liters

Foudre/Fuder   Belgian liquid measure, equal to 30 hectoliters (300 liters); 792.52 U.S. gallons

Fuder   Large cask or liquid measure:

German	900 liters (9 hectoliters)	328 U.S. gallons
Prussia	824.42 liters	217.8 U.S. gallons
Württemburg	293.92 liters	77.6 U.S. gallons

Gallon,   In the U.S., standardized at 8 pounds; 3.63 kilograms of wheat as early as 1303. A U.S. gallon holds **dry or grain** 4.24 pounds, 1.93 kilograms.

Gallon...   (Elizabethan Beer or Ale) Archaic British volume measure equal to 1.22 U.S. gallons; 4.621 liters.

Gallon, Imperial   British volume measure designed to hold exactly 10 pounds of water. Equal to 1.20095 U.S. gallons; 4.55 liters.

Gallon, Scottish   4 Scots quarts, or 3.6 U.S. gallons; 13.63 liters.

Gallon, U.S.   3.7853 liters

Gill   British Imperial measure of 5 fluid ounces; 147.9 milliliters; in the U.S., 4 fluid ounces; 118.3 milliliters.

Hectoliter   Metric volume measurement of 100 liters or 26.417 U.S. gallons; as a dry measure for malt, 92 pounds; 41.73 kilograms.

Himpen   German dry measure similar to a bushel, roughly 8.5 U.S. gallons, holding 53 pounds; 24 kilograms of wheat or 30 pounds; 13.61 kilograms of malt. Also used for hops; by my estimation, 11 pounds of whole hops tightly packed, or half that if loose.

Hogshead   A large oak cask. They have varied in size over the years from 54 to 140 gallons. Presently a hogshead is equal to 63 U.S. gallons; 238.5 liters; 54 imperial gallons (UK).

Hundredweight   112 pounds; 50.8 kilograms

Kilderkin   British half-barrel cask holding 20.61 U.S. gallons; 78.02 liters; 18 imperial gallons

Leaguer   Dutch measure of 153 U.S. gallons; 579.2 liters

Livre   French term, equal to a pound avoirdupois; 454 grams

Mud   Dutch measure for grains, equal to 3.53 cubic feet, or 2.38 U.S. bushels.

Brewing Measures and Weights

Mutchkin	Scottish term, equal to 1 pint; 473 milliliters
Noggin	(British) 5 fluid ounces; 148 milliliters.
Ohm	Not the electrical unit, but another volume measure:

Alsace	50 liters/13.2 gallons
Baden	150 liters/39.6 gallons
Bavaria	128 liters/33.9 gallons
Germany	150 liters/39.6 gallons
Saar	144 liters/38 gallons
Switzerland	40 liters/10.6 gallons

Oxhofd	German barrel size of 206.106 liters; 54.5 U.S. gallons

Hamburg, Germany	226 liters; 59.7 US gallons
Russia	221.389 liters; 58.5 US gallons

Oxhoofd	Dutch barrel of 232.8 liters; 61.5 gallons. Also spelled "okshoofd."
Pfd.	Abbreviation for Pfund, below.
Pfund	German word for pound. Since 1873, equal to 500 grams, or 1.104 pounds, but formerly varied from province to province. Viennese Pfund equaled 560 grams; 1.2 pounds.
Pint	Imperial, 568.261 milliliters, 1.201 U.S. pints; U.S.: 473.176 milliliters, .8327 Imperial pints
Pin	British 1/8 barrel, 3.93 Imperial gallons; 5.4 U.S. gallons; 20.4 liters
Poensel	Belgian fut or cask of 230 liters; 60.8 gallons, used for Brune d'Aarschot
Pond	Dutch pound, equal to 500 grams; 1.3 pounds
Pony	U.S. quarter barrel, 7.75 gallons; 29.34 liters
Pot	Dutch term, equal to 1 liter
Pottle, Potell	(British) 3.3 Imperial pints; 3.96 U.S. pints; 1.87 liters (U.S. and UK before 1826); later standardized to 4 imperial pints; 4.804 U.S. pints; 76.86 fluid ounces; 2.27 liters
Puncheon	British cask holding 72 U.S. gallons (beer/ale)
Quarter	British dry measure equal to 8 bushels, currently standardized to: malt, 336 pounds; barley, 448 pounds
Runlet	A somewhat variable British cask size, eventually standardized at 15 imperial gallons, 18.5 U.S. gallons
Scheffel	German dry measure eventually standardized to 50 liters or 1.4189 bushels; roughly equivalent to 48.24 pounds; 21.88 kilograms of malt.

Bavaria	222.36 liters
Prussia	54.96 liters
Württemburg	177.22 liters

Brewing Measures and Weights

Schepel Dutch dry measure standardized to 10 liters; originally 0.75 U.S. bushel, or 26 liters; holds 25.5 pounds of malt.

Seidel An Austrian 3/4 pint vessel.

Septier, Sextier A medieval volume measure. In Lorraine it equaled 130 to 150 pounds; 59 to 68 kilograms of malt. In Strasbourg, 23.985 liters; 6.3 gallons; holds 26.9 pounds of malt.

Setier French volume measure. Dry, 1.561 hectoliters; liquid, 0.465 liters. Swiss, 37.5 liters.

Sester Anglo-Saxon measure originally of honey, based on the Roman sextarius, about a pint (tenth century), then later twice that or as much as 2 U.S. gallons; 7.6 liters, depending on who you ask. Variably applied to wine and ale, and generally growing: thirteenth century, 4 gallons (of wine); 1521, 14 gallons (of wine). As a dry measure it was also called a "seam," and was more or less equivalent to a quarter (see previous). The Scottish sester was equal to 3 gallons (of wine) in 1150; 12 gallons/51 pounds/23.1 kilograms of grain in 1450, and was equivalent to the "ald (old) boll"

Skåppe Danish dry measure equal to 0.494 U.S. bushels; 18.8 pounds; 17.407 liters

Skep Old British term for bushel; equivalent to modern British bushel

Skjeppe Norwegian dry measure equal to 0.493 U.S. bushels, or 17.370 liters; 16.8 pounds; 7.6 kilograms

Thrydendale English measure of a pint and a half

Tierce Old English barrel size, equal to 1/3 butt, or 42 U.S. gallons, approximately 159 liters

Tønde Danish barrel size, equal to 36.72 U.S. gallons, or 139 liters.

Tonneau French ton, a weight measure equal to 979 kilograms or 1.070 U.S. tons; 1,284 pounds.

Tun British vat, 252 U.S. gallons; 954 liters; 2 pipes or butts; 4 hogsheads.

Vat Dutch cask size, 932 liters; 247 gallons; In Belgium, equal to 1 hectoliter.

Vedro Russian measure of 12.39 liters; 3.3 U.S. gallons

Wine Gallon British measure adopted in the U.S. as the standard gallon size (see above).

Wispel German dry measure. In Braunschweig it equaled 24 Scheffel, or about 13 hectoliters; 36.9 bushels; 1,225 pounds of malt

Zentner/Centner Metric unit of weight equal to 50 kilograms, or 110.231 pounds

Ztr. Abbreviation for Zentner, above

Some Compound Terms Relating to Hops:

Pounds per British Barrel	1.85 oz/ 52 g per 5 gal/19 l
Pounds per U.S. Barrel	1.35 oz/38 g per 5 gal/19 l
Pounds per Hogshead	2.7 oz/77 g per 5 gal/19 l
Pfund (500 g) per Hectoliter	3.3 oz/95 g per 5 gal/19 l

1880, permitting "any wholesome material" as a substitute for malt. This opened the floodgates of cheap corn and rice grits and led to the thinner, less full-flavored beers of modern times. It's not exactly happy news, as it meant the brewery accountants were getting the upper hand, but it is important to keep all this in your mind as you go about recreating older styles.

Yeast is a big unknown. We know from genetic studies that today's brewing yeasts are direct descendents of the brewers' yeasts of ages past, but as you know if you've tried a few strains, there are plenty of differences. Figuring out which ones were used at that particular time and place is next to impossible for the guys in the lab coats. Lager yeasts, on the other hand, are all very closely related. And even though there are slight variations in flavor emphasis from strain to strain, they're not all over the ballpark as is the ale tribe.

Most fermentations prior to 1900 were carried out with multiple strains, and so it was a very big deal in the 1880s when Emil Christian Hansen isolated a single cell culture and propagated it into a pitchable quantity. Wild or spontaneous fermentations were widespread, especially in white ales or small beers that would be quickly consumed, and where the refreshing qualities of some lactic sourness would be welcome. When fermenting in wooden vessels, it is pretty much impossible to keep the wild things away. Fortunately, a stable, if somewhat unpredictable, ecosystem can usually be established in time. Various approaches can be employed to ensure palatable beers, such as the blending used in lambic production, or limiting the use of wild fermentations to weak beers that will be consumed before getting too sour. And it doesn't hurt to have a plan B in place, as with oversoured lambic, which makes a fine polish for copper kettles.

HITTING THE BOOKS

Even though the recipes or descriptions in the old books can be confusing or maddeningly incomplete, it has never been easier to get your hands on the texts. Several—including some very rare ones—have been reprinted commercially; others have been scanned or transcribed; and then placed online as academic or personal projects.

And although there is still a wealth of junk information on the Web, the number of high quality sites is increasing, as is the depth of information available on list servers such as the Historical Brewing Digest. If you're searching for something in particular, don't forget to search the groups as well as the Web at large. People in other countries, particularly in Scandinavia, are also very interested in this topic, and you can use either Google's "translate" feature, or take the text to one of the free Web-based translators such as BabelFish.

If you're going to be doing brewing research in a foreign language, it will be very helpful to

Resources for Historical Research on Brewing

Libraries: public, university, and private

Used bookstores

Alibris and other Internet book search resources

Reprinted texts, Internet and for sale

Trading photocopies of out-of-copyright (100 years old +)

Society for Creative Anachronism and other recreationist groups

Historical brewing newsgroup: hist-brewing@pbm.com

Various hobbyist and academic Internet sites

find a brewing lexicon in that language; a dictionary of chemical terms will be easier to find (and cheaper) and should include most of the common brewing terms.

There's no need to stick strictly to brewing texts. There are old "receipt" books, which offer up concoctions for everything from liniment to buggy polish, and sometimes these include a beer or two as well. They invariably contain recipes for compounded cordials, and some of these spice mixtures translate very well to beer or mead recipes. My notorious chanterelle ale came from such a schnapps recipe. Look for these in old bookstores; they're neither hard to find nor expensive.

VERY ANCIENT BEERS

As has already been noted, the Egyptians and Sumerians were crazy for beer, and it played an important role in ritual as well as daily life. There is some evidence to suggest that brewing was perhaps underway even earlier in the Kurdistan region of what is now southeastern Turkey and northern Iraq. This is backed by the notion that the region appears to have been home to several of the wild grasses domesticated about the time people were learning to brew beer. It's an iconoclastic idea, one that the Sumerologists are having a hard time choking down.

Whatever was happening up north, the Sumerians must have been very busy. They had seventy-seven terms relating to beer, twenty-two for malt, fifty for yeast, and nine for malt cakes. According to records, their god of wisdom, Enki, was drunk a lot.

A number of different grains were available to ancient peoples, including two-, four-, and six-row barleys; emmer and einkorn wheat; spelt; and various types of millet. Some of these grains made pretty lousy bread, and were undoubtedly used for brewing. There's a four-thousand-year-old cake of coarse barley on display in the Oriental Institute in Chicago, so rough it makes your gums bleed to look at it. Such cakes were a preliminary step to brewing, thankfully, so the ancients wouldn't have had to pick the husks from their teeth, and used a more tender grain for their daily bread.

In addition to fermentables

> *"The mouth of a perfectly contented man is filled with beer."*
>
> — Egyptian inscription, 2200 B.C.E.

Sumerian Beer Terms

Kash or Kás	Basic word for "beer"; literally, "what the mouth desires"
Kashdùg or Kashdu	Sweet /fresh beer (as opposed to sour, perhaps?)
Kashgíg	Black beer
Kashgíg-dùgga	Fine sweet/fresh black beer
Kashkal	High quality strong beer
Kassi	Red-brown beer
Kashbir	Small/sweet beer, literally "beer to sniff"
Kash-sig	Fine quality beer
Kash-sur-ra	Pressed out beer (perhaps lautered as opposed to fermented mash?)
Ebla	Light beer; literally, "lessens the waist"
Ulushin	Emmer beer

In addition, these brewing-related terms are particularly interesting: *sa-sa* = reddish roasted barley; *udun-she-sa-a* = barley roasting kiln; *zíd-sig* = cracked barley mixed with wheat flour; *bappir*=beer bread made from barley dough, mixed with malt to make mash; *dabin* = coarse (?) barley flour. *titab* = beer mash; *kirash-i* = emmer wheat for brewing; *gakkul* = clay brewing-vessel, mash tun; *kíkkin* = milling; mill house; adj. for milling women; *imhur* = foam; *titab* = mash for beer; *sa-shè* = to roast barley; *é-lunga* = beerhall or brewery, literally "house" + "brewer."

"Se-bar-bi-gig-dug-ga!" (Bring me a dark one)

—Sargon to his royal cupbearer, 2300 B.C.E.

Papyrus Zoismus, 300 C.E.

"Take well-selected fine barley, macerate it for a day with water, and then spread it for a day in a spot where it is well-exposed to a current of air. Then for five hours moisten the whole once more, and place it in a vessel with handles, the bottom of which is pierced after the manner of a sieve.

"The remainder must be ground up and a dough formed with it, after yeast has been added, just as is done in bread-making. Next, the whole is put away in a warm place, and as soon as fermentation has set in sufficiently, the mass is squeezed through a cloth of coarse wool, or else put through a fine sieve, and the sweet liquid is gathered. But others put the parched loaves into a vessel filled with water, and subject this to some heating, but not enough to bring the water to a boil. Then they remove the vessel from the fire, pour its contents into a sieve, warm the fluid once more, then put it aside."

from grain, other sources of fermentable sugars existed in the form of dates, grapes, figs, palm sugar, honey, and other minor sources.

Spices and herbs were widely used as well. In the Bible one finds this overflowing cupboard, most of which have been used as seasonings for beer at one time or another, right up to the present day.:

anise, cumin, sweet flag, caraway, cassia cinnamon, citron, coriander, dill, hyssop, juniper, mallow, mint, myrtle, myrrh, nettle, rue, saffron, thistles, and wormwood,

Recent chemical evidence has shown that ancient peoples were very adventurous and willing to try all manner of combinations. Analysis of residues found at the famous Minoan king Midas' burial feast on the island of Crete suggests a beverage made from malt, honey, and grapes. When this was recreated by Dogfish Head Brewing, they added saffron, a spice known to have been growing in Phrygia in ancient times.

An Egyptian medical text called the *Ebers Papyrus*, dating to 1552 B.C.E. (but believed to be a copy of a much earlier document) lists several hundred substances, including acacia, basil, bayberry, cardamom, cubeb pepper, fenugreek, licorice, mustard, tamarind, and thyme. The ancient people were very industrious, and it's pretty safe to say that they had rounded up and tasted just about every plant and animal part they could get their hands on. The ones that were palatable in beer would have found their way into the brewer's pot, although availability and price would have restricted expensive items like saffron to luxurious uses—for priests and potentates only. The garlic-scented mandrake root, which was also dangerously psychotropic, was also used in Egyptian brewing.

The Thracians, at the intersection of present day Greece, Turkey, and Bulgaria, had a barley ale called Brytos or Bryton, a tradition they shared with the Peonians and the Phrygians.

Babylonian beer was made from various grists of malt bread, toasted, soaked, and fermented with the addition of rye and spelt. At least three types are known: black beer from one-fifth spelt and the rest malted bread; good black beer with more spelt; and a red beer with more than a quarter spelt, other grains, and malted bread. A tablet at New York's Metropolitan Museum of Art mentions dark, pale, red, and three-fold (triple?) beers, as well as recording beers with and without a head. Honey is also mentioned in some ancient texts as a beer ingredient. At least sixteen different beers were brewed in ancient Babylon. Big shots got special treatment as long, golden straws.

Nubian beer was one of six named varieties of beer described on the *Anastasi Papyrus of Pelusium* in Egypt, circa 2017 B.C.E. The pictures show a man offering a tablet to another who is taking a meal. Surely this was the first beer list. It is recorded as being bitter and not of long keeping.

So what can we say about the beers of the ancient world?

• Varying mixtures of malted and unmalted grains as mentioned previously, mostly sun-dried, but sometimes baked into coarse cakes that would have added: 1) color; 2) Maillard flavor; and 3) perhaps some smokiness. References to red and black beers in several ancient cultures bear this out. Malt was kilned in kernel form as malt kilning ovens are mentioned in texts.

• Just like today, every available grain was put into service in beer. Suitability for brewing or for other foodstuffs, seasonality, availability, fashion, and other factors would affect which ones got into a beer at any given point in time.

• Natural sugar sources such as honey and dates were used to boost the strength of certain types of beer.

• Strong and weak, pale and dark, fresh and aged, clear and cloudy, flat and carbonated, sweet and dry versions are mentioned in various sources. Many would have been sour, but a number are specifically called "sweet." An Egyptian pharaoh is promised in the afterlife: *"bread which doesn't crumble and beer which doesn't turn sour."*

• In Egypt (and possibly elsewhere) a distinction was made between filtered and unfiltered beer. The unfiltered stuff was pretty coarse, with chunks of husk and other bits, and was served to working stiffs for whom any and all nutrition would have been welcome. The premium stuff was reserved for the bigwigs.

• Carbonation and foam were known, but it seems unlikely that ancient people would have been able to maintain these qualities in anything other than very fresh or still-fermenting beer. However, it's not completely out of the question that a sealed, heavy ceramic jug could have held some pressure.

• Fermentation was left to wild or semi-domesticated sourdough strains that also performed leavening duty in the bakery, which was usually right next door. Sourdough yeast strains from the Middle East can be purchased today (see Appendix).

• Detailed recipes don't exist, so we're kind of on our own as far as trying to bring these ancient beers to life, and it will be impossible to know if we ever get it right.

An interesting pursuit, either for a club or an individual, would be to team up with a researcher specializing in the ancient world and collaborate on brewing a beer under his or her guidance. This has been done by commercial brewers a couple of times to great fanfare, but with the skill and process flexibility possessed by many homebrewers, the results should be rewarding.

GREECE AND ROME

While beer was known to the classical world, it seems they never got too excited about it. The Romans' most famous utterance about it was from the Emperor Julian, who said beer *"...smelled of goat."* So screw them.

After the beer-drinkers took over their empire, there was that whole long Dark

Gold Beaker, Ur/Tell al Muqayyar, 2550-2400 B.C.E.

We can't say for sure if this was a beer cup, but the Sumerians did have a goddess for the stuff.

"Beer I bear to thee, column of battle! With might mingled, and with bright glory: 'tis full of song, and salutary saws, of potent incantations, and joyous discourses."

—Brynhild to Sigurd,
The Nibelung

Chewsuran Drinking Vessels

Woodcuts from Arnold's *Origin and History of Beer and Brewing*, 1911.

Ages thing, where longstanding Bronze Age traditions were melded with a Romanized (I refuse to say "civilized") culture. Of course the details of the brewing practices are quite lost, but interesting glimpses do exist in ancient literature such as *Beowulf* and the *Kalevala*, already quoted in Chapter 4.

CHEWSURES AND THE LUDI OF OSSETIA

The world is a large place with many places to hold fast to ancient traditions. The following excerpt gives us an eyewitness account of what Bronze Age brewing may have looked like, even if it offers little information on the beer itself. This is from a book entitled *The Origin and History of Beer and Brewing* by John P. Arnold, published by the Wahl-Henius Institute in 1911. He's quoting G. Radde, *Die Chewsuren und ihr Land*, Kassel 1878.

Dr. Radde was the director of the Caucasian Museum in Tiflis, and in that capacity journeyed through the Caucusus. The result of one of these journeys was his book, in which he tells us, among other things, about the Chewsures and their manners and customs. One of the things he comments on is their religious ceremonies and worship, being, as was the case with other races and tribes, intimately connected with their beer and their practice of brewing, and it is this which is of special interest to us...

"Where clumps of ancient trees are massed in close array—oak, maple, and ash—we have before us the sacred groves of the Chewsures, preserved by them with veneration; and within them may be found their pagan sacrificial altars, as well as their beer breweries." Then he circumstantially describes the two sacred groves near Blo, to which he undertook excursions while stopping at the village. One of these groves is dedicated to Saint George, the other to Saint Michael.

"At the lower edge of the small wood, close to the field of barley, which together with the adjoining meadows, is held the property of Saint George, there stands a roughly constructed hovel, the place for sacrificing. This poor structure is low, dark inside, carelessly put together from flat slabs of slate, and for the moment it was not guarded by anybody. All the implements kept inside, especially the huge beer-tubs, tankards, drinking cups, and the manifold apparatus for brewing, are also looked upon as the property of the guardian angel in question. In the other sacred grove to the east of Blo, they happened to be brewing beer against the approaching holidays; that was why I went thither to be an eye witness to the process.

"From the brewery of Saint Michael there escaped a continuous cloud of smoke. Malting was going on there, and the acrid smoke, occasioned by the damp brushwood which had to serve as fuel, together with the escaping steam wrapped the brewhouse completely in a dusky mantle. The brew-house, too, was built in the rudest way, low and insufficiently lighted. There, by a mighty chain, hung the huge copper brew-kettle. Its form is peculiar, and everywhere the same. In its form it most closely resembles a giant top, being from 1 1/2 to 2 arsheen high (3 1/2 to

4 1/2 feet) and at its greatest width about 1 1/4 arsheen (3 feet) wide. It begins to belly out at a point above the middle. Artisans of Telaw fashion caldrons like these, their value being somewhere between 100 and 200 roubles. Laterally, this caldron is held up by carelessly joined stone rubble, while sooty flame licked at it in front and behind. The mash was bubbling in it at a uniform rate, and was stirred now and then. Water was conveyed from the nearby brook through a small pipe that was laid against the outer edge of the cauldron. The crushed barley that is used for the mash is coarse, and is boiled steadily for several days at an even temperature. Then the brew is run into woolen bags, and the latter are fastened above the rim of a vat, using wooden hoops for the fastening, so that the liquid slowly runs into the vat below. The fresh brew thus made, is turbid, rather insipid, and sweetish in flavor. It is poured into tubs 3 or 4 feet high, and 2 to 2 1/2 feet wide, made of one piece (from sections of tree trunks hollowed out), basswood being mostly used for this purpose. Then the required amount of Kakhetian wild hops is added, and the liquor, well covered up, is allowed to stand for 5 or 6 days.

Chewsure, 1911

These isolated people held on to ancient brewing practices until a just a century ago.

"Everything about these consecrated breweries is grimy with smoke and soot, as is also the case with the dwellings and watchtowers of the Chewsurians, and all the implements to be found upon the sacrificial altars and the breweries is considered the personal property of the guardian angel, and is correspondingly venerated."

Radde further relates that women were excluded from the groves, shrines, and breweries. Female participants in festivals remained behind boundaries, with beer and food served to them there.

The brew incorporated wild hops and malted barley that is dried—and develops color—over the course of several days, on racks positioned in the eaves of the houses, above the heat of the hearth. Fermentation was done in capacious earthenware pots buried in the ground, large enough for a man to descend into using a ladder.

The beer was described as brown in color, reminiscent of dark Bavarian beer, although "imperfectly clean."

THE AGE OF GRUIT

Gruit beer was the dominant beer of the European Middle Ages, and is intimately connected with the power and prevalence of the church. It gave way to hopped beer during the fifteenth century, only shortly before the Reformation, when church power faded. This gruit concession was held by a monopoly, either a church or government power, although sometimes licensed out to politically connected breweries. Since its use was mandatory, gruit served as an early form of taxation on beer. Evidence of its power to enrich the fat cat may still be seen in Bruges, Belgium, where a lavish gruithouse remains to this day an absorbing tourist destination.

Gruithuis, Brugge

This moon guards the entrance to this opulent building, and serves as a symbol for a local brew, Straffe Hendrik.

The Three Gruit Herbs

Bog Myrtle   *Myrica gale*

A low-growing marsh plant from northern climes with a resiny, eucalyptus aroma. It has anti-oxidant properties and a long history as an insect repellent as well as a beer ingredient. Its aromatic components are mostly terpenes, a class of compounds also prominent in hops, along with plenty of tannins. Various sources report that it was added to increase the potency of the beer, but I can find no evidence that psychoactive properties have been documented.

Wild Rosemary   *Ledum palustre*

Another marsh plant thriving on the wet edges of boggy spots in the far north. Generally viewed as inferior to bog myrtle. Not considered safe to consume internally. Used by Shamans in Siberia (the Tungusi and other tribes) in a smoke form as an inebriant. Not hallucinogenic; more of a hypnotic. The active ingredient may be palustride, a coumarin glucoside ester—a toxic relative of modern blood-thinning drugs, and nothing to toy around with. Like *Myrica gale*, loads of tannins.

Yarrow   *Achillea millefolium*

A tall, spindly herb with masses of small flowers, widely available as an ornamental perennial. Related to chamomile, it has been known to trigger hay fever-type allergic reactions. Otherwise no health issues.

The exact recipe for gruit was a closely held secret. Three herbs are always mentioned in association with gruit (see sidebar), and a great number of other herbs and spices were part of the mix as well, including juniper berries, ginger, caraway, wormwood, aniseed, and others. Generally, the spices were mixed together with malt flour or other starchy material, which helped to conceal the true nature of the mix.

Some argue that wild rosemary was just a poor substitute for bog myrtle and there may be some truth to that. The flavors of both are along similar resinous, bay-and-camphor lines, but wild rosemary is much harsher and more medicinal. The growing habitats are not that different, and it's clear from what information we have that all three herbs were not always used, and that the choice of herbs tended to vary on a regional basis. But the psychoactive properties of wild rosemary may have been reason enough to keep it in the mix. It's a hard problem to sort out, especially with such limited information at hand.

Little useful information is available on the beer itself. Like all medieval ales, it was likely to be strong, dark, smoky, and possibly a bit sour from long contact with wooden casks and tuns. Various strengths of beer were brewed, as in all ages, dark or not. To our tastes, the three most important seasonings—wild rosemary, yarrow, and bog myrtle—are not all that tasty, with resinous, medicinal aromas topped off with a load of tannic bitterness.

Gruit was displaced most everywhere by 1500, although it held on in Bremen until the early eighteenth century.

THE HEATHER ALE OF SCOTLAND

Heather is actually a number of different low-growing heath plants adapted to cold and otherwise barren landscapes of the North. Scotland is creepy with them, as is Scandinavia and elsewhere. These plants have small, aromatic flowers that bloom in late summer and have been used to flavor ales and other drinks for a very, very long time.

The flower tops are redolent of resin and perfume, with a complex honeyed character—quite delicious as a beverage seasoning. The flowers are somewhat delicate, and start to lose their aroma as soon as they are picked. Heather is mentioned in con-

Swedish Label, c. 1900

Once again, the Scandinavians set the mood.

RECIPE — Do It To It Gruit

A modernized—that is to say, drinkable—gruitbier.

Gravity: 1.054 (13 °P)

Alcohol/vol: 4.5 to 5.2%

Color: Brown

Bitterness: 10 IBU (or less)

Yeast: Belgian or German ale

Maturation: 6 to 8 weeks

Hops may be added for preservative value, but they were not traditional in this brew. If using, I suggest the lowest alpha variety you can find, which is typically Saaz. Between 0.5 and 1 ounce, boiled the full 90 minutes, ought to do.

All-Grain Recipe:

5.0 lb (2.3 kg)	47%	pale malt
4.5 lb (2 kg)	42%	aromatic/melanoidin
1.0 lb (0.45 kg)	9%	smoked malt
0.25 lb (113 g)	2%	brown or pale chocolate

Extract + Mini-Mash Recipe:

5.0 lb (2.3 kg)	74%	amber dry malt extract
0.5 lb (227 g)	7%	dark crystal
1.0 lb (0.45 kg)	15%	smoked malt
0.25 lb (113 g)	4%	brown or pale chocolate

Mash for an hour at 154° F (67° C).

To the last five minutes of the boil, add: 2 ounces crushed juniper berries; 5 grams each of bog myrtle (*Myrica gale*), caraway, mugwort (*Artemesia vulgaris*), and winemaker's grape tannin or grape seeds; 3 grams each of rosemary, ground cloves, and cardamom; and three whole California bay laurel leaves. Note that I have omitted the yarrow and wild rosemary (*Ledum palustre*), which were invariably mentioned as gruit components. From a health standpoint, these are questionable, and I can't recommend them. If you want to add them for authenticity, you're on your own.

nection with drinks from Scandinavia and the other places it grows, but it is in Scotland where heather ale is legendary.

Heather ale is associated with the Pictish tribes of Scotland, the land's original inhabitants who were eventually pushed aside by the Celts. Archaeological evidence in the form of pollen dates heather ale to at least 1000 B.C.E. *Calluna* and *Erica* heather have been chemically identified on a crusty potsherd, along with meadowsweet and royal fern.

It is hard to say whether the mythic status of heather derives from the beautiful carpet of blossoms, the lovely aroma, or the powdery psychoactive fungus—called fog, or fogg—that adheres to it. An observer writing about heather honey in 1804 says, "*I well remember, however, that, for two years that I used it, it almost always rendered me drowsy. Sometimes it composed me to sleep as effectually as a moderate dose of laundanum would have done.*" The honey may have contained some of the fungus from the heather.

Mind-altering substances have often been central in beer, and let's keep in mind that alcohol is no slouch in that area—even hops have a reputation for inducing sleep. You and I are in it for much more than the kick, but people in other times and places have had all kinds of relationships with their drinks.

The poem quoted at right recounts a mythic episode set in the era of the Celtic con-

From the bonny bells of heather,
They brewed a drink longsyne,
Was sweeter far than honey,
Was stronger far than wine.

—Robert Louis Stevenson,
Heather Ale

Heather Plants

Bell heather, also known as bonnie bells. There are two species of importance: *Erica tetralix* and *E. cinerea.*

Ling or broom heather, *Calluna vulgaris.*

quest over the original Pictish inhabitants of Scotland, which occurred around the sixth century. The Pictish king, back against the precipice, chooses to plunge to certain death rather than reveal the secret of heather ale. The legend is centered around Mull, which is at the southern end of a long, narrow peninsula, just the sort of place to make a last stand. Different versions of this tale are told across northern Europe, sometimes with gold or another treasure rather than beer as the focus.

The legend is very noble, but a bit melodramatic. You can just imagine the Celtic invaders looking across miles and miles of nothing but heather, heather, heather, scratching their chins and muttering to each other, "Now, where on earth are we going to find something to spice up this ale?"

Invasion notwithstanding, heather ale survived as a rustic folk brew, but it doesn't seem to have ever been brewed on any commercial scale. After the English defeated the Scots once and for all after the battle of Culloden in 1746, all things Scottish were banned, heather ale among them (and also subject to a 1707 English law that forbade

---

RECIPE — Heather Ale

Yield: 5 gallons (19 liters)
Gravity: 1.065 (15.5 °P)
Alcohol/vol: 5.3 to 6.2%
Color: Amber
Bitterness: 11 IBU
Yeast: Scottish ale
Maturation: 6 to 8 weeks

All-Grain Recipe:

8.0 lb (3.6 kg)	65%	pale ale malt
3.0 lb (1.4 kg)	25%	amber malt
0.25 lb (113 g)	2%	brown malt
1.0 lb (0.45 kg)	8%	honey, preferably heather, added to secondary

Mash at 155° F (68° C) for one hour.

Extract + Steeped Grain Recipe:

3.5 lb (1.6 kg)	45%	pale dry malt extract
3.0 lb (1.4 kg)	39%	amber dry malt extract
0.25 lb (113 g)	3%	brown malt
1.0 lb (0.45 kg)	13%	honey, preferably heather, added to secondary

Hops & Spices:

1.0 oz (28 g)	60 min	Saaz (3% AA)
2.0 oz (57 g)	end of boil	heather flower tops
0.25 oz (7 g)	end of boil	meadowsweet

---

the use of substances other than hops as bittering agents). With the industrialization of brewing that occurred about this time, many quaint and curious old brews passed into oblivion.

Which is where it would have remained, had it not been for a Scottish homebrew shop owner named Bruce Williams, who became interested in the style and managed to get his hands on an old family recipe. He brewed up some heather ale, which he

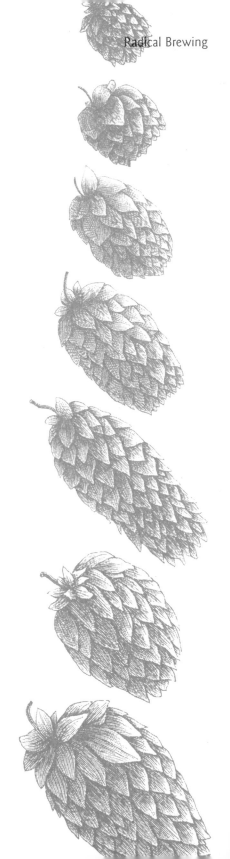

called Fraoch, after the Gaelic word for heather. His version—now a commercial product—is 5 percent alcohol by volume, deep amber in color, with the sweet honey-like fragrance of heather blooms. Fraoch is seasoned with sweet gale (bog myrtle) and meadowsweet along with the heather, which goes through a cleansing process to remove the powdery "fog" that might provide an unwanted thrill here in the modern world.

Heather is harvested in August and September, and the flowers lose their perfume rather quickly. They are best treated as aroma hops, tossed into the kettle as soon as the heat is turned off, and allowed to steep for a while. As they have a delicate flavor, a relatively large quantity is needed.

OLD INGREDIENTS AND QUANTITIES

We always think of ourselves as quite superior in our modern age. So it's very interesting to see that when Richardson first brought the use of the saccharometer (or hydrometer) into the profession of brewing in 1777, he recorded percentages of yield from contemporary barley malts at very similar levels as today, at least for the best grades available at that time. There must have been some incredible inefficiencies in pre-industrial brewing, as well as a lot of variation from brewer to brewer. Some of the quantities of ingredients called for in pre-1800 recipes were truly staggering. In brewing such concoctions, make your best guess at what the strength really was, then follow the proportions and use reliable utilization figures to hit your target.

Hops—at least traditional low-alpha aroma varieties—also may not have been drastically different in centuries past. The first hop extract production plant went into service in 1873, and the measurement of hop alpha acid came some decades later, although cruder measures were available. Serious scientific efforts to breed hops began at that time, and the first commercial high-alpha varieties were introduced in 1917. Up until that time a new variety may have made it into production every century or so, and growers were selecting for desirable agricultural properties and aromatic character, not particularly for high bitterness. And since there was no incredible difference in cultivation that would occasion a dramatic increase in alpha content over a century or two, I am inclined to believe that the traditional breeds of hops back then were not dramatically different from today, at between 3.0 and 4.5 percent alpha acid. There have certainly been improvements in year-to-year consistency and storage, which might knock a percent or two off, so we might look at the 1.5 to 3 percent (effective) alpha acid range as a good guesstimate. That's my story and I'm sticking to it.

It is important to consider the context of the beers in the old stories. Throughout history, brewers have made a range of beers: small, medium, strong, and sometimes extra strong. Our notion of this is not radically different from times past, so if a beer seems to be a everyday drinking beer, then a strength of between 1.040 and 1.060 is probably called for, and so on up and down the scale. I know this is vague, but given the incredible imprecision of old recipes (and our grasp of them) even such guesstimates can be comforting—and useful.

Brewing is generally a very conservative profession, and accepts new ideas, ingredients, or technologies only when there is a clear and proven need for them. This is so unlike our modern industrial world, which has jettisoned pretty much everybody *except* the Department of Improvements, which is exhorted to whip out the latest gee-gaws at a dizzying pace. It is comforting to be engaged in an endeavor in which it it is actually possible to roll back the clock a bit.

FINNISH SAHTI

There are so many dead beers out there, it's great when you find an old-timer alive and kicking. Sahti claims to be the oldest continuously brewed style of beer in the world, which may be arguable, but it's certainly the oldest in Europe. Brewing in Scandinavia goes back a thousand years at least, probably much earlier. Sahti barrels were found on sunken Viking ships dating to the ninth century, and there is hard evidence of malting just a little later. Rye was unknown in Finland until the twelfth century, so it's a "modern" addition to the recipe. Hops show up in the fourteenth century and gain widespread acceptance over the next couple of centuries, as elsewhere in Europe.

Even with the addition of hops to the sahti tradi-

RECIPE — **Sahti**

Yield: 5 gallons (19 liters)

Gravity: 1.062 (15 °P)

Alcohol/vol: 4.2 to 5%

Color: Amber

Bitterness: 8 IBU

Yeast: Compressed bread yeast, no more than one-fourth small cake

Maturation: 2 to 4 weeks

All-Grain Recipe:

8.0 lb (3.6 kg)	71%	Pilsener malt
1.0 lb (0.45 kg)	9%	aromatic/melanoidin (dark Munich)
1.0 lb (0.45 kg)	9%	malted rye
0.75 lb (340 g)	7%	extra dark crystal/special B
0.5 lb (227 g)	4%	malted rye, smoked over pine, spruce, and juniper berries

No Equivalent Extract Recipe

Hops & Spices:

0.3 oz (9 g)	60 min	Northern Brewer
1.0 oz (28 g)	60 min	crushed juniper berries

Boil juniper branches in the mash liquor. Mash procedure: step mash, with 15-minute rests at 104° F (40° C), 130° F (54° C), 148° F (64° C), 172° F (78° C), and a mash out at 190° F (88° C). This is normally accomplished by small additions of boiling water, resulting in a very thin mash at the end. Lauter over juniper branches placed in the bottom of the mash tun.

tion, it never edged juniper out of the limelight. Branches are used as a filter aid and as a flavoring in the mash liquor, and berries are used as a seasoning in the mash. The earliest description of the brewing process dates to 1780, and by that time sahti was already somewhat of a quaint beer. The brewing process was similar to present-day techniques. The same author (Asplund) also mentions the use of fresh raspberries in the southern Tammisaari region of Finland.

Unlike other European countries such as Poland and Lithuania, laws in Finland have allowed home and farm brewing over the centuries (with just a few interruptions), so that sahti has remained a living tradition. There is a commercial tradition of sahti brewing as well, including brewery pubs and export to faraway places like Uppsala, Sweden, and wherever that cask on the Viking ship was heading. There are several commercial breweries producing and packaging sahti today.

Sahti is amber in color, relatively strong, with a sweet maltiness countered by a strong juniper aroma. Hopping is quite light. Various strengths are sometimes brewed—including a lighter "women's sahti"—but the normal gravity is around 1.070 to 1.080. It tastes lighter than it is. In its traditional form it is uncarbonated, although, because it is consumed quickly, it may retain a bit of prickle from an active secondary fermentation. A month is the extent of the shelf life, due in large part to not boiling the wort.

Many sahti brewers in Finland use a premixed malt that includes 85 percent Pilsener malt, 10 percent pale crystal, and 5 percent two-row enzyme malt, although many brewers add 10 percent or more rye malt to this, often toasted for color and flavor. None of these malts are smoked, as they are in other Scandinavian folk-brews.

A scant armful of juniper branches, preferably with berries on them, are placed into a kettle full of water, which is then brought to a boil, and this hot liquor is used to mash in. The traditional mash is an upward step infusion, with small amounts of boiling water added every half hour for up to six hours, constantly raising the mash temperature bit by bit, although the temperature falls during the rests so there's a prolonged period at or near conversion temperatures (149 to 155° F or 65 to 68° C).

The mash is drained through juniper branches using a long trough called a kuurna, made from a hollowed-out log. It is common to use the first runnings for a stronger beer, then make a smaller beer with the sparged runnings.

Bread yeast is often used, and a certain sourness is appropriate. This can come from lactobacillus lurking in the unboiled wort or in wooden fermenters such as butter churns, or may be introduced in a more controlled manner via sourdough starter or pedigreed lactobacillus starter. Bread yeast is commonly used, with the caution that only a very small amount is needed. I used a quarter of a small foil pack of caked bread yeast when I did mine, and it was plenty. Sourdough starters are usually a little more sluggish, so a normal pitching quantity ought to be fine with them.

Keptinus Alus Literally "baked beer" in Lithuanian, this is a surviving relic of an ancient brewing tradition of using bread as a starting point for everyday beer. I can't seem to find much in the way of details, but there may be similarities to the French *kiszlnschtschi* recipe, in which the mash is literally baked in an oven. Barley, rye, and/or wheat were all used, along with hops, and sometimes sugar and peas, said to increase

Finnish Kuurna

The traditional lauter tun for sahti is made from a hollowed out log. Juniper branches are laid upon the slats in the bottom.

the froth of the head. A small beer similar to kvass, called *salde*, was made from malted or unmalted rye, or brown rye bread.

DEVON WHITE ALE

This beer was a curious remnant of medieval culture that managed to survive until around the middle of the nineteenth century. Brewed in both Cornwall and Devonshire, there are a number of tantalizing references to it, starting as early as the reign of Henry VIII (1509 to 1547), where the invention of it was ascribed to a German military officer.

Ich am a Cornishman, ale I can brew

It will make one cacke, also to spew.

It is thick and smokey and also it is thin

It is like wash as pigs had wrestled there in

—Andrew Boorde, 1540

London and Country Brewer, 1736:

"Their white Ale is a clear Wort made from pale Malt, and fermented with what is called ripening, which is a Composition, they say, of the Flower [flour] of Malt, Yeast, and Whites of Eggs, a Nostrum made and sold only by two or three in those Parts, but the Wort is brewed and the Ale vended by many Publicans, which is drank while it is fermenting in Earthen Steens, in such a thick manner as resembles butter'd Ale, and sold for Twopence Halfpenny the full Quart. It is often prescribed by Physicians to be drank by wet Nurses for the encrease of their Milk, and

---

RECIPE	Devon White Ale	
Yield: 1 gallon (3.8 liters)	4.0 lb (1.8 kg)	Pilsener malt
Gravity: 1.024 (6° P)	3.0 oz (84 g)	wheat flour
Alcohol/vol: 2 to 2.5%	0.5	egg white
Color: Cloudy pale straw	0.2 oz (6 g)	kosher (non-iodized) salt
Bitterness: None	*Grout:*	
Yeast: Bread Yeast, 1/4 cake compressed (ale yeast may be used instead)	1 small cake	bread yeast
	0.25 oz (7 g)	freshly ground coriander
Maturation: 1 week	0.25 tsp (1 g)	powdered ginger
	0.12 tsp (0.5g)	caraway

Note that this a 1- gallon recipe.

---

also as a prevalent Medicine for the Colick and Gravel."

A description written in 1808 goes thus:

"The brewing of a liquor called white ale, is almost exclusively confined to the neighborhood of Kingsbridge: its preparation, as far as could be learnt by the

Surveyor, is 20 gallons [75 pounds] of malt mashed with the same quantity of boiling [sic] water; after standing the usual time, the wort is drawn off, when six eggs, four pounds of flour, a quarter of a pound of salt and a quart of grout, are beat up together and mixed with this quantity of wort, which, after standing twelve hours is put into a cask and is ready for use by the following day. The beverage produces a very intoxicating quality, and is much admired by those who drink not to quench thirst only."

It is commonly reported that the houses in this area lacked cellars, as they were situated on solid bedrock. The white ale was fermented indoors in 5-gallon crocks or "steens," mainly by local women who paid half a guinea annually for the privilege of being able to sell it.

We can only guess what mysterious ingredients formed the core of the grout; observers in the past never seemed privy to the secret. I suppose it will take a molecular anthropologist to scrape a bit of crust off an ancient crock. So I'm just going to take a wild stab at it, and suggest a combination of spices known to be in use then and in white beers of the Continent.

KVASS

This is an ancient Russian drink, part of the worldwide family of small beers that have been made throughout the ages using the smallest possible amount of the cheapest local ingredients. Kind of like...well, you know, it comes in cans. Cheap, weak, refreshing, and usually a little sour, they are above all safe to drink. From peasants to Czars, everybody drank kvass. In the firmament of Russian food and drink, it was the second most treasured staple, next to sauerkraut.

In the very old days, kvass was made simply by mixing water with flour, then allowing it to sour. Various types of grain were used—whatever was handy, including rye, barley, wheat, and buckwheat, sometimes with sugar added. Stale rye bread is also a common starting point. At one time street vendors sold it from pushcarts

RECIPE	Kvick Kvality Kvass

Yield: 5 gallons (19 liters)

Gravity: 1.024 (6 °P)

Alcohol/vol: 2 to 2.5%

Color: Pale gold

Bitterness: 11 IBU

Yeast: Bread yeast, one-fourth cake compressed (ale yeast may be used instead)

Maturation: 1 week

All-Grain Recipe:

1.75 lb (0.79 kg)	37%	rye flour
1.0 lb (0.45 kg)	25%	six-row malt
1.0 lb (0.45 kg)	25%	rye malt
9.0 oz (255 g)	13%	buckwheat (kasha), toasted

No Equivalent Extract Recipe

Mix with warm water and hold for a one hour mash at 150° F (65.5° C). Seasonings, added to the mash: 0.12 oz (3.5 g) peppermint (be aware that fresh mint in the grocery store is spearmint); juice and zest of one lemon. The wort is traditionally unboiled.

equipped with tanks. Various seasonings were used, but peppermint emerged as the favorite. Raisins were commonly added. Lemon slices or juice is a more modern addition.

As it became more of a commercial product, spontaneous fermentation was replaced by cultured yeast, but some kind of souring material is needed to get to the 0.15 to 0.5 percent lactic acid content. Today it may be found bottled like soft drinks, and it is in fact alcohol-free in this form. It's lightly spritzy, a sort of malty ginger ale kind of thing, less sweet than regular soda pop. Nice enough, but sanitized and simplistic compared to the real stuff from the old days.

Here's the traditional manner of homebrewing: boiling water is poured over rye bread and allowed to stand twenty-four hours. Then sugar, cream of tartar, and a sour starter made from wheat flour and brewing or baking yeast is added. As soon as it starts to ferment, it is bottled. In a few days it's ready to drink. Alcohol content should be in the range of 1 to 2 percent.

The following is based on an 1896 recipe from a German brewing journal, a commercial recipe made from grain rather than bread. I'm making this a little on the strong side, just to kind of go with the homebrew spirit, but you can cut the quantities of everything but water by two-thirds and still be in the range.

There's no reason you couldn't scale it up either. If I were doing that, I would replace the rye flour with half barley malt, half rye malt, and conduct more of a conventional brewing and fermentation process.

There is a British small beer similar to kvass called "bee's wine," with no connection to either bees or wine, but which was made from stale bread and sugar.

Kiszlnschtschi is an elegant, spritzy variation on kvass. Wagner's description (1877) gives us a pretty good idea.

"The colorless kiszlnschtschi* is essentially a sparkling kwass with less nutritive value than the actual kwass; it is a delight for the taste buds, a refined kwass, which is quite beloved for its carbonation in the summer. Called 'grain champagne,' it's prepared from barley, wheat, and rye malts, plus wheat flour, pearl barley and buckwheat, which are mixed together with boiling water and mashed for 6 hours.

"The quantity of mash water is about three times the grist. After a quantity of boiled and cooled water is mixed in, it is aromatized with peppermint, then clarified by pouring through a filter into a barrel, whereupon the liquid ferments and develops a good sourness, but before it is completed, it is removed from the fermenter and filled into champagne bottles. Into each one is placed a bit of sugar and 2 grapes. The bottles are well corked and wired, then stored in ice cellars to pressurize and to incorporate the flavors of the added materials."

* "kiszlh" means sour and "schtschi" means cabbage soup.

A French book, circa 1800, gives us this recipe for Kislischis:

"Take 20 kg barley, plus 1 kg of barley malt or rye malt; moisten this mix a little, and stir until it has acquired the consistency of molasses. Place it in large iron

pots, and put them in a preheated oven with the embers joined together and moved to the sides; four hours afterwards, you will remove the pots from the oven, and then sprinkle the mixture little by little into a tun of approximately 70 bottles [14 gallons] capacity, then ladling in more hot water and two ladles of dried mint: agitate the whole during a quarter of an hour on several occasions; the barrel is covered, and after two or three days, the liquor can be tapped. The klisischis will still be bubbling slightly. It is a little tart, with a very agreeable taste."

OLD MOSCOW BROWN ALE OR MOSKOVSKAYA

Accurately called "One-Day Beer" in nineteenth century Moscow, this is a folk beer, rich and full of yeast and carbohydrates. It was brewed at home, serving as nutrition for villagers, especially women and infants. In a harsh climate full of very poor people, this brew must have really fit the definition of "liquid bread."

The description I have seen (Wagner, 1877) calls for a mixture of 93 percent by volume of barley flour or meal, and 7 percent wheat malt. It is not clear whether either of these are roasted, or whether a colored sugar syrup is used, but the color was described as "brown."

A related black beer was brewed from a "...mixture of barley and rye malt," using a thin mash and very little in the way of hops. This was top-fermented, and finished very sweet. Again, no description of which ingredient provided the black color, but roasted rye is a traditional product that is still available from German maltsters.

These heavy brown beers form a family of nutritious, partially fermented brews that stretched from Russia to England, roughly the same territory as white beers. Most of them died out before 1900, although a few, such as Belgian diest, managed to survive a few decades more.

ALES AND BEERS OF JOLLY OLD ENGLAND

This is the England of our archetypal dreams—at a crossroads between the medieval and the modern, the Industrial Revolution and the smoky conviviality of the country pub. Toby jugs, John Bull, a mighty nation forcing itself on the world, but longing only for a humming pint by the fire on a damp winter's night.

This dichotomy still may be encountered in England, as elsewhere in Europe. In the invention of America, the ancient taproots needed to sustain such crusty quaintness were severed completely, and this has only heightened our nostalgia for the "good old days." Such constructs are always a bit dishonest, but in the end, they reflect desires for something simple and timeless. The craft brewing movement harnesses this as a prime motivating force.

Melodramatics aside, there were some really interesting beers back then.

The period between about 1680 and 1840 was a unique era when there were plenty of quaint old brewing traditions, now extinct or within living memory. But thanks to the Industrial Revolution, the means existed for the first time to produce books at reasonable costs, which means that a lot of information has survived to this day.

Russian Label, c. 1900

"Bung, Ho!"

—Old British toast

English Tall Ale Glass, c. 1800

Just the thing for strong old ale.

DORCHESTER BEER—FILLING A 300-YEAR-OLD BOTTLE

I recently acquired what was described as a "three-hundred-year-old beer bottle," unearthed from beneath a seventeenth-century cottage in Cerne Abbas, Dorset, England. It is crude and heavy, off-round, with a lopsided neck, holding about a pint and a half.

Nothing about its appearance suggests more than a passing relationship with the Industrial Revolution. Its salt glaze is uneven; there are chips, exploded bubbles, stones, even traces of handprints from the potter who threw it. Crude, heavy, and ugly, this relic drew me into its tale. I tried to imagine it full, corked, and holding a well-aged brew, warming some beer-lover's heart on a chilly night in Dorset. What would such a beer taste like? Strong, weak, hoppy, herbed? It could have been any of those.

Cerne Abbas is a famous place noted for its hillside chalk figure of a giant with a huge erection, carved into the hill by some hairy Druidic race now long vanished. Newlyweds and other couples seeking children are advised to go out and avail them-selves (wink, wink, nudge, nudge) of the power of the aforementioned member as a fertility charm.

The region is Dorset, a short hop south of London, famous among beer aficiona-dos as the home of Eldridge Pope, makers of the barley wine named for their favorite son, Thomas Hardy. By now many of you are familiar with his famous quote describ-ing Dorset beer, written in 1870:

> "It was of the most beautiful color that the eye of an artist could desire; full in body, yet brisk as a volcano; piquant, yet without a twang; luminous as an autumn sunset, free from streakiness of taste; but, finally, rather heady. The masses worshipped it, the minor gen-try loved it more than wine, and by the most illustrious country families it was not despised. But its whole army of brewers have passed away, its flavor is forgotten except by a few aged men, and the secret of its composition appears to have been completely lost as that of Falstaff's beverage."

A writer praised Dorset beers in 1700, "...the people here have learned to brew the finest malt liquors in the kingdom, so delicately clean and well tasted that the best judges...prefer it to the ales most in vogue as in Hull, Derby, Burton, &c." At that time, a great deal of Dorset beer was being shipped to London, the porter revolution there having not yet begun.

I wish I could say that this recipe was copied intact from some ancient scrap of goatskin. The cold, hard fact remains that we will never really know what was in this bottle. What you see here represents a "could have been" approach.

The color of Dorchester beer was described in 1737 as "bright amber." We'll be using a base made of half pale ale malt, and half amber malt. The latter was once widely used for a vari-

RECIPE   Giant Ale of Cerne Abbas

Yield: 5 gallons (19 liters)

Gravity: 1.096 (23 °P)

Alcohol/vol: 7 to 8.3%

Color: Deep amber

Bitterness: 61 IBU

Yeast: Alcohol-tolerant English ale

Maturation: 4 to 8 months

For a real authentic tang, use a packet of *Brettanomyces* or mixed lambic culture once the beer has settled down, and age on this for six months to a year. This recreates the flora found in the wooden casks such beers were aged in, and can be tasted still in such beers as Gales Prize Old Ale.

All-Grain Recipe:

13.0 lb (5.9 kg)	68%	amber/biscuit malt
6.0 lb (2.7 kg)	32%	pale ale malt

No Extract Equivalent Recipe

Hops & Spices:

3.0 oz (85 g)	90 min	East Kent Goldings (5% AA)
3.0 oz (85 g)	10 min	East Kent Goldings (5% AA)
0.25 oz (7 g)	end of boil	fresh sage

Infuse the mash with 7 gallons of hot water at 170° F (76.5° C). This should give a strike temperature of 151 to 153° F (66 to 67° C). Hold for two hours, as starch conversion is apt to be slow. You can test with iodine (if it turns blue, it's not yet converted); once you get conversion, run off the mash. Once this first mash is run off, add 2 to 3 gallons of 180° F (82° C) water to the mash to make up to 6 gallons of wort, which will boil down to a little over 5.

Ferment with your favorite English yeast strain, built up into a starter, or better yet, pitch from the sediment of a recently emptied secondary.

The Cerne Abbas Giant

Carved through the turf to reveal white chalky soil, this big guy has been doing his thing for millennia.

ety of beers in England, including some early porters. Described these days as "biscuit," it has a unique toasted, nutty taste unlike anything else. About 20 to 25° L, it was formerly made by kilning malt over a straw fire, which produced a clean, unsmoked taste.

The yield of this beer was noted as "two barrels per quarter," meaning that 336 pounds of malt made 86.4 U.S. gallons, or 19.5 pounds in a 5-gallon batch. Pretty beefy. This recipe also calls for "Kentish" hops at the rate of 6 or 7 pounds to the quarter, which translates into the quantities that follow. This is a moderate rate for a strong beer like this.

One other recipe for Dorchester beer mentions the use of sage, sassafras, and checkerberry as ingredients. Although by 1700 hopped beers were the norm, I'm tossing in a bouquet of spices as a nod to earlier days.

Brewing in England at that time was done in a "parti-gyle" manner, meaning that the runnings from the mash tun were not all mixed together, but were fermented into two or even three different beers. We'll use the first two-thirds, which will give us a rich, strong brew. The remainder can be tossed, or made into a small beer by the addition of a pound or two of molasses or cooked sugar, or re-mashed with a couple of pounds of additional amber malt before sparging the small beer.

I have a French recipe from about 1800 for Dorchester Ale, which used 100 percent amber malt exclusively, was highly hopped, and included large quantities of ginger, salt, and licorice.

SOME ODDS AND ENDS OF OLD ENGLISH BEER STYLES

English Names for Strong Ale

Stingo	Huffcap
Dagger	Hum-cup
Dragon's Milk	Nipitatum
Clamberskull	Rug
Humming Ale	

Hogen Mogen A strong English ale, most likely spiced, popular in the mid-seventeenth century. Sometimes also called "rug" (which was also a generic term for any strong ale). The famous host and gadabout, Horace Walpole, was famous for his homebrewed Hogen. Dryden in 1663 laments: *"I was drunk, damnably drunk with ale, great hogen mogen bloody ale."* The name derived from a Dutch form of formal address that meant "high and mighty." If there is an extant recipe for this, it is still hiding from the present-day brewing community.

R E C I P E — Oh, Your Highness Windsor Ale

Yield: 5 gallons (19 liters)

Gravity: 1.076 (18 °P)

Alcohol/vol: 7.2 to 8.3%

Color: Medium gold

Bitterness: 29 IBU

Yeast: English ale

Maturation: 8 to 12 weeks

All-Grain Recipe:

12.0 lb (5.4 kg)	92%	pale ale malt
1.0 lb (0.45 kg)	8%	honey (added at end of boil)

Mash 1 hour at 152° F (67° C).

Extract and Steeped Grain Recipe:

7.0 lb (3.18 kg)	78%	pale dry extract
1.0 lb (0.45 kg)	11%	pale crystal
1.0 lb (0.45 kg)	11%	honey (added at end of boil)

Hops & Spices:

1.0 oz (28 g)	90 min	East Kent Goldings (5% AA)
1.0 oz (28 g)	20 min	East Kent Goldings (5% AA)
1.0 oz (28 g)	end of boil	East Kent Goldings (5% AA)
0.5 oz (14 g)	end of boil	ground licorice root
0.25 oz (7 g)	end of boil	crushed coriander
0.1 oz (3 g)	end of boil	dried orange peel
0.1 oz (3 g)	end of boil	grains of paradise
1.0 tsp (4 g)	end of boil	ginger, grated
1.0 tsp (4 g)	end of boil	caraway

Engligh Ale House Window, Date Unknown

Note the *putti* with tails and the donkeys in the shield!

Windsor Ale This is one more of the regional private house brewing recipes that crop up in the books of the period, about 1800:

> *"Take 5 quarters of the best pale ale malt, half a cwt. of hops, 8 pounds of honey, 1 pound of coriander seed, half pound of Grains of Paradise, half pound of orange peel, and two-and-a-half pounds of liquorice root. . . six ounces of ground ginger, and six ounces of ground caraway seed."*

"The drugs above mentioned are forbidden, under the penalty of two hundred pounds, and the forfeiture of all utensils; but of course private families are at liberty to use whatever they please. Nothing but malt and hops are permitted to public brewers, except the colouring extract; and the druggists who sell to brewers are subject to a penalty of five hundred pounds."

Amber This beer showcases a once-popular malt type with the same name. Now more commonly known as "biscuit," this moderately toasted malt will produce a beer with a toasty brown flavor, making it more in line with what we think of as a nut brown ale. Amber was lightly hopped, and it appears as if it was the direct descendant of the unhopped ales which were universal in England prior to the introduction of hops in the sixteenth century. Still being sold at the time when porter rose to

---

RECIPE — Welsh Ale, c 1800

In ancient and Medieval times, Welsh ale meant a type of bragot, a beer with a large proportion of honey. By the early nineteenth century this connection had vanished.

Yield: 5 gallons (19 liters)

Gravity: 1.072 (17.5 °P)

Alcohol/vol: 7 to 8.3%

Color: Deep gold

Bitterness: 24 IBU

Yeast: English ale

Maturation: 8 to 12 weeks

All-Grain Recipe:

13.0 lb (5.9 kg)	98%	pale ale malt
0.5 cup (4 oz)	2%	molasses, added at end of boil

Extract Recipe:

8.0 lb (3.7 kg)	97%	pale dry malt extract
0.5 cup (4 oz)	3%	molasses, added at end of boil

Hops & Spices:

1.0 oz (28 g)	90 min	East Kent Goldings (5% AA)
0.5 oz (14 g)	20 min	East Kent Goldings (5% AA)
0.5 oz (14 g)	end of boil	East Kent Goldings (5% AA)
0.25 oz (7 g)	end of boil	grains of paradise, crushed
0.25 oz (7 g)	end of boil	liquorice root, ground

---

prominence, it was eventually displaced by the newer pale ales. Amber appears to have been the beer that in eighteenth-century London was called "twopenny," and which was one of the blending components of "three threads." Amber was also used as a base for *purl*, below.

Purl Contained wormwood, gentian root, sweet flag, snake root, horseradish, dried orange peel, juniper berries, orange seeds, and galingale. Purl was normally made by infusing amber ale also called "twopenny" with these spices mentioned, typically hung in a muslin bag inside the cask as the beer matured. It was sold along the canals and other waterways in England in the eighteenth century by vendors called "purlmen."

Copper Ale Pot, English, c. 1800

Weaterwald Stein, late 1800s.

China Ale Ale infused with coriander and "China root" (ginger). Spices were usually placed in cloth bags and hung in the barrel.

THICK GOOEY BEERS

This is a family of thick, dark, highly nutritious beers brewed all across northern Europe. Some of these were more or less like normal dark beers, although on the sweet side. Some, like the Danziger Jopenbier described below, are the strange, mutant monsters of the beer family tree.

These were not everyday beers, but nourishing fortifiers drunk by the likes of nursing mothers. And in the case of Jobenbier, it wasn't drunk by itself at all, but used as a seasoning, either for a lighter beer, or for soups and gravies.

Danziger Jopenbier Danzig is the German name for the city of Gdansk, now in Poland, but for a long time it was a part of Germany, as was the rest of Prussia. Its beers have a longstanding reputation for strength. Doctor Knaust reports in 1614 that the barley beer of Danzig *"is the queen and surpasses all other red beers. Although there are in Prussia many delicious and good beers, the Danzig beers overtops them all; and in fact, there is not found in the whole of Germany a stronger beer among the barley beers, a thing which cannot be denied, no matter what else may be claimed."* And boy, this is a strange one!

According to observers in about 1900, this was a beer brewed with conventional ingredients and processes, except for the massive gravity that was achieved by large amounts of malt, and a boil that lasted ten hours or longer. By the time the wort was turned out, the gravity was at a syrupy 45 to 55 °P! The beer was hopped at a rate of 7 to 8 gallons per kilogram (0.13 ounces per pound) of malt. Then things get really weird.

Fermentation was said to have taken place in cellars completely covered with mold, which was carefully guarded against cleaning. No culture yeast was pitched, and the beer went through a five-stage process completely by spontaneous means. Brewing was allowed only between October and April, fermentation in summer being considered too vigorous.

First, a thin white film of mold formed, then changed to bluish green, which accounted for the first two weeks. Then, bubbling gas started coming up from the wort and broke up the film, which, in turn, further sped up the fermentation. This proceeded very vigorously for ten to fourteen days, and provisions needed to be made to retain and return the overflow to the fermenter. In the third phase, the yeast kind of settled out. Then another film formed on the surface—white at first, then dark brown, then at last green, growing and thickening, folding itself up into great ridges as it floated on the surface.

An important part of this very ugly fermentation seems to have been the development of certain oxidized flavors that are normally associated with port or sherry, caused by yeast that lives on the surface of the liquid. At this point it's two or three months old. Aging continues for up to a year, and at the end it is slowly forced through a cloth filter bag and placed into 13-liter crocks or jugs.

Lager, ale, and sherry-type yeasts were present, as well as *Penicillum* and *Mucor* molds, lactobacillus, and possibly other microorganisms. A real zoo. Alcohol was very low, at 2.3 to 7 percent; lactic acid was fairly high (about like lambic) at 2 percent, although given the incredible amount of residual sweetness, it couldn't have been too assertive.

Jopenbier was widely exported to as far away as England, where it seems to have been used as a seasoning for soups and gravies. In Germany it was a popular additive to normal beer, as a flavor booster. As far as I can tell, it is no longer made anywhere today, which is a shame. It really was a unique product.

Haarlem, Holland also claims a jopenbier, this one brewed with a large proportion of oats, more than half in 1500, the remainder being split between malted wheat and barley. A revival version is being brewed by the Haerlemsch Bierbrouwerij, an amber beer of 6.5 percent alcohol, lightly hopped and seasoned with coriander.

Dutch Black Buckwheat Beer I have just two tantalizing references to this, both English, and around 1700:

"...Buckwheat makes also an excellent drink, and is very much used in Holland..."

"as the Hollanders do their thick Black Beer Brewed with Buck Wheat."

Mumme An herb tonic brewed from barley malt created in Braunschweig, Germany, but also very well known— and brewed—in England. Here's the famous English recipe John Bickerdyke dredged up from *The Receipt Book of John Nott*, 1723 (although Bickerdyke dates it to 1682):

"To make a vessel of sixty-three gallons, we are instructed that the water must be first boiled to the consumption of a third part, then let it be brewed according to art with seven barrels of wheat-malt, one bushel of oat-malt, and one bushel of ground beans. When the mixture begins to work, the following ingredients are to be added: three pounds of the inner bark of fir; one pound each of the tops of the fir and birch; three handfuls of Carduus Benedictus, dried; two handfuls of flowers of **Rosa solis** *[sundew]; of burnet, betony, marjoram, avens, pennyroyal, flowers of elder, and wild thyme [Thymus drucei], one handful and a half each; three ounces of bruised seeds of cardamum; and one ounce of bruised bayberries. Subsequently ten new-laid eggs, not cracked or broken, are to be put into the hogshead, which is then to be stopped close, and not tapped for two years, a sea voyage greatly improving the drink."*

Some of these medicinal herbs, especially Carduus (blessed thistle), are excruciatingly bitter—"bitter as gall," as one poem stated. As for the rest: "...there is scarcely any disease in nature against which some of them (ingredients) are not a sure specific..."

This kooky recipe notwithstanding, mumme was one of the thick beers (dictbiers) like jopenbier brewed in several places in northern Germany. Like jopenbier, mumme featured an immensely thick wort, spontaneously fermented and aged for at least a year. Analysis around 1900 gave the gravity at between 48 and 65° Plato, and 0 to 3 percent alcohol, indicating some versions were unfermented.

But earlier, mumme was a drinking beer. Hohberg, who in 1687 dismisses the English recipe above as "...*surely no Brunswick Mumm*..." lays out the following by way of a recipe:

> "*You must take two Brunswick* **Wispel** [2500 pounds total] *of perfectly sound and well-roasted barley malt, and put this in a kettle with sufficient water, letting it slowly boil [brew?] for 5/4 hours. Then, ladle it out into a vat, and let it stand for a while, after which you will pour it again into the kettle, but only the liquid part, not the malt), and let it once more boil for another three hours, together with 15 "Himpen"*[100-150 pounds] *of good rustic hops. After letting the whole mass cool in the vat, and after allowing it to ferment for the proper time...From this is generally obtained 4 1/2 barrels.*"

"Barrels" (*faß*) in this recipe is a vague term relative to seventeenth-century Braunschweig, but generally, whole barrels tend to be in the 25 to 40 gallon range everywhere. After the metric system was introduced, 100 liters became the standard barrel, so if we take a stab and use that figure of about 26.4 gallons per barrel, this comes to 119 gallons for the batch, for the stupidly large 21 pounds per gallon. If "faß" means something more like a butt (126 gallons), then the total batch comes to 567 gallons, or 4.4 pounds per gallon, a high but not ridiculous figure.

The description indicates a no-sparge method, and this will typically produce wort in the 1.080 to 1.090 range. A three-hour boil will bump this up to perhaps 1.085 to 1.100 (20.2 to 25 °P), still only half of the gravity of more recent versions. A mid-nineteenth-century source says that "...hops, molasses, juniper berries, dried prunes, and several aromatic herbs..." were added to the wheat and barley malt base. Sounds kind of tasty to me.

Koyt A Dutch gruit beer, now recreated commercially by a small brewery in Haarlem, Netherlands. Its present incarnation is interpreted from a 1407 recipe, a dark spiced beer brewed from barley malt, wheat, and oats, showing lots of fruity overtones, and strong at 1.074 OG. The old recipes indicate that bog myrtle was the dominant herb.

OUTLAW ALES OF NORTHERN GERMANY

We think of the *Reinheitsgebot* as a German law, but it has only been so since 1877, a few years after Bavaria joined the German Union. This means that in other parts of Germany, especially the Northeast, unique local beers incorporating oats, molasses, honey, spices, and even salt were still being brewed when the new—well, old, actually—law came into force. This left many of the former styles orphaned and worse; by World War II, they had pretty much vanished. A few enterprising craft breweries in Germany and elsewhere are recreating a few of them, but much more work remains to be done.

Northern Germany was a part of a cultural continuum that stretched all along the North Sea. In the medieval period, powerful city-states banded together for trade and

protection in a body known as the Hanseatic League. This gave brewers in Hansa towns a powerful tool for selling beer: access to foreign markets. Guilds of both red (barley) and white (wheat) beer brewers jostled for market share, and cities usually became famous for one or the other. As was true all over the medieval world, limited contact between people and the extreme cost of shipping everyday beer meant that every town had its own unique beer. Dr. Lintner's list (right) gives us a tantalizing glimpse. Many of these local specialties lingered on until 1900 or so; now there are just a handful. Even today, Germans cling to their local beers, although not so much for the uniqueness of them as for simple civic spirit.

The old brewing books give us glimpses of some of these old timers. The more popular styles of the nineteenth century are documented sufficiently to brew replicas of some. Others get just a passing mention, maddening for recipe collectors like myself. But we know how to brew, and there's no shame in cooking up a recipe based on just a sentence or two.

Broyhan Alt A very pale, all-malt middling table beer similar to some of the northern wheat beers. In the seventeenth century and earlier it had been a wheat beer; by the late 1800s, it had turned into a barley beer. It is described as having a "vinous aroma, and a salty-sour taste." It was brewed with a three-step infusion, with rests for glucans, proteins, and starch conversion. An unusual feature was a series of hop infusions, in which hops are soaked for eight to ten hours, the hoppy liquid being used as brewing liquor.

Single and double versions were made. Figures in 1884 showed 1.037 (8 °P) and 1.054 (13 °P) wort gravities, respectively, and those same measurements showed lactic acid contents between 0.06 and 0.15 percent, which is enough to taste, but not extremely sour.

Mysterious German Local Beer Names

The famous Doctor Lintner provided this list for us in 1867. Many of these are just local nicknames for a more widely brewed type of beer, but some of them do refer to beers using unique recipes or brewing methods.

These now largely outdated names, which people in Germany have always attached to their different beers, are idiosyncratic and revealing. A list of German local beer names is just as fascinating as it is linguistically important. The most famous beer names are:

Alter Klaus (Old Nick) in Brandenberg, at the edge of Berlin

Auweh (Oh dear) in Lützerode, near Jena, Hanover

Angst (Worry) in Garden

Bauchweh (Tummy-ache) in Grimma, southeast of Leipzig

Beissdenkerl (Thought-bite) in Boitzenburg, southeast of Hamburg and Lübeck

Bind den Kerl (the fine fellow) in Boitzenburg, Prussia

Blak (Soot/Smoke) in Kohlberg

Block in Kohlberg

Brausegut (Shower-good), Brauseput, Brauseloch, Bruselock in Beneckenstein and Harz

Bocksbart (Goat's-beard, a plant: *Tragopogon pratensis*) in Wartenburg, near Basel, Switzerland

Bitterbier in Zerbst (near Magdeburg)

Broihan in Halberstadt, a type of altbier

Bürste (Brush) in Osnabrück

Daus in Ratzeburg

Dorfteufel (Village Devil) in Jena

Duckstein (Duck-stone) in Königslutter, near Braunschweig, a top-fermented beer aged on or in beechwood. A beer by this name is still being beechwood-aged.

Dicktbier (Thick-beer) in Danzig. See earlier text referring to Jopenbier.

Filz (Felt, beer-mat) in Rostock (North Sea coast, near Lübeck)

Fried und Einigkeit (peace and unity) in Kyritz (northwest of Berlin)

Hansla (teaser?) in Bamberg, North-Central Bavaria

Hund (dog) in Bremen, Dasseln, Corvey

Hosenmilch (trouser-milk) in Dransfeld (S. of Hanover)

O wonderful harvest beer,
you fest of Freedom and desire!
Because of your beer tap folk
wean babies from the breast!

—Song to Harvest Beer

Kotbüsser A special type of German ale, another cousin to the grand family of white beers. It was, at least after 1877, an outlaw beer because of the addition of oats, honey, and molasses. The name derives from Kotbüss, the town in which it was brewed. Both single (1.032, 8 °P) and double (1.054, 13.5 °P) versions were brewed. The recipe that follows is for 5 gallons of the double, which better suits our home-brew palates.

Kotbüsser is a crisp, deep golden beer, moderately hopped, with just a hint of sugary complexity from the honey and molasses. Wheat and oats give it a monumental, near-permanent head, and contribute to the soft, creamy texture. Think of it as an alt-bier with a twist.

You could bump up the flavor level of the honey and molasses by adding them to the beer as a sort of kräusen, after primary fermentation is complete.

RECIPE — Kotbüsser

Yield: 5 gallons (19 liters)

Gravity: 1.055 (13° P)

Alcohol/vol: 4.5 to 5.2%

Color: Medium gold

Bitterness: 27 IBU

Yeast: German ale

Maturation: 4 to 6 weeks

Primary at 62 to 67° F (16.5 to 19.5° C), secondary/lagering at 40 to 45° F (4 to 7° C) for three weeks or longer.

All-Grain Recipe:

6.0 lb (2.7 kg)	57%	German or Belgian Pils malt
3.5 lb (1.6 kg)	33%	wheat malt
13.0 oz (369 g)	8%	oatmeal
2.0 oz (57 g)	1%	light molasses
2.0 oz (57 g)	1%	honey

Traditional mash is triple decoction. Two-step would be adequate. Protein rest at 122° F (50° C) for one hour, step up to 152° F (66.5° C) for one hour. Sparge to collect 6–7 gallons and boil for two hours, which should reduce it down to just over 5.

Extract + Mini-Mash Recipe:

2.0 lb (0.90 kg)	26%	pale dry malt extract
3.5 lb (1.6 kg)	43%	wheat extract syrup
1.0 lb (0.45 kg)	12%	U.S. six-row malt
0.5 lb (227 g)	6%	pale crystal malt
13.0 oz (369 g)	10%	oatmeal
2.0 oz (57 g)	1.5%	light molasses
2.0 oz (57 g)	1.5%	honey

Hops:

1.0 oz (28 g)	120 min	Tettnang (4% AA)
0.5 oz (14 g)	30 min	Tettnang (4% AA)
1.0 oz (28 g)	5 min	Tettnang (4% AA)
0.5 oz (14 g)	5 min	Saaz (3% AA)

Scheps of Breslau This a beloved beer that inspired more poetry than beers from most cities, but faded from glory after about 1700. This would be a great project for somebody to research. The word "*schep*" means "scoop."

Einfachbier, or Single Beer This was 3 to 4 °B, less than 1 percent alcohol. Widely brewed, especially in the North, but little reported in the books.

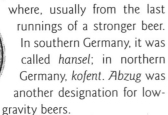

Light beers were made everywhere, usually from the last runnings of a stronger beer. In southern Germany, it was called *hansel*; in northern Germany, *kofent*. *Abzug* was another designation for low-gravity beers.

Potsdamer Bier Brewed in nineteenth-century Berlin, this wheat beer is described as luminously clear, tinged with amber, and seasoned with cloves, coriander, and cinnamon.

Erntebier, or Harvest Beer This was a fairly strong German ale, brewed for use during the harvest, as a fortifier and reward for farm workers. Gravity was 1.050 to 1.059 (12 to 14 °P). Although it was an ale, it was fermented fairly cool and then lagered for several months. Unusual for a dark beer in Germany, it was highly hopped, which added to its thirst-quenching qualities. This gives it certain similarities with Düsseldorfer alt-bier (especially the strong *sticke* version), although I can find no information about what specific malts might have been typical.

A 1682 reference gives a hop rate of approximately 0.3 ounces (9 grams) per pound of grain, or 3.0 ounces (85 grams) per 5-gallon batch, which works out to roughly 40 IBU.

Modern harvest beers seem to be popping up at smaller breweries all over Germany, and are paler and weaker (surprise) than the old version. Today it seems to be a marketing term for individual breweries rather than an actual style.

Mysterious German Local Beer Names

Israel in Lübeck

"Ich weiß nicht wie" (**I do not know how**) in Buxtehude

*Jamme*r (**Misery**) in Ostpreussen

Junker (**Squire**) in Warburg (near Düsseldorf)

Kater (**Wildcat/Tomca**t) in Stade

Kamma (**Crest or crown**) in Herfort. Some of the old books refer to a "kamm'"yeast, which the context indicates may have been like a sherry flor, which would indeed float on top as a crown.

Keuterling in Wettin

Klatsch (**Splash**) or *Klotsej* in Jena

Klotzmilch (**Block/lump/log milk**) in Bautzen

Krabbelanderwand in Eisleben Krabbel an der Wand

Kniesenack in Güstrow

Kühle Blonde (**Cool Blonde**) The famous Berliner weisse of Berlin

Kuhschwanz (**Cow-tail**) in Delitz (Bohemia)

Kukuk in Wittenbe

Lorch (**Larch**) in Livland, a steinbier, mashed with glowing stones

Lumpenbier in Wernigerobe, south of Braunschweig

Luntsch in Erfurt

Masnotzt in Teschen, a weizenbier

Maulesel (**Mule**) in Jena

Menschenfett (**person-fat**), *bestes Dorfbier* (**Village beer**) in Jena

Moll (**Minor**) in Rimwegen

Mord und Totschlag (**murder and homicide**) in Kyritz

Plunder (**plunder**) in Zugenbrück

Plutzerl in Horn, Austria, near Vienna, oat beer

Pohk in Pattensen

Preussing in Jena

Puff (**brothel**) in Halle

Puss (**fuss**) in Halle, west of Leipzig

Rammenach in Glückstadt

Rammeldist in Ratzeburg

Mysterious German Local Beer Names

Rastrum or Raster (grid) (a brown beer) in Leipzig

Rummeldaus in Ratzeburg

Sehtdenkerl or Stähldenkerl (steel-thinker) in Hadeln

Schlagnach or Schlacknack (strike-neck) in Rügen

Schlung or Schüttelkopf (shaker-head) in Riddigshausen

Schweinepost (pig-mail) in Strassburg Austria, southeast of Salzburg

Stürzebartel (beard-fall) in Merseburg, west of Leipzig

Schepps/Scheps/Schoeps (clatter or scoop?) in Breslau, Munich

Stier (bull) in Schweidnitz

Störtenkerl (trouble-fellow) in Dornburg

Todtenkopf (deathhead, skull and crossbones) in Schöningen, east of Braunschweig

Weil es im Leibe knurrte in Dassel

Wirkt Wunder (wonder worker?) in Gehirn

Witteklaus in Kiel

Wollsack (wool-sack) in Brockhusen

Würze (spice) in Zerbst, southeast of Magdeburg, near Berlin

Zitzenmille (thousand-teat) in Naumburg, southwest of Leipzig

Zoigl in Eslarn

Again, Dr. Lintner: *"Without doubt there are many other names for the national beverage, in whose inventiveness and constant transformation the peoples humor is inexhaustible."*

He finishes with a list of categories:

"The designations: **Hausbier** *House beer;* **Zapfbier** *tapping beer;* **Krugbier** *jug beer;* **Flaschenbier** *bottled beer;* **fassbier** *keg beer (in Breslau, an ordinary sort of brown beer);* **Klosterbier** *monastery beer;* **Tischbier** *table beer;* **Festbier** *fest beer; ***Dorfbier** *village beer;* **Stadtbier** *city beer;* **Füllbier** *filling beer; (for the topping up of the keg);* **Hochzeitsbier** *wedding beer;* **Freibier** *free beer (tax free);* **Kirmesbier** *parish fair beer;* **Kräuterbier** *herb beer;* **Kufenbier** *vat beer;* **Landbier** *land beer,* **Maibier** *May beer;* **Morgenbier** *morning beer; and these explain themselves automatically, and so there is still another quantity of folk names."*

Weizenschalenbier A top-fermenting beer brewed in Breslau, Germany, at least until 1860, that added 10 percent wheat husks to the barley malt grist. This beer gained large distribution as a popular bottled table beer. It's not clear what they were getting out of the husks, as the normal use for them in the mash is as a filtering aid, usually employed in wheat beers.

Merseburg Beer This a strong dark top-fermented ale, bittered with gentian root in addition to hops. The only reference I have seen is from a French book (P. Boulin) from about 1885.

German Porter Porter was such a huge phenomenon, brewers everywhere were trying it out and adapting it to their own vernacular. Even in what we think of as a somewhat hidebound Germany, this was happening. The information I have is from around 1900.

Two sorts were brewed, a sweet one and a hoppy one, both at 1.071 to 1.075 (17 to 18 °P). Top-fermented and lager versions were brewed, and the color was obtained from various mixtures of colored malt and caramel sugar. Single, double, and triple decoctions were used, in contrast to the infusions of English versions, and this would have given them a deep, caramelly underpinning. The highly hopped version used the equivalent of about 4 ounces (113 grams) per 5-gallon (19 liter) batch, and was dry-hopped. It appears as if this style may have been subsumed into the schwarzbiers of Kostritz and Kulmbach. Wagner (1877) refers to the former as "Englisher Kostritzer," a hint of its British inspiration.

Voyage Étrange Bière dEmbarcation (Export beer, c 1800)

Yield: 5 gallons (19 liters)

Gravity: 1.048 (11.5 °P)

Alcohol/vol: 4.4 to 5.1%

Color: Deep amber

Bitterness: 42 IBU

Yeast: French or German ale

Maturation: 4 to 6 weeks

*The original recipe called for 100 percent amber malt. To hedge against the possibility that earlier amber was paler—and more easily converted—than modern biscuit, I have included a little pale malt to make conversion easier.

All-Malt Recipe:

5.0 lb (2.3 kg)	59%	amber/biscuit malt
2.5 lb (1.1 kg)	29%	pale ale malt*
1.0 lb (0.45 kg)	12%	raw sugar (Barbados, Muscovado, etc.) added to kettle

No mashing details were given in the original recipe, so let's just go with a standard one hour at 150° F (65.5° C) infusion mash.

No Equivalent Extract Recipe

Hops:

2.0 oz (57 g)	90 min	Strisselspalt (3% AA)
1.5 oz (42 g)	30 min	Strisselspalt (3% AA)
2.0 oz (57 g)	5 min	Strisselspalt (3% AA)

1.25 fl oz (37 ml) cheap brandy, added at bottling or kegging

A FEW FRENCH DELIGHTS

France is generally sniffed at by the real brewing countries, and indeed its glory has always rested on wine, not beer. I guess the scorn is not undeserved, as a reference around 1800 describes beers showcasing grass, coconut, parsnips, beets, potatoes, carrots, and every form of sugar then known. If all that's not bad enough, the same book also described a "bastard-beer" made from cooked unmalted barley and molasses, brewed circa 1774 to cover a shortfall in cider supplies. Overall, pretty appalling.

THE HORRORS OF COLONIAL ALE

We tend to picture America's colonial days in a very romantic light. Quaint craftsmen banging out horseshoes and silver pots, retiring to the gentlemanly confines of a cozy tavern to puff on their pipes, quaff a few strong, malty brews, discuss politics, and plan a revolution. Undoubtedly such reveries existed at certain times and places, but for most settlers, things were very different.

For a start, beer was not universally available. It was unprofitable to ship from England. The raw materials for good beer could not be grown everywhere in

Corn, *Zea mays*

The New World's most important, if not most delicious, contribution to beer.

the Colonies, and the infrastructure for transporting it didn't exist. There was a lot of interest in brewing early on, as the settlers held tightly to their beer culture.

Brewing commercially was a struggle. Well-intentioned laws either forbade the importation of malt or prohibited malting due to scarcity, and were occasionally in force at the same time. So what happened? Rum became the drink of choice for the masses, as well as a standard medium of exchange, especially in New England. Except for a few years leading up to the Whiskey Rebellion, distilled spirits were entirely untaxed until 1861, and their cheapness, durability, and portability made them by far the preferred drink. As a contemporary observer put it: *"All drank as t'were their mother's milk, and not a man afraid."* Farther south in Georgia, the peaches they have become so famous for were not used for pie, but for a fiery brandy that was the dominant tipple there.

It was only in states such as Pennsylvania and New York, with their beer-infused German and Dutch populations, that beer brewing existed as a serious industry. The Dutch started early in New Amsterdam, which the English renamed New York in 1664.

America's unique—some would say dubious—contribution to the world of brewing is the use of corn, more properly called maize, as an ingredient. Experiments with

---

If barley be wanting to make into malt,

We must be content and think it no fault,

For we can make liquor to sweeten our lips,

Of pumpkins, and parsnips, and walnut-tree chips.

—Colonial ditty

RECIPE — Sweet Lips Colonial Ale

Yield: 5 gallons (19 liters)

Gravity: 1.060 (14.5 °P)

Alcohol/vol: 5.3 to 6%

Color: Pale amber

Bitterness: 33 IBU

Yeast: English ale

Maturation: 4 to 6 weeks

*Cambium is the growing layer of the tree, just inside the bark, and has been used as a flavoring in beverages for centuries. Quantity: 0.5 to 1 ounce (14 to 28 grams). Chopped black walnuts (1–4 ounces) may be added to the mash instead.

All-Malt Recipe:

6.75 lb (3.1 kg)	46%	U.S. two-row lager malt
2.0 lb (2.3 kg)	13.5%	amber/biscuit malt
2.0 lb (0.90 kg)	13.5%	flaked corn
2.0 lb (0.90 kg)	13.5%	baked pumpkin (see p. 182)
2.0 lb (0.90 kg)	13.5%	roasted parsnips (same method as pumpkin)
1.0 lb (0.45 kg)	—	rice hulls

This will be a goopy mash. Let it go 1.5 hours at 148° F (64.5° C), and be patient while sparging.

No Equivalent Extract Recipe

Hops & Spices:

1.5 oz (43 g)	90 min	Fuggle (5% AA)
2.0 oz (57 g)	10 min	walnut leaves or cambium*

---

corn as a beer ingredient began before 1550, almost as soon as there was brewing in the Colonies. Thomas Heriot made this remark about maize in 1585: *"The graine is about the bignesse of our ordinary English peaze and not much different in forme and shape: but of divers colours : some white, some red, some yellow, and some blew. All of* them yeelde a very white and sweete flowre: beeing used according to his kinde it maketh a very good bread. Wee made of the same in the countrey some mault, whereof was brued as good ale as was to be desired. So likewise by the help of hops therof may bee made as good Beere." So this goes back a ways.

Beer was brewed on the plantations, but it appears to have been mostly of the very meager small beer represented by George Washington's crummy recipe (see p. 264). Such beers functioned as the soda pop of their days, providing water in a safe and quenching form, and as such they seem to have been regarded as a duty and little else by their makers.

Although his wife Martha brewed small beer every two weeks early in their marriage, Thomas Jefferson got interested in brewing at Monticello rather late. A shipwrecked English brewer, Captain Joseph Miller, ended up at Jefferson's door in 1813, and helped to set up a brewery there. An architectural plan in Jefferson's hand exists, but it is not known if the building was ever built.

But they were brewing beer, and as ever, TJ had higher aspirations: "I wish to see this beverage become common instead of the whiskey which kills one third of our citizens and ruins their families." Records suggest that *The London and Country Brewer* and Combrune's *Theory and Practise of Brewing* were among his references. By the way, *The London and Country Brewer* is available for downloading online if you want to dig into it yourself.

Barley being poorly suited to Virginia's Piedmont climate, malted wheat and Indian corn were used. Jefferson referred to the product there as an ale rather than a porter, suggesting it was a pale beer. One bushel of malt for 8 or 10 gallons of ale was the normal proportion there, a little stronger than the commercial breweries produced.

Futurale

The airlock made an unconfident, shuddering noise, then beeped and opened smoothly. Inside, lights were low and moving hypnotically across the room, little colored balls without apparent source. There was room at the bar, so I wiggled up on the pedestal and locked on. "Beer," I snuffed.

"Jeepy creeps, goomer," the bartron said. "Weegot dizzy choices. Likyalips wonnerful beears, yessy. Firstoff, you wanna syntek or natferment?" I'd had the syntek far too many times, and I still had a few scars on my spleen from it. Besides, all nineteen brands of it were made by the Syllamub Brewing Company. Pure natural interplanetary H_2O, with refreshing "replicated" natural essences and other undisclosed headbanger additives. Pictronic foam. The jolt just wasn't worth it anymore.

"Natferment, man. I'm hardcore nowtimes."

"Oooeee, real customer, bygol. Sure. RubAlt, IPB, Eisblu, Greenie, Belgoman...Yah we got pretty much everything."

"Oakies?" I probed, knowing this could get me into trouble. His head clicked into place as he scanned me at a higher res. Barrel-fermented beers were banned in a number of colonies, but the ban was unevenly enforced. Wood was out of its element in space, rare as flamptonite.

"Big spendee, nodowt, you are. Weeget close, maybe-maybe. Here, I show." He flipped around the visipad and touched the sensor with his thumb. A dazzling array of the finest commercially made replales scrolled past: Gol Zizol Ale, Madam's Picklebock, Oval Rackish, Sahara Novata Palale, Relegator, Voodel; the list was impressive, but strictly from marketing. I figured I could do better.

"I got the thirsties for some Oakie TruFerm. You know, realtime headscrew. Bugs in it. I got the creds. Whatcha got that ain't on the screen. Blow me up, sugar man."

"Pay to talk, good customer." I flipped him my credpak. He slurped out a twenty with a gentle whir. "Welcomy bru central, myolpal." A small panel rotated silently around to reveal six small containers, code lights blinking softly. "Weegot Blondies, Hoppers, and Ecstout Double X." He winked mechanically.

"You tindog! True bugs? Hydroponic barlmalt, zopcones, the works?" He nodded. I could see my credpak start to quiver in anticipated dessication. "Lemee start with the Blondies and work up."

The codelights changed pattern on one of the vaultlets; the panel flipped around again as soon as he had it poured and stowed. It was a thinga'byootee. Class K golden color, a dash of shimmering haze from the contraband micros. Real bubbles—from the actual beer, far more enticing than the microholographic ones in the syntek. Ah! The smell of real byproducts. This was as close to heaven as a sector seven transship loopdock could ever be. I put the foaming essence to my lips.

As I did, my reverie was broken by a rough voice: "Marketing Enforcement, sector seven-point-two. I'm Officer Adolphus, this is Officer Frederick. We need to talk to you about that unadvertised beer..."

George Washington's Small Beer

To Make Small Beer

Take a large Siffer [Sifter] full of Bran Hops to your Taste.—Boil these 3 hours then strain out 30 Gall[ons] into a cooler put in 3 Gall[ons] Molasses while the Beer is Scalding hot or rather draw the Melasses into the cooler & St[r]ain the Beer on it while boiling Hot. Let this stand till it is little more than Blood warm then put in a quart of Yea[s]t if the Weather is very Cold cover it over with a Blank[et] & let it Work in the Cooler 24 hours then put it into the Cask—leave the bung open till it is almost don[e] Working—Bottle it that day Week it was Brewed.

It's hard to estimate how well the grain was malted, what the mashing efficiency was, even whatever they were using British (40 pounds, 18.1 kilograms) or American (34 pounds, 15.4 kilograms) bushels at that time, but the beers were likely in the 1.065 to 1.085 (14.5 to 20.5 °P) range. Hop rate was described as three quarters of a pound per gallon, or 6 to 7.5 ounces (170 to 213 grams) per 5-gallon batch, which

might translate to bitterness somewhere between 40 and 70 IBU—again, with many factors being impossible to predict. But overall, the Monticello brews were something we would today recognize as a craft brew

PENNSYLVANIA SWANKEY

Pennsylvania was one of the great brewing states of the young country, due largely to its population of beer-thirsty Germans. Swankey was a curious specialty that managed to survive up until about 1900. A corruption of *schwenke*, meaning a *schank* or light beer, swankey was a very weak beer fermented partially, then chilled to preserve some sweetness and keep the alcohol low at around 2 percent. Original gravity was about 1.028 (7 °P); at 1.020 (5 °P) the casks were stopped up and allowed to prime, and then the beer was chilled and sent out to be sold. The resulting beverage

RECIPE	Plug Nickel—Thomas Jefferson's Pale Ale

Yield: 5 gallons (19 liters)

Gravity: 1.069 (16.5° P)

Alcohol/vol: 5.2 to 6.2%

Color: Pale amber

Bitterness: 44 IBU

Yeast: English ale

Maturation: 6 to 8 weeks

All-Malt Recipe:

9.0 lb (4.1 kg)	75%	pale ale malt
2.0 lb (0.90 kg)	17%	Indian corn, ground to grits and precooked
1.0 lb (0.45 kg)	8%	biscuit/amber malt

An infusion mash—1 hour at 154° F (68° C)—will work as long as the corn grits are precooked (as you would rice), and it's not likely that TJ and his English brewmaster were doing anything more complicated than this. A mini-mash version can be brewed by reducing the pale malt to 2 pounds (0.90 kilograms) and adding 4 pounds (1.8 kilograms) of pale dry malt extract to the kettle in lieu of the missing malt.

Hops:

2.0 oz (57 g)	60 min	U.S. Fuggle (5% AA)
1.5 oz (43 g)	10 min	U.S. Fuggle (5% AA)

was very much like a sort of licorice root beer.

You can brew this as a normal-strength brown ale (1.042 to 1.050, 10 to 12 °P), and for the last five minutes of the boil, add 1 to 2 teaspoons (4 to 6 grams) of aniseed, plus 0.25 to 0.5 teaspoons (1 to 2 grams) of star anise. A small amount of basil, caraway, and/or fennel will add complexity, although I can't imagine this is authentic.

KENTUCKY COMMON BEER

This is a top-fermenting everyday-beer that was popular up and down the Ohio River in the vicinity of Louisville. Little is known of its makeup. As the Wahl-Henius *Handy Book* describes it, *"Its color is dark, being about the same as that of average Bavarian [dunkel] beers. The beer should possess a pronounced malt flavor, be full to the palate, of some-what sweet taste, and mild in character."*

Gravity was light to medium, at 1.040–1.055 (10 to 12.5 °P). It was brewed from 25 to 35 percent corn adjuncts in addition to pale malt, and colored with black and caramel malts, but cooked sugar (caramel) was also employed. Hopping was light, at 0.5 to 0.75 pounds per barrel, which works out to 1.25 to 2 ounces per 5 gallons (38 to 57 grams per 19 liters), about half the amount used for stock ales of the day.

Kentucky common was fermented with the addition of some "rod" bacteria that intro-duced some souring. This was specified as an ale yeast containing about 2 per-cent bacteria, otherwise "this taste would become too pronounced, which not alone would make the product obnoxious, but also endanger its brilliancy and stabili-ty." The fermentation was carried out at 68 to 70° F (20 to 21° C) over a period of about a week.

Although this style died out commercially long ago, the Bluegrass brewing company in Louisville has brewed it anew, as have some homebrewers.

"To Make Beer and Ale From Pea Shells"

"No production of this country abounds so much with vegetable saccharine matter as the shells of green peas. A strong decoction of them so much resembles, in odour and taste, an infusion of malt (termed wort) as to deceive a brewer. This decoction, rendered slightly bitter with the wood sage, and afterwards fermented with yeast, affords a very excellent beverage.

"Fill a boiler with the green shells of peas, pour on water till it rises half an inch above the shells, and simmer for three hours. Strain off the liquor, and add a strong decoc-tion of the wood sage, or the hop, so as to render it pleasantly bitter; then ferment in the usual manner. The wood sage is the best substitute for hops, and being free from any anodyne property, is entitled to a preference. By boiling a fresh quantity of shells in the decoction before it becomes cold, it may be so thoroughly impregnated with saccharine matter, as to afford a liquor, when fermented as strong as ale."

—Mackenzie's *Five Thousand Receipts*, Philadelphia, 1829

Brewery Tray, c. 1910

This regional style was in decline by this point, and never made it past Prohibition.

SAVE THE BEES!

A BIT ABOUT HONEY

Honey is the concentrated nectar of flowers made by bees for use as a storable form of food for the hive. The high water content is one of the things that makes it stable; few organisms can survive the immense osmotic pressure of such a strong solution of sugar. Honey also has anti-microbial chemical properties, and this provides an extra challenge for the would-be meadmaker.

The type of flower from which the nectar is collected determines the character of the honey, and there is a huge range available. Honey may be nearly clear to seriously brown; however, the color is not an accurate gauge of flavor intensity. The specific gravity is 1.41, or in brewer's terms, 1.410, which translates to 11 pounds, 12 ounces per gallon; 2 pounds, 11 ounces per quart; or 1.4 kilograms per liter. A pound of honey will contribute between 1.0070 to 1.0075 OG (1.7 to 1.8 °P) to a 5-gallon (19 liter) batch, although some types may be as high as 1.0079 or as low as 1.0064.

Many scholars believe mead may have been the first fermented beverage. And the fact that the same Indo-European root word, *medhu*, means "honey," "sweet," and "drunkenness" is further evidence for this. Honey won't ferment in its natural concentrated form, but as soon as it is diluted—when combs are washed out, for example—it starts to ferment. There is, in fact, no ancient technology capable of stopping it more than temporarily. With no cooking or crushing needed, it's the simplest alcoholic beverage to make, and probably appeared just as soon as humans created something to put it in. The rock art of one Neolithic society, at Tassili-n-Ajjer in Algeria, prominently features a zoomorphic "bee-man," which is suggestive of their familiarity with the other sort of buzz that bees create. Never mind the fact that he is covered head-to-toe with magic mushrooms as well.

This buzz is not always simply from alcohol. Many plants with toxic and/or psychoactive components exude them in their nectar, which is then concentrated by the bees into a kind of narcotic honey that Pliny the Elder called *meli mœnomenon*, or "mad honey." Datura, belladonna, cannabis, wild rosemary, rhododendron, and a large number of tropical plants are capable of producing mind-altering honey, and the ethnobotanical connections for many psychoactive honeys are well documented. Fortunately, such honeys are rare, and pose little danger (or opportunity) for mad meadmakers.

Despite its great antiquity, mead has only rarely been an everyday drink, and has never been industrialized on any significant scale. It was either, as with the Beaker Culture or the Vikings, the strong drink of warriors and other elite, or a quaint country beverage made and enjoyed in the boondocks. In fact, mead can't ever be commercialized on the scale of beer because honey is really a minor by-product of agriculture or the local ecosystem, and getting more honey isn't simply a matter of plowing up more fields. Even if there is a good quantity available, there is the issue of consistency, as the flowering of plants is quite seasonal, making honey dramatically different from month to month. That means more fun for us homebrewers, but not something to build a national distribution system around.

Mead comes in a variety of subtypes. Most kinds may be made either sweet or dry, and still, sparkling, or in-between. The level of sweetness is controlled by adding sugar (honey) to the point where yeast can't handle it and give up. For this reason, natural carbonation is not feasible, so sweet meads are usually made in the still style. The amount of sugar that yeast can handle depends on the yeast type, but it's between 13 and 20 pounds of honey in a 5-gallon batch.

The close connection with agriculture means that mead was usually made from the local honey *du jour*, dolled up with whatever else was available in the neighborhood: herbs, fruit, and/or grains. Since mead has never had much commercial importance, very little about it was ever recorded in books, which means our sources for creative inspiration are pretty limited except to try to imagine the settings in which it was brewed, what the possibilities *could have been*, and go from there.

Honey Beverage Types	
Braggot	Any combination of honey and malt
Brochet	Mead made from honey that has been boiled down and darkened; "burnt sack mead"
Cyser	Mead and apple cider fermented together
Eismead	Made by removing ice from partially frozen mead, concentrating alcohol and flavors. Considered distillation by the federal government, and technically illegal.
Hippocras	Mead fermented with grapes or grape juice, and spices
Hydromel	Lighter-gravity, or "small" mead
Mead	The generic term covering all forms, or more specifically, made from honey alone
Melomel	Mead fermented with fruit or fruit juice
Metheglin	Mead flavored with herbs and/or spices
Miodomel	Hopped mead
Pyment	Mead made with grapes or grape juice (or raisins)
Sack Mead	Heavy sweet mead with Sherry (sack) characteristics
Weirdomel	Non-traditional mead made with unusual ingredients. See Atomic Fireball Mead recipe.

A FEW TECHNICALITIES

Mead is much easier to make than beer. Older recipes recommended boiling the honey and water mix (or must); newer recipes recommend heating it just to pasteurization temperature (145 to 150° F or 63 to 65.5° C) and holding it for thirty minutes before cooling and pitching. Modern thinking suggests that even this gentler cooking is unnecessary, plus it can drive off a lot of desirable aromatics.

Honey is loaded with sugar, but like a continuous diet of candy bars, yeast need more than sugar to be healthy. Unlike beer wort, which is a rich stew of nourishment, honey is barren. Minor nutrients like amino acids, lipids, vitamins, and trace minerals are missing. A good yeast nutrient will provide them easily, but they are not all created equal. Some types are simply forms of soluble nitrogen (di-ammonium phosphate); others are made from yeast or a mix of chemicals and have a greater range of benefits to offer. Quantities are important, so be sure to follow the manufacturer's instructions.

The Honey Bee, *Apis Mellifera*
The start of it all.

A Few Honey Varieties

Acacia	Ultra pale, lightly fruity, tropical hints
Alfalfa	Extremely pale color, delicate flavor
Basswood	Complex and elegant, hints of cedary wood
Blueberry	Delicate, fruity
Buckwheat	Dark and very intense; malty, molasses character
Clover	Familiar middle-of-the-road flavor
Cranberry	Bright and fruity, hints of floral perfume
Fireweed	Very pale; delicate, tea-like, with buttery overtones
Heather	Pale, yet intense, resinous; gel-like *thixatropic* properties
Orange Blossom	Floral and perfumey, hints of orange blossoms
Sage	Three varieties of varying color; all have an elegant floral character
Snowberry	Delicate, complex, perfumey
Tupelo	Complex floral/fruity flavors; high in fructose
Wildflower	Highly variable, but often strongly flavored; may also originate from soybeans or other unglamorous crop

From a flavor standpoint, two other major things are missing from honey: acidity and tannins. These don't affect fermentation in a huge way, but mead without them can taste flat, thin, and, as they say in the wine world, flabby. When fruit juice or pulp is incorporated, it often adds both acidity and tannin, but sometimes the mead still needs to be adjusted to get the proper flavor. With pure meads, acid is usually needed to balance any residual sweetness, and a little grape tannin may be used to add structure. It is best to do this after fermentation. This avoids the creation of conditions that are too acidic for the yeast, and allows you to better determine the sweetness of the finished mead, and therefore how much acid (and maybe tannin) is needed to create a balanced flavor. Tartaric, malic, and citric acids may be used, or a commercial mixture called "winemaker's acid blend."

To avoid wild yeast contamination, the mead can be either pasteurized by heating or dosed with sulfite prior to fermentation. Older recipes direct you to boil the must, which is no longer recommended because it drives off a lot of important aroma compounds. Pasteurization is a gentler heating—thirty minutes at 145 to 150° F (63 to 65.5° C)—and is sufficient to kill any wild yeast present. If the sulfite method is used, Campden tablets are the typical means; dosing is between three and eight tablets per 5-gallon batch, depending on pH. They are simply added to the honey and water and allowed to stand overnight before pitching the culture yeast.

There are mead-specific yeasts, although any ale or wine yeast can be used. Ale yeasts are less tolerant of alcohol, and will start to produce a sweet mead at about 10 percent alcohol (13 pounds per 5 gallons). Wine or Champagne yeast may go as high as 16 to 19 percent before slowing down and allowing unfermented sugar to remain. Because of its antibiotic properties, mead fermentations tend to go slowly. And because mead strengths tend to be higher than beer, relatively long aging is required for a mellow and mature product. For a mead of 10 percent alcohol, a year is about the minimum.

Mead made without heat pasteurization may take longer to clear, and may even require the use of a fining agent like gelatin. Or, if you're planning a long aging and can deal with sediment, just let time do its thing. Racking a few times can also speed things up.

New Zealand offers some interesting honeys. Here, *Tawari*, which has a lingering buttery flavor; and *Kamahi*, with a full-bodied complexity.

Fruit is lovely in mead—melomel, actually—and the techniques are much the same as for fruit beers (Chapter 13). One thing to pay attention to is the amount of acidity in the finished melomel, as the fruit can taste lifeless without enough acidity. You can take a conservative stab at adding some acid blend—mix, taste, then add more if it seems to need it. Or you can conduct a small-scale test, using a known solution of acid dosed with a pipette calibrated in 0.10 milliliters into a small (1 ounce or 25 milliliter) sample. Once you determine the correct amount of acid per ounce, just scale up to the full batch size.

Mead is most often bottled, although it is possible to put it on draft just like homebrewed beer. Still (non-sparkling) mead can be dosed with potassium sorbate, which will prevent fermentation from restarting. This is usually done in combination with sulfite, as sorbate does not inhibit malolactic bacteria, which can produce gas and off flavors in a closed environment like a bottle. Wait until fermentation has ceased and mead has dropped clear before bottling, and add 2.5 teaspoons of potassium sorbate at that time. The sulfite chart is above.

Campden Tablet Dosing by Must* pH	
pH	No. Tablets/5 gallons
3.0	3
3.2	4
3.4	5
3.6	6
3.8	8

Based on 75 ppm free SO_2 per tablet per gallon

*Must is the term for unfermented wine or mead

Typical Honey Analysis	
Component	%
Water	17.1
Glucose	31.0
Fructose	38.2
Maltose	7.2
Longer sugars	4.2
Sucrose	1.5
Minerals, vitamins, enzymes	0.5

Sparkling mead can be put up just like beer, although for Champagne-like sparkle, carbonation levels need to be four to six times higher. Note that heavy sparkling wine bottles are needed for this; regular beer bottles can't handle that kind of pressure. Sparkling wine is disgorged, a process that starts when the yeast is induced to settle onto the caps of bottles stored inverted. The neck of the bottles are frozen in a brine solution, then turned upright and uncapped, shooting the plug of yeast out. The bottles are corked or capped, and the mead can be served sparkling clear, unmarred by muddy sediment.

MEAD, GLORIOUS MEAD

An Arabic medicinal mead Although alcohol is forbidden in contemporary Islam, this was not always so. In fact, the very word, al-kohl, is Arabic, and distilling reached Europe through the Islamic world.

The following mead recipe is loosely based on a beverage described in a medieval medicinal text, the *Aqrabadhin*, attributed to Al-Kindi in the ninth century. The drink as he describes it is more of a flavored syrup, as he advises to mix grape juice and honey, then boil it down to half its volume. This mix is then spiced and bottled for

Neolithic Cave Painting, c. 6000 B.C.E.

This image of a honey gatherer from Cueva La Araña, near Valencia, Spain, may be the earliest image of humans interacting with bees.

RECIPE	Call Me Al —an Islamically Inspired Mead

Yield: 5 U.S. gallons (19 liters)

Gravity: 1.104 (25 °P)

Alcohol/vol: 10 to 13% (depending on yeast)

Yeast: Mead

Maturation: 6 to 10 months

Rather than recommend something unpalatable to modern tastes, I am reworking it into something inspired by Al-Kindi, rather than directly from his hand.

10.0 lb (4.5 kg)   orange blossom honey

46.0 fl oz (1.4 L)   muscat juice concentrate

0.5 oz (14 g)   winemakers acid blend

Plus 0.1 oz (3 g) each, coarsely crushed and placed in a hop bag: green or white cardamom; black cardamom*; cinnamon (true Ceylon cinnamon, see p. 160); cloves; long pepper (*Piper longum*; substitute black pepper or grains of paradise, see p. 162 & 275). Place this in the kettle at the end of the pasteurization, and allow to steep in the hot must for 10 minutes

After primary fermentation, saffron is added. The original recipe called for 0.3 oz (9 g) of saffron—a king's ransom from your local grocery store—and pretty overwhelming. One gram ought to add plenty of saffron flavor.

* Known in medieval days as "greater cardamom," it's available from Indian markets. The pods are twice the size of ordinary cardamom and have a chocolate brown color. It has a strong, smoky, astringent taste. You might want to cut the quantity down by half or so.

Black Cardamom, *Amomum subulatum* (See above recipe)

More astringent and pungent than ordinary green or white cardamom.

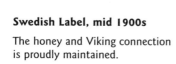

Swedish Label, mid 1900s

The honey and Viking connection is proudly maintained.

immediate use. In its original form it appears to have been non-alcoholic.

The base of this recipe was originally a cooked grape juice, or *must*. Although aromatic grapes are somewhat out of favor today except as sweet dessert wines, perfumed varieties such as Muscat were treasured in ancient times—up until a century or two ago. Concentrated muscat juice is available from home winemaking suppliers.

Dwojniak Mead This is a Polish specialty made from a 1:1 mixture of honey and water, and aged for five to seven years. Honey contains osmophilic strains of yeast (*Zygosaccharomyces*), which can only ferment solutions between 50 and 82 percent sugar, and this is used in making dwojniak. The resulting mead is very sweet, with a deep toasty complexity and a sherry-like aroma. Another Polish sweet mead called *trojniak* is made with twice as much water (1:2) and fermented with *Malaga* yeast. It matures in three years. Cornflower honey is the preferred variety.

"Mjød" is the Scandinavian version of the word mead, and can mean different beverages according to context. More recently the term has referred to a low-gravity commercially brewed specialty item that is popular around Christmas. This is a middle-of-the-road interpretation; current artisanal products can be as high as 19-percent alcohol by volume. Alcohol-free versions that also included malt were once made many decades ago by brewers at holiday time. If you can't find Spalt, use Tettnang hops. Half a pound of cooked sugar or caramelized honey (see p. 198) may be used in place of the crystal malt.

Mead, a German recipe, 1898 "Add 2.1 liters (14.3 pounds) honey to 5 gallons of water, and add (unspecified amounts) hops, coriander, sage, nutmeg, pinks (*Dianthus armeria*), cinnamon, and galangal." Spices were placed in a cloth bag and suspended

RECIPE	Mjød	
Yield: 5 U.S. gallons (19 liters)	3.0 lb (1.4 kg)	honey, added to kettle for full boil
Gravity: 1.100 (24 °P)	0.5 lb (227 g)	pale crystal malt, steeped, then removed before the boil
Alcohol/vol: 10 to 13% (depending on yeast)	0.75 oz (23 g)	citric acid, added to kettle
Bitterness: 23 IBU	10.0 lb (4.5 kg)	honey, added to kettle as soon as boil is finished
Yeast: Mead	*Hops:*	
Maturation: 6 to 10 months	1.5 oz (43 g) 60 min	Spalt (4% AA)
	1.5 oz (43 g) end of boil	Spalt (4% AA)
	Yeast nutrient, per manufacturer's instructions.	

in the mead for a few weeks. Other recipes of the same time period included pepper and grains of paradise.

Miodomel A medieval Polish hopped mead, the specialty of the monks of Saint Basil. Since this is all we know about it, we're free to concoct whatever sort of beer fits that description. We'll be looking at barley wine strength and barley wine hopping, except there's no malt in it. A modern interpretation might be to use 15 pounds of a medium-intensity honey such as clover or tupelo, and 2 to 4 ounces of Polish Lublin (substitute: Saaz) hops. Boil a couple of pounds of honey with the hops, using half in the full boil for bitterness, and the other half tossed in at the end of the boil for aroma. A few ounces of a cooked sugar (p. 198) may be used to add an ancient amber glow. This mead will require a couple of years to come into its own. It may be improved by giving it some exposure to toasted oak, easy to handle in the form of winemaker's cubes or chips (see p. 91).

RECIPE	Chuck's Atomic Fireball Mead	
Yield: 5 gallons (19 liters)	15.0 lb (6.8 kg)	lightly flavored honey such as clover
Gravity: 1.125 (25 °P)	50	Atomic Fireball jawbreakers, soaked in hot water overnight, then added to water in kettle and dissolved before the honey is added
Alcohol/vol: 10 to 13% (depending on yeast)	1 to 2 boxes	Celestial Seasonings Red Zinger tea (for color), added at the end of pasteurization and allowed to steep for 10 minutes
Yeast: Mead		
Maturation: 6 to 10 months	1.0 oz (28 g)	cinnamon oil, added to the secondary or at bottling
Made by Chuck Boyce of the Bloatarian Brewing League in Cincinnati, and the damndest thing I ever tasted. Sounds just awful, but tastes really good.	For an extra kick, a little cayenne pepper may be added.	

Herb Tea Mead There are a large number of commercially made herb and spiced teas out there that have great-tasting combinations of flavorings that can be showcased well in an elegantly simple mead. Three to ten teabags per batch would probably be appropriate, and these could be added to the mix during pasteurization, or if you're doing the cold-prep method, then make the tea first and add it to the honey and the rest of the water before fermentation. Earl Grey tea contains bergamot, an exotic citrus fruit. It makes an excellent tea mead.

BRAGOT AND OTHER HONEYED BEERS

Honey as a fortifier for beer goes all the way back to the beginning of brewing, in the ancient Near East. It is mentioned in the *Hymn to Ninkasi*, the praise-poem that is actually a fairly detailed brewing procedure, although

RECIPE	Crancrabapple Mead

Yield: 5 gallons (19 liters)

Gravity: 1.120 (29 °P)

Alcohol/vol: 10 to 13%

Yeast: Epernay Champagne yeast

Maturation: 6 to 10 months

15.0 lb (4.5 kg)	Cranberry (or blueberry) honey
5.0 to 8.0 lb (2.3 to 3.6 kg)	Crabapples, frozen then thawed (to soften the texture)

This recipe solves the problem of the lack of acidity and tannin in honey, as crabapples have them both in spades. Fermented bone dry, then carbonated very highly, the overall impression is of a *blanc de noirs* Champagne, a white wine made from red grapes, and displaying a soft, fleshy blush. This recipe works equally well with cranberries substituted for the crabapples. A gallon of pressed-out juice of either fruit may be used if you have access to a press.

American Label, c. 1938

Despite the name, it's unclear whether this beer had any honey in it. Honey has rarely been a part of mainstream beers.

there is some possibility that the word "honey" in this context may also refer to date syrup. The *Hymn* was used several years ago as a guide in the brewing of an ancient beer, a project involving Anchor's Fritz Maytag and Sumerian scholars Miguel De Civil and Solomon Katz.

Moving forward a thousand years or so, we find ourselves in Phrygia, in what is now Turkey, circa 700 B.C.E. In 1957, King Midas' tomb was found intact, with the remains of a grand funerary feast still intact. Recently, the University of Pennsylvania's Patrick McGovern ran scrapings of the drinking vessels through a chromatograph and found markers for wine, beer, and honey all in the same vessel, suggesting a mixed beverage. Sam Calagione of Dogfish Head Brewery worked with McGovern to reinvent a recipe for this ancient brew, and that beer is now a regular commercial product called Midas Touch.

Beers fortified with honey often share a similar ancient Irish (*brach*) or Welsh (*brag, bragio*) root word meaning "to sprout." This leads to many words for honey beer: bragget, bragaut, brackett, bragot, and bragawd. The fact that the word refers to the grain portion of the beverage attests to the

RECIPE	"Phunny You Don't Look Phrygian" Raisin Honey Beer

Yield: 5 gallons (19 liters)
Gravity: 1.080 (19 °P)
Alcohol/vol: 8.6 to 10%
Yeast: Wine
Maturation: 4 to 6 months

4.0 lb (1.8 kg)	30.5%	pale malt
1.5 lb (0.68 kg)	11.5%	amber/biscuit malt

Add to brew kettle at the end of the boil:

4.0 lb (1.8 kg)	30.5%	light-flavored honey, preferably from some old-world plant—sage?
46 fl oz (1.4 L)	27.5%	muscat grape concentrate

great antiquity of honey beers. Chemical analysis of the residue found in a birch-bark bucket buried with a woman more than three thousand years ago at Egtved in the Jutland region of Denmark showed signs of the presence of honey, wheat, cranberries, and the fruit of the bog myrtle shrub.

The Roman historian Cornelius Tacitus (C.E. 55 to 117), reported that the Germanic people: *"... lie on bear skins and drink mead or beer brewed with honey from large drinking horns. They can bear hunger and cold weather easily, but not the thirst."*

Bronze Age Bragot The crud scraped out of that bucket doesn't give us as much information as we'd really like, but it's enough to cook up something pretty tasty. I've used cranberry honey before, and it has a really nice fruitiness. It stands to reason that

Bronze Situla, c. 700 B.C.E.
This was used to dip King Midas' drink from the royal cauldron.

RECIPE	Bronze Age Bragot

Yield: 5 gallons (19 liters)
Gravity: 1.100 (24 °P)
Alcohol/vol: 12 to 13.5%
Yeast: Wine
Maturation: 8 to 12 months

All Malt Recipe:

8.0 lb (3.6 kg)	47%	malted wheat
8.0 lb (3.6 kg)	47%	cranberry honey
1.0 lb (0.45 kg)	6%	six-row lager malt

Extract Recipe:

6.0 lb (2.7 kg)	43%	liquid wheat malt extract
8.0 lb (3.6 kg)	57%	cranberry honey

Spices:

0.1 oz (3 g)	60 min	bog myrtle
1	End of boil	wintergreen Lifesaver, plus a few drops of liquid smoke (to simulate the effect of the birch bark)

6.0 lb (2.7 kg)   cranberries, frozen then thawed (to soften the texture), and added to the secondary. These should remain in the mead for 2 to 4 weeks. Then, rack the mead off into another carboy and allow it to drop clear. A half-gallon of pure cranberry juice may be used instead of the whole fruit, in which case it is simply added to the secondary.

where there are cranberries, there is cranberry honey. This will be a little on the strong side, suitable for a journey to the next world. In the Bronze Age, this obviously wouldn't have been carbonated, so to be authentic, you'd want to serve this flat. Authenticity isn't everything, so feel free to put it into whatever kind of condition you see fit.

Other appropriate herbs are meadowsweet and heather, both of which were known to have been used by Northern people in ancient times.

I have not specified smoked malt, although it is likely that Bronze Age wheat malt would have been at least a little smoky. If you want to add this authentic touch, then skip the wintergreen candy and smoke some of the malt over a birch fire. Be sure to use the bark as well as the wood, as they still do in the brewing of the rustic Swedish beer, *gotlandsdrickå*.

Welsh Bragawd As time flowed on, honey became more of a marginal player in beer. The one final famous incarnation of it was in Wales. From ancient times the Welsh were famous for their honey beer, bragawd, and this lasted right up until the Industrial Revolution, when most of the rustic old-time brews faded away. By 1800, the recipes for Welsh ale include no honey (see p. 274). A Welsh ode to a drinking horn recounts in 1056:

> *Cup-bearer, when I want thee most,*
> *With duteous patience mind my post,*
> *Reach me the horn, I know its power*
> *Acknowledged in the social hour;*
> *Hirlas,* thy contents to drain,*
> *I feel a longing e'en to pain;*
> *Pride of the feasts, profound and blue.***
> *Of the ninths wave's azure hue,*
> *The drink of heroes formed to hold,*
> *Wih art enrich'd and lid of gold!*
> *Fill it with bragawd to the brink,*
> *Confidence inspiring drink.*

* name of the horn
**referring to the silver from which it was made

But as famous as it was, I can't find anything like a recipe for Welsh bragawd, so if you want to make one, you'll just have to get creative.

English Bragot John Bickerdyke* (1888) did a lot of research and concluded that, *"To define bragot with any degree of preciseness would be as difficult as to give an accurate definition of 'soup.'"* He does come up with an old recipe for a honey and spice infused beer, which is supposed to originate in the fourteenth century, but by the language appears to be circa 1500:

> *'Take to x galons of ale iij potell of fyne wort, and iij quartis of hony, and put thereto canell [cinnamon] oz: IIIj, peper schort or long oz: IIIj, galingale oz: i,*

RECIPE	An English Bragot, c. 1500

Yield: 5 gallons (19 liters)

Gravity: 1.104 (24.5 °P)

Alcohol/vol: 10.5 to 11.5%

Color: Deep brownish amber

Yeast: Alcohol-tolerant English ale

Maturation: 8 to 12 months

All-Malt (& Honey) Recipe:

12.0 lb (5.4 kg)	60%	amber/biscuit malt
6.0 lb (2.7 kg)	30%	pale malt
2.0 lb (0.90 kg)	10%	honey, added to secondary

Spices, added to the secondary:

0.8 oz (23g)	each: cinnamon, plus black or long pepper (see below, and p. 162 & 275)
0.8 oz (22 g)	chopped candied ginger
0.2 oz (6 g)	each: galingale, cloves

As this was made with ale, hops would not have been used. If you want them for their preservative value, add 0.5 ounce of a low-alpha English hop such as East Kent Golding, for a one-hour boil.

and clowys [cloves] oz i, and gingiver oz ij"

In modern terms, the following quantities would make a 5-gallon batch: 2.3 gallons (8.7 liters) ale, 2.6 gallons (9.8 liters) wort, 2 pounds (0.90 kilograms) honey. But to brew it in a more rational way, see above.

This form of bragot was popular in London during the mid-sixteenth century. In other recipes, mace and nutmeg replace the pepper and galingale. There were various methods for making bragot. The simplest involved adding the honey to the fermented ale, and suspending the spices in a bag in the barrels. Another approach was to re-boil the already fermented ale with the new wort and honey, which seems like a uselessly cumbersome process unless you were trying to save an ale that was going sour. Bragot/bracket was sometimes made entirely with unfermented wort and spices, which would have produced a very sweet beverage. Bragot survived until the mid-nineteenth century in Lancashire and then winked out, not to return until the explosion of homebrewing and craft brewing in the last twenty years.

Long Pepper, *Piper longum*

This relative of black pepper was once quite popular as a culinary spice in Europe. Available at Indian markets. Shown a little over twice life size.

A FEW MORE HONEY BEERS

RECIPE — Buckwheat Honey Black Beer

Yield: 5 gallons (19 liters)

Gravity: 1.068 (16 °P)

Alcohol/vol: 7.5 to 8.5% (depending on yeast)

Color: Deep chestnut brown

Bitterness: 38 IBU

Yeast: Belgian ale, perhaps saison

Maturation: 4 to 6 months

This next recipe is inspired by references to Dutch beers a few hundred years ago, although they used buckwheat with no honey. It should have a deep chestnut color and a rocky, cream-colored head. This should be fermented at a reasonably warm temperature (70 to 76° F).

All-Grain (& Honey) Recipe:

3.0 lb (1.4 kg)	25%	flaked spelt
2.0 lb (0.90 kg)	17%	six-row malt
2.0 lb (0.90 kg)	17%	biscuit malt
1.0 lb (0.45 kg)	8%	chocolate malt
1.0 lb (0.45 kg)	8%	buckwheat, toasted 20 minutes at 300° F (see p. 224)
0.5 lb (227 g)	—	rice hulls
3.0 lb (1.4 kg)	25%	buckwheat honey, added to the kettle at the end of the boil

No Equivalent Extract Recipe

Hops & Spices:

1.5oz (43 g)	90 min	Northdown (6.5% AA)
1.0 oz (28 g)	end of boil	coriander, crushed
0.25 oz (7 g)	end of boil	caraway, crushed
0.1oz (3 g)	end of boil	cardamom seeds, crushed

RECIPE — "A Perfect Ten" Wheaten Honeywine

Yield: 5 gallons (19 liters)

Gravity: 1.100 (24 °P)

Alcohol/vol: 10 to 11% (depending on yeast)

Color: Medium gold

Bitterness: 36 IBU

Yeast: German weizen

Maturation: 6 to 10 months

This will be a good vehicle to show off the honey, so pick a variety with a pleasing and delicate aroma and a pale color. The honey will add a nice aroma and cut the thickness of the wheat.

All-Malt (& Honey) Recipe:

11.5 lb (5.2 kg)	70%	wheat malt
2.0 lb (0.90 kg)	12%	six-row lager malt
3.0 lb (1.4 kg)	18%	honey, added at end of boil

For an extract recipe, substitute 9.5 lb (4.3 kg) of liquid wheat extract for the malts.

Hops:

2.0 oz (57 g)	60 min	Tettnang (4% AA)
1.5 oz (42 g)	30 min	Tettnang (4% AA)
1.0 oz (28 g)	end of boil	Tettnang (4% AA)
0.1 oz (3 g)	end of boil	lemon zest

RECIPE   Ruby You Hot Little...Schwarzbracket

Yield: 5 gallons (19 liters)

Gravity: 1.100 (24 °P)

Alcohol/vol: 9.5 to 11%

Color: Deep-ruby brown

Bitterness: 23 IBU

Yeast: Bavarian lager

Maturation: 8 to 12 months

All-Malt (& Honey) Recipe:

9.0 lb (4.1 kg)	81%	Munich malt
2.0 oz (57 g)	1%	black patent malt
1.0 lb (0.45 kg)	9%	honey, cooked down to a medium amber color (see p. 198)
1.0 lb (0.45 kg)	9%	strongly flavored honey, added to secondary

No Equivalent Extract Recipe

Hops:

2.5 oz (71 g)	60 min	Hallertau (3.5% AA)

RECIPE   Crystal Malt Old Bracket

Yield: 5 gallons (19 liters)

Gravity: 1.133 (32.5 °P)

Alcohol/vol: 13 to 14.5%

Color: Tawny amber

Bitterness: 23 IBU

Yeast: Sherry or Madeira

Maturation: 12 to 18 months

This recipe can also be made with caramelized honey (see p. 198), sugar, or malt extract augmenting or replacing the crystal malt.

This will be a hopped bracket, using a small amount of crystal malt and no other grain. Place 2 to 3 gallons of cold water in the brew kettle.

2.0 lb (0.90 kg)	12%	medium crystal malt, as per steeped-grain procedure
14.0 lb (6.4 kg)	88%	moderately full-flavored honey, added at end of boil

Over the course of 45 minutes, slowly bring the pot to a boil, pulling the grain bags out shortly before boiling, then squeezing and draining any remaining malt juice back into the kettle.

Hops:

2.0 oz (57 g)	90 min	Challenger (7.5% AA)
1.0 oz (28 g)	30 min	Challenger (7.5% AA)
1.0 oz (28 g)	end of boil	Challenger (7.5% AA)

For an authentic old-ale character, add a packet of *Brettanomyces* culture after the primary is finished. This will be a strong mead that will require a minimum of a year's aging—five would probably be a lot better. Bottle this uncarbonated.

DON'T TRY THIS ALONE

THE GLORY OF BREW CLUBS

One of the great pleasures of homebrewing is its social aspect. Like a magic magnet, it draws interesting, passionate people into its foamy vortex. If you've been brewing for a while, you probably know what I mean. If you're new to the hobby, I urge you to get in touch with other brewers through your local homebrew shop, the American Homebrewers Association (find them at www.beertown.org), or by searching online for a club in your area.

Even if you're not generally a "joiner," you may find in a homebrew club the kind of warmth and easy familiarity the Germans call *Gemütlichkeit*. It's certainly been my experience.

One brewer, in a kitchen or garage, can make beer equal to the best commercial brews, which is a pretty good achievement. But if you put a group of brewers together, even more amazing things can happen.

American Homebrewers Association

The national club. Find them at www.beertown.org.

Club Activities	
Featured Beer Style	Commercial and homebrewed versions are compared, and the history and style guidelines are reviewed.
Crystal Malt Tasting	Many different varieties are laid out for tasting.
Invite a Local Brewer	Who's going to turn down free beer? Most of these guys brewed at home before going pro.
Equipment Party	A group build for wort chillers, keg kettles, or other gear. Rent a TIG welder if anybody knows how to use it.
Beer & Food Pairings	Cheese, chocolate, salsa—there are so many possibilities.
Mashing Demo	Just to show people it's nothing to be afraid of.
New Brewer Day	Brew class and demo of brewing for the novices.
Bad Beer Tasting	Have people save their bad beers.
Local Beer Historian	Many cities have somebody who really knows about the local brewing tradition. You might even make a replica beer to serve.
Judging Practice	Have judging forms and style guides available. More experienced judges should be paired with newer ones.

Club Activities (continued)

Local Water Workshop
Work out ways to treat the local water for different beer styles.

Yeast Culturing Demo
Plating, making slants, culturing from bottles—there's a lot to do.

Invite a Beer Author
Most of them enjoy talking to homebrewers, and I've never heard of anyone charging a fee, but travel expenses may need to be paid.

Brewers Open House
Several people with interesting systems or methods all brew simultaneously, and people go from house to house checking things out. End the day with a potluck or pizza.

Homebrew Invitational
A competition in which identical kits of ingredients are given to some of the better (and better known) brewers in the area, who then brew beers for a walka-round competition. Other brewers who wish to enter may purchase the kit. The usual rule is that brewers don't have to use everything in the kit, but must also incorporate a set quantity of a specialty ingredient, which can be grain, vegetable matter, a box of break-fast cereal, candy, and so on. Loads of fun.

Hop Variety Smell-Off
Assemble many different hop varieties for a walka-round sniffing.

Malt Roasting Demo
Run through a number of different times and temper-atures, and taste the results. Send the grains home to be brewed and have a tasting when the beers are ready.

Sugar Cookdown
Sugar is cooked in a heavy pan until it darkens (see p. 198) for use as a brewing ingredient. Flavors and col-ors are compared. Honey and malt extract may be treated this way, too.

Sugar Tasting
Gather a number of different sugars, and lay them out for tasting. For part two, brewers can take sugars home and brew with them, then bring the finished beers back a few months later for tasting.

Smoked Malt Tasting
People smoke malt with different woods, and for dif-ferent times. Compare the results in a walkaround format.

Judge Exam Preparation
Review beer styles and brewing technique. You have to drink to get the styles, so it's a pretty fun study hall.

Clubs, Clubs, Clubs

While the largest cities tend to have the largest clubs, active and sophisticated clubs can be found all around the country.

GREAT BIG BARRELS O' BEER

Whiskey Barrel Beers The idea of aging a strong beer in a bourbon barrel originated with a group of suburban Chicago homebrewers, although it has come to be the rage among the *avante*-micro crowd. Now it even has its own festival.

First, obtain a recently used bourbon barrel. Since these 50-gallon charred oak containers can't be reused for bourbon, they're fairly cheap. Most are disassembled and shipped off to Scotland, Mexico, and the Caribbean to age whiskey, tequila, and rum, but they find uses here, split into planters or sawn up into bulky barstools. The Internet is a good source, but if you're within striking distance, a road trip to bourbon country can be fascinating and fun. If your barrel is somewhat dried out, you may want to refresh it by adding a bottle of inexpensive but respectable bourbon.

Line up enough brewers to produce 53 gallons (plus a little more for topping up occasionally) of stout. Everyone can brew separately, or can gang up on brew day for one massive assault. Strongly flavored beers such as strong stout, barley wine or imperial pale ale can best stand up to the rich bourbon and vanilla flavors the cask will contribute. Let the separate batches of beer ferment out through the primary before adding to the barrel. Then fill it up and let it age. Make sure it is on solid footings, because it will be very heavy when full. After a few months, have everyone assemble for a massive bottling party, or just rack off the stout into soda kegs and enjoy something wonderful.

Barley Wine Solera This is just a way to procure a supply of blended ancient and new barley wine. Obtain a large demijohn or barrel, from 15 to 50 gallons. As in above, brewers rotate brew duty. There are two rules: One, the vessel must be kept full, or oxygen will allow vinegar bacteria and/or mold to spoil the beer; and two, the beer must be at least a certain gravity, which in my opinion should be ridiculously high. Give this beer a special name, make ritual offerings to it on beer holidays—worship it, really—and serve it only for very special occasions. The result will be very, very fine, and sharing a beer is guaranteed to hold a group together.

You can do this on a smaller scale as well, using a corny keg and keeping the beer carbonated, which avoids the problem of air in the headspace.

If the solera is inoculated with a *Brettanomyces* or mixed lambic culture, the wild complexity will increase as time goes by, tempered by additions of fresher, sweeter beer. Be sure to keep the cask in a cool place where temperature swings are minimal— a cellar is the obvious solution if you have one. Also, be sure to keep the cask topped up, as evaporation will occur, and air is an invitation to vinegar-producing bacteria.

STONE BEER

In the days when wooden vessels were the norm for brewing, getting the heat of the fire into the mash or the boil wasn't as easy as just swinging the cauldron over the fire. The problem was solved by heating stones and then placing them in the tubs along with the mash or wort.

This practice survived from ancient times in Carinthia, the southern part of Austria. Two commercial breweries made steinbier until 1917, although twenty-six stone breweries had been active in the area in 1750. According to research, pine or other softwood was used to heat the stones, giving them (and the beer) a somewhat resinous quality. Here's an eyewitness account from 1908:

"The mash is put into a wooden mash-tub, is then heated up by means of stones brought to a glow, and this subjected to boiling. The stones used for the purpose, on the average size of a human head, are heated in a wood fire for two or three hours, and when they begin to be red-hot, the smaller ones are placed on the bottom of the mashtub, this bottom having first been covered with thoroughly soaked juniper brush-wood. Next the hops and some water are added, and after the hops have several times brought to the boiling point, the doughing-in commences. The larger stones are now submerged in the mash, using for this purpose peculiarly shaped forks, and stirring the mash at the same time. The 'Steinbier' brewer knows from experience just how many of these stones are needed to get his wort to the right temperature. Thermometers and iodine tests are anachronisms for him. After the mash is ready it remains at rest for an hour, branches or twigs of juniper having been first placed into the mash in a vertical position, to promote straining. Then the mash is drawn off, the plug of the mash-tun only loosened somewhat to that end. The wort is ladled back from the underback until it runs off clear.

"Meanwhile water has also been heated in a second tub by means of hot stones, and the sparging is done with this water. Next the first wort and the spargings are both put into smaller tubs, where the wort is to cool off, since surface coolers do not exist in this 'Steinbier' brewery. [The wort is] pitched with yeast at [66 to 77 °F or 19 to 25° C]. At this temperature, then, it is pitched, of course with a rather unclean top-yeast. Next day the beer is racked from the tubs into smaller casks, where it undergoes a secondary fermentation, and in three or four days it is ready for consumption.

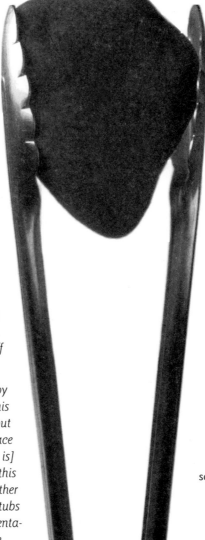

Stone beers are a fun and scary group project, as well as an ancient tradition.

"Malting methods are just as primitive as the brewing and the malt takes on a smoky odor or taste in consequence of the smoke of the kiln-fire, similar to the Graetzer beer of Posen, which enjoys great reputation, and is distinguished by its intensely smoky taste. Stone beer is turbid, but of pale color, and is popular because of its thirst-quenching, refreshing and carbonic qualities. Mostly it is drunk in mugs or tankards, with a bit of gin or fruit brandy, just as is often done with 'Weissbier.'"

Such beer was traditionally made from two-thirds oats and one-third malt, often wheat rather than barley. A German brewing magazine reported in 1910 that the amount of grain used was about 4.5 pounds per 5-gallon batch, in homebrew terms, putting the gravity somewhere in the neighborhood of 1.020 (5 °P). A very small beer, indeed, as were many other related wheat- and oat-based beers of the day such as witbier and Berliner weisse.

The rocks normally employed (a heat-resistant metamorphic sandstone called graywacke) create a mountain of steam when plunged into the wort. A concretion of gooey caramelized sugars penetrates the pores, coating the rocks as the wort boils. The rocks are then placed into the lagering tanks to stimulate a secondary fermentation, giving off caramel, toffeelike, and finally smoky flavors as the sugars dissolve in the beer.

Rauchenfels Steinbier is commercial steinbier inspired by the Carinthian tradition, although employing beechwood instead of pine, plus several other changes that bring it into line with more modern tastes. The brewery makes two versions, a pale amber lager Steinbier, and a lighter colored Steinweizen, which exhibits more smoky character. Both are of conventional gravity at 1.048 (11.5 °P), with modest hop bitterness.

As you might imagine, the brewing of steinbier is a spectacular crowd pleaser, with giant fires, plenty of steam, and dangerously hot boiling liquids. And because of the intense caramelization of the wort by the hot rocks, the beer's a delight as well.

My friend Ray Spangler used to organize a stone beer demo at the infamous Oldenburg Beer Camp. He employed fist-size granite stream cobbles. These are reasonably stable and not prone to flaking as are rougher rocks. Finer-textured rock tends to hold together best. The best candidates are dense, igneous (volcanic) rocks such as granite or basalt, and I've heard that quartzite works as well. Avoid limestone or other sedimentary rock, as it is porous, prone to cracking, and soluble in beer. For a 5-gallon batch, you'll need about 7 to 8 pounds of rocks, about 0.5 to 1 pound each. It's a good idea to preheat stones at lower temperatures before putting them in the fire, to reduce the risk of shattering. A couple of hours in a conventional oven at 350° F ought to do it, or you can put them near the fire at first and move them in gradually, rather than just plopping them in the coals.

GROUP GROPES

Just getting everybody's equipment together for a brew can be a lot of fun, whatever the beer. While this usually takes place in backyards and driveways, it can be much more extreme. The American Homebrewers Association sponsors an event on

Holy Temecula, Brewman!

Put two homebrewers and a few well-crafted beers together, and you've got a rocking party. Put fifteen hundred of them in a park in southern California for three days in May, doing what homebrewers do, and it's a sublime state of bliss, a sort of worty Woodstock. The Southern California Homebrew Festival, with ever more elaborate serving displays, and ever more beer, topped off with lectures, barbecue, and even a homebrewed band, is the largest gathering of homebrewers on the planet.

A similar event called the Northern California Homebrewers Festival takes place in the foothills of the Sierra Nevada mountains. It features much of the same kind of camaraderie, and even includes a gourmet beer dinner in the woods.

RECIPE	Carinthian Steinbier

Yield: 5 gallons (19 liters)

Gravity: 1.038 (9 °P)

Alcohol/vol: 3 to 3.5%

Color: Pale straw

Bitterness: 16 IBU

Yeast: German weissbier; lactic culture optional

Maturation: 3 to 5 weeks

This has been modernized into something more palatable, while trying to preserve some of the character of this old-timer. As outlined in the previous description, the process is pretty complicated, and I'll leave it to you whether you want to follow the whole archaic ordeal. I think it's reasonable to skip the stones in the mash, and just do that part conventionally.

WARNING: Be aware that any rock can shatter violently when heated, especially when the heating or cooling is rapid. Be sure that everyone nearby is wearing goggles or safety glasses. There's bound to be some splashing, even a boilover, so suit up— this is a good cold-weather spectacle.

All-Malt Recipe:

5.0 lb (2.3 kg)	67%	oat malt
2.5 lb (1.1 kg)	33%	smoked wheat malt
Armful		juniper branches (preferably with berries on them)
	or	
4.0 oz (113g)		crushed juniper berries

Hops:

1.5 oz (43 g)	60 min	Saaz hops (3% AA)

Procedure:

Place 2 gallons (7.5 liters) of water into your brew kettle, add the juniper branches (or berries) and the first dose of hops, then bring to a boil, which should last half an hour. This can be done with the hot stones as described, or over a flame. Transfer this liquid, branches and all, into your mash tun, add the grain, and add more boiling water as needed to bring it up to a rather high (155° F or 68.5° C) saccharification temperature, then let it rest for an hour. Sparge as normal, not worrying too much about wort clarity. Bring the wort up to a simmer.

Meanwhile, you should be heating your rocks, either in a campfire or on a propane burner. **Be sure to make everyone involved wear goggles and long sleeved clothing when you're doing this! A waterproof apron is a good idea for those within splashing distance.**

Place the stones in the fire and heat them until they're as hot as you can get them—glowing red or white. Use long tongs or a shovel to transfer the stones into a basket made from stainless steel strapping or heavy screen mesh, with chains attaching the basket securely to a pole that two people can handle. Then, slowly lower the rocks into the brew. There will be a dramatic release of steam; people will ooh and aah. After a minute or two, pull out the basket of stones and allow the sugars to caramelize, then lower them back in the wort. Repeat this a few times until the rocks have lost most of their heat. Complete the boil with a conventional heat source. Allow the rocks to cool to room temperature, then you can either place them in the primary fermenter, or put them in plastic bags and store them in the freezer, then add them to the beer in the secondary, where it's likely to retain more of the caramelized flavors.

the first Saturday in May called Big Brew. Sites around the country host brewers and their rigs for a giant brew-in, which also usually includes a big ol' party. Definitely worth checking out, and you don't have to brew to attend.

Cincinnati's Bloatarian Brewing League has a campout—Beer & Propane—that culminates in a mystic late-night campfire ceremony, complete with holy relics, silly hats, and the pounding of the symbol of Evil Order (as represented by a can of mega-brew) into the earth.

An apple-smashing party can be a lot of fun in the fall. Rent or borrow a cider press, and set it up, hopefully at somebody's house where there's an apple or pear tree, as the fruit is much cheaper that way. Ask everyone who comes to bring apples, pears, quinces, crabapples, or anything squishable, and start squeezing. This really makes for a great fall day.

OR, YOU CAN GET COMPETITIVE

**Beer Judge
Certification Program**

This organization tests and certifies judges and sanctions competitions. Go to bjcp.org for details and loads of other useful beer information.

The Gulf Coast Region seems to produce very competitive-minded clubs. A series of homebrew competitions that double as mini conferences in Dallas, Orlando, and Houston occupy much of the year for brewers down South. These events are run with much passion and good humor. At Houston's Dixie Cup, homebrew legend Fred Eckhardt has been cast as an alien, bandito, dominatrix, and ghoul in "Night of the Living Fred." The boundaries also get pushed with special competition categories like "The Beer That Burns Twice," for chile beers, of course.

There are hundreds of homebrew competitions at the local, regional, and national levels. The Beer Judge Certification Program qualifies and tracks judges as well as sanctioning competitions. Many local competitions tie together to award regional "best of" awards; the Gulf Coast is one such circuit. MCAB (Masters Championship of Amateur Brewing) awards point to individuals at sanctioned competitions, then brings the best of the best together for a final gundown. The American Homebrew Association National Competition is the biggest of all, three thousand beers, fed into a number of regional first-round sites, and culminating in June at the AHA National Conference where the finalists are chosen and crowned. Competitions are the surest way to hone your brewing skills. The ruthless honesty of a blind judging gives you feedback your pals never will. You improve or else.

There are other possible formats besides sanctioned competitions. Beer & Sweat, the world's largest keg-only homebrew competition, rocks Cincinnati in August with about one hundred and fifty entries. Here in Chicago, we have hosted invitational brewoffs, extending invitations and a kit of ingredients to a number of well-respected brewers; others were free to buy the kits and compete as well. Contestants didn't have to use everything in the kit, and they were required to add something to the brew—one year it was a box of breakfast cereal—which made for a fun and fascinating tasting. For a competition like this, judging can be by celebrity panel or popular voting.

Homebrewers do more than homebrew; they're in the vanguard of promoting interest in quality commercial beer as well. The most active Washington D.C. area club, the Brewers United for Real Potables (BURP), hosts a specialized beer conference called "The Spirit of Belgium" on a roughly every-other-year basis. My own club, the Chicago Beer Society—a beer appreciation club run mostly by homebrewers—helps Ray Daniels put on the Real Ale Fest, the largest gathering of real ales outside of Britain, and hosts five or six other commercial beer events a year. A favorite is the Brewpub Shootout, where local brewpubs compete fiercely for best beer, best food, and best pairing.

BEYOND BEER DRINKING: BEER TASTING

This is very simple to do at home with your friends. All you need is some small glasses, a loaf of bread or crackers, some beer enthusiasts, and, of course, beer. Tastings come in many formats. They can be blind or not. They may focus on a single style or be very diverse. See the list on the following page for some suggestions.

Glasses Four- to 6-ounce clear glasses work best. Champagne or small wine-glasses are perfect, but little tumblers will do. Have at least two glasses for every person. Clear plastic cups are serviceable for a larger group. If you are using glass, make sure that it is squeaky clean, with no traces of detergent that can affect the aroma and collapse the head.

Water A really good idea. Use bottled or filtered—tap water usually has a lot of chlorine in it.

Dump Buckets Have empty pitchers or small buckets for dumping rinse water.

Bread or Crackers These help to clear the palate between tastings. They're a must-have in a judging situation, more optional in an informal tasting. Best are very simple products such as water crackers or plain French bread. Serving butter along with them is a definite no-no, as this can affect flavor and cause the untimely collapse of an otherwise faultless head.

Focus The world of beer is very large. Tastings are usually more informative if a theme is chosen, rather than a random assortment of beers. Check the accompanying box for a list of possibilities.

Reference Material Have a book handy, such as Michael Jackson's *World Guide to Beer*, to provide background information on the beers at your tasting. Most breweries now post information on their Web sites about their products, so putting together a custom handout shouldn't be all that difficult.

No Smoking! Tobacco smoke can make it very difficult to properly evaluate the nuances of fine beer. On the other hand, beer and cigar tastings have been held with some degree of success, usually by concentrating on massively powerful beers.

Freshness Counts Beer is highly perishable, and may easily succumb to the ravages of time, heat, and fluorescent light. Try to make sure the beers you're tasting are as fresh as possible.

Serving Temperature This makes a lot of difference. Lagers should ideally be served at about 40 to 45° F, ales at 50 to 55° F. Except for lawnmower beers, none should be served ice-cold.

Pour for a Good Head Straight down the center of the glass is the preferred method for pouring beer. This may create what seems like an excess of foam, but when it settles down, you'll have a tight, creamy head and plenty of aroma.

Small Pours are Best A 2- to 4-ounce sample is adequate for judging and evaluating beers. Larger amounts make it difficult to do very many. Six to 8-ounce glasses allow room for the head, and to collect the aroma.

Black Oil Porter and Brain Death Barley Wine

Souvenirs of Houston's Dixie Cup homebrew competition. Labels by Bev Blackwood.

Beer Tasting Themes

By Country/Region:

Germany

Belgium

USA—Microbreweries

Britain

Mexico

Southern Hemisphere beers

The beers of Asia

By Season:

The beers of summer

Oktoberfest beers

Winter beers

Bock beers

By Character:

By color

By strength

By yeast—lager, ale, weizen, etc.

By Beer Styles:

Lagers

Scotch ales

Monastery beers

Wheat beers

Stouts and porters

Pale ales

Beer with Food:

Pitch-in pairings

Chili cook-off and the perfect chili beer

National beer and food

Score Sheets These make a tasting slightly more formal, but they force participants to consider each important aspect of the beer. Wine tastings have been done this way for years. Why not think about beer in the same considered fashion? Ask for an extra copy of a judging form, and you can copy it for your own tasting.

Blind is Best for Rating If you're trying to evaluate beers objectively, this is a must. Cover the labels or pour the beers out of sight of the tasters

Limit the Number of Beers Even experienced judges experience palate burnout over about a dozen beers. You can have a very nice tasting with only half that amount.

YOU CAN TAKE IT WITH YOU!

One of the early icons of modern homebrewing was a photo of the legendary Charlie Papazian and his band of merry pranksters cavorting in the surf, homebrew in hand, in Fiji of all places. Staring at this photo brought to mind a rush of possibilities. If one's nose could be thumbed at rampant commercialism by drinking homebrew at the very ends of the earth, then nothing was impossible. Homebrew is universal! As brewers, it is our privilege, even our duty, to carry it to the distant corners of the globe.

At the simplest, you just toss a few bottles in the knapsack and go. But sometimes, glass is forbidden. Sometimes you want to bring a whole lot more than a six-pack. Sometimes, you even want to brew it there!

Most venues and events don't really want you bringing your own beer to the game. But in an effort to become more "family-friendly," many have relaxed their standards, allowing coolers as long as they contain "no glass, no cans." Your weapon in this little game is the plastic soda bottle. With your dark beers in cola bottles and your pale ones in ginger ale bottles, you can walk through the checkpoint as cool as a well-chilled Pilsener.

You may bottle and prime plastic bottles as you would glass or fill them with draft beer from the tap. The Carbonator Cap (available from most homebrew shops) allows you to give the draft beers an extra squirt of gas, replacing what you lose when you draw off the tap. To reduce foaming, I have found it helpful to extend the tap with a piece of hose long enough to reach the bottom of your bottle. Release most of the pressure on the keg, using 3 to 5 psi to get the stuff to flow.

Even when you're not in a surreptitious mode these bottles are a good choice, as they are light, cheap, and unbreakable. But be advised that some soda flavors linger in the plastic and can give your beer the startlingly inappropriate aromas of root beer, grape, or orange. Cola, lemon-lime, and ginger ale bottles seem to be fine, though.

BREWING IN THE WILD

I have a friend who brews beer on the first day of his annual group canoe trip, consuming the beer at the end of the week. It sounds impossible at first, but brewing away from home just takes a little extra planning and special technique.

If you're traveling heavy, you can transport your whole rig, including multiple propane burners and a generator for your pumps. But you can make beer with much less. Wood fire served our ancestors for a million years or so. A fermenter can be made from a couple of clean trash bags lining a cooler. Gravity works really well in the forest. If you have a lot of time on your hands, do as the Finns do and hack a brewing/fermenting vessel out of a log.

The only big trick is fermenting and finishing the beer in a short time. Bottling is out of the question; you need a draft setup for this trick. Here's what you can do to speed up the process:

1. Brew a low-gravity beer With less work for the yeast to do, you get a palatable beer more quickly. An amber or dark beer will hide the inevitable cloudiness, if you're concerned about esthetics.

2. Pitch plenty of yeast Use three or four packets of fresh dry yeast, properly rehydrated, or a big gob of the stuff from a starter or previous batch.

3. Crash it Two days before serving, rack it into a soda keg (unless your primary is in a vessel that can be easily iced), and chill it as close to freezing as you can manage. This will drop the yeast from suspension, largely clearing your beer. Then rack back to the primary (be sure to save some extra trash bags to use for liners), clean the settled yeast out of the keg, and rack the beer back into it.

4. Jam it Force carbonate to 40 to 50 psi, rocking or shaking for fifteen minutes or longer. Leave it on the gas overnight at this pressure and the next day it will be carbonated enough to thoroughly enjoy. Be sure to keep it cold all through this process.

That's all there is to it, although the logistics of wort chilling and sanitation will be challenging, to say the least. A nice touch is to add a taste of the natural bounty of your location: raspberries, wild ginger root, birch bark, sassafras, or even chanterelle mushrooms. For the sake of time, most of these are probably best added at the end of the boil. Pull out the Euell Gibbons and see what's available.

So you see that there is no need to stay locked in your cellar this summer in order to be near a source of decent beer. Don't be afraid to pack up your cooler, get out, and enjoy the sunshine!

Chapter 20

The Buckapound Brewery

There comes a point for many homebrewers when the basic starter equipment kit just doesn't cut it any more. The mysterious urgings of the brewer's art often send many of us scurrying from junkyard to laboratory supply shops in search of the pieces from which to build the perfect homebrewery—some dusty but beautiful stainless steel vessels, bits of tubing, valves, screen, and the like. At some point during this quest the aspiring brewery engineer is faced with the intimidating problem of how to put it all together.

For many homebrewers, equipment is simply a means to an end—simple, functional, something that has to be addressed before the real work of brewing can begin.

For me, it's a little different. Of course I enjoy making and sharing homebrew, but I also love the hardware. The thrill of a good scrounge combined with the rewarding handwork of cutting, shaping, and fusing stainless steel suits me perfectly. Part NASA, part Frankenstein's lab, and part Snuffy Smith, I view my Buckapound Brewery as functional kinetic art.

It's called the Buckapound Brewery because for a long time this was the price of scrap stainless. Now the price is $1.25, but that just doesn't have the same ring.

I've been working on this outrageous brewery-building path since 1986 or so, and have gone through numerous variations, not all of them successful. I now have it to the point that it's functioning smoothly; it's a rare brew day that I have to get out the tool kit. Parts of it are still pretty rough looking—prototypes, really. My current thrust is toward making it all attractive as well. The lauter tun is the first piece of this better-looking gear; wood cladding will complete the classic look. A copper and stainless brew kettle is in the works.

How I ever ended up with a hobby that involves so much plumbing is a cosmic mystery I'll never fathom, except to acknowledge that the universe does have a sense of humor.

I thought it might be amusing, or possibly even informative, to share some of my principles and practicalities with you. Few would want to follow me all the way down this path, but I think there are ideas here that are well worth considering, no matter what sort of homebrewery you're assembling.

One more thing. I am an artist by training, not an engineer. So those of you without technical training should know that this deficiency is no barrier to making the homebrewery of your dreams. Hooking a mash tun up to a computer is beyond most of us, but there are plenty of things you can just work out through trial and error. The engineers that specified the castoffs I'm using can laugh if they want, but this thing does brew beer.

PLANNING AND GOALS

You can just start building stuff willy-nilly, but the beginning is a good time to pause and decide what you are trying to accomplish with all this grinding and welding. You will want to formulate some sort of a plan.

Some possible goals are (some of these may conflict):

- Shorter brew day
- Less effort/attention
- More complete control
- Special processes like adjunct mashes, decoctions
- Really cool looking
- Built around a unique found object/vessel/part
- Historical authenticity

You will also have some limitations to deal with:

- Skill areas
- Access to tools—your own or otherwise
- What's available for $1 per pound
- Available space
- Energy source(s)

Cool Looks

A basic brew kettle with artful, stylized details.

You also have to ask the hard question: will the new doojiemaflopper work for me? It's easy to make brewing more difficult as things get more complex. There are issues of coordination and reliability; the more pieces you have, the more time it takes to hook it up, and then take it apart. And more to wash, at the very least. You need to coldly decide if the benefit is worth the effort.

RAW MATERIALS

Brew-friendly materials are often hostile to deal with. The ingredients that make stainless durable also make it challenging to shape and join. What works for one material is often a disaster for another. A little knowledge and the proper tools can mean the difference between a shiny new brewery and a smoking pile of expensive junk on the basement floor.

Stainless Steel This is the best material for almost everything for all stages of the brewing process, from mashing to lagering. It is resistant to all chemicals used in brewing and cleaning, with the caution that extended contact with chlorine-based cleaners will cause corrosion. It is a poor heat conductor, but adequate for most brewing purposes. It is expensive when new, but since it's so enduring, there are lots of vessels, parts, and pieces on the surplus market.

There are two types you will most often come across: 304 and 316. The latter is the higher-grade material, with extra manganese for better resistance to corrosion.

Brewery Safety

The combination of electricity, water, heat, gas, and motors offers a tremendous number of potential hazards. Here are a number of them, but no list can replace good common sense in building or operating your brewery equipment.

• Electricity and water can be a deadly combination. Use the kind of electrical boxes meant for outdoor use, and always be sure the equipment is grounded. The use of a GFCI-protected outlet or extension cord is essential; be sure to test it regularly. If you install sensors like float switches or thermostats, use low voltage for the signal circuits, stepping it up to line voltage with a relay placed well away from the water. Use good sense as far as the way things are constructed, using waterproof boxes and connectors when that is a concern, and heat-resistant wire and other hardware when that is appropriate.

• Propane is often used to fire burners. It should never be used or stored indoors, as it is heavier than air, and should a leak develop, it will crawl along the floor until it finds a pilot light and then…blam. It is obvious that gas hoses of any kind should be checked often and kept well away from the heat when the burner's on.

• Fire from these large burners can put heat where you don't want it: above, below, and beside the pot, so make sure you keep flammable (or low melting point) materials well away. Install heat shields if needed.

• A natural gas or propane burner can generate dangerous amounts of carbon monoxide if it's burning poorly. Yellow flame or soot on the kettle are dead giveaways (literally). Some burners (wok burners, for example) don't like to be turned down too low, or they'll start putting out carbon monoxide. If you brew indoors, get a CO monitor/alarm and use it.

• A common source of injury in commercial breweries is the boilover. When the wort comes to a boil, it can turn from placid to raging in an instant, so you need to be watching the heat very carefully at this critical point. Hops provide nucleation sites for bubble formation, adding to the problem. Add a pinch at first, let the boil settle, then add the rest—and be ready to lower the heat.

• Moving hot liquids through tubing can be dangerous, as the heat may cause the tubing to soften, and it may pop loose from its fitting, squirting scalding water randomly. Pumps multiply the hazard. Make sure your tubing can handle the heat, check the hose clamps when the tubing is warm, and retighten if needed.

• Rotating motors connected to things like stirring paddles can be dangerous, so try to design them in such a way as to keep fingers out of the way as much as possible.

• Although there are plenty of safe and effective brewery cleaning chemicals, if you can't resist the urge to occasionally use the more traditional chemicals like caustic soda (lye) or strong acids, you should make sure to use goggles, gloves, and other protection.

Either type is fine for any conceivable homebrew purpose.

Stainless steel is hard, and when it gets hot it gets even harder. This is a key point. This is the reason for the smoking drill bits and melting saber saw blades you may have encountered when trying to cut or drill the stuff. Slow speeds are recommended.

For drilling, the secret weapon is a cobalt drill bit. They cost more than regular bits, but they're virtually indestructible. Any large hardware store should have them. Tungsten carbide bits aren't meant for drilling stainless steel, but a carbide rotary file or burr is a useful tool to chuck into your drill to clean up rough-edged holes and saw cuts.

If you're tapping (threading) stainless, get the most expensive taps you can find—high-speed steel, at least—and be very careful. It's easy to break off a small tap in the process of trying to thread a hole (broken taps in stainless or copper can be dissolved with acid, by the way). A good lubricant is essential. It's also important to back the tap out frequently, to keep the hole clear of chips.

Unless it's very thin, stainless is too tough to cut with tin snips, and must be cut with a saw or abrasive disk. In a saber saw, use a type of blade called bimetal, which features high-speed steel teeth on a flexible backing. A variable-speed saber saw or a reciprocal saw with a bimetal blade is a workable choice. Watch the speed carefully, because the blade can get red-hot trying to chew through the stuff, and will dull (or melt) rapidly. Carbide grit blades work pretty well, too, and are the blade of choice with a single-speed saw.

Abrasive disks work better than saws. I like a 3" diameter, 1/16" thick disk on a die grinder, which will cut through just about anything.

Stainless steel requires an exotic and expensive welding process as well. TIG welding uses an inert gas to prevent oxidation of the weld. Before you take your job to the welder, make sure he has this capability.

Stainless (and other materials) can be joined by brazing with silver-based alloys. This is strong, but is not as corrosion-resistant as welding. It is suitable for affixing a pipe fitting to the bottom of your boiling kettle, which is the thing you'll be most likely to need. You can do this at home with a MAPP or propane torch. Make sure the brazing filler is compatible with food and drink. For stainless, you need special flux. Just call the welding supply shop and tell them what you're doing, and they'll sell you the right stuff. Since the braze is water-thin when molten, it will not fill gaps. A very tight fit-up is mandatory for good results.

Copper This is the traditional material for boiling kettle construction, due to its excellent heat conductivity. It is resistant to acids, but easily damaged by contact with alkaline materials such as chlorine cleaner and lye. It is suitable for anything on the hot side of the brewery, but is not serviceable for fermentation because it reacts with the common materials used in cleaning and sterilizing. That great coppery luster on traditional brew kettles requires a lot of elbow grease, as copper tarnishes quickly.

Brass and Bronze These are alloys of copper: brass with zinc; and bronze with tin, silicon, or other metals. They are most commonly used for such pieces as tube fittings and valves. All the precautions about the corrosiveness of copper apply to these metals too. Most ordinary yellow brass contains lead as a lubricant to make it machine better, so this is not such a great material for extended contact with acidic or alkaline liquids, although for things like brew kettle valves it poses no great hazard.

Aluminum It is cheap, available, and an excellent conductor of heat. It is passable as a boiling kettle material, but not recommended due to its reactivity. Aluminum corrodes violently on contact with alkalis such as chlorine cleaner and lye, but is resistant to acids. It is okay for heating water (for strike and sparge) but not too great for any other use.

Solder Watch out. Ordinary solder is a mix of tin and lead, both of which are toxic to yeast and powerful haze-formers as well. Don't use it for anything that comes in contact with wort or beer. The lead-free solder you can get is less toxic, but is mostly tin, which may be leached out by the acidic wort or beer. So-called "silver" solder is mostly tin, too. If you can avoid solder, do so.

Iron/Steel Contact with beer should be avoided, as iron can be a source of bad flavor and a significant haze-former. It's fine for stands and other structural uses. Enamel canning kettles are steel underneath, so if they're chipped, they're capable of contaminating your beer.

Copper Stein, c. 1900
The burnished glow of copper has long caught the drinker's eye as well as the brewer's.

Glass Brewery Piping, Zatec, Czech Republic
Bohemia, famous as a glass blowing center, is phasing out these old pipes.

Glass It's a beautiful material, inert, and inexpensive; in many respects an ideal material for fermentation vessels such as carboys. It is resistant to all cleaning and sterilizing materials you would ever use. The one caution is that glass will become etched from long contact with strong solutions of caustic (lye), so it's best to limit the soaking time if you're using that cleaning material. Its extreme brittleness makes glass impractical to cut and drill.

Polyethylene and other Plastics Polyethylene is inexpensive and abundant. Of course it is not at all heat resistant, but it's fine for water treatment and storage, mashing, sparging, and wort collection vessels. High density or linear is the premium grade—it's harder, tougher, and stands up to heat better than the garden variety. Often used for primary fermenters, polyethylene is highly resistant to all common cleaning and sanitizing materials, but after some use it will develop minute scratches that can be a safe haven for contaminating microbes. White kitchen trash bags, fresh from the box, are relatively sterile and may be used as liners for primary fermenters.

Nylon, polycarbonate, polypropylene, and other types are available in sheets or slabs of varying thicknesses, and make good structural materials for brewery equipment.

Flexible tubing is an essential brewery material. Most is PVC (polyvinyl chloride). It's very important that it is of food grade material, which is more expensive and sometimes can't be found at the hardware store, but the cheap stuff can leach toxic chemicals into your beer. If it is not specified as food grade, it probably isn't. Tubing of other materials such as polyethylene and silicone are useful as well, and sometimes show up as industrial surplus.

INTERCHANGEABILITY, MODULARITY

This is crucial for an easy-to-use system. Standardize all hose connections with the same type of connector. I like 3/8" Swagelok type compression fittings. Other, quicker disconnects are available, but are usually pretty expensive, even on eBay. Valuable components such as pumps need to do multiple duty, making an even stronger case for a unified system of hookups.

On larger vessels it is helpful if components, especially electrical stuff, can come off for cleaning. I have installed sanitary (Tri-Clover type) fittings to all my larger vessels, so thermometers and large valves can quickly pop on and off for cleaning or reconfiguration. You will see this as we tour the brewery later on.

Reliability It's a problem sometimes with surplus, but more often it's:

- Poor planning
- Improper usage
- Quickie (duct tape) construction

Take the time to install something properly, and resist the urge to put something to use as soon as you can.

Hot and cold water can be hooked up with readily available (and inexpensive) garden hose disconnects.

Left, NPT threaded plumbing fittings, not quick; center, Swagelok type tubing fittings, sort of quick; right, quick disconnects, expensive and hard to clean.

Simplicity? Well, this is a beautiful idea, and I highly recommend it to others, but it's really not the path for me!

AUTOMATION

My own goals are these, in order of importance:

- Faster brewing
- Easier setup/takedown/cleanup
- Better beer, more flexible process

The length of the brew day is important, but also how much energy and attention is required for each stage. I like to have things running without a lot of intervention, so I can do something else while a process is taking care of itself.

Temperature Control I have implemented some temperature control measures in these areas: mashing, sparge water, and fermentation. Fortunately, this is a common occurrence in the industry, so the parts and pieces are readily available on the salvage market.

Mechanical Mixing This has been a big success at the Buckapound. I always hated stirring, but with flame-heated step mashes, the scorching and sticking required constant stirring, and even that wasn't enough. There are geared motors available with speed reduction built in. You want something around 60 rpm or somewhat lower. If you can find a reversible one, even better. The bigger problem with stainless vessels is the scorching. I solved this by cutting out the bottom of the vessel and replacing it with 0.090" thick copper sheet. This isn't easy to do, but silicon bronze or aluminum bronze rod with a TIG process will stick permanently to both metals.

I have installed a solenoid valve on my filtered tap water line. This may seems like a pointless luxury, but when controlled by a float switch at the top of my kettle or liquor back, it saves me hours of mopping up water that used to spill out when I forgot to stand there and monitor the fill level.

I have a couple of other uses for float switches. One, in the lauter tun, monitors the sparge water level and kicks on a pump to keep the bed from drying out. The second is attached to the grant, and when a certain level is reached, turns on a pump that moves the wort to the brew kettle. With these two devices, I can let the sparge go almost completely unattended, freeing me to get the next stage of brewing set up.

These float switches cannot handle the 110 volts needed for things like pumps. They must be wired to switch on (or off) a low-voltage signal, and this is fed to a relay, which delivers the line voltage the pumps require. This is a necessity, but it's also a great safety feature as it keeps the line voltage high and dry on the wall or ceiling. I have one freestanding relay box, and another one built into the control box of a pump.

Mercury Thermoregulator

There are many different types of devices that may be used to switch devices on and off according to temperature. This is one of the more elegant types, usually used for incubators and other laboratory setups.

CIP (Clean-In-Place) Unit Built by the Author

3-way valves allow recirculation, fresh water, and pumping to the drain. Carboys and soda kegs may be inverted on top for cleaning.

A pair of pumps

Above, a direct-drive centrifugal pump that will move several gallons a minute. Below, a magnetically coupled self-priming gear pump used for wort transfer.

Float Switch

Used to switch a valve or pump according to liquid level.

A NOTE ON SURPLUS

It is a sign of the great abundance of our civilization that massive quantities of perfectly useful industrial parts and pieces are scrapped out and end up for sale for just pennies on the dollar. Most cities of any size have an industrial surplus outlet, and these are well worth searching out. Many of these operations now have a presence on the Web, and of course eBay has become a tremendous source for just about anything you need to put a really crazy, wonderful brewery together.

THE BUCKAPOUND BREWERY—AN OVERVIEW

This is a current snapshot of my own brewing setup. As noted in the text, there are many different ways to put a brewing system together—this is just how I solved the problem, based on my skills and the junk (sorry, *stuff*) I found during the process.

Virtually all of this equipment is made from stainless steel, from junkyards and surplus shops.

The hose connections are 3/8" compression fittings, and the valves and thermometers are connected to the vessels with sanitary fittings, which are easy to remove for cleaning.

1a Mash kettle with copper bottom

1b Reversible stirring motor

1c 2" ball valve for transferring mash to lauter tun

2a Lauter tun made from stainless sheet metal. This is fitted with an insulating jacket and an outer oak cladding, both of which are removed for clarity.

2b Sprinkler head for sparge water

2c Vacuum gauge measures pressure on bottom of lauter screen (too much suction is bad)

2d Water coils circulate sparge water around the tun to keep temperature of mash up. These may be bypassed when recirculating (*vorlaufing*).

2e Float switch monitors level of water on mash, turns on pump when level gets low.

3a Grant made from industrial pressure ves-

sel. It holds the wort that drains from the lauter tun.

3b Float switch in grant turns on pump when level gets too high, sending wort to kettle.

4a Pump positioned to transfer wort from grant to kettle.

4b Transfer pump moving hot water to sparge sprinkler. Note that this is shown attached to boil kettle. In practice, the mash kettle is cleaned out and used as a hot liquor tank.

5a Boil kettle made from castoff beer kegs—a quarter barrel welded on top of a half barrel. The kettle rests on top of a home-built stove, featuring a wok burner fueled by natural gas. This kettle features a copper bottom like the mash kettle.

5b Light fixture. With a kettle this deep, it really is a helpful feature to see how the boil is coming, or to get it clean.

5c 2" valve feeds wort, hops and all, into the hop back.

6 Hop back made from soda carbonator keg. Inside is lined with a fine perforated mesh, which catches the hop cones and particles.

7 12-gallon cylindroconical fermenter made from a stainless steel milk container. It has sanitary fittings top and bottom, as well as a soda-keg hatch for cleaning access.

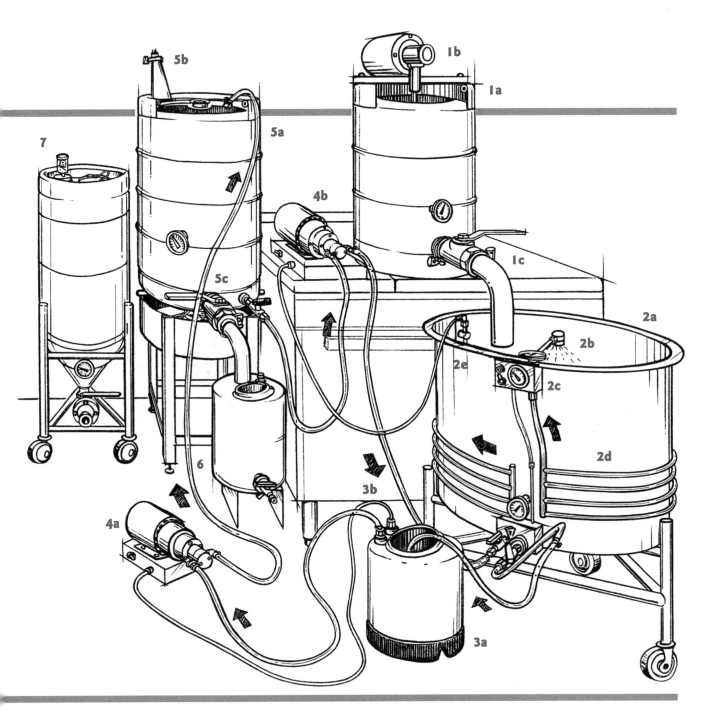

Chapter 21

A Few Words on Beer and Food

Drink now the strong beare,

*   cut the white loaf here,*

The while the meat is shredding,

For the rare mince pie,

*   and the plums stand by,*

To fill the paste that' a-kneading.

—Herrick

Finding foods and beers that go well together has been elevated to an arcane metaphysical art of late, and I do have to say that when you find a great combination it can be magical. But let's not over think this, folks. There's nothing about finding great combinations that should be mystical or intimidating. The dirty little secret? There is no *perfect* pairing; something else would always work. So the pressure's off. Now, let's figure out how to go about it.

We beer aficionados are fortunate to have a product to work with that is kaleidoscopic in its range of color, strengths, flavors, and textures—especially when you include the radical realm. The available range of beers covers just about every food possibility, from eels to peanut butter cups.

I'm outlining a set of rules, but you have to keep in mind that rules are meant to be broken. The most important thing is to be conscious about your choices, and pay attention to the flavors and the way they play against each other while you're enjoying them. This will eventually lead you to your own set of preferences, ideas, and epiphanies.

MY RULES OF MATCHING FOOD AND BEER

One should not overwhelm the other. Find beers of the same intensity as the food. A salad obviously needs a lighter accompaniment than a steak.

Look for resonance. See if you can find similar flavors in the food and beer that can play off each other and add up to a greater whole—pairing a spicy dunkelweizen with a delicately spiced gingerbread, for example. Or to ramp it up, maybe a weizenbock with a sauerbraten in its traditional gingersnap gravy. There are lots of possibilities: toasted savory flavors, buttery richness, herbal or spicy aromas, creamy textures, smokiness, and roasted chocolate flavors. The list goes on and on.

Do a balancing act in your mouth. Everything's going to end up there anyway, so consider the food and beer as one thing, not two. Once you match the intensity, you can find foods and beers that will play off each other's eccentricities. A remarkable example of this is to pair a sweet carrot cake with a crisply bitter imperial India pale ale. They have a similar intensity, but one is very sweet, the other intensely bitter. A mouthful of one demands a swig of another, and on and on it goes.

Cut the fat. Many foods are rich in delicious fat that leaves the mouth coated and longing for something refreshing to cleanse the palate. Crisp, well-carbonated, and especially bitter beer slices through any greasiness, and leaves the diner ready for another bite.

Consider bitterness. This is a flavor found in only a few foods, for a very good reason. In nature, bitterness is a marker for toxic chemicals such as alkaloids, many of which evolved as a defense by plants against being eaten. We can learn to like it, as most of us new-beer fanatics have, but it does go against the grain, especially in food. Also, the taste buds that sense bitterness are much larger than the rest of the buds, which means that bitterness takes longer to register, and lingers on the tongue long after the other tastes have faded. Bitterness may be balanced by sweetness, acidity, or salt, so these are things to look for in pairings. In general, very bitter beers (50 or higher IBU) can easily overwhelm food flavors. Indian cuisine and IPA notwithstanding, I also think that bitterness tends to magnify spicy heat, and that slightly sweeter, maltier beers are better for hot food. Vienna/märzen with Mexican food is the classic historical example.

A Sidewalk in the Hallertau
This region takes its food very seriously.

Look to tradition. Cuisines evolve, and this means that traditional combinations tend to be pretty agreeable. Stout and oysters is something that might take an adventurous person a lot of experimenting to stumble on, but the English already worked this out for us. Tradition isn't always a sure bet, though. There are lots of new foods out there with no traditional beer companions. And in many food traditions, one beer serves for all foods, which is obviously better for some dishes than for others.

Desserts are really interesting with beer. Roasted flavors and sweetness can be built upon, and bitterness can be balanced against the sweet flavor of desserts. Additionally, beer (except for lambic and other intentionally sour beers) is less acidic than wine, so it works with chocolate and some of the heavier butterfat flavors better than wine does. Sometimes you want something bright and acidic, and the lambics, especially fruit lambics, come through, and are ideal companions to fruit tarts, shortcake, and lighter desserts.

COOKING WITH BEER

In food, beer works like other kinds of liquid ingredients: to richen the dish, to add flavors and aroma, and possibly color as well. There is a great range of flavor strength available, which by this point should be obvious.

A Few Great Beer & Food Combinations

Belgian Dubbel	Barbecued Ribs
Brown Ale	Smoked Trout
Rauchbier	Black Forest Ham
Maibock	Roasted Pork Shank
Strong Witbier	Poached Salmon
Stout	Oysters
Porter	Roast Pork Loin
Pale Ale	Grilled Steak
Belgian Pale Ale	Mussels and Frites
IPA	Blue Cheese
Foreign Stout	Well-aged Cheddar
ESB	Uncomplicated Goat Cheese
Hoppy Pilsener	Triple-crème Cheese
Barley wine	Stilton
Imperial India Pale Ale	Carrot Cake
Imperial Stout	Chocolate Truffles
Belgian Strong Dark Ale	Milk Chocolate Hazelnut Truffles
Barley wine	Chocolate Mousse Cake
Cherry Brown Ale	Black Forest Cake

Shop Display, Brussels

Chocolate shaped like beer.
You just gotta love this
place!

Uses of Beer in Cooking

Usage	Typical dish
Replace liquid in recipe	Beer bread Chocolate cake
To add air, lightness	Beer batter Sabayón sauce
As sauce base	Carbonnade Flamande Welsh rarebit
To richen	Chili and soups Bread dough Couscous Stuffing
For basting	Roast fowl and meats Barbecued shoulder or brisket
To deglaze pans	Sautéed chicken Roast pork
Marinade	Barbecue ribs, other grilled foods Brining base for poultry, pork loin
Poaching/steaming	Salmon, snapper, other fish Crabs, clams, other shellfish Bratwurst, other mild sausages Vegetables such as endive or Brussels sprouts
As primary flavor	Kriek (cherry ale) ice cream Framboise cheesecake Stout float

Chicago's Brewpub Shootout

Chefs fine-tune their creations
before the competition.

Because the aromas of beer are volatile, it is sometimes a good idea to add some fresh beer right at the end of cooking

Bitterness is the big drawback beer poses as an ingredient, but there are workarounds. First, choose low-bitterness beer unless it will be used in a way (like in a chocolate dish) that a little extra bitterness will not be noticed. Second, resist the urge to reduce beer as you would a wine-based sauce, because even a lightly bittered beer can get unpleasant. Reduce pan sauces first, then add beer right at the end. Should you end up with a little more bitterness than you'd like, it can usually be countered by sweetness, salt, or some combination added before serving.

When choosing cooking beers, look for freshness, good clean flavor, and plenty of it. For most uses, beers with low bitterness are desired; even very sweet beers will taste much drier when incorporated into a recipe.

Mainstream American beers are okay for beer batter and other situations where you don't want a lot of flavor. Although purists say not to cook with anything you wouldn't drink, this is not necessarily true. But skunked beer (usually in clear or green bottles) will introduce unpleasant, rubbery flavors into your food, so chuck 'em.

Beer ingredients, as opposed to beer itself, can also be used for cooking. One versatile component is malt extract in syrup or powdered form. It is richly flavored, like the malted milk of our childhood, and can be used where a little sweetness is needed. It's great in bread dough, as it kind of supercharges yeast, and is used commercially for that purpose. Use as a base for sauces or glazes for ham, duck, and other dishes where a slightly sweet sauce is appropriate. Be sure to use an unhopped variety for zero bitterness; liquid or dry will work equally well in most cases. Dry extract is less messy to deal with in the kitchen when you're doling it out a scoop at a time.

Crystal malt has a glassy, sugary crunch and is very sweet, with great nutty, caramelly flavors. The different degrees of kilning give it lots of versatility. Crystal malt is especially good added to bread or rolls, where it adds a nice grainy texture and complex sweetness. Just crush it coarsely and add it to dough, perhaps a cup for a 1-pound batch. Many people use spent grain for a similar purpose, but I have to say there is no comparison. They don't call it "spent" for nothing.

Other malts may be used as well. Black or Carafa malt may be powdered finely and sieved, then used to dust the outside of truffles, which are hopefully made with the addition of imperial stout or barley wine.

Good Beers for Cooking

Beer Style	Character in Cooking
Brown Ale	Soft complex toastiness
Oktoberfest	Sweetish, caramelly, mellow
Porter	Rich, creamy; softer versions not bitter
Weissbier	Delicate but flavorful, not bitter
Doppelbock	Very rich and sweet—good for basting
Wheat Bock	Unique spiciness, plenty of caramel character
Lambic	Acidic, full of unique aromas
Fruit Lambics-Cherry (Kriek) Raspberry (Framboise)	Acidic, bursting with fruitiness
Imperial stout	Very rich and full flavored—great in chocolate desserts
Flanders Sour Brown	Sharply acidic, complex, fruity aromas
Belgian Dubbel	Rich, malty, uniquely spicy
Belgian Tripel	Intense, crisp, spicy
Rauchbier	Sweetish, with mellow beechwood smoke
Munich Helles	Pure, clean maltiness without a lot of bitterness

A Few Dishes Prepared with Beer

Pork roast with apples and Kriek (cherry) lambic

Duck glazed with doppelbock

Chocolate stout truffles rolled in powdered black malt

Malt extract and mustard-glazed ham

Marinated grilled salmon, served with white beer cream sauce

Gingerbread stout cake

Pork chops in bock with mustard and onions

Pork ribs in smoked beer barbecue sauce

Chicken sautéed in Flanders sour brown ale and cherries

Grilled steak marinated in pale ale and green peppercorns

Bocked beans

Cheddar cheese spread made with India pale ale

Dinner rolls with bock and crystal malt

Chicken baked with dried apricots and wheat bock

Beef roasted in Christmas beer

Cafe, Zatec, Czech Republic
Despite the unintended message, things there are looking up.

Chapter 22

What's Next?

We homebrewers are as varied as the beers we brew, and we're lucky to be involved in a hobby that offers us so many different ways of enjoying it. If I've accomplished even half of my mission, this book has opened your eyes to some facets of brewing you hadn't considered before, and given you some ideas as to where to go next to keep growing as a brewer. From engineering to art, plus a host of tangential paths, there's a whole splendiferous world of beer out there. So get going. The future of beer is what we make it.

Get an education Your desire to get the details exactly right will ultimately lead you on a quest for more authoritative sources. Fortunately for us, generations of really smart people have dedicated their lives to unraveling the inner mysteries of the brewing arts, and their work is out there for us to profit from in the form of books, journal articles, lectures, and educational courses of varying lengths and levels. The old books are always interesting and usually useful. Since we're brewing on a somewhat primitive level compared to a modern 25-million barrel production brewery, there is much of practical value for us going back as far as one hundred and fifty years or more. The newer books are useful as well, especially in the areas of yeast and biochemistry.

Seminars and conferences can be extremely useful. Many of the larger competitions and other gatherings of homebrewing feature guest speakers. Usually these sessions are fascinating as well as useful, and have the added benefit of being able to ask questions and engage in conversations with others who have experience in a subject. I shouldn't need to mention that these gatherings of homebrewers are a blast as well, and put you in contact with many new beers and friends. If you're part of an active club, you might even consider staging your own mini-conference. It's a lot of work, but it's a fun way to network with brewers with all kinds of interests on many different levels.

There are more professional ways to pursue a brewing education. Independent brewing schools such as the Siebel Institute and university-affiliated programs such as the University of California at Davis offer programs of varying length, right up to a four-year or advanced degree, the ultimate being the beer engineering diploma from Weihenstephan in Germany. Many homebrewers sign up for the short programs; the longer ones require a commitment of time and money that pretty much limits them to those advancing a career rather than a hobby. Web-based learning programs such as the Siebel/Doemens World Brewing Academy are becoming ever more substantial.

Teach someone to brew Besides being the honorable thing to do, this may actually have tangible benefits. First, your new brewer trainee is probably one of your non-brewing pals who's been shamelessly mooching off of you, so this will help take the pressure off your brewhouse. If you help him get going, you can be sure his beer will be worth mooching back. Just as important, you actually improve your own understanding by having to explain a thing to someone else.

Enter some competitions Sure, you can pass your beer around and ask people what they think, but it is impossible to get a straight answer out of them. Even if they don't feel the need to be polite, you're not likely to get the kind of thoughtful feedback you need and that a competition assessment delivers. Beers are judged according to category by experienced judges, and a detailed score sheet is filled out and returned to you. Don't hyperventilate over the numerical score; this can vary widely. But do pay close attention to the descriptions, category fit, flaws, off-flavors, and other comments. Look for patterns that may indicate opportunities for improvement, and take them to heart. Work on your problem areas. Keep brewing, keep improving, and sooner or later you'll strike gold.

Become a beer judge This takes some discipline and effort, but can put you at a much higher level as a brewer. It just makes sense. How can you improve your brews if you don't have the experience and knowledge to make critical evaluations of styles, technique, off-flavors, or other important aspects of brewing? The Beer Judge Certification Program (www.bjcp.org) is a volunteer-run organization that tests and certifies judges at several levels as well as sanctioning homebrew competitions. There is a wealth of information on their Web site. I should mention that they offer a detailed study guide for the exam, and the style guidelines are very helpful to brewers of any level. Many brewers get together and form a study group, then meet regularly at a bar with a good international selection and taste their way through the twenty-six categories and numerous substyles. For study hall, not too bad!

Learn to weld I know this a radical idea, but you can help save the dying Industrial Arts departments in this country by signing up for an adult/continuing education class. There may be a class available in your area; these usually give you access to a full metal shop as well as welding equipment at a ridiculously low price. You won't be doing sanitary welds in stainless for a while, but the usefulness of the stuff you make will amaze you and everyone around you.

Hang with the beeries I have made this point before, but it bears repeating. Beer is a fundamentally social product, and segregating yourself from the larger homebrew community deprives you of one of its most important joys. No matter where you live, there are ways to get involved at a local or global level. There's no excuse in being shy. Without a doubt, homebrewers are the friendliest species on the planet, maybe in the whole universe. So make that call, click that Web button, or just show up at the next meeting with a six of your latest creation and get ready to be welcomed into the ancient and honorable (and fun, too!) community of brewers.

Homebrewers have a large hand in running some of the most well-respected beer festivals.

Fabulous Beer Festivals

Great American Beer Festival®
Denver, September/October

Great British Beer Festival
London, August

Oktoberfest
Munich, September

Mondiale de la Bière
Montréal, June

Bokbierfestival
Amsterdam, October

Oregon Brewers Festival
Portland, OR, June

Real Ale Fest
Chicago, March

Great Taste of the Midwest
Madison, WI, August

The Great Alaska Beer & Barleywine Festival
Anchorage, January

Colorado Brewfest
Fort Collins, CO, June

Become a yeast hunter Tracking down exotic yeast from the far corners of the brewing world gives some people exquisite pleasure, and the skill set you'll develop trying to do it successfully will serve you well in dealing with this most important aspect of brewing. Most yeast hunters have a little kit with the vials and other gear needed to bring 'em back alive.

Get into events Whether you're just a volunteer server, or the chairman of the event, beer tastings, dinners, and festivals can be enjoyable and rewarding for homebrewers and other beer lovers. It's a chance to help spread your passion for beer and brewing, as well as an opportunity to rub elbows with pro brewers and other important players in the beer community. Plus, there's the beer. Established festivals are always looking for people to help at every level, although you may have to pay your dues pouring beer before you get on the organizing committee.
Just get in touch and offer up your time, enthusiasm, and expertise.

For homebrew clubs, commercially-oriented beer tastings and festivals offer a number of benefits. First, they offer a chance to help out the beer community in a meaningful way. Public events attract the kind of people who may be interested in becoming homebrewers, so they can be a great recruiting tool. Properly run events can provide a considerable boost to the club treasury. And despite the hard work required, the challenge of staging a tasting can bond the organizers together into deep and lasting friendships.

Even as a spectator, beer tastings and festivals are just about the best way to learn about—and enjoy—beer. Many of the events in this country and elsewhere are major events worthy of a long journey and such a beerfest can be the centerpiece of any vacation. Start your trip at the fest if possible, then you can mine the experts you meet about what else you should see while you're in the area.

GOING PRO: SO YOU WANT TO WEAR THE RUBBER BOOTS

This isn't every homebrewer's dream, despite the glamour of hefting heavy bags of malt and hanging around for long hours in steamy brewhouses and dank conditioning rooms. Oh, and did I mention low pay? Well, despite all this, the right brewer's job offers a certain freedom and opportunity for self expression, plus the chance to hang around with attractive members of the brewpub wait staff, many of whom have fascinating personal problems. Honestly, of all the people I know, brewers spend the least time moping and whining about their jobs.

Breweries hire people of all skill levels. There is a lot of grunt work, especially endless amounts of cleaning. So if you want to escape up to the next rung, a little brewing education will go a long way. Being an accomplished homebrewer is a good start, but either doing an apprenticeship in a brewery or taking one of the professional programs mentioned previously (or both) would round out your résumé and give you a shot at a more respectable, less back-breaking job. Knowing your way around a petri dish might even land you a cushy lab job at a production brewery.

The ideal situation for many brewers is to own a piece of the action. This puts you right up there with the rest of the management, sharing the risks and rewards of the business. Scary, yes, but it's a chance to build something of value as your career develops, rather than just being the employee. Starting your own place from the ground up is another possibility; just about every microbrewery in the country began as a gleam in some homebrewer's eye. You can probably guess that this is a difficult thing to do, and besides losing the family fortune, there's that problem whereby the fun gets sucked out of something when it goes from being a hobby to a business. Despite that, there are still opportunities to thrive for people with vision, creativity, and solid business skills.

A FINAL EXHORTATION

If you've made it all the way to the end of this book, you have a fair idea of some of the breadth and depth of brewing through the ages. I hope you have found inspiration, as I have, from the creativity and resourcefulness of brewers both modern and ancient. Use the tools available here and elsewhere to develop your own voice as a radical brewer. Brew to surprise, to thrill, to seduce, to shock, to satiate. This is the power of radical brewing. Brew with seriousness, but don't forget to have fun. Pour your heart and head into your brewing and something wonderful will always appear in the glass.

I raise a radical brew to you.

HOMEBREW WRECKED MY LIFE

I've been brewing night and day for just about a year,
Seven hundred batches of a nectar strong and clear.
I've filled up every corner of this home that was so sweet,
But now my honey's gone and set my kettle on the street.

I spent the baby's trust fund on a tank of stainless steel,
And sold the faithful doggie just to put the thing on wheels.
I guess I'd do it differently if I could do it over,
I'd skip the wheels and get myself a bottler with rover.

Homebrew wrecked my life today,
This brewer's name is mud.
I'll give my brewing vats away,
And buy a case of Bud.

I've lined the walls with plastic, and epoxied all the floors,
Put in ultraviolet lasers to protect the beer from spores.
And everything was going great, the brewing never stopped,
Until my sweetie found her walk-in closet filled with hops.

Homebrew was a blast until it finally wrecked my life,
Nineteen thousand bottles really aggravates a wife.
And when they started goin' off, they tore the house apart,
Now my baby's gone and wrecked the mash tun of my heart.

Homebrew wrecked my life today,
I've brewed my final batch.
I'll leave behind the homebrew way,
And start a garden patch.

Now I'm on the sidewalk with my last remaining beer,
The neighborhood is quiet, all the windows dark from fear.
A soggy pile of bricks and glass commemorates my house,
And me without a carboy or a hop back or a spouse.

I'm sorry for the state of things, you know I really am.
My passion was excessive, and my plans a little grand.
I'd gladly make it up to her, if I could find some malt,
I'd brew her up a special batch directly from my heart.

Homebrew wrecked my life today,
She walked right out that door.
But since my baby's gone to stay,
I might brew just one more...

—R.M.

PPENDIX

For the Radical Brewing Web links, go to:

www.radicalbrewing.com

LINKING UP

Due to the transitory nature of many Web sites, I have decided it is better to keep an online links page rather than list a lot of dead URLs.

The scope, depth, and accuracy of Web-based information continues to grow. I found a large number of sites that were helpful to me during the course of research-ing this book, and you may also find them interesting and useful as well. And as I have stressed already, the quality and enjoyment of the brewing hobby will likely be height-ened if you connect with others with similar passions, so there are lots of links to var-ious organizations on the Radical Brewing page. Also, the uncommon ingredients in some of the recipes in this book can usually be found at online retailers.

The following is a list of categories of sites that radicalbrewing.com will link to:

- Academic sites dealing with beer and brewing subjects, including transcribed and facsimile texts
- Sites on spices, herbs, grains, and other related materials used in brewing
- Translation and conversion resources
- Hobbyist sites on brewing and meadmaking
- Online forums for brewing and related subjects
- Beer and brewing organizations, homebrew clubs, and competitions
- Commercial beer and homebrewing festivals
- Manufacturers and retailers of ingredients and supplies

In addition, there are a few other useful items available at radicalbrewing.com:

- Downloadable brewing worksheet
- Photographic tour of the Buckapound Brewery
- In time, some additional recipes
- Info and ordering of my hard-to-find first book, *The Brewer's Companion*

BREWING ORGANIZATIONS

American Homebrewers Association: www.beertown.org/homebrewing/about.html
Association of Brewers (craft brewing trade assoc.): www.beertown.org
Beer Judge Certification Program: www.bjcp.org
Home Brew Digest (online discussion group): www.hbd.org
Campaign for Real Ale (British enthusiast/preservation group): camra.org.uk
Home Wine & Beer Trade Association: hwbta.org

LIST OF RECIPES

Names in solid black are complete recipes.
Name in shaded text *indicates abbreviated recipe.*

BIBLIOGRAPHY

Fredrick Accum, *A Treatise on Adulterations of Food* (London: Longman, Hurst, Rees,Orme & Brown, 1820 edition) Transcribed by James Sumner, June 2001

George Stewart Amsinck, *Practical Brewings: A Series of Fifty Brewings*, (London: published by the author, 1868)

John P. Arnold, *Origin and History of Beer and Brewing*, (Chicago, IL: Alumni Association of the Wahl-Henius Institute, 1911)

John P. Arnold and Frank Penman, *A History of the Brewing Industry and Brewing Science in America*, (Chicago, IL: Wahl Henius Institute and G. L. Peterson, 1933)

Heinrich Joseph Barth, Christiane Klincke and Klaus Schmidt, *The Hop Atlas: The History and Geography of the Cultivated Plant* (Nuremberg: Joseph Barth & Sohn, 1994)

Judith M. Bennett, *Ale, Beer and Brewsters in England: Women's Work in a Changing World 1300–1600*, (Oxford and New York: Oxford University Press, 1996)

John Bickerdyke (Pseudonym for Charles Henry Cook and J. G Fennel), *The Curiosities of Ale and Beer*, (London: Spring House, 1965 reprint of the original 1889 edition)

P. Boulin, *Manuel Practique de la Fabrication de la Bière*, (Paris: Bernard Tignol, 1880)

M. L. Byrn, *The Complete Practical Brewer*, (Philadelphia: Henry Carey Baird, 1552; 2002 reprint by Raudins Publishing)

Sanford C. Brown, *Wines & Beers of Old New England: A How-to-Do-It History*, (Hanover, NH: The University press of New England, 1978)

Jean de Clerck, *A Textbook of Brewing*, Translated by Kathleen Barton-Wright (London: Chapman & Hall Ltd., 1957)

Samuel Child, *Every Man His Own Brewer*, fourth edition, (London: 1794?) Transcribed by James Sumner, January 2002

John Combrune, *Theory of Brewing*, (London, Vernor and Hood, Longman and Rees, Cuthell and Martin, and J. Walker, 1804)

Martyn Cornell, *Beer: The Story of the Pint* (London: Headline Book Publishing, 2003)

H.S. Corran, *A History of Brewing*, (London: David & Charles Ltd, 1975)

Ray Daniels, *Designing Great Beers*, (Boulder, CO: Brewers Publications, 1996)

Max Delbrück, *Illustriertes Brauerei-Lexicon*, (Berlin: Verlagsbuchhandlung Paul Parey, 1910)

William Ellis, *London and Country Brewer*, second edition, (London: Fox, 1736) Online scans thanks to Jim Liddil

George A. Fix and Laurie A. Fix, *An Analysis of Brewing Techniques*, (Boulder, CO: Brewers Publications, 1997)

George Fix, *Principles of Brewing Science*, (Boulder, CO: Brewers Publications, 1989)

John Gardner (Editor), *The Brewer, Distiller and Wine Manufacturer*, (Philadelphia: P. Blakiston, Son & Co., 1883)

Guinard, Jean Xavier, *Lambic*, Classic Beer Styles Series (Boulder, CO: Brewers Publications, 1990)

H. Lloyd Hind, *Brewing, Science & Practice*, (London: Chapman & Hall Ltd. 1938)

J.S. Hough, Briggs, R. Stevens, *Malting & Brewing Science*, (London: Chapman & Hall Ltd. 1971)

Michael Jackson, *The Beer Companion*, (Philadelphia, PA: Running Press 1993)

Michael Jackson, *The Great Beers of Belgium* (CODA, Antwerp, Belgium: 1992)

Mark Edward Lender and James Kirby Martin, *Drinking in America: A History*, Second Edition, (New York: The Free Press, 1982, 1987)

Carl J. Lintner, *Die Bayrische Bierbrauer*, (Munich: Verlag von F. H. Gummi, 1867)

Oscar Mendelsohn, *Dictionary of Drinks and Drinking* (New York: Hawthorne Books, Inc., 1965)

Alexander Morrice, *Practical Treatise on the Brewing of Various Sorts of Malt Liquors*, (London: Printed for Sherwood, Neely, and Jones, 1819)

Randy Mosher, *The Brewer's Companion* (Seattle, WA: Alephenalia Publications, Second Edition, 1995)

James Lightbody, *Every Man His Own Gauger*, (London: Printed for G. C., [1695])

U. J. Olberg, *Der vollkommene Brau-und Malzmeister*, (Vienna and Leipzig: U. Hartleben's Verlag, 1937)

Annie Perrier-Robert and Charles Fontaine, *Beer by Belgium, Belgium by Beer* (Esch/Alzette Luxembourg: 1996)

Roger Protz, *The Ale Trail: A celebration of the revival of the world's oldest style*, (Orpington, Kent, UK: Eric Dobby Publishing Ltd, 1995)

Christian Rätsch, *Urbock: Bier jenzeits vom Hopfen und Malz*, (Licerne Switzerland, EMB-Service für Verleger, 1996)

Cindy Renfrow, *A Sip Through Time: A Collection of Old Brewing Recipes*, (Cindy Renfrow, 1994)

John Richardson, *The Philosophical Principles of the Science of Brewing*, (Printed for G. C. and J. Robinson, London (and others), 1788)

Hermann Rüdiger, *Die Bierbrauerei und Die Malzextract-Fabrication*, (Vienna:U. Hartleben's verlag, 1887)

George Saintsbury, *Notes on a Cellar-Book*, (New York: The MacMillan Company, 1933)

Pamela Sambrook, *Country House Brewing in England 1500–1900*, (London and Rio Grande, OH: The Hambledon Press, 1996)

Franz Schönfeld, *Obergärige Bier und ihre Herstellung* (Berlin, Verlag von Paul Parey, 1938)

Ken Schramm, The *Compleat Meadmaker*, (Boulder, CO: Brewers Publications, 2003)

Gualtiero Simonetti, edited by Stanley Schuler, *Simon & Schuster's Guide to Herbs and Spices*, (New York: A Fireside Book published by Simon & Schuster, 1990)

Julius E. Thausing, *Die Theorie und Praxis der Malzbereitung und Bierfabrikation*, third edition, (Leipzig: J. M. Gebhardt's Verlag, 1882)

Gallus Thoman, *American Beer: Glimpses of Its History and Description of Its Manufacture*, (New York: United States Brewers' Association, 1909)

John Tuck, *Private Brewer's Guide to the Art of Brewing Ale and Porter*, Second Edition (London: Printed for W. Simpkin and R. Marshall, 1822; Facsimile edition by Zymoscribe)

Ladislaus von Wagner, *Handbuch der Bierbrauerei*, (Weimar, Germany: Bernhard Friedrich Voigt, 1877)

Edward Whitaker, *Directions for Making Malt Liquors*, (London, Printed for J. Nutt, 1700)

William Worth, *Cerevesia Comes: or the New and True Art of Brewing*, (London: Printed for J. Taylor and S. Clement, 1692)

Wahl, Robert & Max Henius, *A Handy Book of Brewing*, (Chicago: Wahl-Henius Institute, 1901)

Richard A. Young and Thomas J. Glover, *Measure for Measure* (Littleton, CO: Blue Willow, Inc., 1996)

INDEX

ABOUT THE AUTHOR

Randy Mosher is a nationally-recognized author and expert in the field of beer and brewing. He writes for virtually all the national beer and brewing-related periodicals, has lectured to audiences across the country, and has taught beer style courses at the Siebel Institute.

He is active in the leadership of the Chicago Beer Society, the American Homebrewers Association, and the Association of Brewers.

His interests in beer and brewing memorabilia combined with his experience as a branding and packaging designer specializing in beer and food have given him the tools to visually express the richness and exuberance of beer and brewing traditions in *Radical Brewing*.

Randy Mosher lives in Chicago with his wife Nancy.

Also by Randy Mosher:

The Brewer's Companion, Alephenalia, Seattle, WA, Revised Second Edition, 1995

The Brewer's Companion is designed to be a ready reference for the serious homebrewer. Information is presented in a highly graphical manner, with numerous charts and tables. Emphasis is on record-keeping and recipe formulation. Several brewing worksheets are included from the simple to the highly detailed. Comprehensive information on ingredients, processes, beer styles and troubleshooting are included in a compact-yet-detailed form. A photographic step-by-step guide to getting started is also included. Numerous illustrations and whimsical homebrew labels enliven the text.

8.5" x 11" 224 pages, softcover. ISBN 0-9640410-1-4